VIEW OVER LAKE WANAKA FROM THE SUMMIT OF ROB ROY PEAK (65 A4).

TRIP PLANNING   2

North Island travel time and distances   2
South Island travel time and distances   3
20 top things to do in New Zealand   4
25 must-see attractions   5
Te Araroa – The Long Pathway   5
DOC campsites   6

NATIONAL PARKS MAPS   8

Te Urewera National Park   8
Tongariro National Park   9
Arthur's Pass National Park   10
Kahurangi National Park   11
Mount Aspiring National Park   12
Aoraki/Mt Cook & Westland Tai Poutini National Parks   13
Nelson Lakes National Park   14
Fiordland National Park   15

NORTH ISLAND REGIONAL MAPS   MAPS 1-36

Far North   map   1-2
Kauri Coast & Whangarei   map   3-4
Kaipara Harbour & Kowhai Coast   map   5-6
Auckland & Coromandel   map   7-8
Waikato   map   9-10
Central Waikato   map   11-12
Rotorua & Bay of Plenty   map   13-14
Eastern Bay of Plenty & East Cape   map   15-16
North Taranaki & Taumarunui   map   17-18
Taupo   map   19-20
Hawke's Bay & Gisborne   map   21-22
Taranaki and River Region   map   23-24
South Taranaki   map   25-26
Napier & Hastings   map   27-28
Manawatu & Horowhenua   map   29-30
Manawatu & Wairarapa   map   31-32
Wellington & South Wairarapa   map   33-34
Cook Strait   map   35
Great Barrier Island   map   36

SOUTH ISLAND REGIONAL MAPS   MAPS 37-80

Nelson   map   37-38
Nelson & Marlborough   map   39-40
Buller & Tasman   map   41-42
Marlborough   map   43-44
Central West Coast   map   45-46
Kaikoura & Hurunui   map   47-48
Glacier Country   map   49-50
Arthur's Pass   map   51-52
Central Canterbury   map   53-54
Ashburton & Christchurch   map   55-56
Southern West Coast   map   57-58
Mackenzie Region   map   59-60
Timaru & Ashburton   map   61-62
Northern Fiordland   map   63-64
Queenstown, Wanaka & Central Otago   map   65-66
Southern Canterbury & Northern Otago   map   67-68
Central Fiordland   map   69-70
Southland & Central Otago   map   71-72
Central Otago & Dunedin   map   73-74
Southern Fiordland   map   75-76
Southland   map   77-78
Coastal Otago   map   79
Stewart Island   map   80

NORTH ISLAND CITY & SUBURBS   MAPS 81-113

Bay of Islands   map   81
Russell   map   82
Paihia   map   83
Whangarei CBD   map   84
Whangarei Suburbs   map   85
Kerikeri CBD   map   86
Auckland CBD   map   87
North Shore Suburbs   map   88
West Auckland Suburbs   map   89
East & South Auckland Suburbs   map   90
Hamilton CBD   map   91
Hamilton Suburbs   map   92
Tauranga CBD   map   93
Tauranga Suburbs   map   94
Rotorua CBD   map   95
Rotorua Suburbs   map   96
Taupo CBD   map   97
Taupo Suburbs   map   98
Gisborne CBD   map   99
Gisborne Suburbs   map   100
Napier CBD   map   101
Hastings CBD   map   102
Napier / Hastings Suburbs   map   103
Palmerston North CBD   map   104
Palmerston North Suburbs   map   105
New Plymouth CBD   map   106
New Plymouth Suburbs   map   107
Wanganui CBD   map   108
Wanganui Suburbs   map   109
Wellington Suburbs   map   110
Wellington CBD   map   112

SOUTH ISLAND CITY & SUBURBS   MAPS 113-128

Picton CBD   map   113
Picton Suburbs   map   114
Nelson CBD   map   115
Nelson Suburbs   map   116
Blenheim CBD   map   117
Greymouth CBD   map   118
Christchurch CBD   map   119
Christchurch Suburbs   map   120
Timaru CBD   map   121
Oamaru CBD   map   122
Dunedin CBD   map   123
Dunedin Suburbs   map   124
Queenstown CBD   map   125
Queenstown Suburbs   map   126
Invercargill CBD   map   127
Invercargill Suburbs   map   128

MOTORHOME DUMP STATIONS

Motorhome/Caravan Park with dump station (wastewater disposal site)   124
Public Motorhome Dump Station (wastewater disposal site)   126

INDEX   128

LEGENDS   INSIDE BACK COVER

TE HOHO ROCK AT CATHEDRAL COVE (8 D13)   ©ISTOCK.COM/TROYANA

Distances are shown in kilometres and assume the most direct route on sealed roads where possible.
Travelling times are shown in hours & minutes and are calculated for a driver travelling at 80-100 km/hr on open stretches, with an allowance for rest stops.

Distance chart — each cell shows distance in kilometres (top) and travelling time in hours:minutes (bottom).

From / To	Cape Reinga	Chateau Tongariro	Dargaville	Gisborne	Hamilton	Hicks Bay	Kaitaia	Masterton	Napier	New Plymouth	Paihia	Palmerston North	Rotorua	Taupo	Taumarunui	Tauranga	Thames	Waikaremoana	Waitomo Caves	Wanganui	Wellington	Whakatane	Whangarei
Auckland	444 / 8:15	342 / 5:35	182 / 3:05	496 / 8:20	124 / 1:55	500 / 9:05	321 / 6:00	626 / 9:20	424 / 6:35	365 / 6:20	237 / 4:15	521 / 7:40	235 / 3:50	284 / 4:05	201 / 4:45	115 / 3:20	390 / 1:50	198 / 7:50	457 / 3:10	652 / 8:00	295 / 9:15	166 / 4:55	— / 3:00
Cape Reinga		786 / 13:50	290 / 5:25	940 / 16:35	568 / 10:10	944 / 17:20	112 / 2:15	1070 / 17:35	868 / 14:50	809 / 14:35	216 / 4:30	967 / 11:50	679 / 12:20	726 / 13:00	728 / 16:05	645 / 11:35	559 / 10:05	834 / 16:05	642 / 11:25	901 / 16:15	1096 / 17:30	739 / 13:10	267 / 5:15
Chateau Tongariro			524 / 8:40	431 / 6:55	218 / 3:40	468 / 8:25	663 / 11:35	314 / 4:00	234 / 4:00	251 / 9:50	579 / 3:10	207 / 2:50	178 / 1:30	94 / 3:45	58 / 0:50	250 / 4:40	311 / 6:05	283 / 2:45	158 / 2:45	138 / 4:45	338 / 4:15	263 / 8:00	508 / 8:35
Dargaville				678 / 11:25	306 / 5:00	682 / 12:10	178 / 3:10	808 / 12:25	606 / 9:40	547 / 9:25	126 / 2:20	705 / 10:45	417 / 6:40	464 / 7:10	466 / 7:50	383 / 6:25	297 / 4:55	572 / 10:55	380 / 6:15	639 / 12:20	834 / 8:00	477 / 1:05	55 / 1:05
Gisborne					385 / 6:30	176 / 3:40	817 / 14:20	452 / 6:45	221 / 3:25	582 / 10:25	733 / 12:35	397 / 6:05	274 / 4:50	337 / 5:25	446 / 7:20	291 / 5:00	402 / 7:05	167 / 2:55	435 / 7:30	469 / 7:15	534 / 8:15	201 / 3:25	662 / 11:20
Hamilton						389 / 7:15	445 / 7:55	504 / 7:25	298 / 4:40	241 / 4:25	361 / 6:10	397 / 5:45	111 / 1:40	158 / 2:10	160 / 2:50	109 / 1:55	110 / 1:50	74 / 1:15	326 / 6:05	528 / 7:30	196 / 3:05	290 / 4:55
Hicks Bay							821 / 15:05	817 / 10:25	397 / 7:05	737 / 11:10	573 / 13:20	278 / 9:45	362 / 5:35	450 / 6:55	295 / 8:50	406 / 5:45	343 / 7:50	439 / 6:35	582 / 8:15	710 / 10:40	205 / 11:55	666 / 4:10	— / 12:05
Kaitaia								947 / 15:20	745 / 12:35	686 / 10:10	109 / 2:15	844 / 13:40	556 / 10:05	603 / 10:45	605 / 9:20	522 / 7:50	436 / 13:50	711 / 9:10	519 / 14:00	778 / 15:15	973 / 10:55	616 / 8:00	155 / 3:00
Masterton									231 / 3:20	341 / 5:15	863 / 13:35	107 / 1:40	430 / 6:35	346 / 5:15	342 / 6:05	502 / 7:40	563 / 8:25	413 / 6:30	442 / 8:00	179 / 2:50	100 / 1:50	515 / 8:00	792 / 12:20
Napier										410 / 6:15	661 / 10:50	176 / 2:40	224 / 3:50	140 / 2:30	252 / 4:55	296 / 5:40	357 / 3:10	182 / 5:05	309 / 3:50	248 / 4:55	313 / 9:35	309 / —	590 / —
New Plymouth											602 / 10:35	234 / 3:35	305 / 5:35	193 / 5:25	309 / 3:30	343 / 5:40	463 / 6:15	181 / 10:00	162 / 3:30	352 / 2:25	393 / 5:10	531 / 7:00	— / 9:20
Paihia												760 / 11:55	472 / 7:50	519 / 8:20	521 / 9:00	438 / 7:35	352 / 6:05	627 / 12:05	435 / 7:25	694 / 12:15	889 / 13:30	532 / 9:10	71 / 1:15
Palmerston North													323 / 4:55	239 / 3:35	235 / 4:25	395 / 6:00	456 / 6:45	358 / 5:50	335 / 6:20	72 / 1:10	142 / 2:10	408 / 6:20	689 / 10:40
Rotorua														84 / 1:20	172 / 2:50	83 / 1:30	168 / 2:40	155 / 4:15	161 / 2:45	304 / 4:25	454 / 6:30	85 / 1:25	401 / 6:35
Taupo															112 / 1:55	156 / 2:25	217 / 3:10	189 / 4:35	169 / 2:35	220 / 3:05	370 / 5:10	169 / 2:45	448 / 7:05
Taumarunui																227 / 4:05	288 / 4:40	301 / 6:30	100 / 1:55	166 / 3:15	356 / 5:15	257 / 4:15	450 / 7:45
Tauranga																	111 / 2:05	238 / 5:45	149 / 2:30	376 / 6:35	526 / 8:00	94 / 1:35	367 / 6:20
Thames																		323 / 6:55	173 / 3:05	425 / 6:55	587 / 8:20	205 / 3:40	281 / 4:50
Waikaremoana																			316 / 7:00	430 / 7:00	495 / 8:00	240 / 5:40	556 / 10:50
Waitomo Caves																				266 / 5:10	456 / 7:10	243 / 4:05	364 / 6:10
Wanganui																					190 / 2:45	389 / 5:10	623 / 10:00
Wellington																						539 / 7:55	818 / 12:15
Whakatane																							461 / 7:55

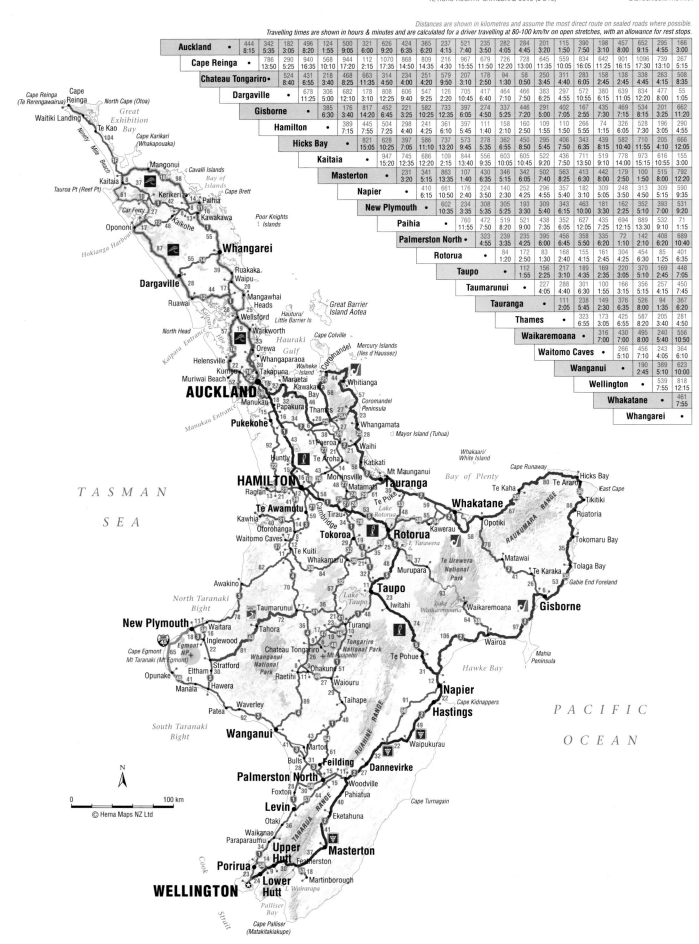

Cape Reinga (Te Rerengawairua)
North Cape (Otoa)
Cape
Reinga
Waitiki Landing
Great Exhibition Bay
Te Kao
Cape Karikari (Whakapouaka)
Ninety Mile Beach
Mangonui
Cavalli Islands
Bay of Islands
Kaitaia
Tauroa Pt (Reef Pt)
Kerikeri
Cape Brett
Paihia
Kaikohe
Kawakawa
Poor Knights Islands
Opononi
Car Ferry
Hokianga Harbour
Whangarei
Dargaville
Ruakaka
Waipu
Ruawai
Mangawhai Heads
Wellsford
Hauturu / Little Barrier Is
Great Barrier Island Aotea
North Head
Warkworth
Orewa
Whangaparaoa
Hauraki Gulf
Cape Colville
Helensville
Kumeu
Takapuna
Coromandel
Mercury Islands (Îles d'Haussez)
Muriwai Beach
Waiheke Island
Whitianga
AUCKLAND
Maraetai
Kawakawa Bay
Manukau
Papakura
Coromandel Peninsula
Thames
Pukekohe
Whangamata
Mayor Island (Tuhua)
Huntly
Waihi
Paeroa
Te Aroha
Katikati
Mt Maunganui
Whakaari / White Island
HAMILTON
Morrinsville
Tauranga
Bay of Plenty
Cape Runaway
Hicks Bay
Te Araroa
East Cape
Raglan
Matamata
Te Puke
Te Kaha
Te Awamutu
Cambridge
Tikitiki
Kawhia
Tirau
Lake Rotorua
Ruatoria
RAUKUMARA RANGE
Otorohanga
Tokoroa
Rotorua
Kawerau
Opotiki
Tokomaru Bay
Waitomo Caves
Te Kuiti
L. Tarawera
Matawai
Tolaga Bay
Whakamaru
Te Urewera National Park
Murupara
Te Karaka
Gabie End Foreland
Awakino
Lake Taupo
Taupo
Waikaremoana
Gisborne
North Taranaki Bight
Taumarunui
Iwitahi
Lake Waikaremoana
New Plymouth
Waitara
Turangi
Wairoa
Tongariro National Park
Inglewood
Tahora
Mahia Peninsula
Cape Egmont
Egmont NP
Chateau Tongariro
Mt Ruapehu
Te Pohue
Hawke Bay
Mt Taranaki (Mt Egmont)
Stratford
Whanganui National Park
Ohakune
Opunake
Eltham
Raetihi
Waiouru
Napier
Manaia
Hawera
Waiouru
Taihape
Cape Kidnappers
Hastings
PACIFIC OCEAN
Waverley
Patea
Waipukurau
South Taranaki Bight
Wanganui
RUAHINE RANGE
Marton
Dannevirke
Bulls
Feilding
Woodville
Palmerston North
Foxton
Pahiatua
Cape Turnagain
Levin
Eketahuna
Otaki
TARARUA RANGE
Waikanae
Paraparaumu
Masterton
Upper Hutt
Porirua
Featherston
Martinborough
WELLINGTON
Lower Hutt
L. Wairarapa
Cook Strait
Palliser Bay
Cape Palliser (Matakitakiakupe)

TASMAN SEA

N
0 — 100 km
© Hema Maps NZ Ltd

TASMAN VALLEY, AORAKI/MT COOK NATIONAL PARK (59 A7) ©ISTOCK.COM/TURNERVISUAL

Distances are shown in kilometres and assume the most direct route on sealed roads where possible.
Travelling times are shown in hours & minutes and are calculated for a driver travelling at 80-100 km/hr on open stretches, with an allowance for rest stops.

Distance & Travelling Time Chart (South Island)

Each cell shows the distance in kilometres (top) and the travelling time in hours:minutes (bottom). Rows are read from the city label on the right.

• Alexandra
km: 648 88 300 260 95 799 139 227 836 233 380 643 202 507 547 137 346 193 923 470 232 772 379 558
time: 11:35 1:25 4:40 4:00 1:30 11:40 2:20 3:20 12:55 3:30 6:20 9:20 2:55 9:45 9:50 2:00 6:50 3:00 16:45 6:40 3:25 11:10 5:45 8:40

• Arthur's Pass
km: 198 511 258 733 568 447 398 345 386 414 853 313 671 101 385 97 616 262 462 473 159 701 420 182
time: 3:03 8:35 4:00 11:05 9:35 7:03 6:04 5:01 6:02 6:35 13:25 4:55 10:00 1:04 6:04 1:45 10:20 4:35 6:05 7:55 2:25 10:03 7:05 2:55

• Ashburton
km: 380 343 79 578 400 420 230 166 509 246 698 264 492 283 478 279 437 444 283 583 91 522 393
time: 6:15 5:25 1:05 8:10 6:40 6:05 3:30 2:15 7:25 3:40 10:30 3:55 7:05 4:35 8:45 4:40 7:30 3:55 8:55 1:05 7:35 5:40

• Blenheim
km: 258 736 472 971 793 27 623 559 116 639 1091 129 885 363 647 323 830 524 676 247 311 915
time: 4:15 11:20 6:45 13:50 11:50 0:25 9:25 7:55 1:45 9:25 15:15 1:50 12:45 5:05 9:35 5:05 11:45 8:45 9:35 4:35 4:35 13:15

• Bluff
km: 885 325 443 190 220 942 376 356 1031 470 310 786 30 744 460 784 96 583 239 1105 613
time: 13:35 5:10 6:30 2:55 3:30 13:40 5:45 5:20 14:45 6:55 5:15 11:30 0:30 11:45 8:40 11:50 1:25 10:45 3:40 16:30 8:40

• Christchurch
km: 330 434 170 669 491 338 321 257 427 337 789 182 583 260 544 256 421 374 501
time: 5:10 6:30 2:10 9:15 7:15 5:00 4:35 3:20 6:15 4:55 11:35 2:50 8:10 4:05 8:55 4:10 7:15 6:55 5:00 7:50

• Collingwood
km: 311 841 662 1127 948 235 813 749 131 829 1247 75 1075 416 1075 577 866
time: 5:20 15:10 10:00 19:50 17:05 4:20 12:25 11:20 1:45 12:45 21:55 6:00 16:00 6:55 11:55 6:10 15:05 9:50 12:50

• Dunedin
km: 660 281 204 295 288 703 237 117 792 331 415 416 555 154 539
time: 10:55 4:25 2:50 4:15 4:25 10:00 3:25 1:40 11:05 4:35 6:35 7:50 3:10 8:05 9:35 8:10 2:15 9:45

• Fox Glacier
km: 302 264 532 536 371 551 371 491 490 465 656 530 545 161 123 201 483
time: 5:25 5:25 8:10 10:00 7:15 9:10 7:20 9:05 8:15 8:25 12:20 9:30 10:15 2:55 2:05 3:40 8:50

• Gore
km: 785 225 355 141 171 857 276 271 946 370 261 701 65 644 360 684
time: 12:10 3:35 5:05 2:00 2:35 12:15 4:20 3:55 13:30 5:30 4:20 10:20 0:55 10:20 6:45 10:25

• Greymouth
km: 101 465 355 737 572 350 495 442 289 511 857 329 746 40 324
time: 1:45 9:05 5:20 13:40 10:55 5:30 8:10 6:55 4:35 8:25 16:00 6:15 11:20 0:45 5:40

• Haast
km: 425 141 409 413 248 674 248 368 613 342 533 653 422 284
time: 7:30 3:20 8:10 7:55 5:10 11:10 5:15 7:00 10:15 6:25 10:15 11:25 8:10 5:00

• Hokitika
km: 141 425 359 697 532 390 499 446 329 511 817 369 706
time: 2:30 8:20 5:15 12:55 10:10 6:15 8:05 6:50 5:25 8:15 15:15 6:35 11:15

• Invercargill
km: 855 295 413 160 190 912 346 326 1001 440 280 756
time: 13:05 4:40 6:00 2:25 3:00 13:10 5:15 4:50 14:15 6:25 4:45 11:00

• Kaikoura
km: 332 607 343 842 674 156 494 430 245 510 962
time: 5:30 9:20 5:00 13:55 11:10 2:15 7:25 6:10 3:35 7:45 16:15

• Milford Sound
km: 958 398 619 120 299 1118 455 532 1146 549
time: 16:50 6:15 9:25 2:20 5:05 18:25 7:45 8:15 18:35 8:55

• Mount Cook
km: 612 207 212 429 264 666 94 214 755
time: 10:00 3:00 3:10 6:30 3:50 9:45 1:10 3:55 10:30

• Nelson
km: 224 754 588 1026 861 104 739 675
time: 3:45 12:45 8:25 16:15 13:30 2:10 9:55 9:35

• Oamaru
km: 543 233 87 412 290 586 120
time: 8:30 3:40 1:10 5:55 4:50 8:20 1:45

• Omarama
km: 596 113 161 342 170 650
time: 9:50 1:55 2:40 5:25 2:40 9:50

• Picton
km: 285 763 499 998 830
time: 4:40 11:45 7:10 16:05 13:20

• Queenstown
km: 673 113 331 179
time: 12:30 1:50 5:35 2:45

• Te Anau
km: 838 278 499
time: 14:30 4:35 7:05

• Timaru
km: 456 274
time: 7:20 4:35

• Wanaka
km: 566
time: 10:45

• Westport

Map place names

Cape Farewell, Collingwood, Golden Bay, Takaka, Rangitoto ki te Tonga/D'Urville Island, Cook Strait, ABEL TASMAN NATIONAL PARK, TASMAN MTNS, Tasman Bay, Motueka, Okiwi Bay, Picton, Nelson, Richmond, Cloudy Bay, Blenheim, KAHURANGI NATIONAL PARK, Kohatu, Renwick, Clifford Bay, Cape Campbell, Karamea, Westport, Cape Foulwind, Murchison, L Rotoroa, St Arnaud, Mt Travers, NELSON LAKES NATIONAL PARK, INLAND KAIKOURA RANGE, PAPAROA NATIONAL PARK, Reefton, SPENSER MTNS, Hanmer Springs, Kaikoura, Greymouth, Lake Brunner, ALPS, Culverden, Waiau, Cheviot, Hokitika, ARTHUR'S PASS NATIONAL PARK, Arthur's Pass, SOUTHERN, Waipara, Rangiora, Amberley, Ross, Pegasus Bay, Oxford, Kaiapoi, WESTLAND/TAI POUTINI NATIONAL PARK, Franz Josef Glacier, Fox Glacier, Lake Coleridge, Sheffield, CHRISTCHURCH, Lyttelton, Mt Hutt, Burnham, Lincoln, Banks Peninsula, TASMAN GLACIER, Aoraki/Mt Cook, AORAKI/MOUNT COOK NATIONAL PARK, Mt Cook Village, Mt Musgrave, Methven, Rakaia, Akaroa, Akaroa Harbour, Lake Ellesmere, Jackson Head, ALPS, Haast, Lake Tekapo, Lake Tekapo, Ashburton, MOUNT ASPIRING NATIONAL PARK, Lake Pukaki, Fairlie, Geraldine, Lake Ohau, Temuka, Canterbury Bight, Mt Aspiring, SOUTHERN, Twizel, Pleasant Point, Timaru, PACIFIC OCEAN, Milford Sound, Lake Wanaka, Wanaka, Lake Hawea, Omarama, L Aviemore, Waimate, Glenorchy, Tarras, DUNSTAN MTNS, Mt Ida, Lake Benmore, Queenstown, Cromwell, Mt Pisgah, Oamaru, FIORDLAND NATIONAL PARK, Lake Wakatipu, Clyde, Ranfurly, EYRE MTNS, Lake Te Anau, Te Anau, Alexandra, Secretary Is, Doubtful Sound, Manapouri, Middlemarch, Palmerston, Resolution Island, Roxburgh, Raes Junction, Mosgiel, Otago Harbour, Otago Peninsula, Dusky Sound, West Cape, Lumsden, DUNEDIN, Clifden, Gore, Clinton, Milton, Chalky Inlet, Winton, Riverton, Balclutha, Owaka, Molyneux Bay, Nugget Pt, Preservation Inlet, Te Waewae Bay, Invercargill, Bluff, Fortrose, Waikawa, Slope Pt, Foveaux Strait, Toetoes Bay, Mason Bay, Halfmoon Bay (Oban), RAKIURA NP, Stewart Island/Rakiura, Port Pegasus, South West Cape

TASMAN SEA

© Hema Maps NZ Ltd

0   100 km

LEGEND

- Motorway
- State Highway - sealed
- State Highway - unsealed
- Major Road - sealed
- Major Road - unsealed
- Intermediate Kilometres — 17
- Alpine Pacific Triangle Tourism Route
- Inland Scenic Tourism Route — 72
- Southern Scenic Tourism Route
- Twin Coast Tourist Route
- Thermal Explorer Tourist Route
- Pacific Coast Tourist Route
- Surf Highway 45
- Forgotten World Tourist Route
- Classic New Zealand Wine Trail
- The Great Alpine Highway

20 TOP THINGS TO DO

1 GREAT WALKS

There are six DOC Great Walks in the South Island: Abel Tasman Coast Track, Heaphy Track, Kepler Track, Milford Track, Rakiura Track and Routeburn Track. The North Island has three DOC Great Walks: Waikaremoana, Tongariro Northern Circuit and Whanganui Journey (a canoe trip).

2 SKI

The South Island has numerous skiing areas, including several near Queenstown and Lake Wanaka. The North Island has three skifields: Whakapapa, Turoa and Maunganui. The season in New Zealand generally runs between mid June and October.

3 FOLLOW WINE TRAILS

The Hawke's Bay region is the North Island's largest wine producing area; other major areas include Waiheke Island, West Auckland, Warkworth/Matakana, Gisborne and Martinborough. The South Island's largest wine producing region is Marlborough, and Central Otago, Nelson and Waipara are other booming areas.

4 CRUISE

In Auckland or Paihia you can charter a yacht or join a boat cruise around local islands. A highlight from Russell or Paihia is the cruise out to the Hole in the Rock. Cruising is also a good way to experience the waterways of Fiordland and Marlborough Sounds.

5 SEE WILDLIFE

Live kiwi displays can be seen throughout New Zealand including at the Auckland Zoo, the Kiwi Encounter at Rainbow Springs in Rotorua, Mt Bruce National Wildlife Centre, the National Kiwi Centre in Hokitika, and at the Orana Wildlife Park in Christchurch. The South Island's West Coast offers tours to see New Zealand's only white heron nesting site, and both coasts offer the chance to see colonies of both blue and yellow-eyed penguins. Spy upon fur seals at Cape Foulwind or along the Catlins Coast, and see the world's only mainland colony of Northern Royal albatross at Taiaroa Head on the Otago Peninsula.

6 SAMPLE LOCAL PRODUCE

Te Puke is New Zealand's kiwifruit 'capital'. Sample mussels and oysters on Coromandel Peninsula, tuatua at Ninety Mile Beach, kumara at Dargaville, honey just south of Warkworth, bacon in Pokeno, cheese in Eltham and Oamaru, and sun-ripened fruits from orchards in Hawke's Bay and Central Otago. Delicious crayfish are a highlight of any visit to Kaikoura, Greenshell mussels are a tasty treat in Havelock, and internationally-famous oysters can be found in Bluff. And don't forget to stock up on NZ's best preserves at Barker's in Geraldine.

KAWARAU BRIDGE BUNGY JUMP (65 G6) NEAR QUEENSTOWN

7 SCENIC FLIGHTS

A scenic flight is a great way to see New Zealand's more remote scenery, like the sounds of Fiordland, and the glaciers of the Southern Alps. It's also a good way to see Australasia's highest mountain and the southern hemisphere's longest glacier located in Mt Cook National Park.

8 ADVENTURE ACTIVITIES

New Zealand is a wonderful country to experience a mind-numbing array of adventure activities from sky diving, bungy jumping, jet boating, mountain biking, and bridge climbing, through to kayaking, skiing, white-water rafting, four-wheel driving, diving, gliding and hot-air ballooning.

9 BUSHWALKS AND TRAMPS

Tramp in the Waipoua Forest, the Waitakere and Hunua Ranges, Whakarewarewa Forest, Tongariro and Whanganui national parks, and the Tararua Ranges in the North Island. Good hikes in the South Island include those found in the Abel Tasman, Kahurangi, Rakiura and Fiordland national parks.

10 THE TRANZALPINE TRAIN JOURNEY

This spectacular four hour journey winds through the breathtaking scenery of Arthurs Pass, en route to the west coast township of Greymouth from the eastern city of Christchurch.

11 GEOTHERMAL PHENOMENON, HOT POOLS AND SPRINGS

Rotorua and Taupo offer numerous geothermal parks, while hot pool complexes can be found at Rotorua, Taupo, Te Aroha, and Kaikohe, and also at Waiwera, Miranda and Parakai near Auckland. In the South Island seek out the spa townships of Hanmer Springs and Maruia Springs in the Lewis Pass.

12 SHOP

Auckland, Wellington and Dunedin offer a good range of designer shopping, and smaller cities offer artworks, gourmet food products and quality knitwear. On the West Coast of the South Island, good quality jade (greenstone) jewellery and carving are brilliant souvenirs.

13 FISH

Trout can be caught at in most fresh water lakes and rivers throughout the North and South Islands. For big game-fishing head to Tutukaka, Whangaroa Harbour, or the Bay of Islands. Salmon can be snared on most South Island rivers and lakes, including the Rakaia River, a world renowned salmon fishing area.

14 EXPERIENCE MAORI CULTURE

Cultural experiences can be found throughout New Zealand including those located at Waitangi, Auckland, Rotorua and Christchurch. There are numerous historic pa sites and marae to see throughout NZ, particularly around the North Island's East Coast.

15 BUNGY JUMP

Bungy jump off the Auckland Harbour Bridge, at Rotorua's Agrodome, or over the Waikato River in Taupo. Numerous jumps can be found in and around Queenstown, including the 134m high Nevis Highwire, Australasia's highest.

16 SURF

On the rough west coast, board surfers enjoy the breaks of Taranaki, Raglan, Piha, Muriwai and Ahipara. Highly recommended surfing venues on the east coast include: Castle Point, Gisborne, Mt Maunganui, Whangamata, Mangawhai Heads, Waipu Cove and Sandy Bay.

17 CAVE

The Waitomo region has extensive cave systems and caves can also be found throughout the nation at key sites including the Waipu Caves, Kawiti Caves, and Te Anau Caves. New Zealand's deepest cave, Nettlebed, is located in the South Island's Kahurangi National Park.

18 GOLF

Premium golf experiences are offered at Kauri Cliffs in Northland, Gulf Harbour north of Auckland, Wairakei near Taupo, and Terrace Downs near Christchurch. To tackle some of New Zealand's toughest holes, head to Clearwater Resort in Christchurch.

19 SCENIC DRIVES

To see the best of New Zealand's scenery, follow designated tourist routes such as the North Island's Twin Coast Discovery Highway, Thermal Explorer Highway and Pacific Coast Highway. In the South Island the Southern Scenic Route, Alpine Pacific Triangle, and Inland Scenic Route offer stunning scenery.

20 MOUNTAIN BIKE RIDES

Mountain bike tracks abound, from sites located at Woodhill and Waiheke Island in Auckland, the Whakarewarewa Forest in Rotorua, through to the Central Otago Rail Trail, and Queen Charlotte Walkway in the south.

25 MUST-SEE ATTRACTIONS

LORD OF THE RINGS MOVIE-SET LOCATIONS
(Throughout this atlas major filming locations are shown with a 🎬 symbol).

CAPE REINGA LIGHTHOUSE (1 A1)
The meeting point of the Tasman Sea and the Pacific Ocean.

KERIKERI'S OLD BUILDINGS (4 A8)
New Zealand's oldest stone building (1833) and New Zealand's oldest house (1822).

POOR KNIGHTS ISLANDS MARINE RESERVE (4 E13)
One of the world's finest dive locations.

AUCKLAND (7 D4)
View the Sky Tower, Kelly Tarlton's Antarctic Encounter and Underwater World, and Waiheke and Rangitoto Islands.

CATHEDRAL COVE AND THE COROMANDEL PENINSULA (8 D13)
For beautiful beaches perfect for swimming, fishing and boating.

WAITOMO CAVES (11 H5)
To see glow-worm caverns and to try caving, abseiling and black-water rafting activities.

MOUNT TARAWERA (13 H6)
See the excavated dwellings of the Buried Village, near Rotorua.

ROTORUA (13 G4)
For colourful geothermal attractions, including hot springs, mud pools and geysers.

CRUISE TO WHITE ISLAND (14 E11)
Take a cruise from Whakatane to walk upon New Zealand's most active volcano.

LAKE TAUPO AREA (19 E4)
Explore this mammoth lake, its wild trout fishery, and geothermal areas.

MOUNT TARANAKI (23 D5)
See New Zealand's 'most climbed mountain' at 2517m.

TONGARIRO NATIONAL PARK (26 A12)
Ski at Whakapapa or Turoa, hike the Tongariro Crossing, and tramp up live volcanoes.

CHAMPAGNE POOL, WAI-O-TAPU THERMAL AREA (13 J5)

©ISTOCK.COM/MATEJAY

©ISTOCK.COM/WILDNEROPIX
SEALY TARNS TRACK IN AORAKI/MT COOK NATIONAL PARK (59 B6).

WELLINGTON (33 F1)
Don't miss the highlights of New Zealand's capital: Te Papa Museum, the Embassy Theatre, Wellington Cable Car, Carter Observatory, and the Wellington Botanical Gardens.

MARLBOROUGH REGION (40)
Visit wineries and kayak or cruise the Sounds.

PANCAKE ROCKS BLOWHOLES (45 B5)
Explore spectacular limestone rocks and blowholes.

FRANZ JOSEF (49 G6) & FOX (49 H4) GLACIERS
Experience massive rivers of ice on foot or by helicopter.

MT COOK NATIONAL PARK (59 A7)
View the Tasman Glacier and Aoraki Mt Cook, Australasia's highest mountain at 3754m.

LAKE TEKAPO (60 D10)
Marvel at the vividness of this turquoise-blue glacial lake.

CHRISTCHURCH (56 D10)
Stroll through Hagley Park, punt on the Avon River, and visit the International Antarctic Centre.

DUNEDIN (74 H11)
Admire the city's wealth of Victorian and Edwardian architecture, and visit Larnach Castle, the Royal Albatross Centre, Penguin Place, and take a ride on Taieri Gorge Railway.

CURIO BAY (78 H11)
Photograph this fossilised forest in the Catlins, dating back from the Jurassic age.

INVERCARGILL'S QUEENS PARK (127 A3)
Meander around this 80ha CBD park, which comes complete with a golf course, the Southland Museum and Art Gallery, an aviary, and rose garden.

QUEENSTOWN (65 H4) AND WANAKA (66 D8)
The Adventure Capital: ride the gondola, cruise the lake on the TSS Earnslaw, discover the wine trails of Central Otago, take a scenic flight, hike in Mount Aspiring National Park, and visit Puzzling World.

MILFORD SOUND (63 C7)
Cruise, kayak or dive at Milford Sound and see the Bowen and Stirling Falls, Mitre Peak, and spy upon bottlenose dolphins, fur seals, and Fiordland crested penguins.

TE ARAROA
The Long Pathway

- Cape Reinga
- Whangarei
- **Auckland**
- Rotorua
- Gisborne
- Wanganui
- Napier
- Nelson
- **Wellington**
- Greymouth
- **Christchurch**
- Queenstown
- Dunedin
- Invercargill

Base image © Geographx 2011

Te ARAROA
THE LONG PATHWAY

A 3,000 KILOMETRE LONG WALKING TRACK running from Cape Reinga to Bluff is now open. Named Te Araroa, which means the Long Pathway, it was created by the Te Araroa Trust in consultation with local authorities and Department of Conservation (DOC) conservancies, by linking existing walking tracks with new routes.

Much of Te Araroa's route crosses countryside and coast that is legally walkable, for example on road reserve that has been surveyed off but not built on, or coastline, or down rivers where canoes are recommended, or across DOC land that is not tracked. Some of the tracks, for example the routes through the Tararua and Richmond Ranges, should only be attempted by experienced trampers. At major rivers, it's up to individual trampers whether they decide to cross and how they go about it. Te Araroa Trust recommends that any trampers who attempt remote tracks or significant river crossings should first consult with the local area office of DOC so they are fully aware of hazards. For safety, trampers must always fill out intentions forms at every hut and shelter they pass, even if they don't overnight there. Trampers should also take advantage of mountain safety and river crossing courses; for more information regarding courses visit www.mountainsafety.org.nz.

For the latest track information and trail maps visit www.teararoa.org.nz.

Legend

Symbol	Meaning	Symbol	Meaning	Symbol	Meaning
	Drinking Water		Picnic Area		Stream Water
	Toilets		Rubbish Disposal		Walking Track
	Fireplace/BBQ		Shower		Fees Apply

- Fully serviced Campgrounds have flush toilets, tap water, showers, rubbish collection, picnic tables and usually some powered sites. Many have barbecues or fireplaces, a kitchen, laundry and shop.
- A fee is charged at most DOC campsites.

NORTHLAND

Name	Map Ref
Cable Bay	4 A11
Forest Pools	3 B6
Kapowairua (Spirits Bay)	1 A2
Maitai Bay	2 F7
Otamure Bay	4 D13
Pandora	1 B2
Puketi	3 A7
Puriri Bay	4 C12
Raetea North Side	3 A3
Rarawa Beach	1 E4
Sunset Bay	4 A11
Tapotupotu	1 A1
Trounson Kauri Park	3 G5
Twilight	1 B1
Uretiti Beach	4 J13
Urupukapuka Bay	4 A11
Waikahoa Bay	4 D12

AUCKLAND

Name	Map Ref
Akapoua Bay	36 D4
Awana Beach	36 D5
Harataonga	36 D5
Home Bay	6 J12
Medlands Beach	36 E5
Motuihe	7 D6
Motuora	6 F11
The Green	36 E4
Whangapoua	36 C4

WAIKATO

Name	Map Ref
Arohena (Landing Road)	12 G10
Billygoat Basin	8 G12
Booms Flat	8 G12
Broken Hills	8 G13
Catleys	8 G12
Fantail Bay	8 A9
Fletcher Bay	8 A10
Hotoritori	8 G12
Kahikatea (certified self-contained vehicles only)	8 H12
Kakaho	19 C2
Ngaherenga	18 B13
Piropiro	18 C12
Port Jackson	8 A10
Shag Stream	8 G12
Stony Bay	8 A10
Totara Flat	8 G12
Trestle View	8 G12
Waikawau Bay	8 B11
Wainora	8 G12
Wentworth	8 J14
Whangaiterenga	8 G12

BAY OF PLENTY

Name	Map Ref
Dickey Flat	10 F10
Hot Water Beach	13 H6
Humphries Bay (1 night, walk/kayak in)	13 G6
Lake Tarawera Outlet	13 H6
Lake Okareka	13 G5
Mangamate	20 C11
Matata	14 D9
Okahu Road	20 D12
Rerewhakaaitu-Ash Pit Road	13 J6
Rerewhakaaitu-Brett Road	13 J6
Sanctuary	20 D11

EAST COAST

Name	Map Ref
Anaura Bay	16 J11
Boulders	15 G3
Manganuku	15 J3
Mokau Landing	21 E2
Omahuru (Ogilvies)	14 J12
Orangihikoia	20 D14
Rosie Bay	21 E2
Te Pakau (8 Acre)	14 J12
Te Taita O Makoro	21 D2
Waikaremoana Motor Camp	21 E3 (Fully serviced)
Whitikau	15 G5

TONGARIRO/TAUPO

Name	Map Ref
Army Road	19 G6
Clements Clearing	19 G6
Clements Road End	19 G6
Kaimanawa Road	19 J3
Kakapo	19 G6
Mangahuia	18 J12
Mangawhero	26 C11
Pokaka Mill	18 H12
Te Iringa	19 G6
Urchin	19 J3
Whakapapa Motor Camp	26 A12 (Fully serviced)

WHANGANUI

Name	Map Ref
John Coull	25 A7
Maharanui	18 H8
Makino	27 F4
Mangapapa	18 J8
Mangapurua	25 A7
Mangawaiiti	25 A7
Ngaporo	26 C8
Ohauora	17 J7
Ohinepane	18 G9
Piripiri	30 A11
Pohangina Base	30 A11
Poukaria	18 G9
Simpsons Domain	26 H13
Tieke Kainga	26 B8
Whakahoro	18 H8

WAIRARAPA/WELLINGTON

Name	Map Ref
Bucks Road	33 C6
Catchpool Valley	33 F3
Corner Creek	33 G4
Graces Creek	33 F3
Holdsworth	34 B7
Kiriwhakapapa	34 A8
Matiu/Somes Island	33 E2
Otaki Forks	33 A5
Putangirua Pinnacles	33 G5
Waikawa	29 H5
Waiohine Gorge (road closed)	33 B7

HAWKES BAY

Name	Map Ref
Everetts	20 J11
Glenfalls	20 J10
Kumeti	30 B11
Lake Tutira	28 A12
Lawrence	28 C8
Kuripapango (Ox Bow)	27 C7
Mangatutu Hot Springs	28 A8
Tamaki West	31 B5
Waikare River Mouth	28 A14

NELSON/MARLBOROUGH

Name	Ref	Notes
Acheron Accommodation Hse	47 E6	
Angelus Hut	42 H12	
Aussie Bay	40 G9	
Butchers Flat	39 H6	
Bay of Many Coves	40 F11	
Black Rock	40 F10	
Blumine Island/Oruawairua	40 F12	
Camp Bay	40 F11	
Canaan Downs	38 F9	
Cannibal Cove	40 E12	
Cobb River	37 H6	
Coldwater Stream	43 J2	
Courthouse Flat	42 C11	
Cowshed Bay	40 G10	
Davies Bay	40 G9	
Elaine Bay	40 E8	
Ferndale	40 F10	
French Pass	40 C9	
Harvey Bay	40 E8	
Jacobs Bay	40 E9	
Kauauroa Bay	40 E10	
Kawatiri	42 F11	
Kenepuru Head	40 F11	
Kerr Bay	42 G13	Fully serviced
Kowhai Point	43 E3	
Kumutoto Bay	40 G10	
Lake Rotoroa	42 G11	
Lake Tennyson	47 C4	
Lucky Bay	40 C9	
Marfells Beach	44 E12	
Mill Arm	40 B9	
Mill Flat	43 C7	
Moawhitu	40 B8	
Moetapu Bay	40 G9	
Molesworth Cobb Cottage	43 J5	
Momorangi Bay	40 G9	Fully serviced
Ngaruru Bay	40 G12	
Nikau Cove	40 F10	
Nydia	40 F8	
Okiwi Bay	48 C14	
Onamalutu	40 J8	
Pelorus Bridge	39 H6	Fully serviced
Penguin Bay	40 B9	
Picnic Bay	40 F10	
Pipi Beach	40 F9	
Puhi Puhi	48 C13	
Putanui Point	40 G9	
Rarangi	40 J10	
Ratimera Bay	40 G11	
Robin Hood Bay	40 H11	
Schoolhouse Bay	40 F12	
Siberia Flat	42 C11	
South Arm	40 B9	
Tawa Bay	40 E8	
Totaranui	38 D9	
Waimaru	40 E10	
Waiona Bay	40 D9	
West Bay	43 F1	
Wharehunga Bay	40 F12	
Whatamango Bay	40 G11	
Whites Bay	40 J10	

CANTERBURY

Name	Ref	Notes
Ahuriri Bridge	67 A4	
Andrews Shelter	52 B10	
Avalanche Creek Shelter	52 B8	
Craigieburn Shelter	52 D9	
Deer Valley	46 E13	
Grey River	53 D7	
Greyneys	52 B8	
Hawdon Shelter	52 B9	

There are many more places to stay in the great outdoors managed by Department of Conservation. For details of Great Walks, walk in campsites near huts, information about huts or any other conservation information contact your nearest visitor centre or visit the DOC website: www.doc.govt.nz

DOC HOTLINE 0800 362 468 For fire, search and rescue call 111

Name	Ref	Notes
Klondyke Corner	52 C8	
Lake Pearson (Moana Rua)	52 C10	
Lake Taylor	46 J12	
Loch Katrine	46 H12	
Mt Nimrod	60 J13	
Orari Gorge	61 E4	
Otaio Gorge	68 B11	
Peel Forest	61 C5	Fully serviced
Pioneer Park	61 F2	
Temple	59 F4	
Waihi Gorge	61 E4	
White Horse Hill	59 B6	
Wooded Gully	52 E14	

WEST COAST

Name	Ref	Notes
Gillespies Beach	49 G3	
Goldsborough	45 H3	
Hans Bay	45 J3	
Kohaihai	37 H2	
Lake Ianthe	50 C9	
Lake Mahinapua	45 J1	
Lake Paringa	58 B12	
Lyell	41 G6	
Marble Hill	46 D12	
Ottos/MacDonalds	49 F6	
Slab Hut Creek	46 B9	

OTAGO

Name	Ref	Notes
Boundary Creek	58 J10	
Cameron Flat	58 G11	
Danseys Pass	67 G6	
Glencoe	68 J10	
Homestead	66 E14	
Kidds Bush	66 A9	
Kinloch	64 F12	
Lindis Pass Historic Hotel Campsite	66 D11	
Macetown	65 F6	
Moke Lake	64 H14	
Papatowai	78 G13	
Pleasant Flat	58 E12	
Purakaunui Bay	79 H2	
Skippers Township	65 F4	
St Bathans Domain	67 F2	
Sylvan	64 E11	
Tawanui	78 E13	
Trotters Gorge	74 B13	
Twelve Mile Delta	64 H13	

SOUTHLAND

Name	Ref	Notes
Cascade Creek	64 G10	
Deer Flat	64 H9	
Hall Arm	69 E6	
Henry Creek	70 B12	
Kiosk Creek	64 H9	
Lake Gunn	64 F10	
Mackay Creek	64 J9	
Maori Beach	80 D5	
Mavora Lakes	71 B4	
Monowai	70 H10	
North Arm	80 E5	
Piano Flat	72 E11	
Port William	80 D5	
Smithy Creek	64 G9	
Thicket Burn	76 D10	
Totara	64 J9	
Upper Eglinton	64 G9	
Walker Creek	64 J9	

SITUATED BETWEEN ROTORUA AND GISBORNE, the remote and rugged Te Urewera National Park contains the largest forested wilderness remaining in the North Island. State Highway 38 links Wairoa on the East Coast with Murupara in the Central North, through the wilderness playgrounds of Te Urewera National Park past Lake Waikaremoana, one of the North Island's most scenic lakes.

The Park is popular with hunters and encompasses Lake Waikaremoana, which is known for its great walking tracks and trout fishing. Although much of the Park is remote and inaccessible, there are several well-maintained and clearly signposted walking tracks, with viewpoints and ridges that provide great photographic opportunities. The three- to four-day Lake Waikaremoana Great Walk follows the lake's shore for most of its 46km length. A moderately easy tramp, this Great Walk provides ample opportunities for swimming and fishing. There are five huts and five camping areas provided along the walk —bookings are essential for both huts and campsites.

Aniwaniwa, on the shores of Lake Waikaremoana, has a comprehensive visitor's centre and fully-serviced Department of Conservation motorcamp. Permits are available from the visitor centre for hunting introduced animals, including deer and pigs.

For centuries Te Urewera has been home to the Tuhoe people, dubbed the 'Children of the Mist' as it is believed they are the offspring of Hine-puhohu-rangi the celestial mist maiden.

See maps 14, 20 and 21 for touring maps.

RAINFOREST IN TE UREWERA NATIONAL PARK

OZSTOCK IMAGES

N

0   10 km

© Hema Maps NZ Ltd

CONTAINING BOTH ACTIVE AND EXTINCT VOLCANOES, Tongariro National Park is New Zealand's oldest national park and a World Heritage area. In Peter Jackson's Lord of the Rings films, the Park's dramatic landscape was the setting for Mordor and Mount Ngauruhoe made an appearance as Mount Doom.

Forming the Park's heart are the active volcanoes: Mt Tongariro with its red, raw craters; the charred cinder cone of Mt Ngaruahoe; and majestic Mt Ruapehu's snowy crown and sinister crater lake. Scenic flights provide excellent views of the mountains' diverse peaks.

The cream of the Park's hikes is the 17km Tongariro Crossing, which provides an opportunity to experience some of the most scenic volcanically active areas. There is the option to climb to the summit of Mt Ngauruhoe or Mt Tongariro en route. It is not a round trip so transport must be arranged at one end, or you can catch a shuttle bus from Turangi, Whakapapa Village or National Park Village.

During the summer, guided walks take you to NZ's largest active volcanic crater lake at Mt Ruapehu's summit, or you can 'self-hike' the Skyline Walk, a one-and-a-half-hour round trip, or the dramatic Meads Wall Walk. Other popular walks include the Tama Lakes and Taranaki Falls.

In winter, snow falls in the park and Mt Ruapehu has three skifields: Whakapapa, Turoa and Tukino.

See maps 18, 19, 26 and 27 for touring maps.

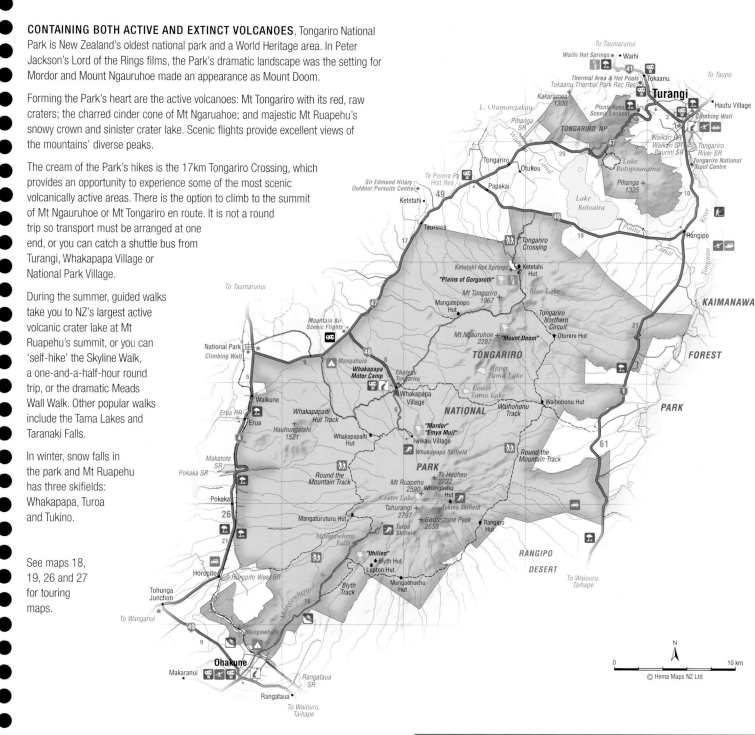

MT NGAURUHOE

VIEW TO MT RUAPEHU

TRAMPERS AND CLIMBERS FLOCK TO ARTHUR'S PASS National Park for its amazing ridges, screes, deep valleys, waterfalls, glaciers and gorges. Sitting right in the heart of the national park, Arthur's Pass village has basic facilities and several accommodation options. The excellent DOC headquarters has detailed maps of all the tracks in the area and enthusiastic trampers can enquire here about overnight trips. There's also a small museum, which gives some historical background, and an old Cobb and Co coach on display. Nearby, at the Alpine Chapel, you can gain great views of the Avalanche Creek Waterfall.

Since Arthur Dobson surveyed the pass in 1864, it has been a popular route linking Westland and Christchurch. Skiers, trampers and climbers have been frequenting the region since the railway was completed in the early 1920s. During the summer experienced climbers flock to Arthur's Pass to climb nearby mountains including Mt Rolleston, Mt Murchison and Mt Franklin. In winter the park is transformed by snow, making it popular with skiers and climbers.

Make sure you stop at the lookout point above the pass to see the native mountain parrots called keas and gain excellent views before heading downhill to Otira.

See maps 45, 46, 51 and 52 for touring maps.

WAIMAKARIRI RIVER RUNNING THROUGH ARTHUR'S PASS.

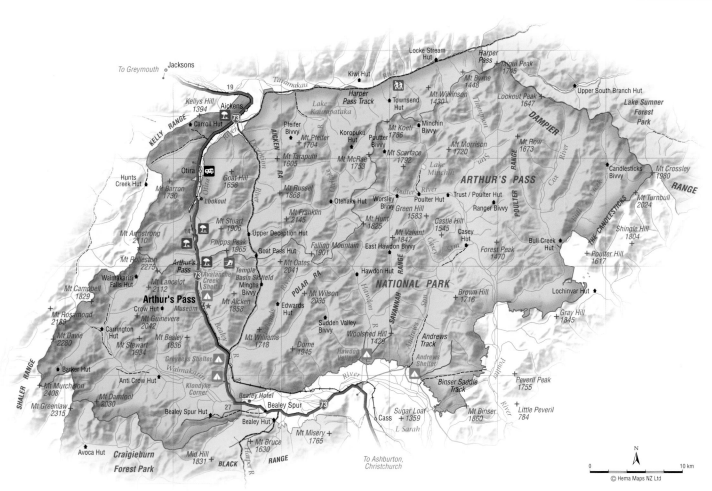

THE VAST KAHURANGI NATIONAL PARK is a 400,000 hectare wilderness of native forest and nikau palms that is a haven for adventure activities. The park contains New Zealand's deepest cave: Nettlebed.

Many tracks cross this isolated park, including the Heaphy Great Walk and the Wangapeka Track. It takes four to six days to complete this Great Walk, and DOC provides seven huts and six campsites. Many a hiker emerges from the national park reporting sightings of great spotted kiwi, short and long tailed bats, and giant land snails. The quiet township of Karamea is both the beginning and the end point of the Heaphy Track.

The beginning of the Heaphy Track provides one of the region's nicest short walks. A suspension bridge crosses the Kohaihai River accessing a 40-minute side-loop that winds through an amazing nikau palm grove where these beautiful palms thrust their smooth, ringed trunks from the pure white sands of a lagoon.

See maps 37, 38 and 42 for touring maps.

WATERFALL AT
AORERE-BOULDER LAKE

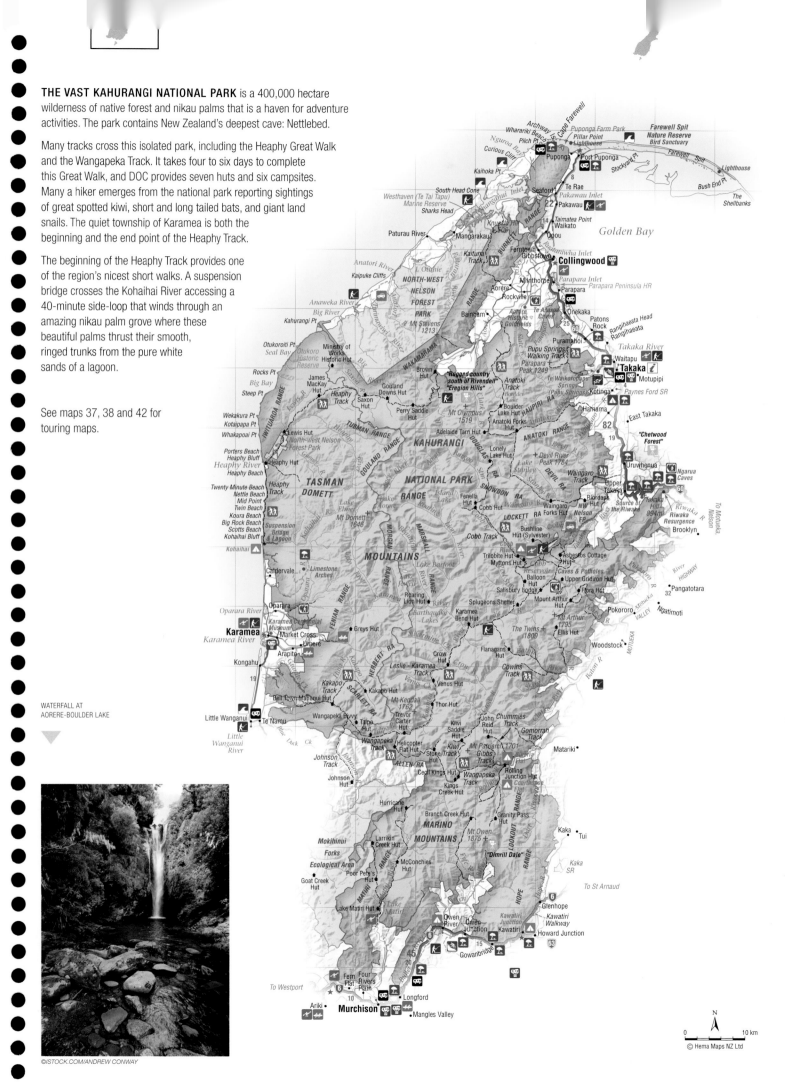

©ISTOCK.COM/ANDREW CONWAY

© Hema Maps NZ Ltd

0   10 km

N

PART OF TE WAHIPOUNAMU, the Southwest New Zealand World Heritage Area, Mount Aspiring National Park has many scenic walks including the Cascade Saddle Route and Rees-Dart Track, a moderately difficult four to five day tramp along the Rees and Dart rivers. Stunning mountain scenery, alpine landscapes and the Dart Glacier are all seen en route. It is also possible to climb Mount Aspiring (Tititea), but peaks such as these and the glaciers are best explored with experienced guides from a reputable trekking and climbing company.

The Routeburn Great Walk journeys through Mount Aspiring National Park and down over Harris Saddle into the Fiordland National Park. The 32km track takes two to three days to complete, and four huts and two campsites are provided along the way.

From Wanaka, SH6 follows the northern shores of Lake Wanaka towards Makarora before the incredibly scenic drive heads through Mount Aspiring National Park then hugs the Haast River into the small settlement of Haast, on the west coast. Be sure to stop at the Gates of Haast to see the river tumbling down over massive boulders.

See maps 57, 58, 64 and 65 for touring maps.

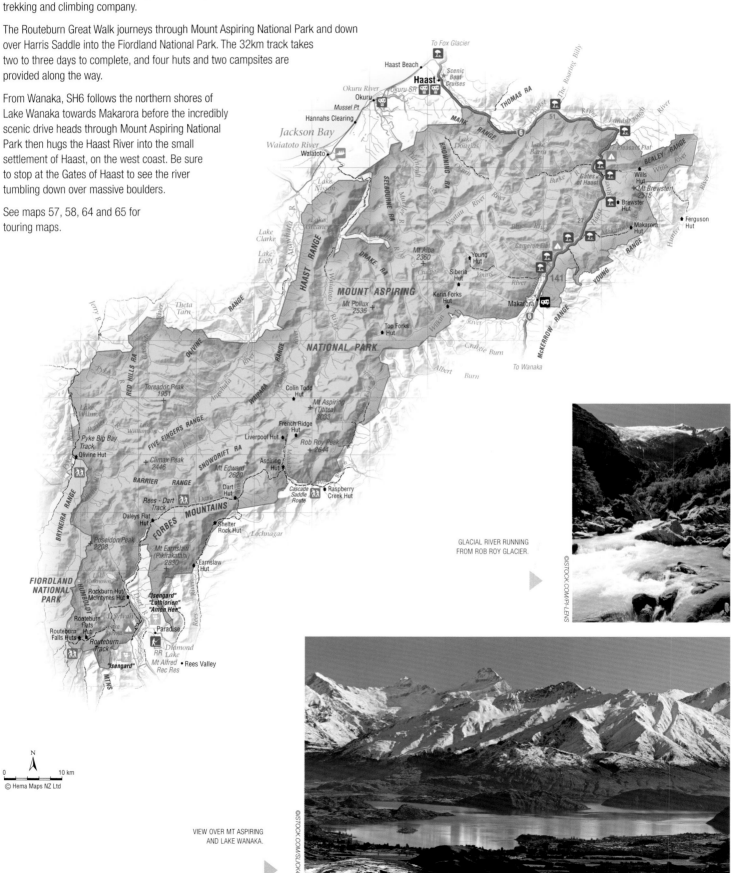

GLACIAL RIVER RUNNING FROM ROB ROY GLACIER.

©ISTOCK.COM/PI-LENS

VIEW OVER MT ASPIRING AND LAKE WANAKA.

©ISTOCK.COM/SLICK479

0   10 km

© Hema Maps NZ Ltd

THE INCREDIBLY SCENIC DRIVE TO MT COOK via SH80 skirts the shores of Lake Pukaki beneath the textured slopes of the Ben Ohau Range. The tiny alpine village of Mount Cook is an ideal base from which to explore the Aoraki/Mt Cook National Park, which boasts Australasia's highest mountain (Mt Cook) and the rumbling Tasman Glacier, the Southern Hemisphere's longest frozen river of ice.

During the winter heli-skiing is a popular pastime and various companies provide options for guided tours. Skiers can also land on the 27km-long Tasman Glacier in a ski plane. Heli-hiking on Mt Dark's rugged ridges and wide open basins is available year round.

In the summer visitors can enjoy 4WD journeys, rock climbing and hiking or an informative cruise on Tasman Glacier Lake, beneath the terminus of the glacier. There are a number of good family walks that leave from the village, including the Bowen Bush Walk, Glencoe Walk, Kea Point and Hooker Valley Track. The Blue Lakes to the Tasman Glacier viewpoint track offers stunning views of the glacier's lunar-like landscape. If you're looking to conquer Aoraki/Mt Cook (3754m) or Mt Tasman (3498m), Alpine Guides can lead you to either summit. Those tackling longer hikes should check in at the DOC Visitors' Centre for a weather update, as conditions can change fast, no matter what the season.

The Westland Tai Poutini National Park encompasses the Fox and Franz Josef glaciers, whose icy tongues are surrounded by rainforest. To really experience these massive rivers of ice, take a guided tour or take a helicopter ride for a bird's-eye view.

©ISTOCK.COM/PH-LENS

From Franz Josef it's a short drive to the glacier's car park. To gain a good view of the Franz Josef Glacier hike to Sentinel Rock (around 10 minutes) or hike the 3km Glacier Valley Walk to the terminal face (around an hour and a half return). You can join a guided tour and hike up the face of the glacier to explore stunning blue ice on the world's steepest and fastest-flowing commercially guided glacier.

Helicopter flights and guided walks of the Fox Glacier are also on offer and it takes around five minutes' hiking from the car park to gain a view of the glacier or 30 minutes to get close to the terminal face.

See maps 49, 50, 59 and 60 for touring maps.

VIEW ACROSS LAKE PUKAKI
TO AORAKI/MT COOK.

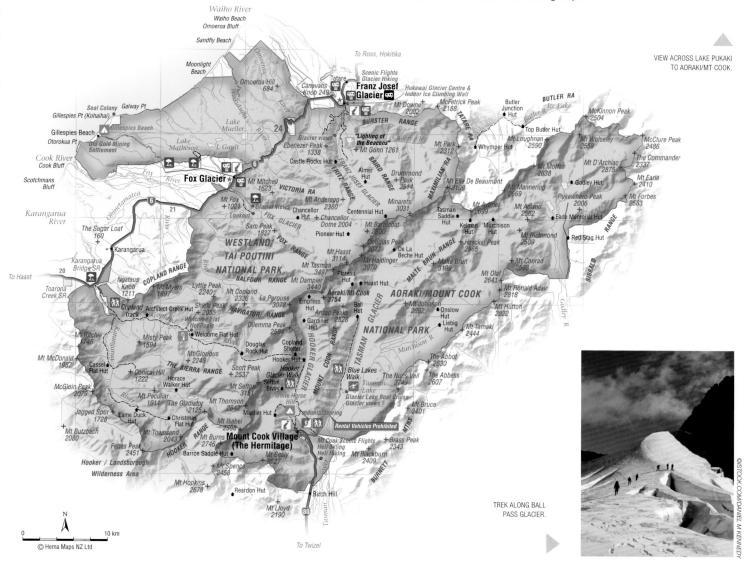

TREK ALONG BALL
PASS GLACIER.

©ISTOCK.COM/DANIEL M KENNEDY

ST ARNAUD, RIGHT AT THE DOORSTEP OF NELSON LAKES NATIONAL PARK, provides a great base for trampers exploring the park's various tracks including the four-to-seven-day Travers-Sabine Circuit. The two- to three-day hike to Lake Angelus, a stunning alpine pond, is also popular. There are also several excellent day hikes, including the Lake Rotoiti Circuit, Mount Robert loop track, St Arnaud Range track, and Whisky Falls track. A commercial water-taxi service on the lake whisks hikers to and from various points or provides cruises of the lake on demand. The latest weather report, maps, hut tickets and hunting permits are available from the DOC visitor centre in St Arnaud.

Located on the lake edge, the Rotoiti Nature Recovery Project is an important conservation site. The Bellbird and Honeydew tracks provide an insight into this work and honeydew nectar can be seen literally dripping from the beech trees.

Hunting in the region is encouraged by DOC and other activities visitors can enjoy include ice-skating, gold panning and mountaineering. There is a small ski club field at Mount Robert, but it can only be accessed by a 1.5 to 2 hour walk. Both Lake Rotoiti and Lake Rotoroa are good for trout fishing, and water-skiing is permitted on Rotoiti.

The wild Buller River, which begins its journey from Lake Rotoiti and flows through Murchison to meet the sea at Westport, is popular with both white-water rafters, white-water kayakers and anglers.

See maps 42, 46 and 47 for touring maps.

© ISTOCK.COM/FKIENAS

HIKER ON THE SABINE TRACK.

VIEW FROM THE JETTY AT LAKE ROTOITI TO MT ROBERT.

© ISTOCK.COM/RAY HEMS

0   10 km

© Hema Maps NZ Ltd

MOST VISITORS TRAVEL TO FIORDLAND NATIONAL PARK TO SEE MILFORD SOUND, but the journey to get there is equally inspiring with lots of wild waterfalls, forested valleys, granite peaks, crystal-clear lakes and friendly townships, like Te Anau and Manapouri, where activities are bountiful. Milford Sound lies within Te Wahipounamu, Southwest New Zealand World Heritage Area, and is totally encompassed by the Fiordland and Mount Aspiring National Parks.

To really experience Milford Sound, a cruise or kayaking trip is essential. Boat trips travel the length of the fiord and take one to two hours. There's the chance to see bottlenose dolphins, fur seals and Fiordland crested penguins, and diving is excellent here where deepwater species, including black corals, are visible at a much shallower depth. Even if you can't dive, you can still explore underwater attractions by visiting the Milford Deep Underwater Observatory.

Some people choose to reach the Sound by hiking the Milford Track, New Zealand's most popular Great Walk. The 54km track takes five days to complete and three huts are provided for overnight stays. Bookings (months in advance) are essential for both independent and guided walkers as numbers are limited.

Fiordland has a wealth of other Great Walks and hiking tracks. The 60km Kepler Track traverses lake edges, beech forest, alpine summits and a glacial valley over three to four days. The 32km Routeburn Track leads from the forested valleys of the Fiordland National Park up over Harris Saddle into Mount Aspiring National Park over two to three days. It is not a circuit so you'll need to consider transport at either end.

Further south, Lake Manapouri provides the launching point for visits to Doubtful Sound. Cruise or kayak the winding arms of this ice-carved fiord and its ever-changing panorama of waterfalls, beech forest and wildlife. Lake Manapouri and Lake Hauroko both provide access to the Dusky Track to Dusky Sound, an 84km track averaging ten days to complete. The Tuatapere Hump Ridge Track is a three-day hike providing a slice of the Fiordland experience.

See maps 63, 64, 69, 70, 75, and 76 for touring maps.

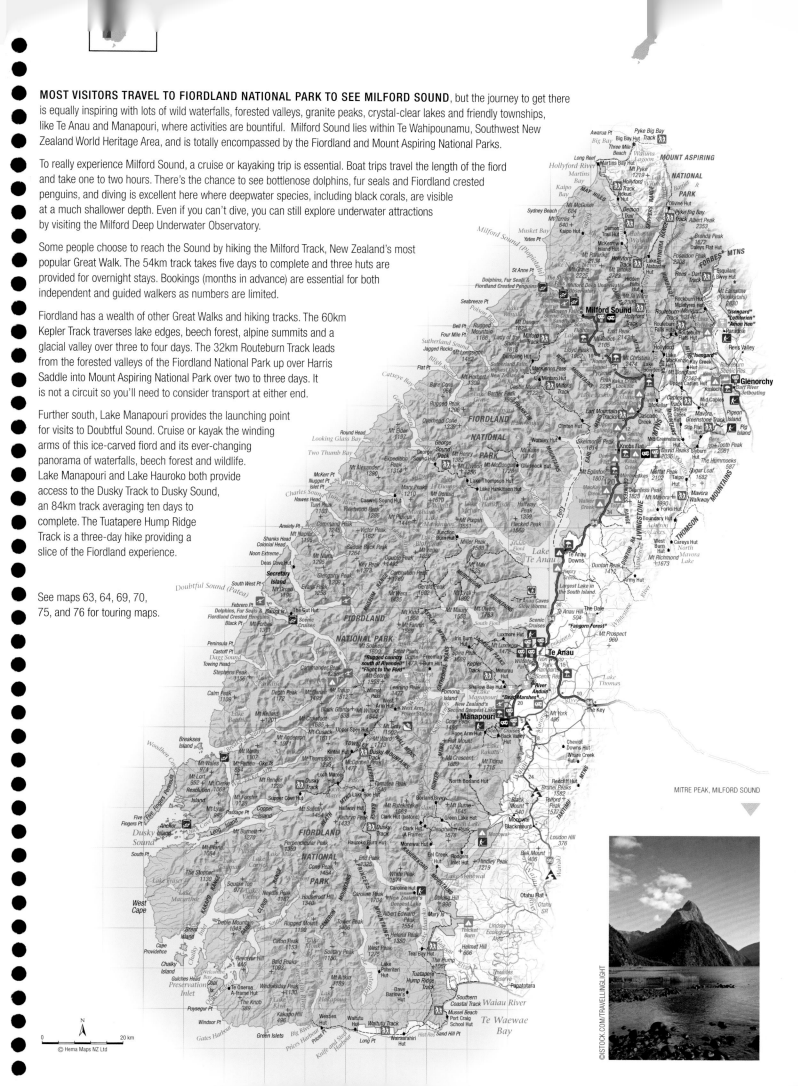

MITRE PEAK, MILFORD SOUND

©ISTOCK.COM/TRAVELLINGLIGHT

© Hema Maps NZ Ltd

0   20 km

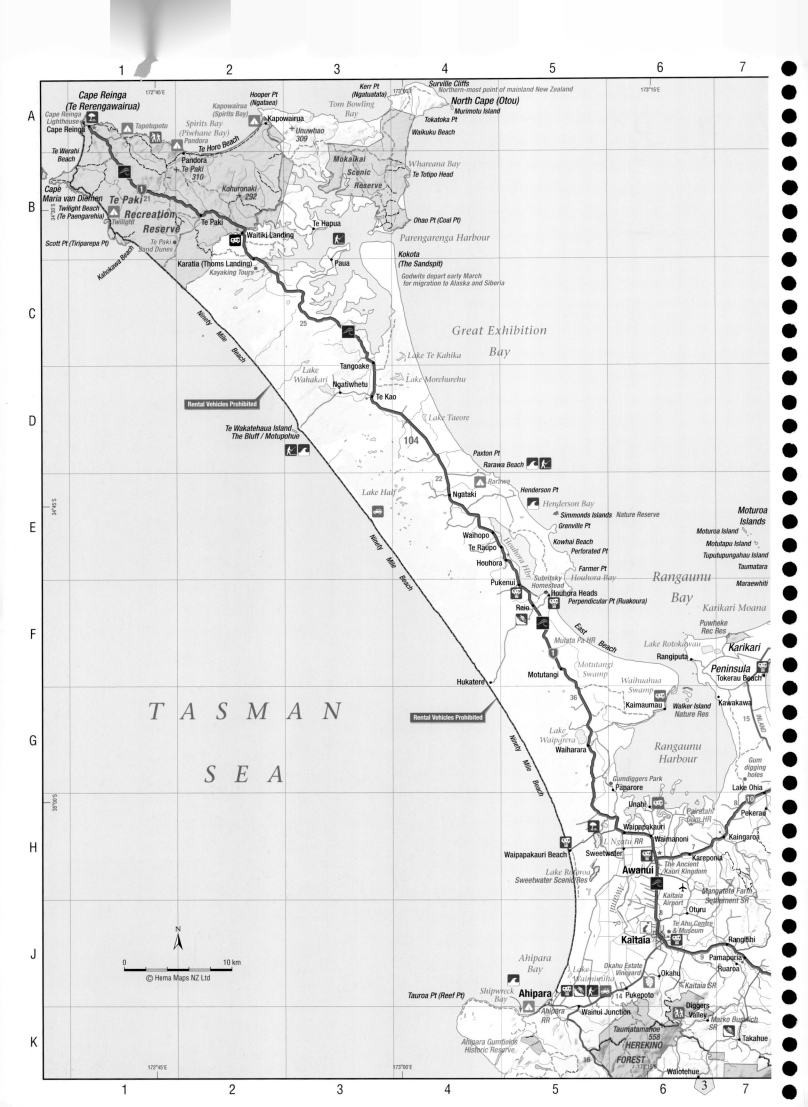

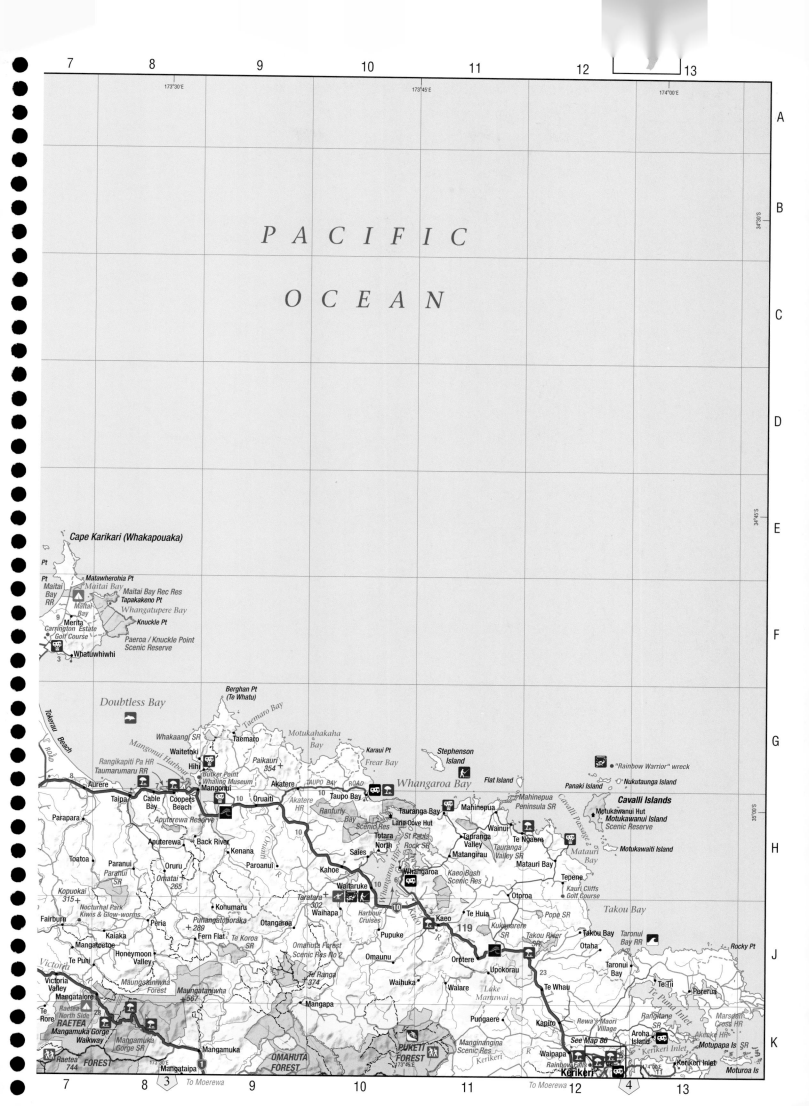

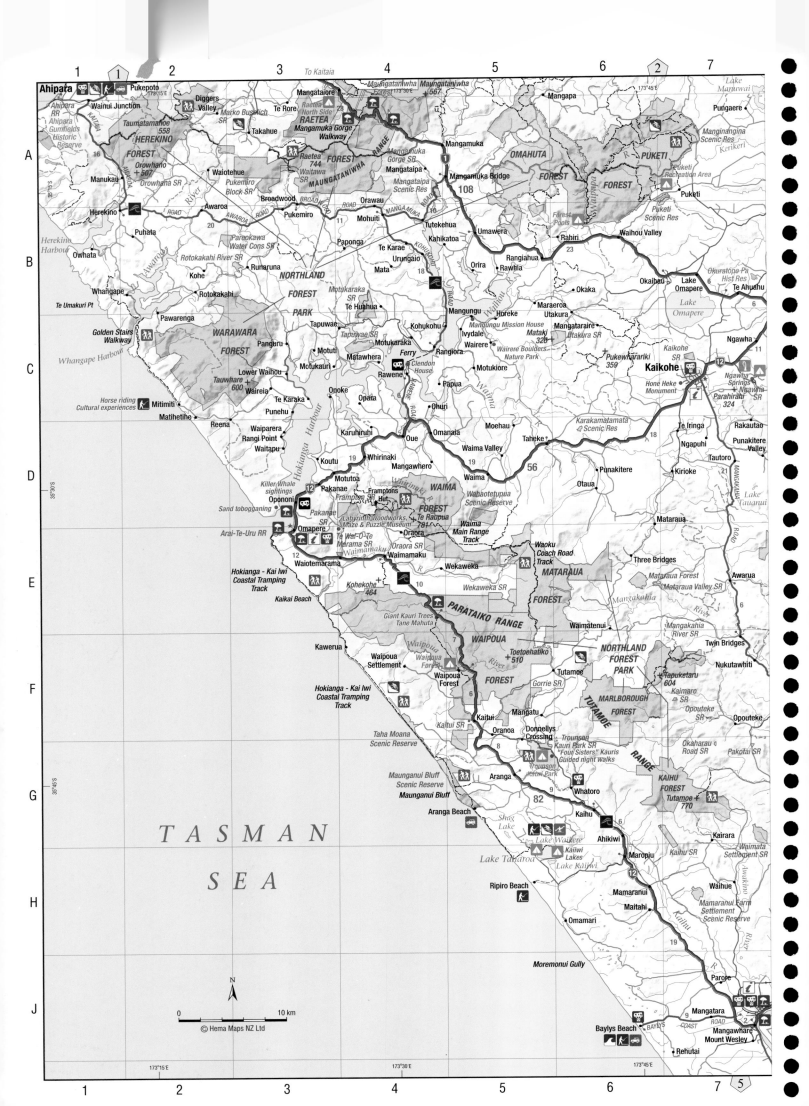

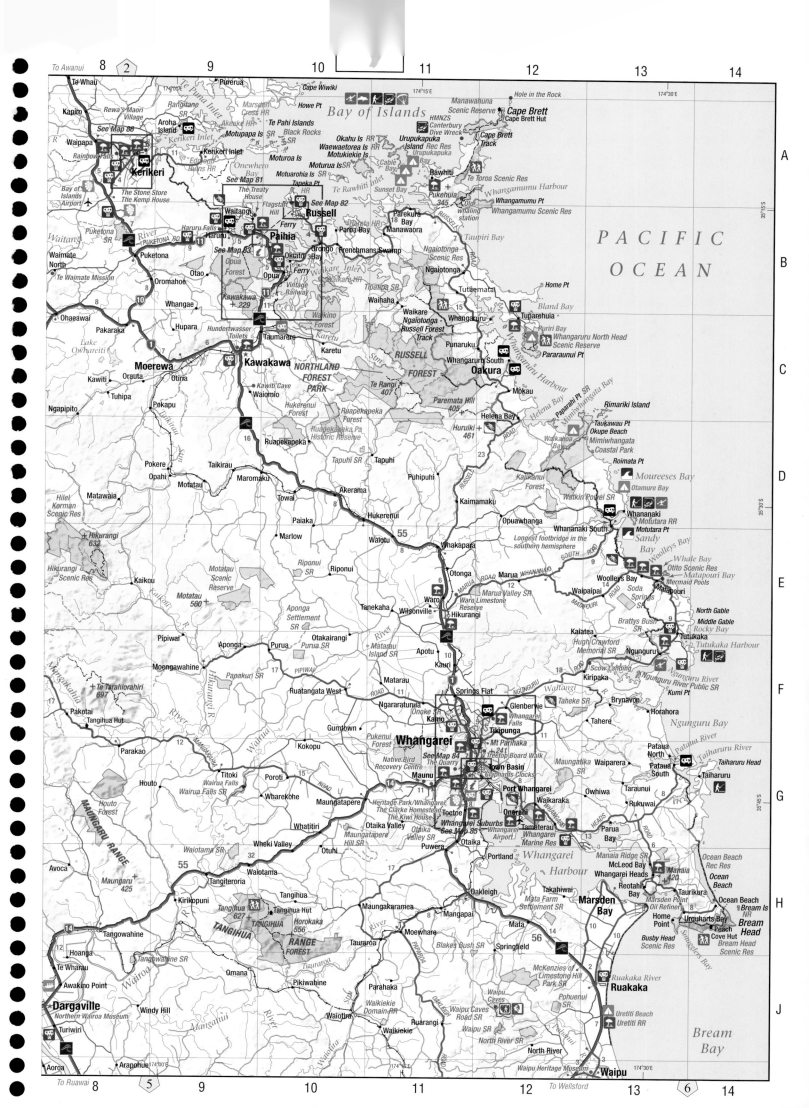

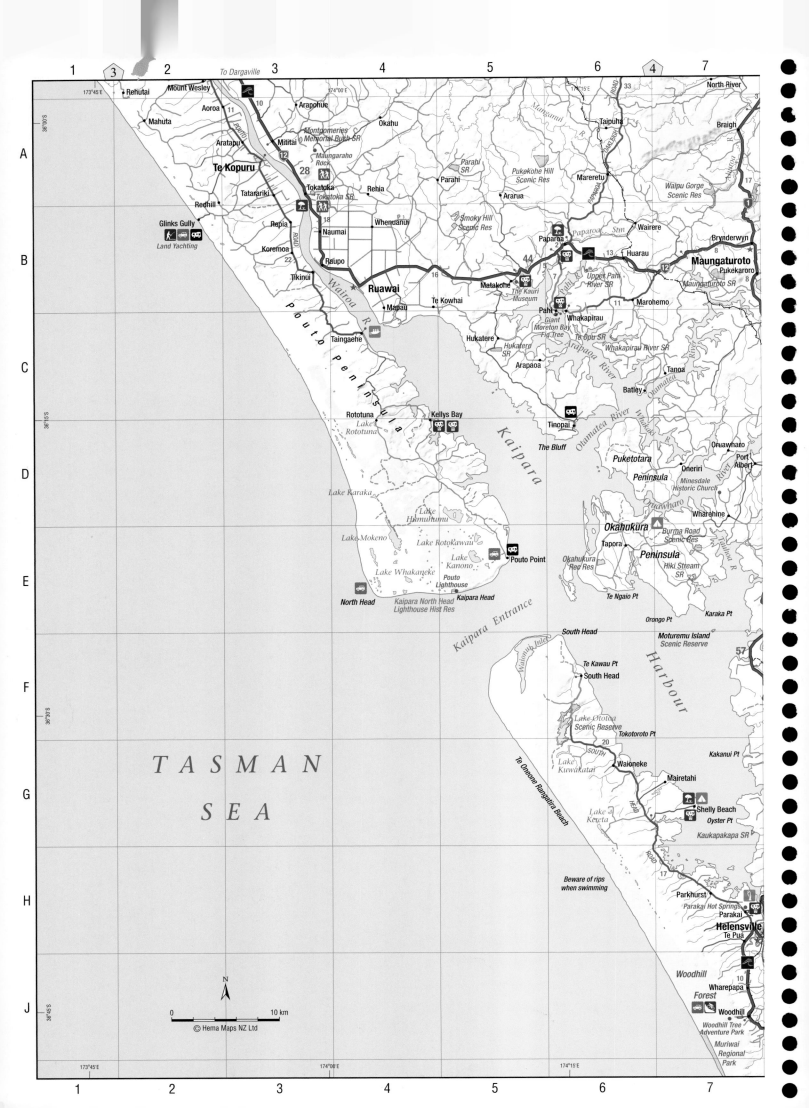

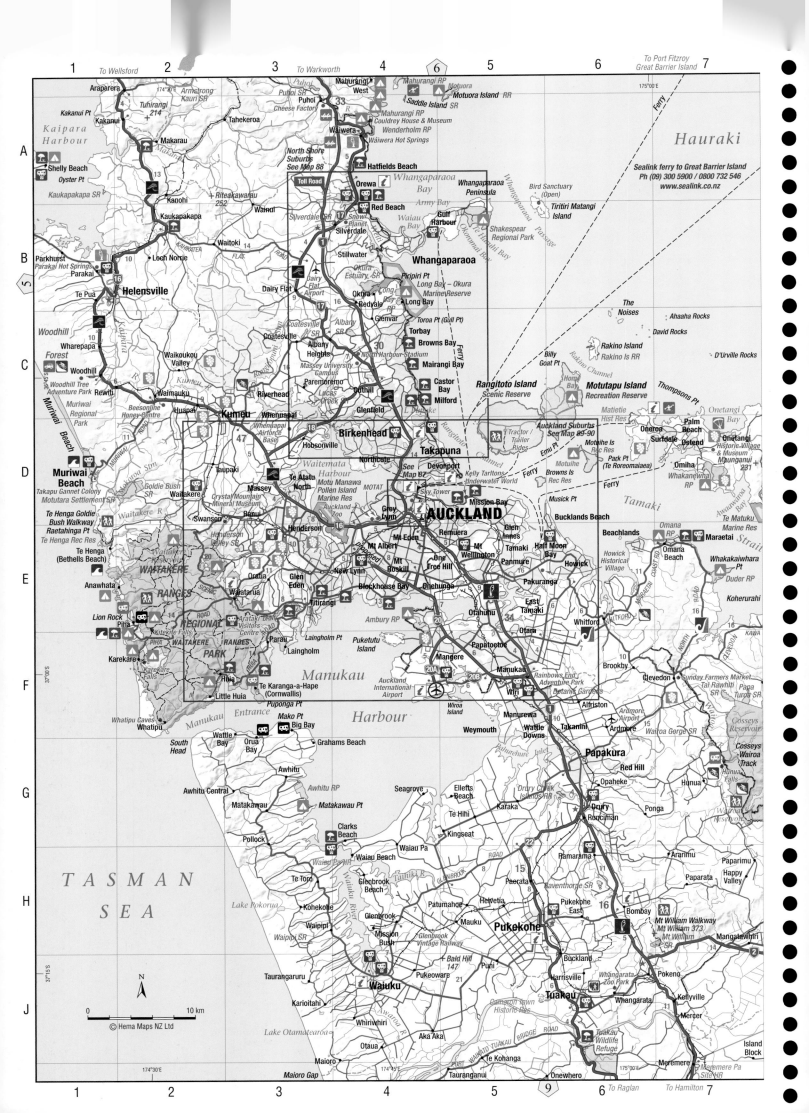

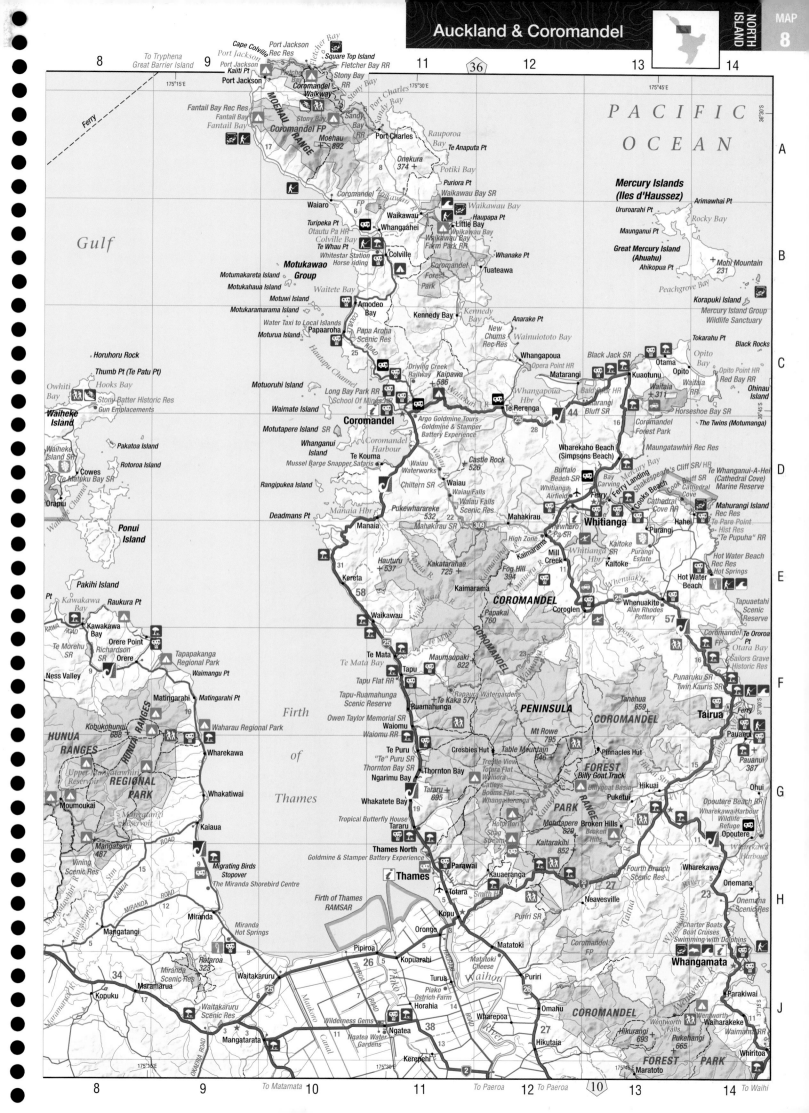

MAP
9
NORTH ISLAND

1 To Auckland 2 To Auckland 7 3 4 175°00'E 5 6 7

174°45'E 175°15'E

A

Manukau
Auckland Suburbs See Map 89-90
Harbour
Puketutu Island
Ambury RP
Mangere
Papatoetoe
Otara
Whitford
Brookby
Wiroa Island
Auckland International Airport
Wiri
Manukau
Rainbows End Adventure Park
Botanic Gardens
Alfriston
Clevedon
Sunday Farmers Market Tai Rawhiti SR
Ness Valley
Papa Turoa SR
Te Morehu SR
Kawakawa Bay
Orere Point
Richardson SR
Orere
Tapapakanga Regional Park
Waimangu Pt
Matingarahi
Matingarahi Pt
Firth

B

Grahams Beach
Awhitu RP
Matakawau Pt
Weymouth
Wattle Downs
Takanini
Ardmore
Ardmore Airport
Wairoa Gorge SR
Papakura
Red Hill
Opaheke
Hunua
Ponga
Arkarimu
Paparimu
Happy Valley
Cosseys Reservoir
Hunua Falls
Wairoa Reservoir
Upper Mangatawhiri Reservoir
Moumoukai
HUNUA RANGES
Kohukohunui 688
HUNUA RANGES
REGIONAL PARK
Mangatangi Reservoir
Waharau Regional Park
Wharekawa
Whakatiwai
Kaiaua
of
Thames

C

Seagrove
Elletts Beach
Te Hihi
Karaka
Drury
Runciman
Drury Creek Islands RR
Clarks Beach
Waiau Pa NR
Waiau Pa
Waiau Beach
Kingseat
Ramarama
Paerata
22
15
Patumahoe
Helvetia
Pukekohe East
Bombay
Mt William Walkway
Mt William 373
Mt William SR
Mangatawhiri
Mangatangi
Mangatangi 487
Vining Scenic Res
Paparata
Miranda
Miranda Hot Springs
Migrating Birds Stopover
The Miranda Shorebird Centre
Te Toro
Glenbrook Beach
Glenbrook
Mauku
Pukekohe
16
Taihiki R
Ravensthorpe SR

D

Waipipi
Glenbrook
Mission Bush
Glenbrook Vintage Railway
Bald Hill 147
Puni
Buckland
Harrisville
Tuakau
Whangarata Zoo Park
Pokeno
Kellyville
Whangarata
Mercer
Island Block
Kopuku
Maramarua
34
Miranda Scenic Res
Rataroa 323
Waitakaruru
Waitakaruru Scenic Res
Mangatarata
Pukeoware
Waiuku
Taurangaruru
Karioitahi
Whiriwhiri
Aka Aka
Te Kohanga
Tuakau Wildlife Refuge
Cameron Town Historic Res

E

Lake Otamateaoa
Otaua
Maioro
Maioro Gap
Maioro Sands
Waikato River
Port Waikato Sand Dunes Rec Res
Port Waikato
Taurenganui
Onewhero
Onewhero Rec Res
Pukekawa
Meremere
Meremere Pa Site HR
Whangamarino
Whangamarino
Orton
Hapuakohe Track
HAPUAKOHE RANGE
Torehape
Kaihere
Matahuru Scenic Reserve
Maungakawa 535
18
26

F

Wairamarama
"Weathertop"
Limestone Downs
Glen Murray
22
Tikotiko
Lake Whangape
Opuatia
Waikare
Rangiriri Wildlife Refuge
Rangiriri
Lake Waikare
Te Kauwhata
43
Taniwha Pa Historic Res
Matahuru
Mangapiko Valley Scenic Reserve
Mangapiko Valley
Waiterimu
Hapuakohe Ecological Area
Ohinewai
Ohinewai RR

G

Te Karaka Memorial Scenic Reserve
Ngatutura Pt
Kaawa
Naike
75
Woodleigh
Ruawaro
Pukekapia
Rotongaro
Te Kauri
Kimihia
Lake Waahi
Waikaretu
Parikotuku Pt
Matira
Waikorea
Renown
Waikokowai
Mahuta
Weavers Crossing
Huntly Power Station
Rakaumanga
Lake Kimihia Pukemore 282
Huntly
Westmere
Mangawara
Orini
Te Hoe
Hoe-O-Tainui
37
Netherby

H

Otehe (Crayfish Pt)
Pepepe
Glen Afton
Rotowaro
18
Pukemiro
Te Akatea
Dunmore
Hakarimata Scenic Res
Hakarimata Walkway
HAKARIMATA RANGE
Taupiri
Hopuhopu
15
Kainui
Komakorau
TAUPIRI RANGE
Whitikahu
Candyland
24
Horsham Downs
Gordonton
Hamilton Suburbs See Map 91

J

TASMAN SEA
Te Akau
Te Akau South
Te Hara Pt
Kauri Flat
Ruakiwi
Waingaro
Waingaro Hot Springs
Glen Massey
Te Puroa SR
Ngaruawahia
Ngaruawahia Domain R
Horotiu
Te Kowhai
39
Te Rapa
Te Rauri
Lake Rotokauri
Rototuna
Puketaha
Eureka
Ohautira
17
11
Kakariki Scenic Reserve
Karakariki
Hamilton Lake
Karakiriki Rec Res
HAMILTON See Map 91
174°45'E 175°00'E 175°15'E

1 2 To Pirongia 3 11 4 5 To Te Awamutu 6 To Cambridge 7

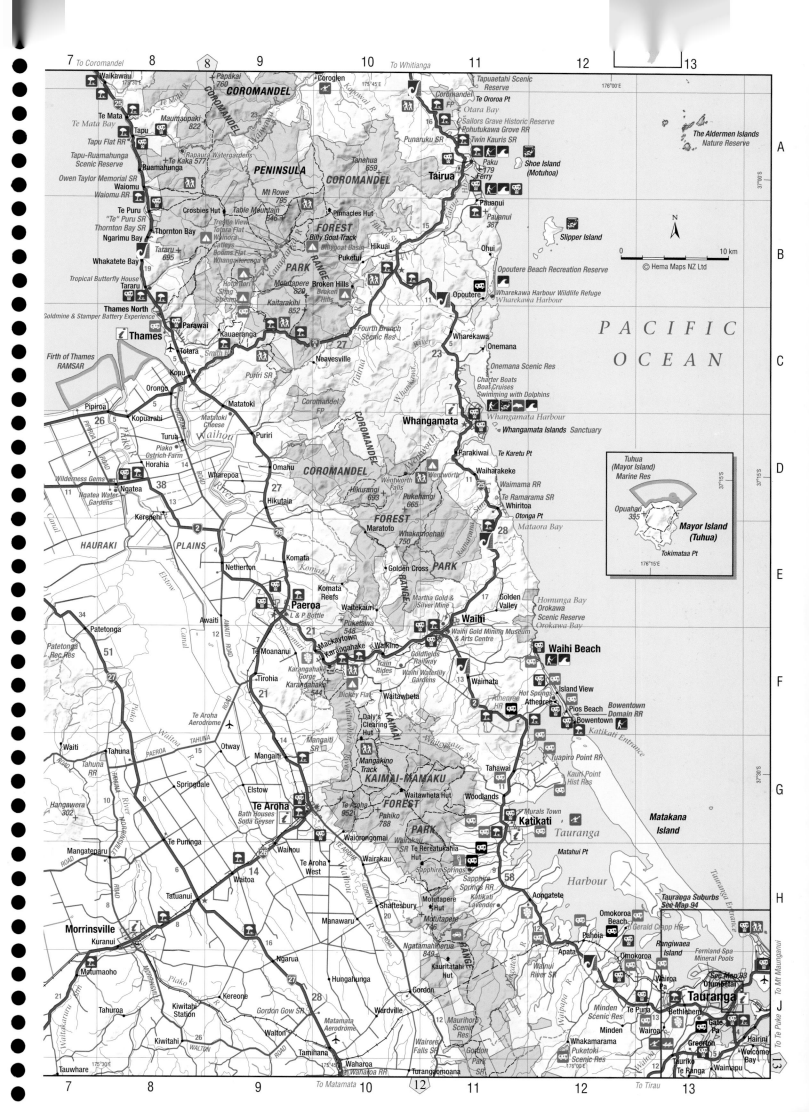

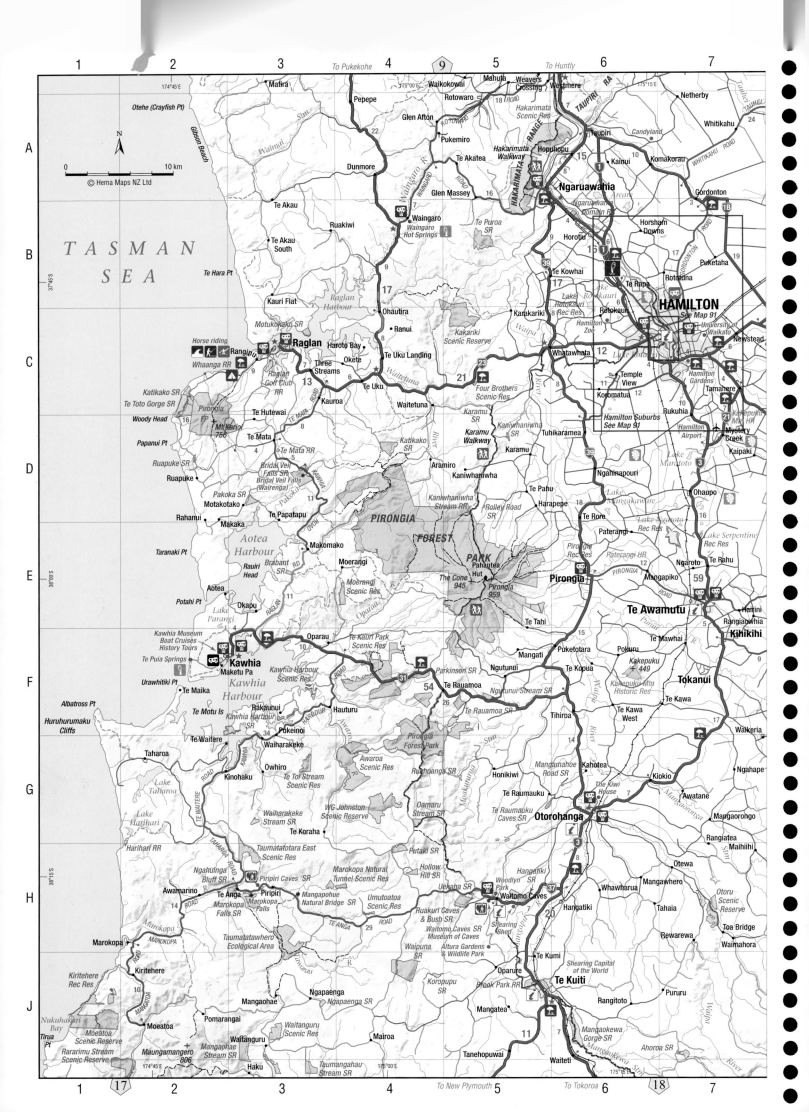

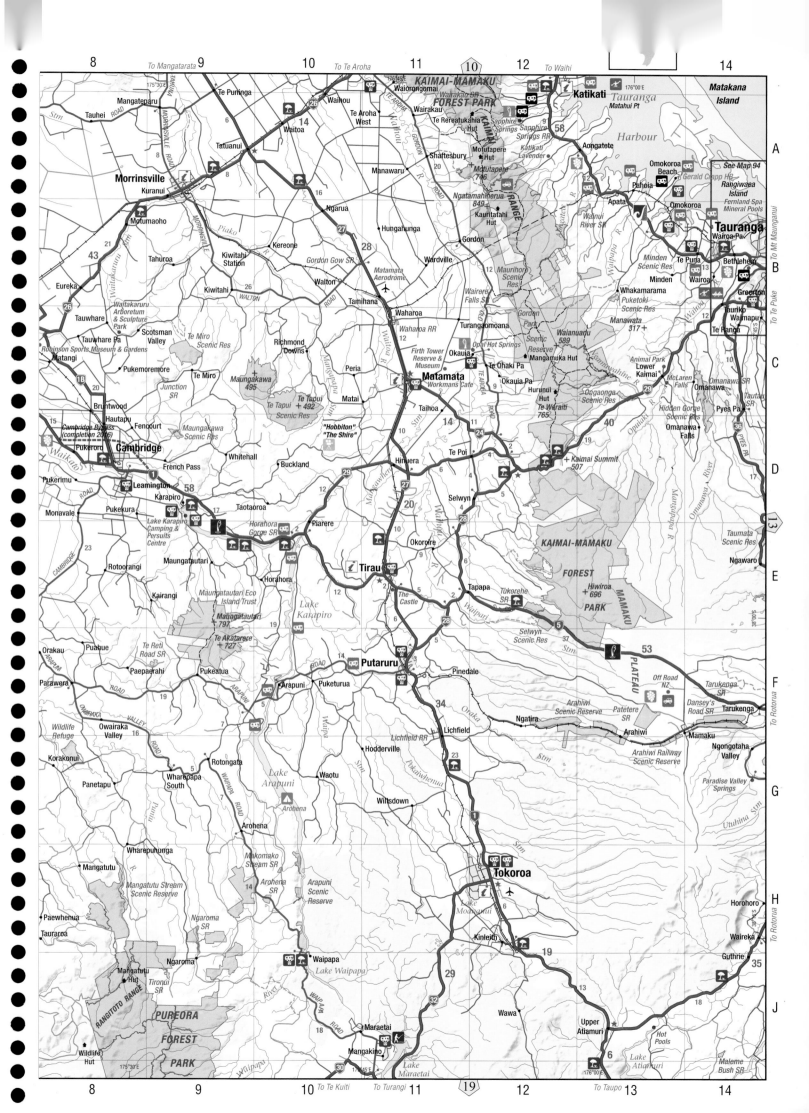

MAP
13
NORTH ISLAND

1 2 10 3 4 5 6 7

To Waihi

Katikati
Tauranga
Matakana Island
176°00'E
Matahui Pt

58
Sapphire Springs
Sapphire Springs RR
Katikati Lavender
Aongatete

Harbour

Omokoroa Beach
Gerald Crapp HR
Pahoia
Apata
Omokoroa
Rangiwaea Island
Wairoa Pa
Motuotau Island SR
Mt Maunganui
Omanu
Te Maunga
Omanu Beach
Tauranga Suburbs
See Map 94
Motiti Island
Tumu Bay
Motuhaku Island
(Schooner Rocks)
Taumataika Pt

Kauritatahi Hut
Wainui River SR

KAIMAI-MAMAKU

Maurihoro Scenic Res

FOREST

Te Puna
Minden Scenic Res
Minden
Whakamarama
Puketoki Scenic Res
Bethlehem
Otumoetai
See Map 93
Taumata
Fernland Spa Mineral Pools
Tauranga
Gate Pa
Greerton
Maungatapu
Matapihi
Papamoa Beach RR
Papamoa Beach
Kairua
35
Blokart Heaven
Taumata 317
Manawata 317
Tauriko
Te Ranga
Hairini
Ngapeke
Welcome Bay
The Monmouth Redoubt & The Tauranga Mission House
Waimapu
Kaitemako
Papamoa
16
Tauranga Eastern Link (completion 2015 toll road)
Okurei Pt
Little Waihi
Maketu
Pukehina Beach

Motunau Island
(Plate Island)

PARK

Gordon Park Scenic Reserve
Waianuaru 589
Mangamuka Hut
Okauia Pa
Hurunui Hut
Te Weraiti 765
Lower Kaimai
Animal Park
McLaren Falls
Omanawa
Omanawa SR
Tautau SR
Pyes Pa
Ohauiti
Kaiate Falls
Kaiate Falls SR
Otawa 564
Otawa Scenic Res
Te Puke
Manoeka
Te Matai
Kiwi 360
Te Puke Vintage Auto Barn
Te Tumu
Pukehina
Ohinepanea
34

Ongaonga Scenic Res
Hidden Gorge Scenic Res
Omanawa Falls
29
40
Kaimai Summit 507
19
Kaimai Summit
To Matamata
To Putaruru
12

KAIMAI-MAMAKU

Tukorehe SR
To Tirau

FOREST

Hiwiroa 696

PARK

17
Otanewainuku 640
Mangatoi
Te Ranga
Douglas Corner
Paengaroa
Longridge Fun Park
Maniatutu
Pongakawa
Pongakawa Rec Res
Pongakawa Valley
31
33
48
Roydon Downs Scenic Reserve
Carrie Gibbons Scenic Res
Manawahe
Pokopoke Stream SR
Lake Rotoehu
L Rotoehu
Lake Rotoehu Scenic Res
Lake Rotoma Scenic Reserve

Taumata Scenic Res
Ngawaro
Mangorewa Scenic Res
Te Pu
Mangapouri Scenic Res
Te Waerenga SR
Rotongata
Penny Road SR
Kaharoa
Hamurana
Okere Falls
Whangamarino
Otaramarae
Matawhaura North SR
Motuoha Pt
Lake Rotoiti
L Rotoiti SR
Gisborne Point
Hinehopu
Rotoehu
Lake Rotoma
9
85
Lake Rotoma Scenic Reserve
30

PLATEAU
53
Selwyn Scenic Res
Waipari Stm
37
Off Road NZ
Tarukenga SR
Oturoa
Hamurana Springs RR
Awahou
Mourea
Hells Gates
Ruato
Haupara Bay
Tikitere
15
Waione Block Scenic Res
Rotoiti
Haroharo 817
Maungawhakamana 728

Ngatira
Arahiwi Scenic Reserve
Patetere SR
Dansey's Road SR
Tarukenga
Waiteti
7
Ngongotaha
Mokoia Is
Lake Rotorua
Mokoia
Te Ngae
Mud Spa
Lake Okataina
Lake Okataina Scenic Reserve
Makatiti Dome Scenic Reserve

Oraka Stm
Arahiwi Railway Scenic Reserve
Arahiwi
Mamaku
Ngongotaha Valley
Mt Ngongotaha Scenic Res
Rainbow Springs & Farm
The Agrodome
Miniature Railway
Rotorua Museum
The Bath House
Orchid Gardens
Holdens Bay
Rotorua Airport
Rotokawa
Hannahs Bay
12
Lake Okareka SR
Lake Okareka
Lake Okareka
Lake Okareka Thermal Valley
Lake Okareka
Miller Bush SR
Humphries Bay
Te Tapahoro RR
Lake Tarawera Outlet

Paradise Valley Springs
Skyline Gondola & Luge
Rotorua
Koutu
Tamaki Tours
Whakarewarewa
Pohutu Geyser
Owhata
Lynmore
See Map 95
Ohinemutu
Utuhina Stm
12
Rotorua Suburbs See Map 96
Waipa Village
Whakarewarewa Lake Tikitapu (Blue Lake) Forest
Lake Tikitapu Lookout
Punaromia
Lake Tarawera
Lake Tarawera Scenic Res
Ruawahia Dome 1111

To Tokoroa

Tokoroa
Kinleith
5
13
30
25
Horohoro
Kapenga
21
The Buried Village
Te Wairoa
Hawaiki Bay
Hot Springs
Lake Rotokakahi (Green Lake)
Lake Rotokakahi SR
Hot Water Beach
Lake Rotomahana
Rerewhakaaitu
Brett Rd & Ashpit Rd
Lake Rerewhakaaitu
Lake Rerewhakaaitu Recreation Reserve

6
19
1
13
35
8
Wairaka
Guthrie
Ngakuru
18
Tamaki Maori Village
Tumunui
Earthquake Flat
Pareheru
Waimangu Scenic Res
Waimangu
Waimangu Volcanic Valley
Rotomahana
Guy Roe Reserve
Ngatamawahine

Wawa
Upper Atiamuri
Hot Pools
Lake Atiamuri
176°00'E
6
Maleme Bush SR
176°15'E
Waikite Valley
Maungaongaonga
Waikite Valley Hot Pools & Thermal Area
Maungaongaonga Scenic Reserve 825
Waiotapu
Waiotapu SR
Rainbow Mtn 566
Rainbow Mtn SR
Kerosene Creek Thermal Area
Lady Knox Geyser
Waiotapu Thermal Area
Paeroa 979
18
176°30'E

To Taupo 19 To Taupo To Murupara 20
1 2 3 4 5 6 7

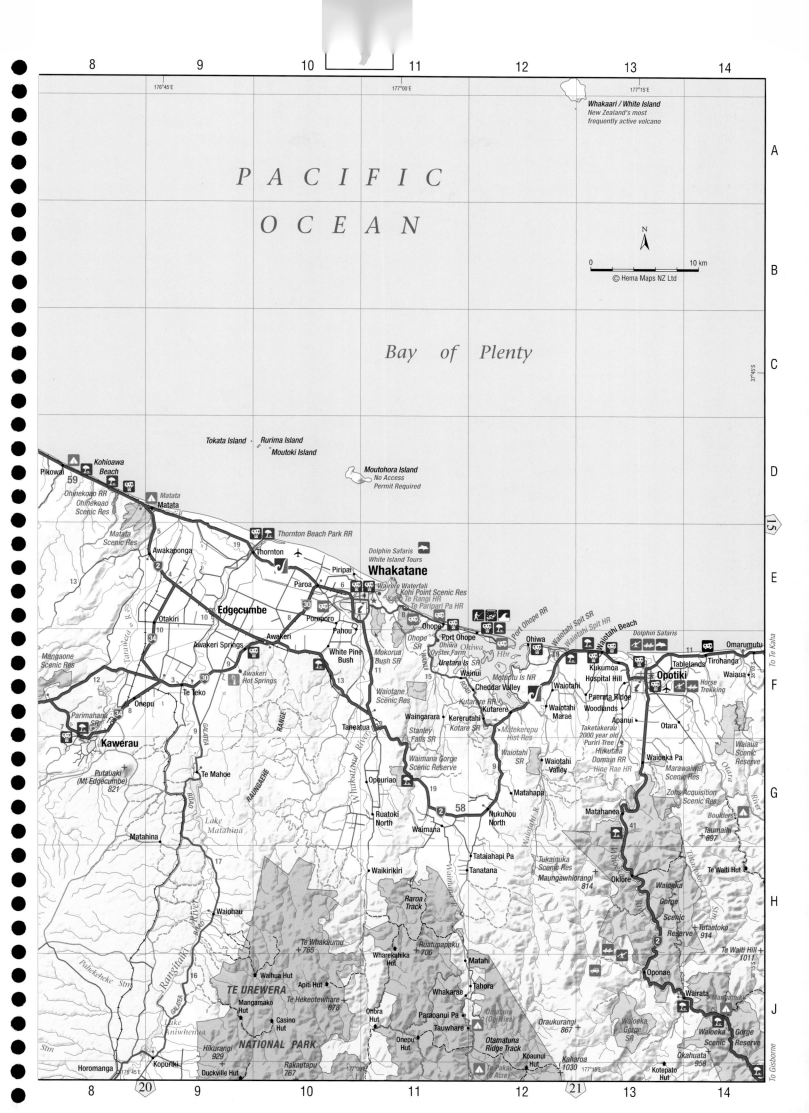

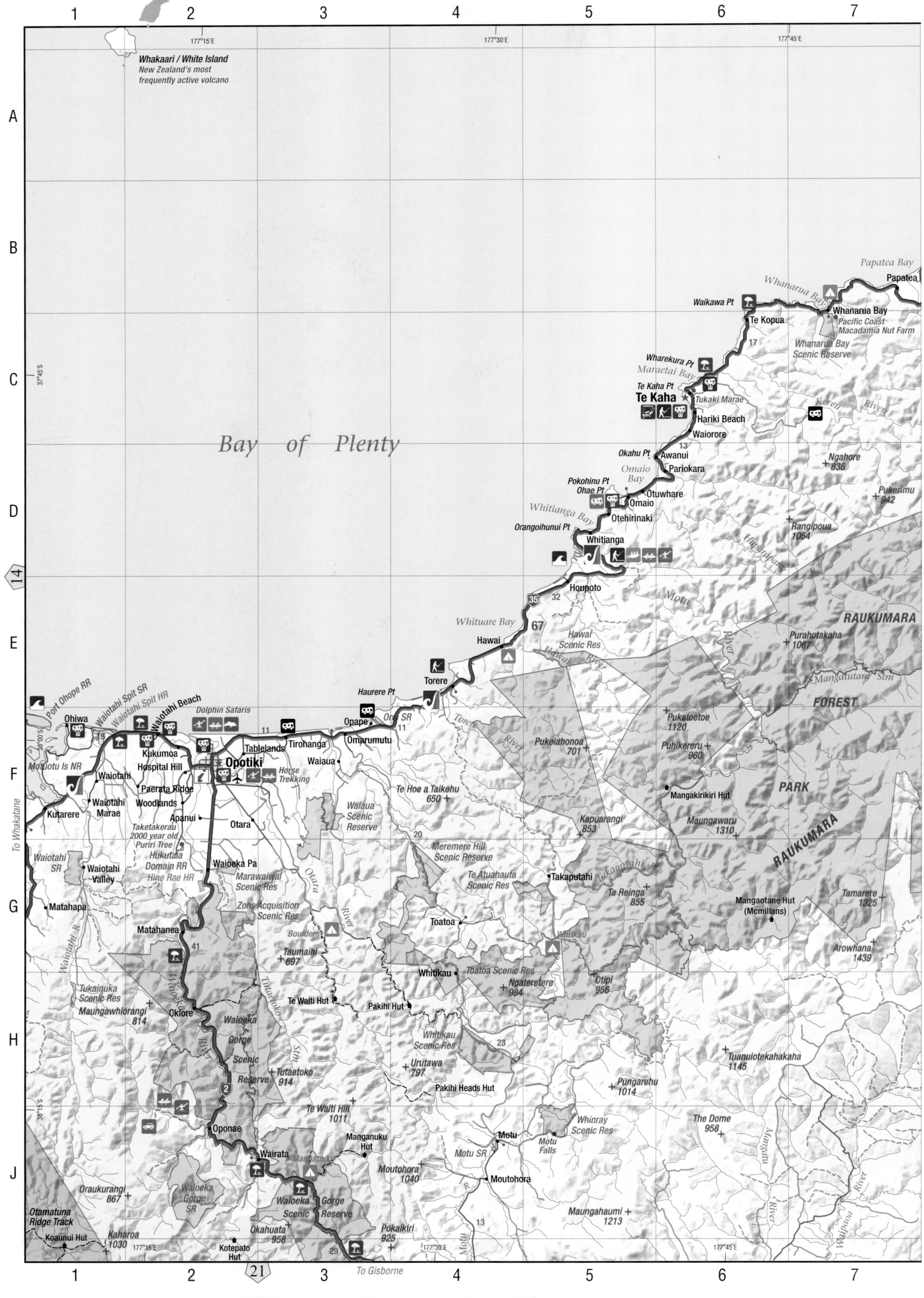

MAP
15
NORTH ISLAND

Whakaari / White Island
New Zealand's most
frequently active volcano

Bay of Plenty

Papatea Bay
Papatea
Whanarua Bay
Waikawa Pt
Te Kopua
Whanarua Bay
17
Pacific Coast
Macadamia Nut Farm
Whanarua Bay
Scenic Reserve
Wharekura Pt
Maraetai Bay
Te Kaha Pt
Kereu River
Te Kaha
Tukaki Marae
Hariki Beach
Waiorore
Okahu Pt
Awanui
Omaio Bay
Pariokara
Ngahore
836
Pokohinu Pt
Ohae Pt
Otuwhare
Omaio
Pukerimu
942
Whitianga Bay
Otehirinaki
Orangoihunui Pt
Whitianga
Rangipoua
1054
Houpoto
Motu
35   32
RAUKUMARA
67
Whituare Bay
Hawai
Scenic Res
Purahotakaha
1067
Hawai
Mangatutara Stm
Torere
FOREST
Haurere Pt
Puketoetoe
1120
Port Ohope RR
Waiotahi Spit SR
Waiotahi Spit HR
Opape
Oru SR
Ohiwa
Waiotahi Beach
Dolphin Safaris
11
11
Pukelahonoa
701
Puhikereru
960
Motiuotu Is NR
Tablelands
Tirohanga
Omarumutu
Waiaua
Mangakirikiri Hut
PARK
Kukumoa
Hospital Hill
Opotiki
Te Hoe a Taikehu
650
Kapuarangi
853
Maungawaru
1310
RAUKUMARA
Waiotahi
Paerata Ridge
Horse
Trekking
Kutarere
Woodlands
Waiotahi
Marae
20
Meremere Hill
Scenic Reserve
Otara
Apanui
Taketakerau
2000 year old
Puriri Tree
Waiaua
Scenic
Reserve
Te Atuahauta
Scenic Res
Takaputahi
Te Reinga
855
Mangaotane Hut
(Mcmillans)
Tamarere
1325
Waiotahi
SR
Waiotahi
Valley
Hukutaia
Domain RR
Hine Rae HR
Waioeka Pa
Marawaiwai
Scenic Res
Matahapa
Zohs Acquisition
Scenic Reserve
Toatoa
Whikau
Arowhana
1439
Boulders
Matahanea
Taumahi
697
Whitikau
Toatoa Scenic Res
Ngateretere
984
Otipi
956
41
Te Waiti Hut
Pakihi Hut
Tuanuiotekahakaha
1145
Tukainuka
Scenic Res
Maungawhiorangi
814
Okore
Waioeka
Gorge
Scenic
Reserve
Whitikau
Scenic Res
23
Urutawa
797
Pungarehu
1014
Tutaetoko
914
Pakihi Heads Hut
Whinray
Scenic Res
The Dome
958
Te Waiti Hill
1011
Oponae
Manganuku
Hut
Motu
Motu
Falls
Oraukurangi
867
Waioeka
Gorge
SR
Wairata
Manganuku
Moutohora
1040
Motu SR
Moutohora
Otamatuna
Ridge Track
Waioeka
Scenic
Gorge
Reserve
Maungahaumi
1213
Koaunui Hut
Kaharoa
1030
Okahuata
958
Pokaikiri
925
13
Kotepato
Hut
29

To Whakatane
To Gisborne

37°45'S
38°00'S
38°15'S
177°15'E
177°30'E
177°45'E

14
9
2
21

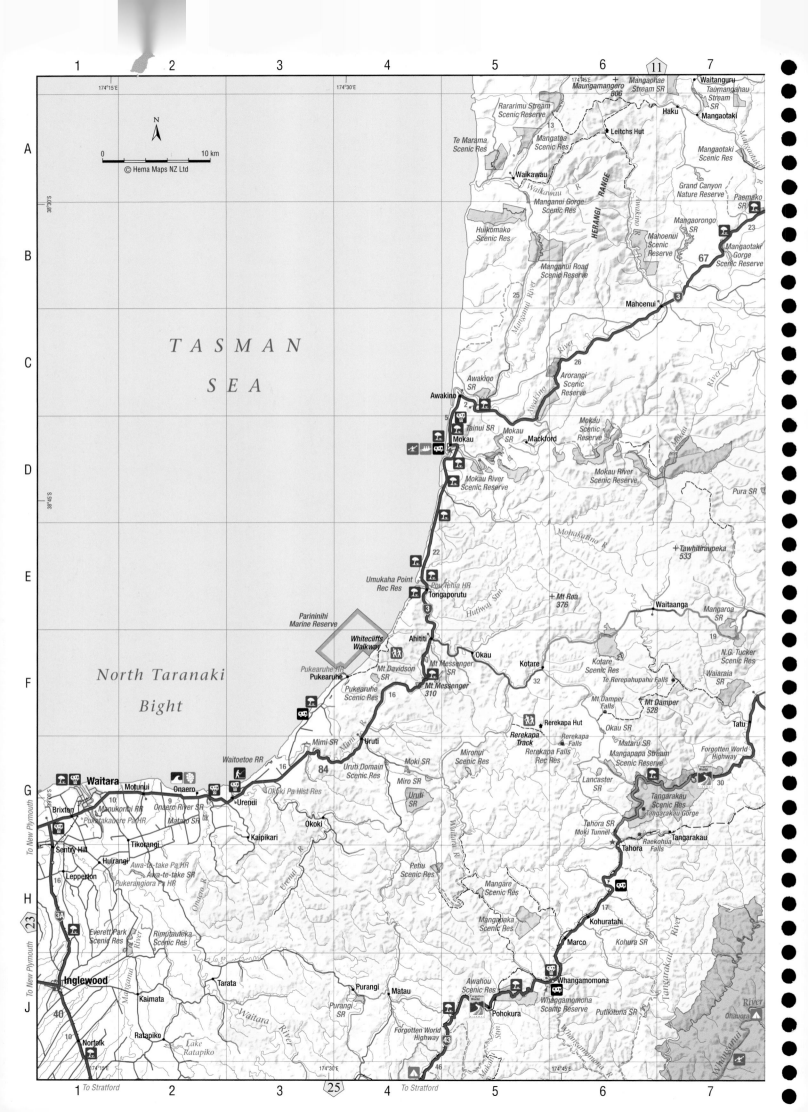

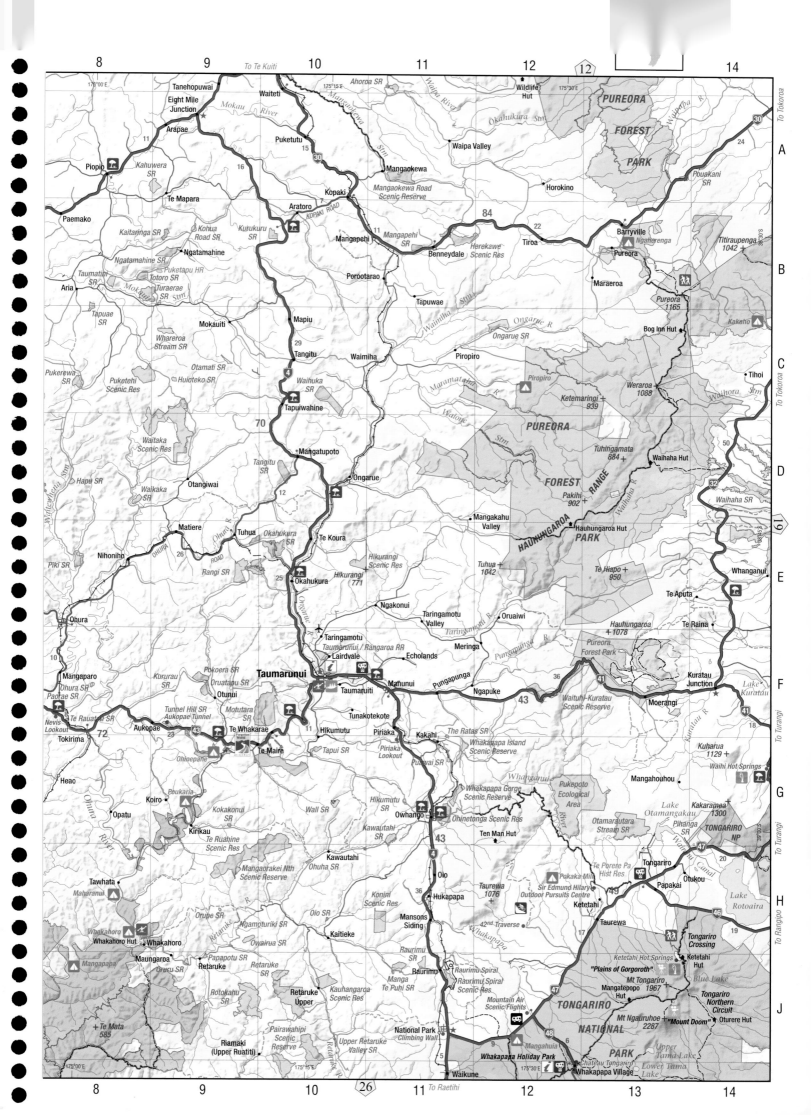

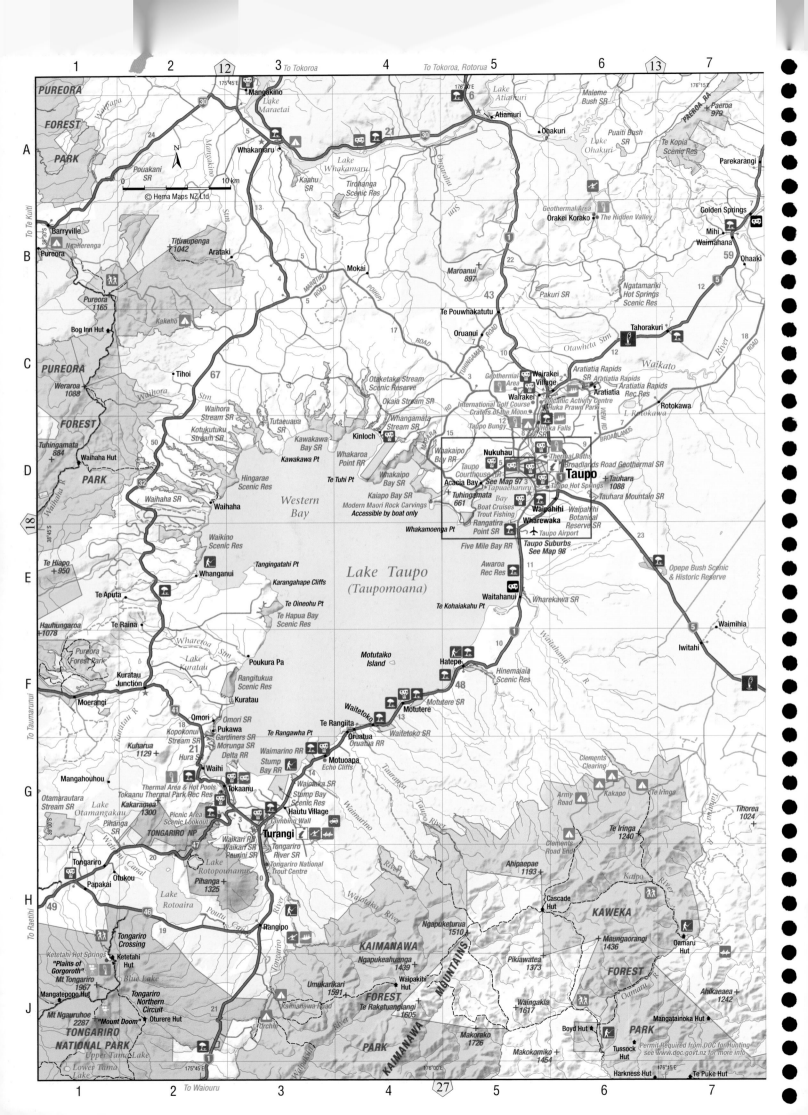

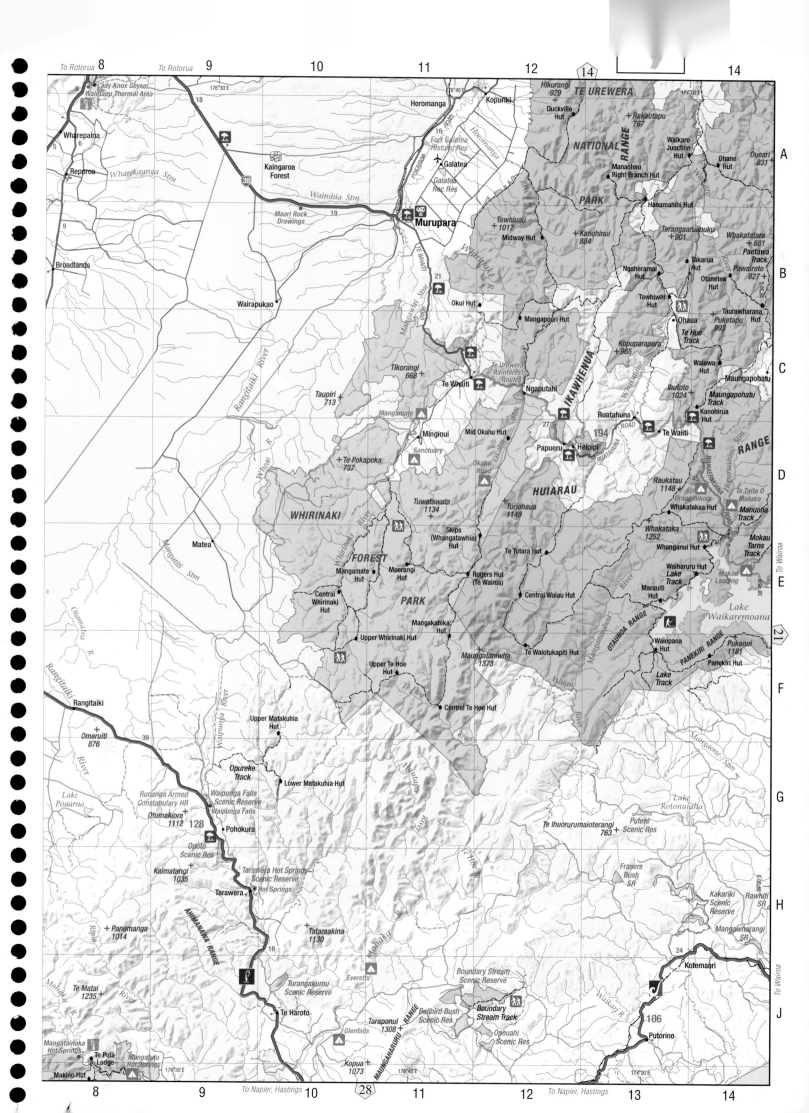

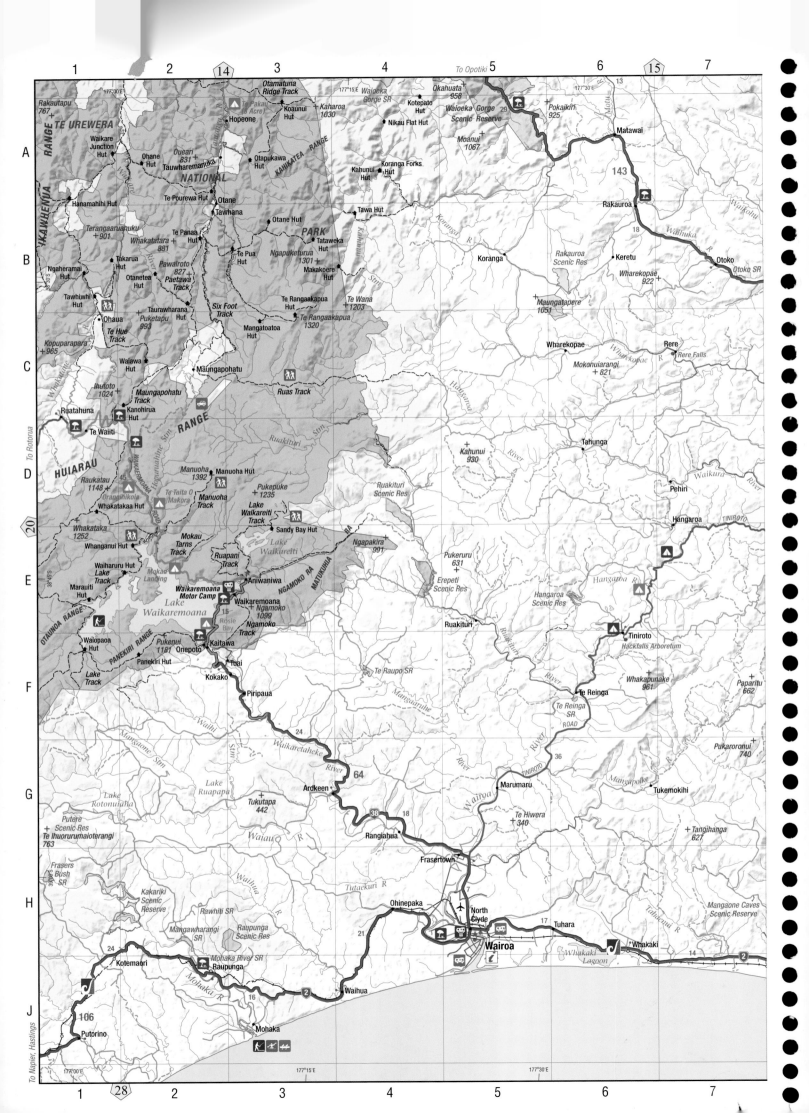

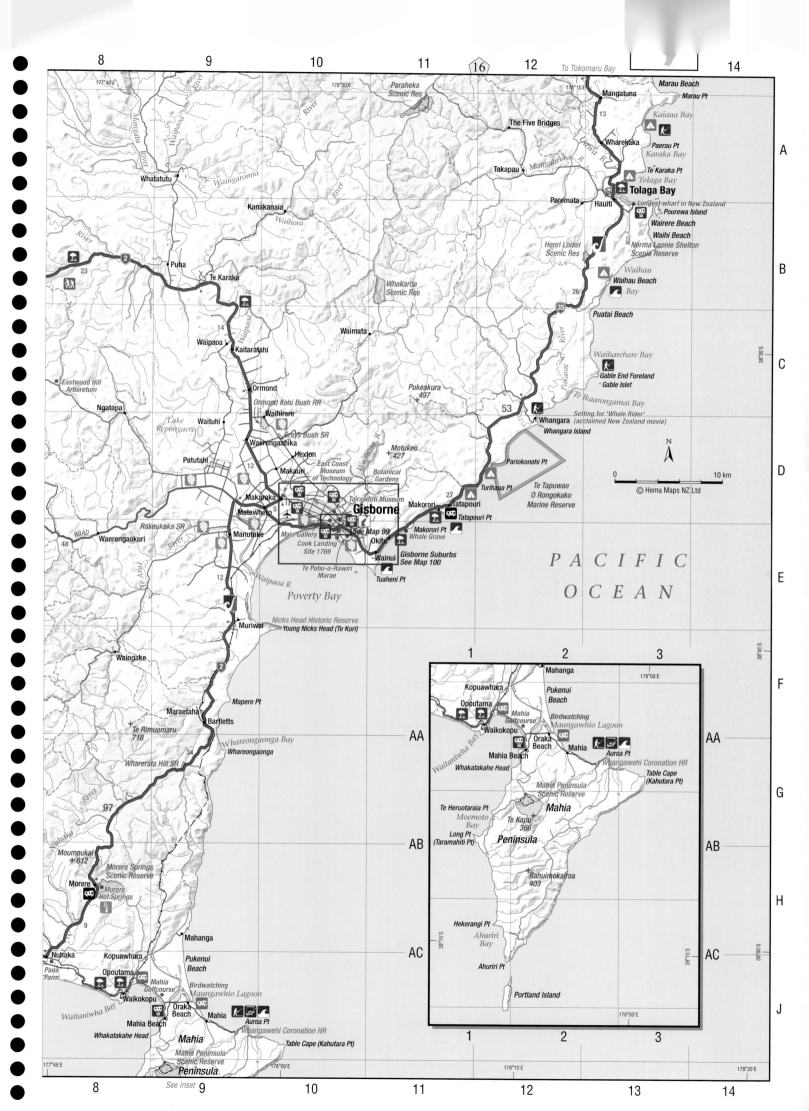

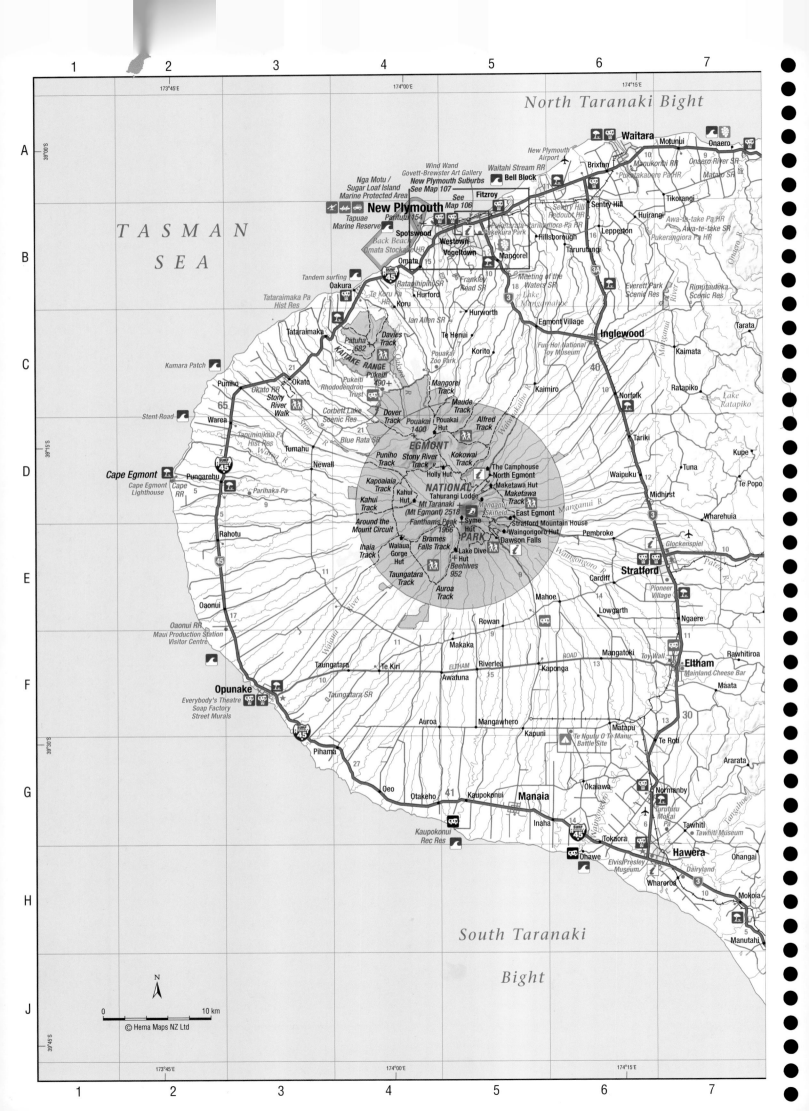

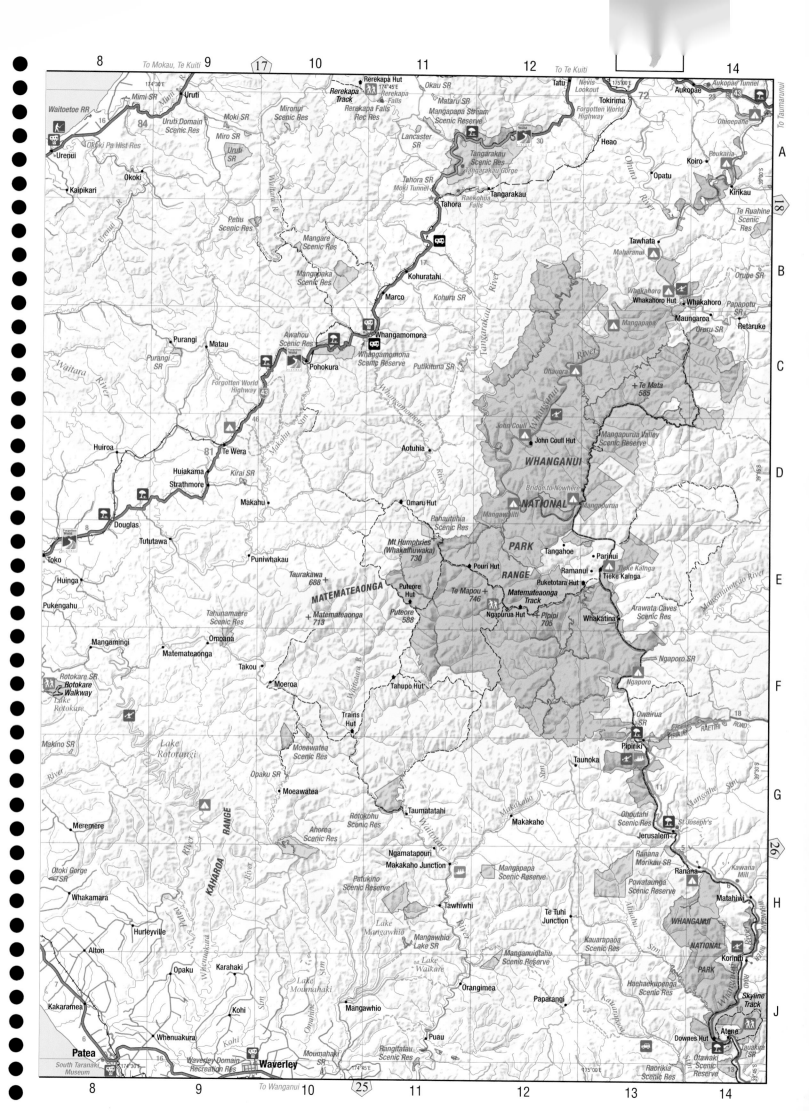

Grid reference numbers (top): 8, 9, 17, 10, 11, 12, 14
Grid reference numbers (bottom): 8, 9, 25, 10, 11, 12, 13, 14
Grid reference letters (right side): A, 18, B, C, D, E, F, 26, G, H, J

To Mokau, Te Kuiti
To Te Kuiti
To Taumarunui
To Ruahine Scenic Res
To Wanganui

Place names and labels:

Aukopae Tunnel
72
Aukopae
Ohinepane
Poukaria
Koiro
Kirikau
Opatu
Tokirima
Nevis Lookout
Tatu
Heao
Forgotten World Highway
30
Tawhata
Maharanui
Orupe SR
Whakahoro
Whakahoro Hut
Papapotu SR
Maungaroa
Oruru SR
Retaruke
Mangapapa
Rerekapa Hut
Rerekapa Track
Rerekapa Falls
Rec Res
Okau SR
Mataru SR
Mangapapa Stream Scenic Reserve
Lancaster SR
Mironui Scenic Res
Moki SR
Miro SR
Uruti SR
Uruti Domain Scenic Res
Mimi SR
Uruti
Mimi
84
16
Waitoetoe RR
Okoki Pa Hist Res
Urenui
Okoki
Kaipikari
Pehu Scenic Res
Mangare Scenic Res
Tangarakau Scenic Res
Tangarakau Gorge
Tahora SR
Moki Tunnel
Raekohua Falls
Tahora
Tangarakau
Ohura River
Ohauora
Te Mata 585
Mangapaka Scenic Res
Kohura SR
Kohuratahi
Marco
Whangamomona
Tangarakau River
Whakahoro
Mangapurua Valley Scenic Reserve
WHANGANUI
Purangi
Matau
Purangi SR
Awahou Scenic Res
Forgotten World Highway
Pohokura
Whangamomona Scenic Reserve
Putikituna SR
Whakaihuwaka
Whanganui River
John Coull Hut
John Coull
NATIONAL
Bridge to Nowhere
Mangapurua
Waitara River
Huiroa
81
Te Wera
46
43
Kirai SR
Huiakama
Strathmore
Makahu
Aotuhia
Pahautuhia Scenic Res
Omaru Hut
Mangawhiti
PARK
Tangahoe
Parinui
RANGE
Ramanui
Puketotara Hut
Tieke Kainga
Tieke Kainga
Douglas
Forgotten World
8
Tututawa
Puniwhakau
Mt Humphries (Whakaihuwaka) 730
Pouri Hut
Te Mapou 746
Matemateaonga Track
Ngapurua Hut
Pipipi 705
Whakatina
Arawata Caves Scenic Res
Mangamingoteao River
Toko
Huinga
Pukengahu
Taurakawa 688
MATEMATEAONGA
Puteore Hut
Puteore 588
Matemateaonga 713
Tahunamaere Scenic Res
Mangamingi
Matemateaonga
Omoana
Takou
Moeroa
Trains Hut
Tahupo Hut
Ngaporo SR
Ngaporo
Rotokare SR
Rotokare Walkway
Lake Rotokare
Moeawatea Scenic Res
Owairua SR
18
RAETIHI ROAD
Pipiriki
Makino SR
Lake Rotorangi
Opaku SR
Moeawatea
Taumatatahi
Makakaho
Taunoka
Mangaehu Stm
11
Meremere
KAHAROA RANGE
Rotokohu Scenic Res
Ahoroa Scenic Res
Waitotara River
Ohoutahi Scenic Res
St Joseph's
Jerusalem
Otoki Gorge SR
Patea River
Whakamara
Ngamatapouri
Makakaho Junction
Patukino Scenic Reserve
Mangapapa Scenic Reserve
Te Tuhi Junction
Ranana / Morikau SR
Ranana
5
Kawana Mill
6
Hurleyville
Tawhiwhi
Lake Mangawhio
Kauarapaoa Scenic Res
Powataunga Scenic Reserve
Matahiwi
Alton
Whenuakura River
Opaku
Karahaki
Lake Moumahaki
Mangawhio Lake SR
Orangimea
Te Tuhi Junction
Manganuiotahu Scenic Reserve
Haehaekupenga Scenic Res
WHANGANUI
7
Kakaramea
Kohi
Kohi Stm
Mangawhio
Puau
Paparangi
Kauarapaoa Stm
NATIONAL
Koriniti
Skyline Track
Patea
South Taranaki Museum
174°30'E
16
Whenuakura
Waverley Domain Recreation Res
Waverley
Moumahaki SR
Oraugine Stm
Rangitatau Scenic Res
174°45'E
175°00'E
Raorikia Scenic Reserve
Atene
Tauakira SR
Otawaki Scenic Reserve
Downes Hut
PARK
10
13

Coordinate labels:
174°30'E, 174°45'E, 175°00'E
39°15'S, 39°30'S, 39°45'S

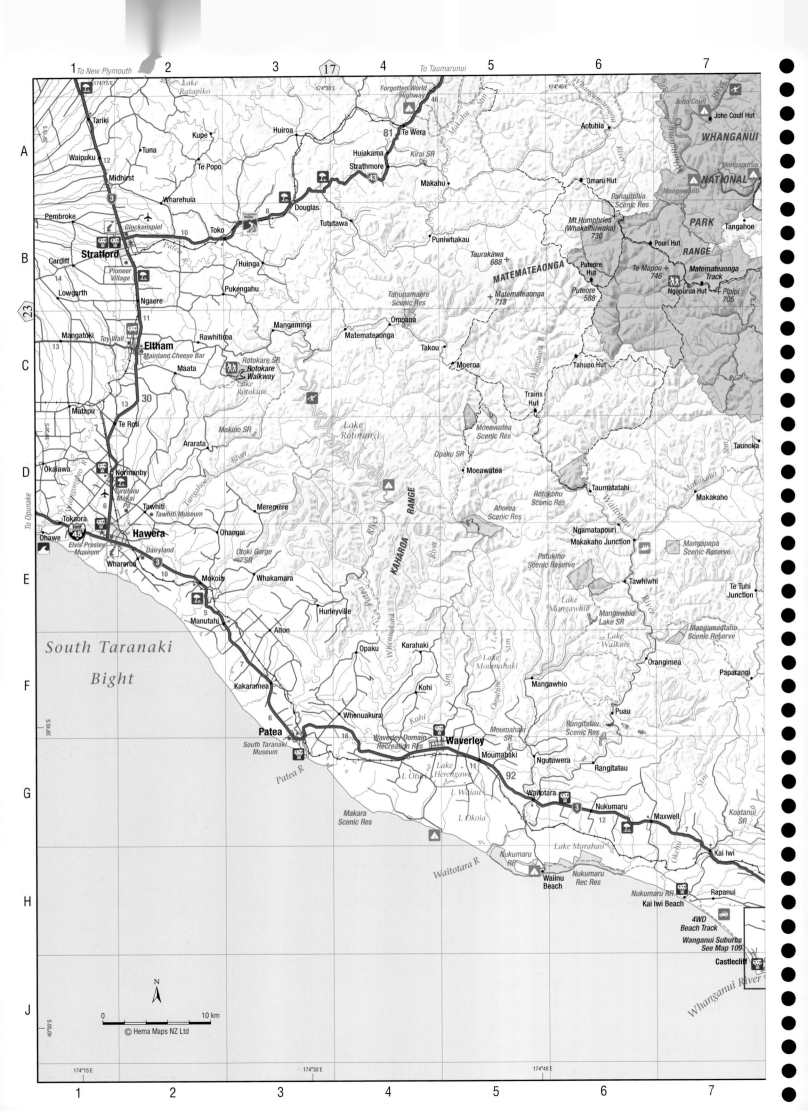

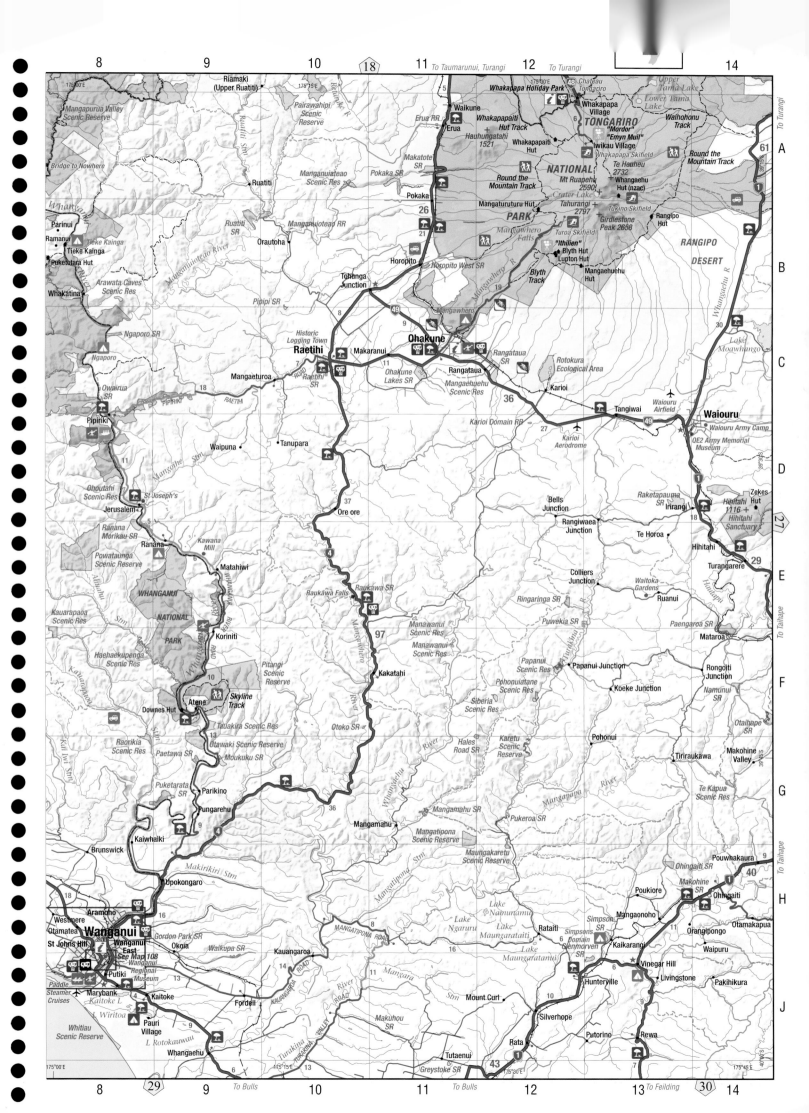

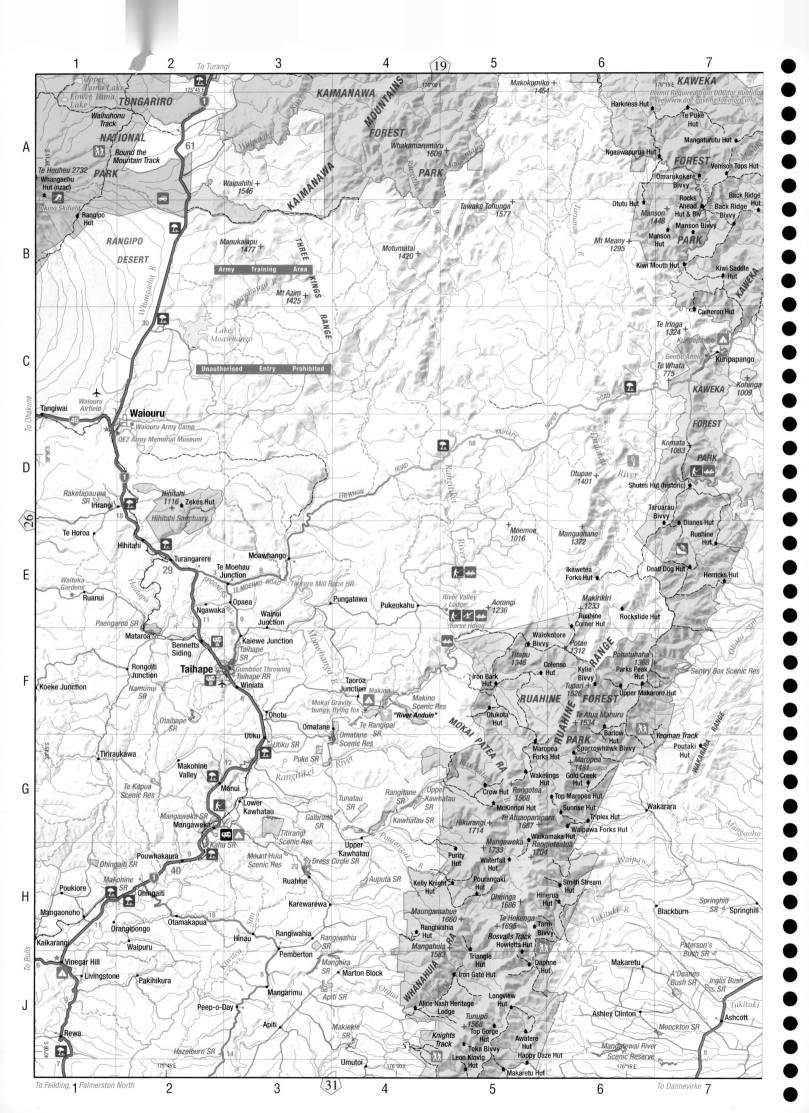

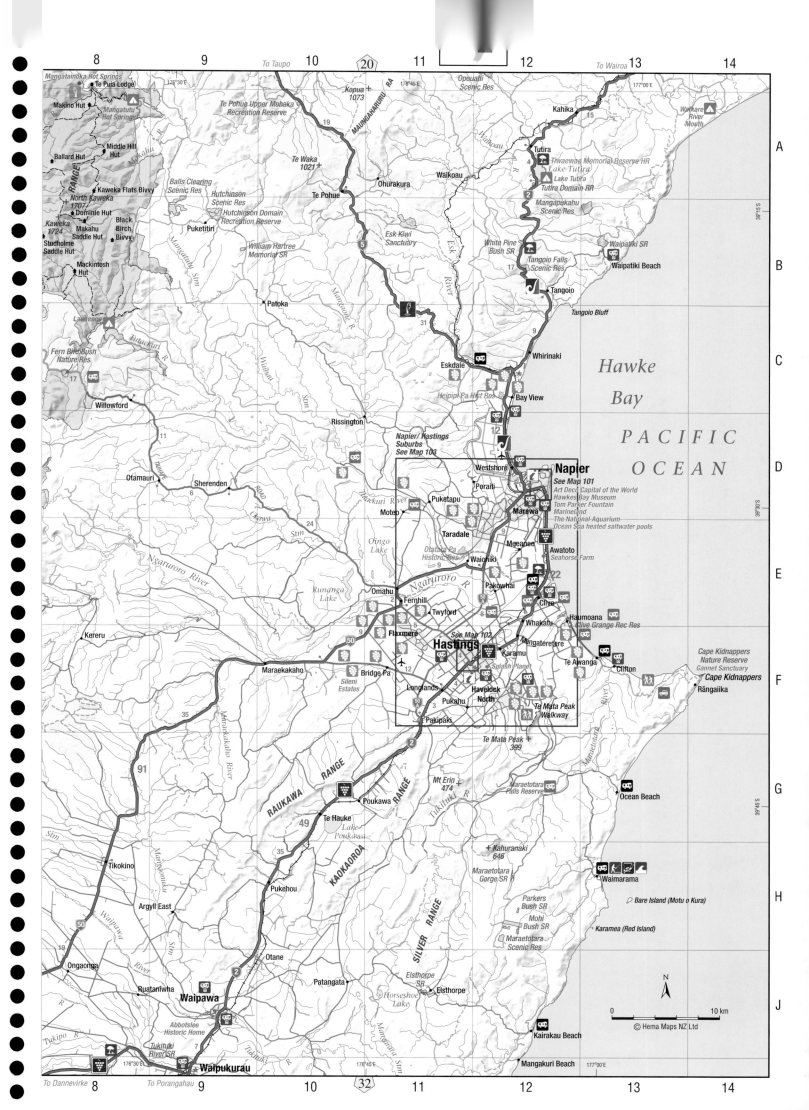

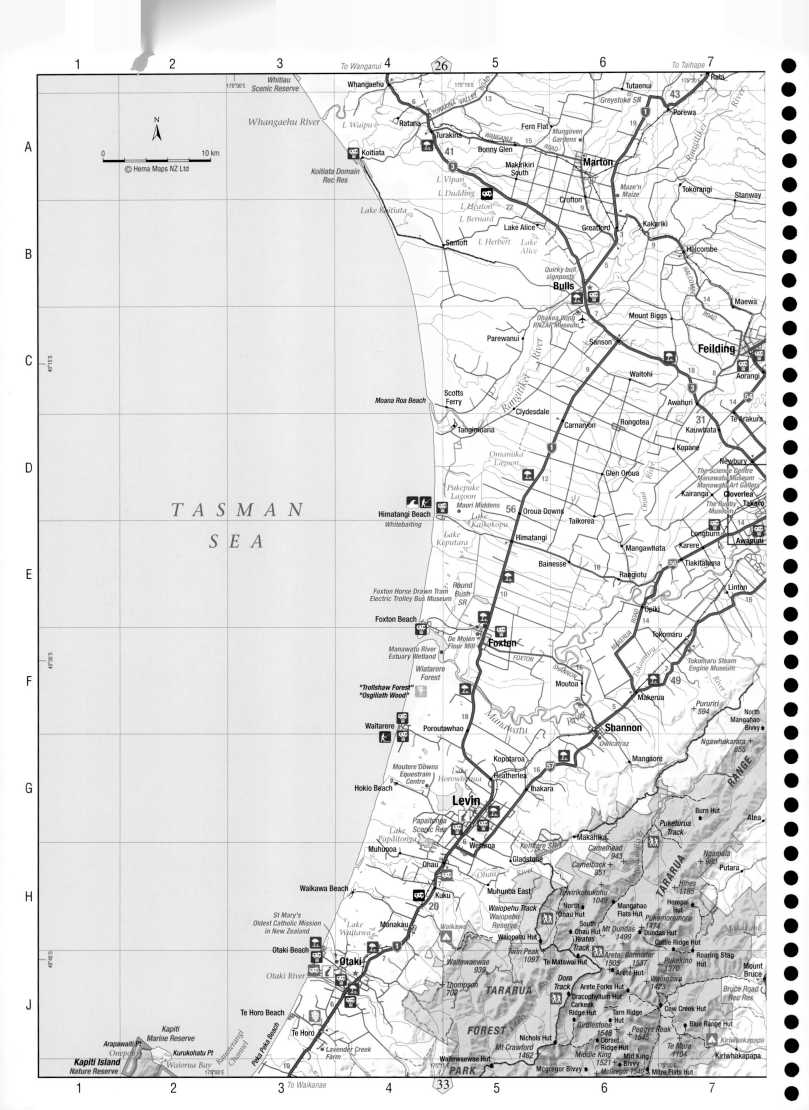

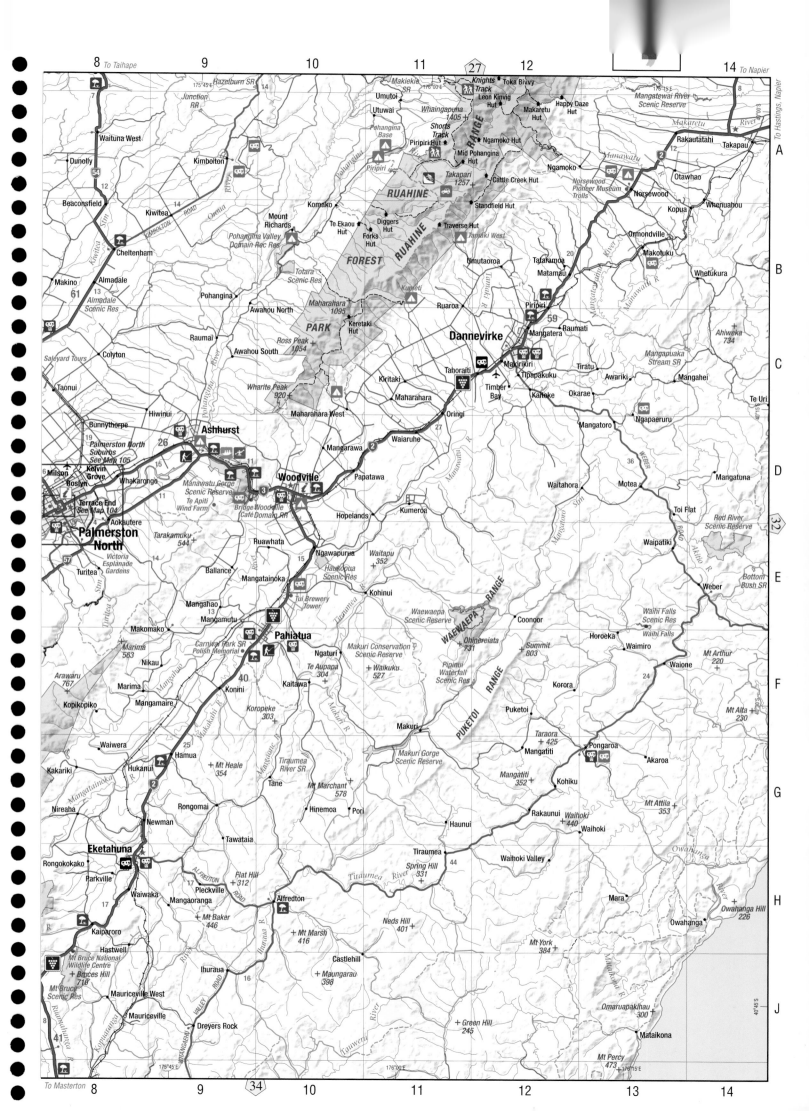

MAP
31
NORTH ISLAND

Grid references: 1 2 3 27 4 5 6 7 (top) / 1 2 3 34 4 5 6 7 (bottom)
Rows: A B C D E F G H J

To Taihape

Rata · Waituna West · Kimbolton · Hazelburn SR · Junction RR · Makiekie SR · Umutoi · Utuwai · Knights Track · Toka Bivvy · Leon Kinvig Hut · Makaretu Hut · Happy Daze Hut · Mangatewai River Scenic Reserve · Makaretu · Rakautatahi

Dunolly · Kimbolton · Whaingapuna 1405 · Shorts Track · Pohangina Base · Piripiri Hut · Mid Pohangina Hut · RANGE · Ngamoko Hut · Ngamoko · Norsewood Pioneer Museum Trolls · Norsewood

Stanway · Beaconsfield · Kiwitea · Mount Richards · Komako · Te Ekaou Hut · Diggers Hut · Traverse Hut · Takapari 1257 · Cattle Creek Hut · Standfield Hut · Ormondville

Halcombe · Cheltenham · Pohangina Valley Domain Rec Res · Forks Hut · RUAHINE · Tamaki West · Umutaoroa · Tataramoa · Matamau · Makotuku

Makino · Almadale · Pohangina · Awahou North · FOREST · Kupreti · Ruaroa · Piripiri

Maewa · Almadale Scenic Res · Raumai · Maharahara 1095 · PARK · 59 · Mangatera · Raumati · Mangapuaka Stream SR

Feilding · Saleyard Tours · Colyton · Awahou South · Ross Peak 1054 · Keretaki Hut · Dannevirke · Makirikiri · Tipapakuku · Tiratu · Awariki · Mangahei

Aorangi · Wharite Peak 920 · Kiritaki · Tahoraiti · Timber Bay · Okarae · Kaitoke · Ngapaeruru

Awahuri · Taonui · Maharahara West · Maharahara · Oringi · Mangatoro

Te Arakura · Kauwhata · Hiwinui · Bunnythorpe · Ashhurst · Mangarawa · Waiaruhe · Papatawa · Waitahora · Motea

Palmerston North Suburbs See Map 105 · Kelvin Grove · Whakarongo · Woodville · Hopelands · Toi Flat

Newbury · Milson · Roslyn · Manawatu Gorge Scenic Reserve · Bridge Woodville Café Domain RR · Kumeroa · Waipatiki

The Science Centre · Manawatu Museum · Manawatu Art Gallery · Takaro · Terrace End See Map 104 · Te Apiti Wind Farm · Ruawhata · Ngawapurua · Waitapu 352

Kairanga · Cloverlea · The Rugby Museum · Aokautere · Tarakamuku 544 · Mangatainoka · Haukopua Scenic Res · Kohinui · Waihi Falls Scenic Res

Longburn · Awapuni · Victoria Esplanade Gardens · Ballance · Tui Brewery Tower · Waewaepa Scenic Reserve · Ohinereiata 731 · Coonoor · Horoeka

Karere · Turitea · Mangahao · Mangamutu · Carnival Park SR · Polish Memorial · Pahiatua · Makuri Conservation Scenic Reserve · Summit 803 · Waimiro · Waione

Linton · Makomako · Marima 563 · Nikau · Ngaturi · Te Aupapa 304 · Waikuku 527 · Pipinui Waterfall Scenic Reserve · Korora · Puketoi

Tokomaru · Arawaru 767 · Marima · Kaitawa · Koropeke 303 · Makuri · Mangatiti · Taraora 425 · Pongaroa · Akaroa

Tokomaru Steam Engine Museum · Pururiri 594 · Kopikopiko · Mangamaire · Konini · Mangatiti 352 · Kohiku

North Mangahao Bivvy · Ngawhakarara 855 · Waiwera · Hamua · Mt Heale 354 · Tiraumea River SR · Mt Marchant 578 · Makuri Gorge Scenic Reserve · Mangatiti · Rakaunui · Waihoki 440 · Mt Attila 353

Kakariki · Hukanui · Tane · Hinemoa · Pori · Haunui · Waihoki

Burn Hut · Nireaha · Rongomai · Newman · Tiraumea · Waihoki Valley

Atea · Mt Marchant · Tawataia · Spring Hill 331 · Mara

Ngamaia 980 · Putara · Rongokokako · Eketahuna · Flat Hill 312 · Tiraumea River

Herepai Hut · Parkville · Waiwaka · Pleckville · Mangaoranga · Alfredton · Mt York 384

Roaring Stag Hut · Kaiparoro · Hastwell · Mt Baker 446 · Neds Hill 401 · Castlehill

Mt Bruce National Wildlife Centre · Mt Bruce Scenic Res · Bruces Hill 710 · Maungarau 398 · Green Hill 245 · Omaruapakihau 300

Mount Bruce · Mauriceville West · Ihuraua · Mataikona

Bruce Road Rec Res · Mauriceville · Dreyers Rock · Mt Percy 473

Kiriwhakapapa

To Masterton

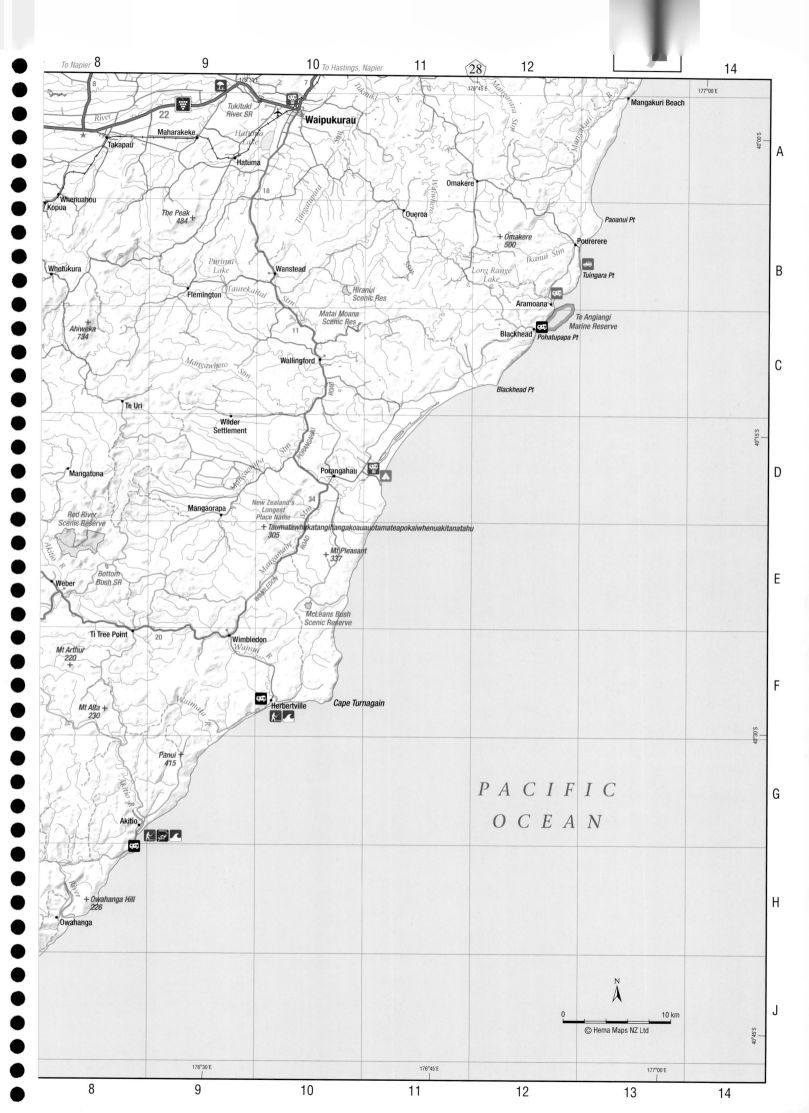

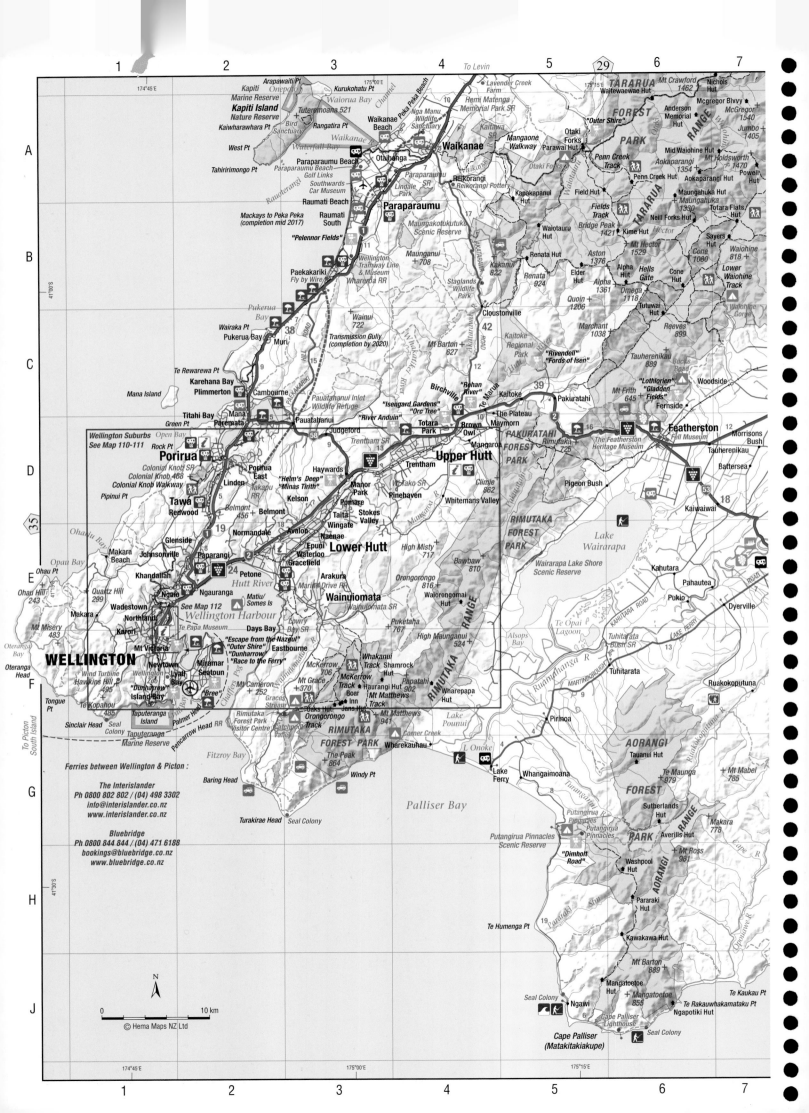

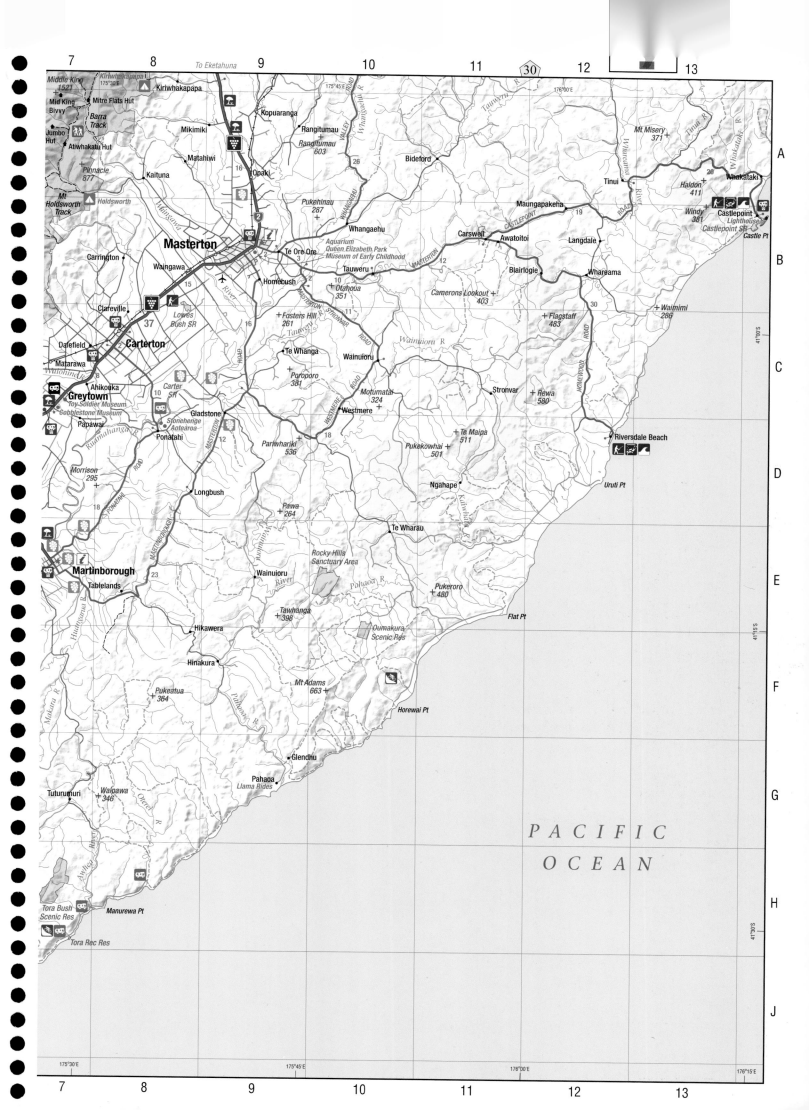

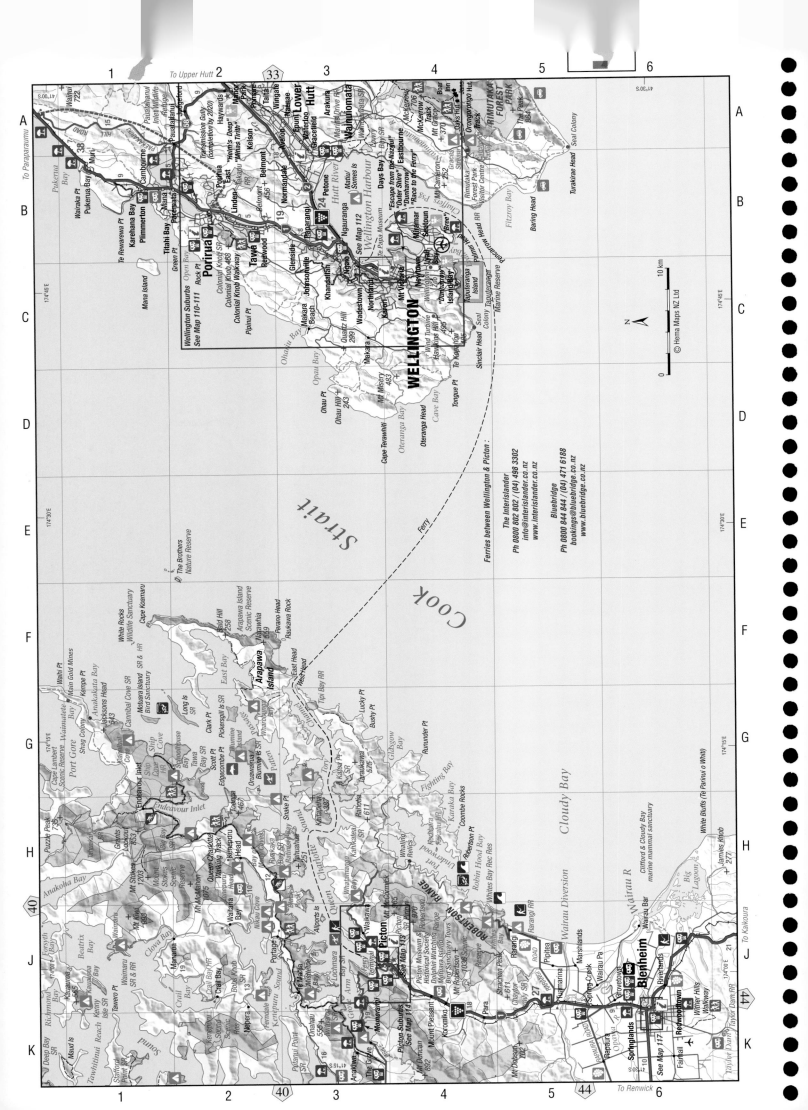

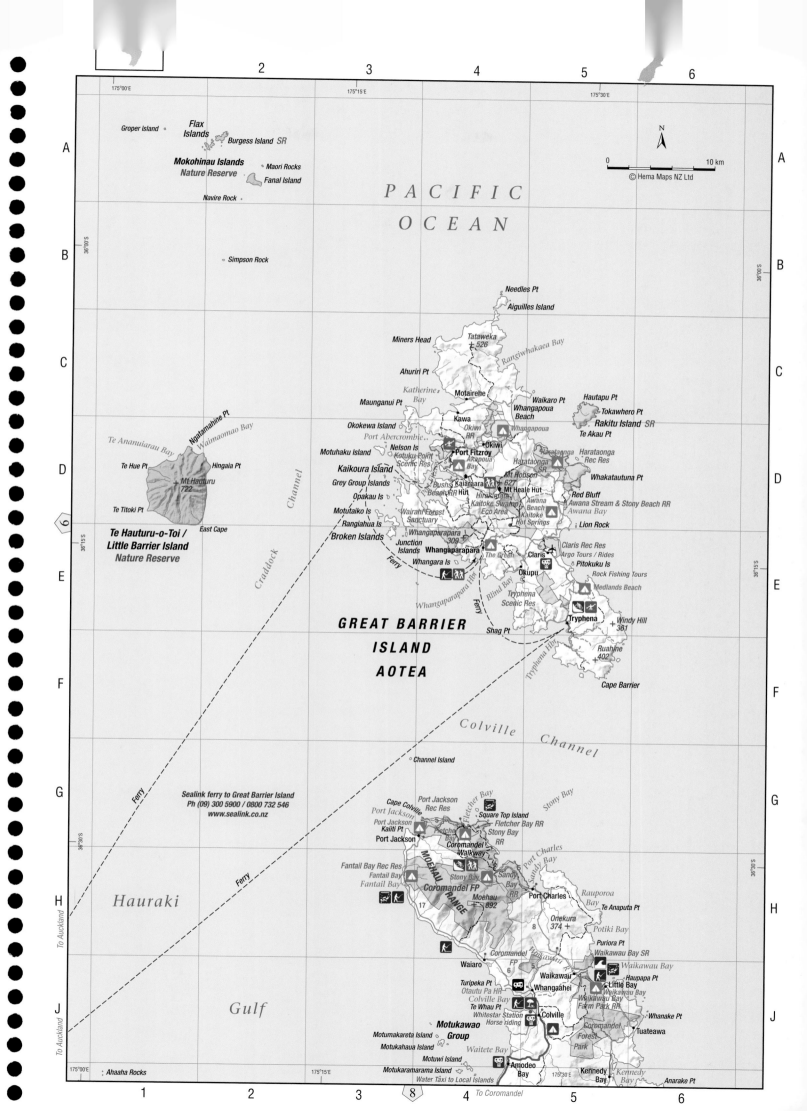

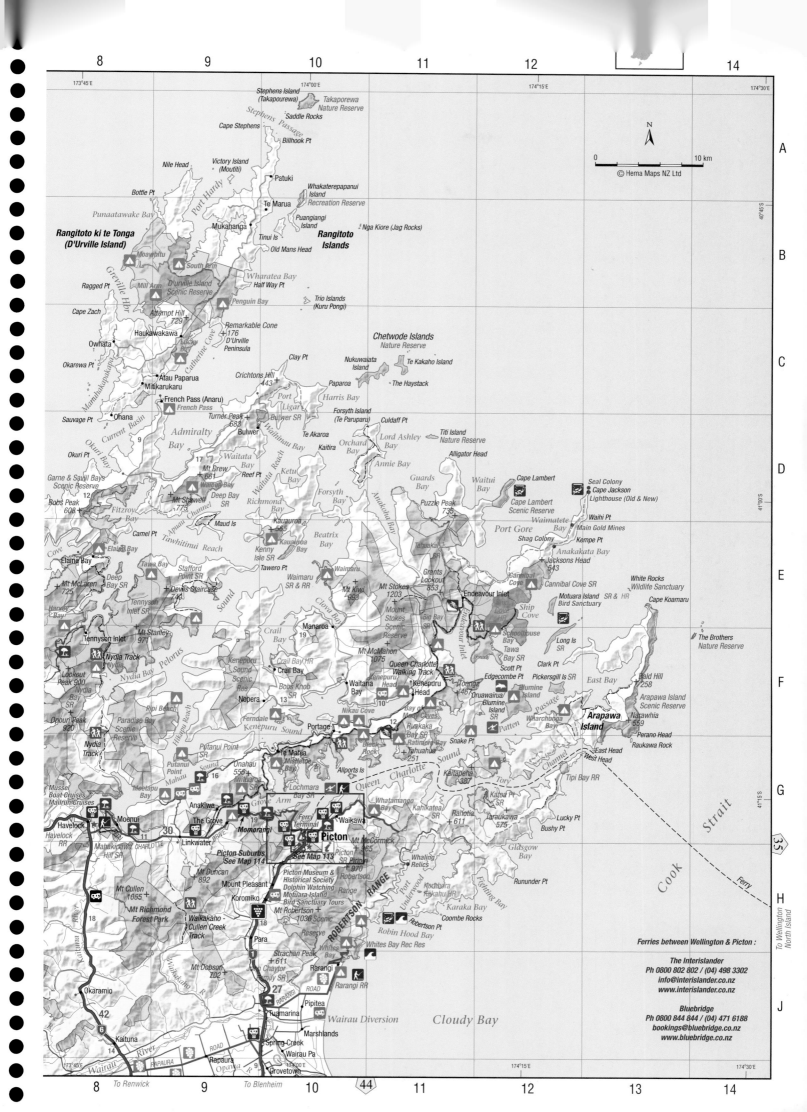

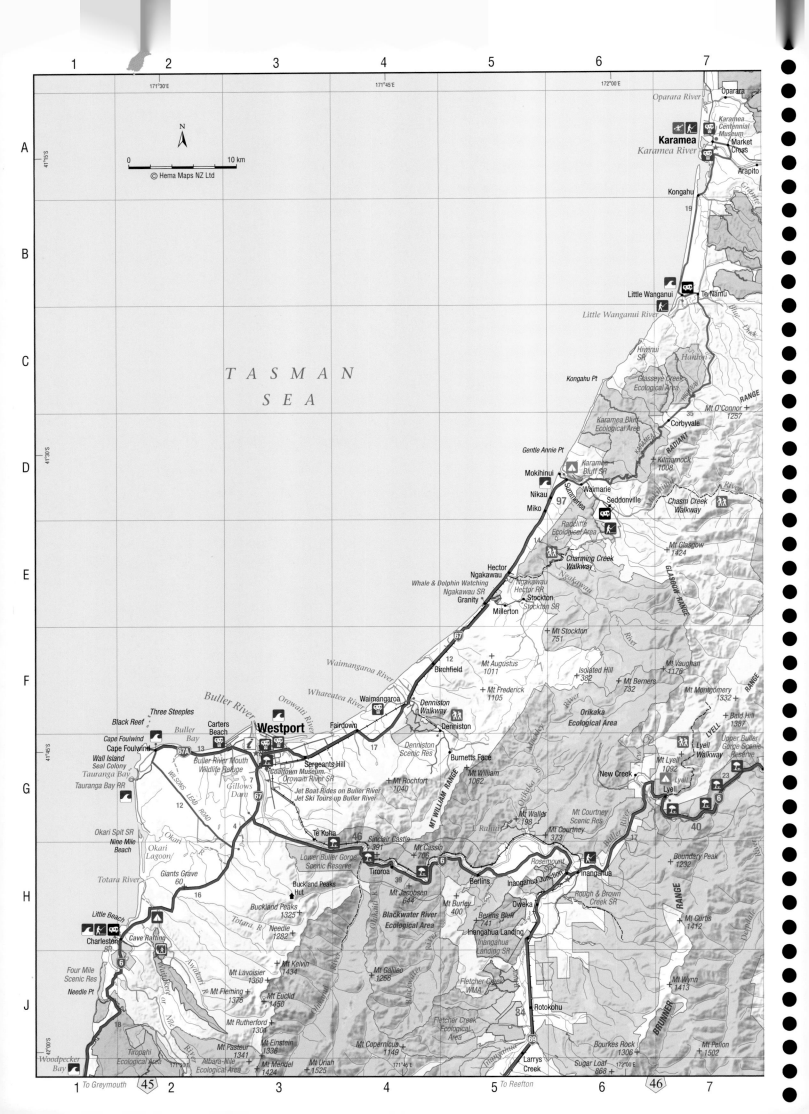

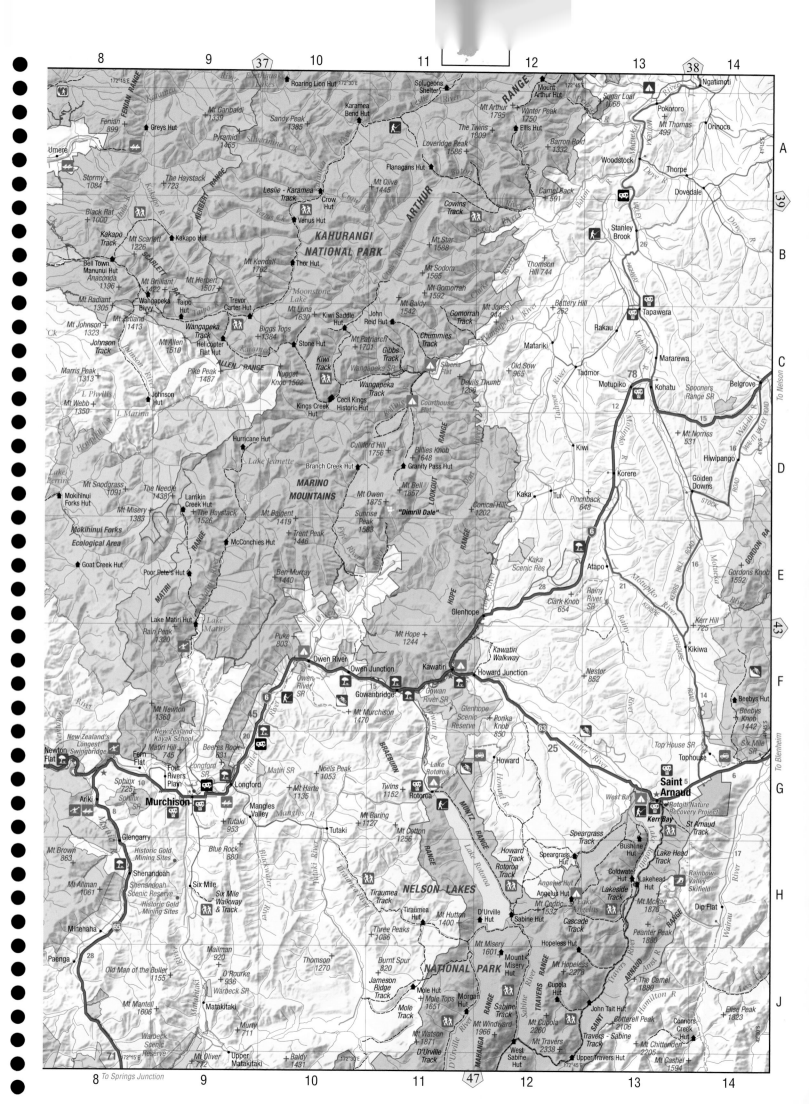

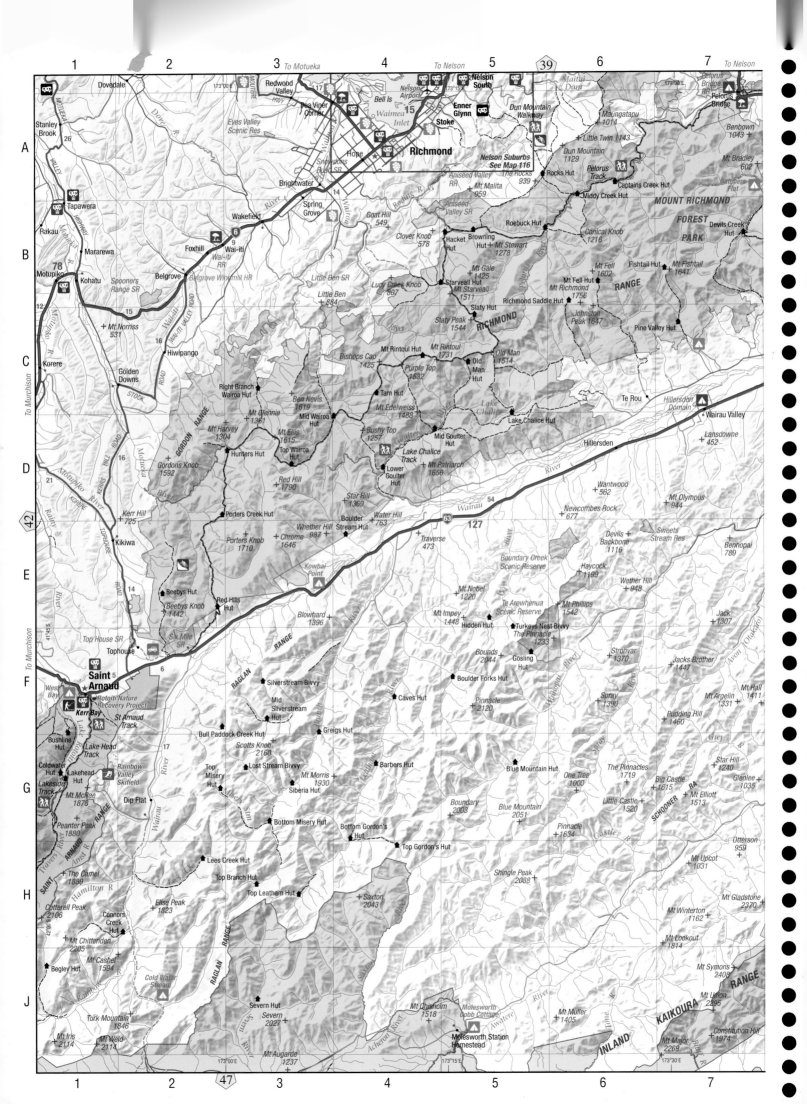

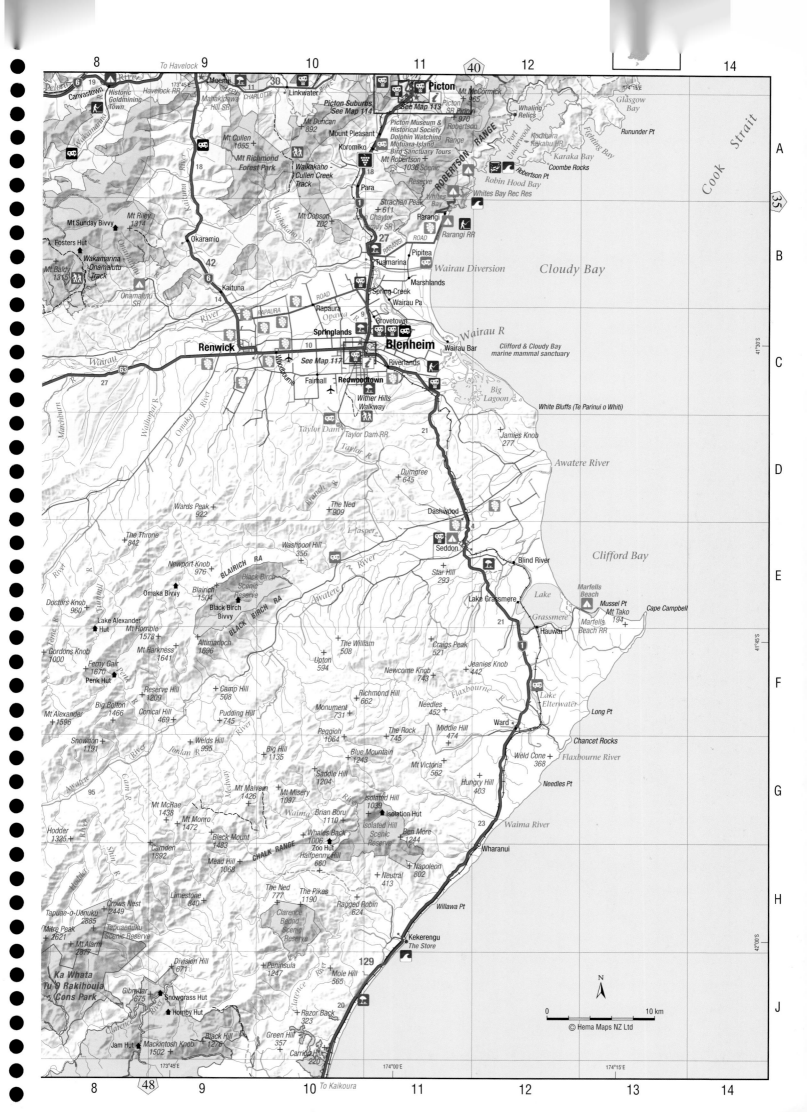

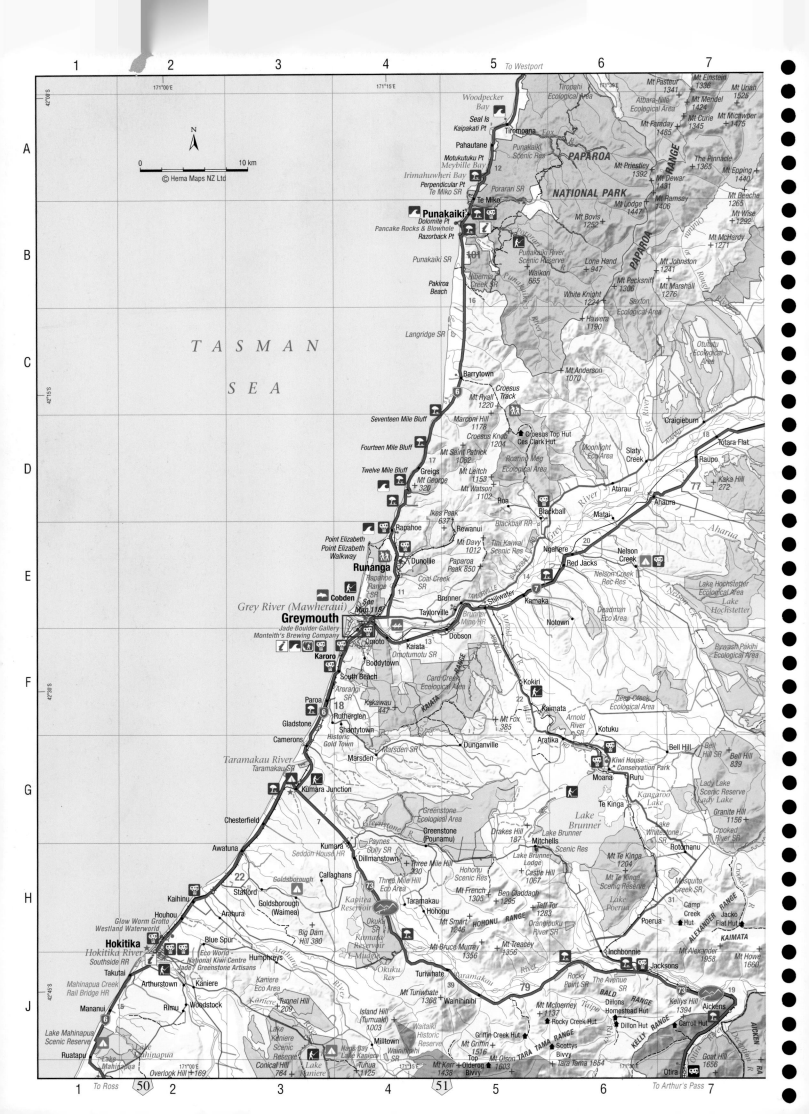

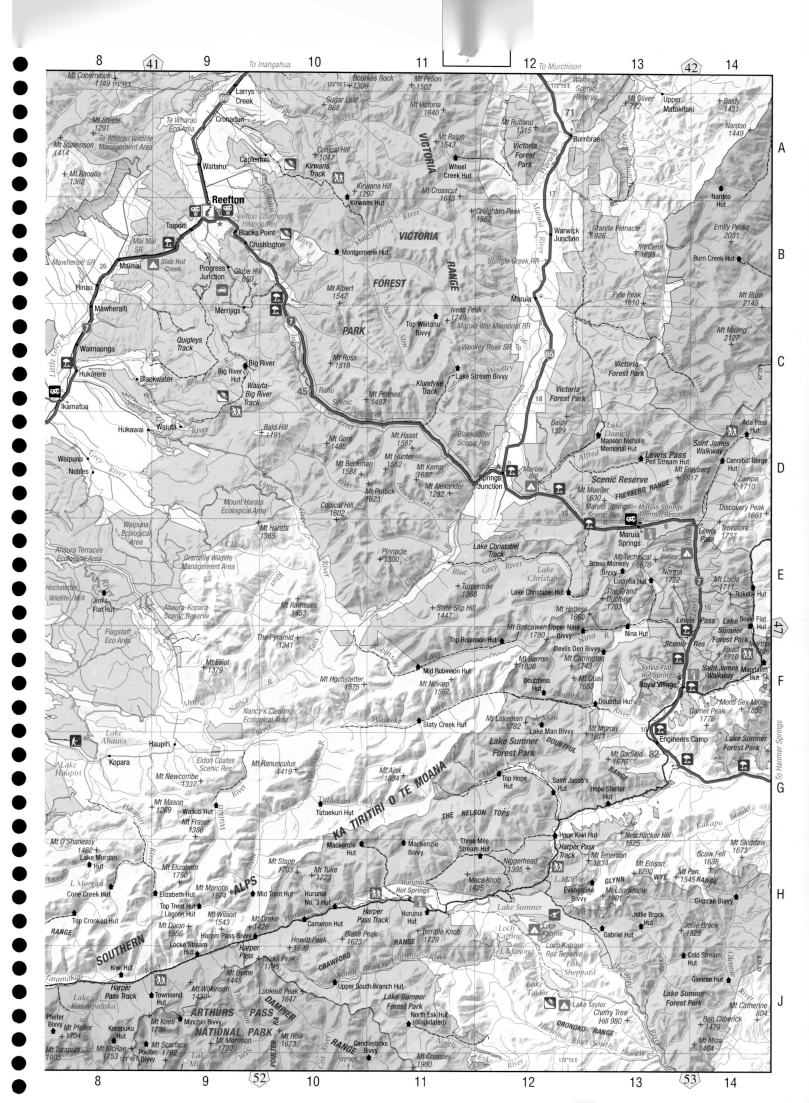

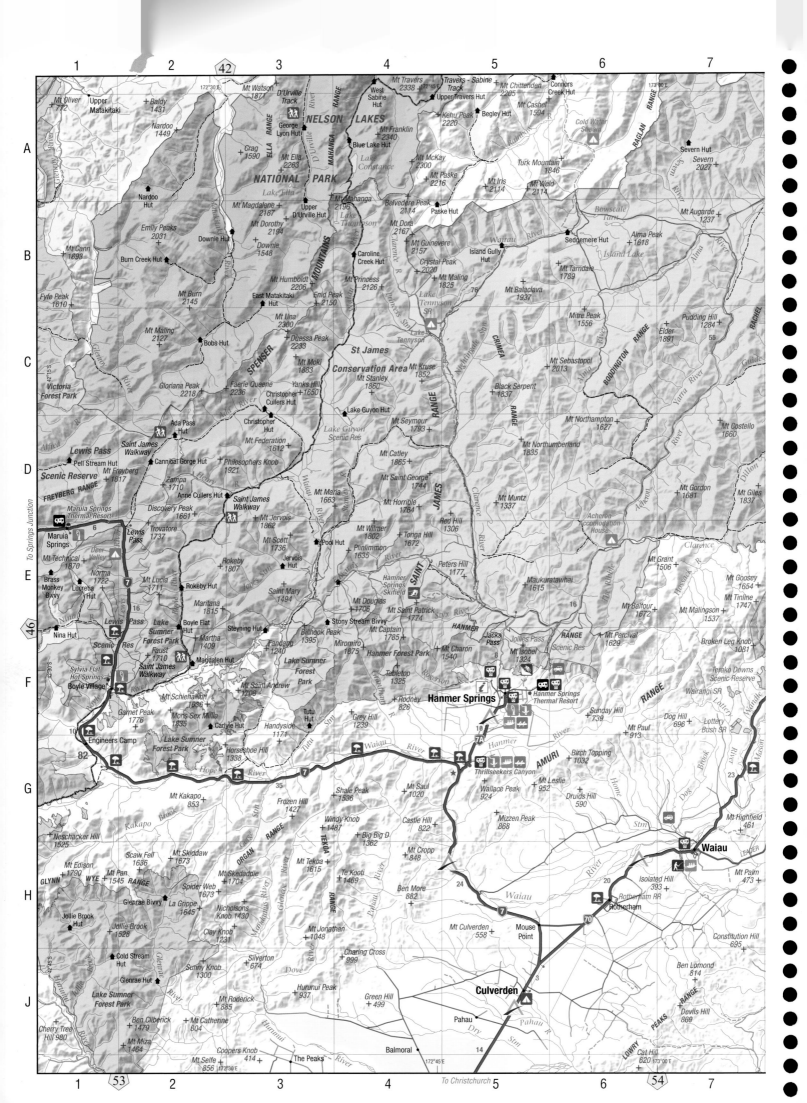

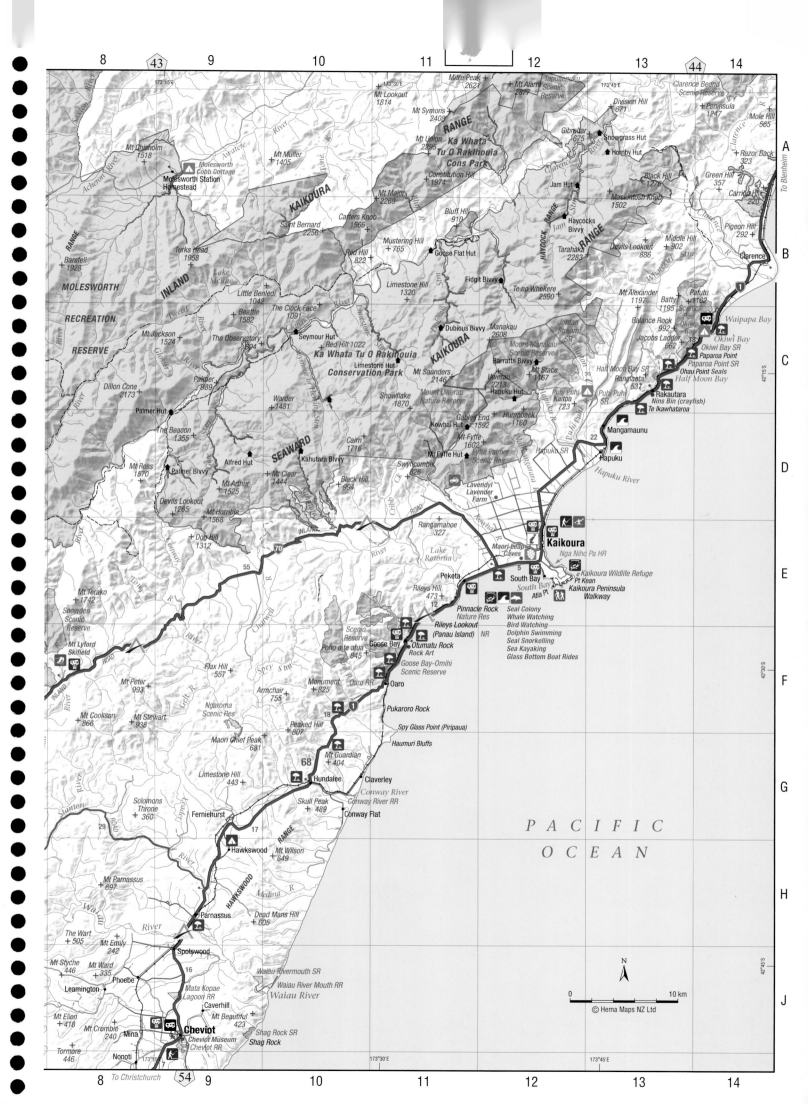

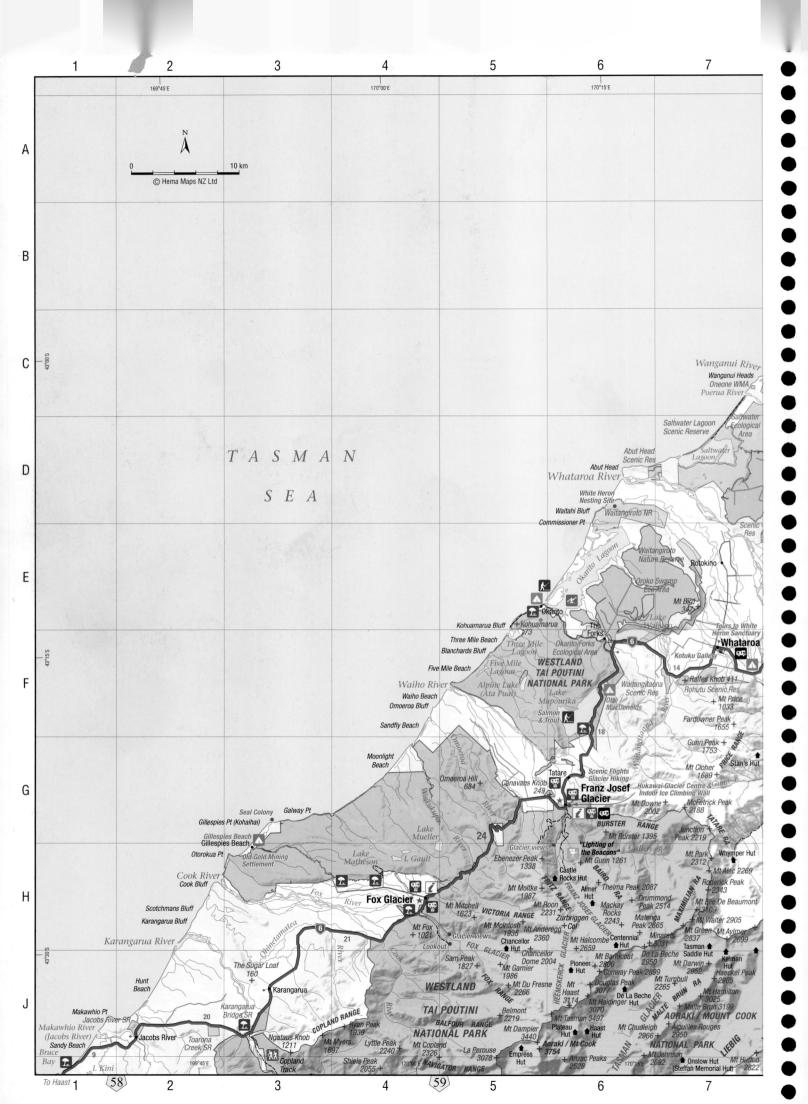

Map grid references and labels

Columns: 1 2 3 4 5 6 7

169°45'E 170°00'E 170°15'E

Rows: A B C D E F G H J

43°00'S

0 10 km
© Hema Maps NZ Ltd

N

T A S M A N S E A

Wanganui River
Wanganui Heads
Oneone WMA
Poerua River

Saltwater Lagoon
Scenic Reserve

Saltwater
Ecological
Area

Abut Head
Scenic Res

Abut Head

Whataroa River

White Heron
Nesting Site

Waitahi Bluff
Commissioner Pt

Waitangiroto NR

Rotokino

Scenic
Res

Waitangiroto
Nature Reserve

Oroko Swamp
Eco Area

Okarito Lagoon

Mt Big?
347

Lake
Wah?

Tours to White
Heron Sanctuary

Okarito

Kohuamarua Bluff + Kohuamarua
673

The
Forks

6

Whataroa

Three Mile Beach
Blanchards Bluff

Five Mile Beach

Waiho River

Waiho Beach
Omoeroa Bluff

Sandfly Beach

Three Mile
Lagoon

Five Mile
Lagoon

Alpine Lake
(Ata Puai)

Okarito Forks
Ecological Area

**WESTLAND
TAI POUTINI
NATIONAL PARK**

Lake
Mapourika

Salmon
& Trout

Kotuku Gallery

14

Waitangitaona
Scenic Res

Otto
MacDonalds

18

Rohutu Scenic Res

+ Ralfes Knob +11

+ Mt Price
1033

Fardowner Peak
1655 +

Gunn Peak +
1753

Stan's Hut

Moonlight
Beach

Omoeroa Hill +
684

Canavans Knob
249

Tatare

Scenic Flights
Glacier Hiking

Hukawai Glacier Centre &
Indoor Ice Climbing Wall

Mt Cloher
1689 +

Seal Colony   Galway Pt

Gillespies Pt (Kohaihai)

Gillespies Beach
Gillespies Beach

Otorokua Pt

Cook River
Cook Bluff

Lake
Mueller

Lake
Matheson

L Gault

Old Gold-Mining
Settlement

24

Waikukupa River

**Franz Josef
Glacier**

Mt Downe +
2002

McFetrick Peak
+ 2188

Glacier views

"Lighting of
the Beacons"

BURSTER   RANGE
+ Mt Burster 1395

Mt Gunn 1261

Ebenezer Peak +
1338

Castle
Rocks Hut

Junction
Peak 2219

Mt Park
2312 +

Whymper Hut

+ Mt Alec 2269

Roderick Peak
+ 2343

Scotchmans Bluff

Karangarua Bluff

Karangarua River

Fox
River

Fox Glacier

Mt Mitchell
1623 +

Mt Fox
+ 1021

Glacier views
Lookout

Mt Moltke +
1987

VICTORIA RANGE

Mt McIntosh
1935 +

Mt Roon
2231 +

Mt Anderegg
2360 +

Zurbriggen
Col

Mackay
Rocks
2243 +

Matenga
Peak 2665

+ Mt Green
2837

Mt Walter 2905

+ Mt Ellie De Beaumont
3109

Drummond
Peak 2514

Centennial
Hut

Minarets
3031

Tasman
Saddle Hut

Mt Aylmer
2699

Sam Peak
1827 +

Chancellor
Dome 2004

+ Mt Du Fresne
2266

Mt Halcombe
+ 2659

Pioneer
Hut

Mt Barnicoat
2800 +

De La Beche
2950

Mt Darwin +
3025

Kelman
Hut

Haeckel Peak
2965

WESTLAND

Chancellor
Hut

+ Mt Garnier
1986

FRITZ RANGE

FRANZ JOSEF GLACIER

**BAIRD
RA**

Thelma Peak 2087

Conway Peak 2899

Douglas Peak
3077

De La Beche Hut

Mt Turnbull
2265 +

Mt Hamilton
2995

The Sugar Loaf
160

Hunt
Beach

Karangarua

COPLAND RANGE

Ryan Peak +
1939

Mt Myers
1697 +

Lyttle Peak +
2240

**BALFOUR
RANGE**

Mt Copland
2326

Belmont
2219 +

TAI POUTINI

NATIONAL PARK

Mt Haast
3114 +

Mt Haidinger Hut

Mt Dampier
3440 +

Plateau
Hut

Haast Hut

Mt Chudleigh
2966 +

AORAKI / MOUNT COOK

Aiguilles Rouges
2950

MALTE   BRUN   RA

Malte Brun 3199

Mt Johnson
2692 +

NATIONAL PARK

LIEBIG

Makawhio Pt
Jacobs River SR

*Makawhio River
(Jacobs River)*
Sandy Beach

Bruce
Bay

L Kini

9

Jacobs River

Toarona
Creek SR

20

Karangarua
Bridge SR

Ngataus Knob
1211

**Copland
Track**

Shiels Peak
2055 +

La Perouse
3078

Aoraki / Mt Cook
3754

Empress
Hut

Anzac Peaks
2528

Onslow Hut
(Steffan Memorial Hut)

Mt Hutton
2822

**NAVIGATOR
RANGE**

Karangarua River

Whetanatea River

COOK GLACIER
HOOKER GLACIER

HEEMSKERCK GLACIER

TASMAN GLACIER

MAXIMILIAN RA

TATARE RA

Te Koroka RA

PRICE RANGE

**FOX
RANGE**

8 9 10 11 12 45 14

To Hokitika, Greymouth

Ruatapu
Lake Mahinapua
Lake Mahinapua
28
13

Totara River
Overlook Hill 169
Kokatahi
Mt Graham 829
Conical Hill 764
Tuhua 1125
Wainihinihi SR
Lake Kaniere
Hans Bay Lake Kaniere
Milltown

A

Ross
Donoghues
Mikonui River
Historic Gold Mining Town
Mt Camelback 569
Kowbitirangi
Lake Kaniere Walk
Dorothy Falls Scenic Reserve
Mt Brown Hut
Mt Upright 524
Mt Harry 564
Spey R
Mid Styx Hut

Moyes Hill 340
Constitution Hill 634
Camelback SR
The Doughboy (Kokiraki) 610
Lake Arthur Scenic Res
Boo Boo Hut

Ross Goldfields Hist Res
Doctor Hill 675
Doctor Hill Eco Area
Hokitika Gorge SR
The Doughboy Scenic Res
Genoa Peak 1503
Pinnacle Bivvy

B

Fergusons Bush SR
22
Mt Greenland 905
Mt Diedrichs 1084
Cedar Flat Huts
Mt Reeves 1779
Crawford Junction Hut

Kakapotahi Ecological Area
Waitaha River
Kakapotahi SR
Fergusons
Bald Hill 1145
Gerhardt Bivvy
Adventure Bivvy
Yeates Hut
Top Kokatahi Hut

Kakapotahi
Silver Peak 1016
Upper Totara Ecological Area
Fraser Peak 1166
Explorer Hut
Rapid Creek Hut
Mt O'Connor 1814
Mullins Hut
Crystal Bivvy
Mt Ambrose 2014
Mt Bannatyne 1808

Greens Beach
Waitaha Scenic Res
Pukekura
Mt Rangitoto 1127
Mikonui Flat Hut
Mikonui Spur Bivvy
Mt Inframeta 1356
Serpentine Hut
Top Toaroha Hut
Mt Ross 1770
Toaroha Saddle Bivvy
Mungo Hut
Mt Eliot 2059

C

Pukutuaro Cliff
Wanganui Coastal Scenic Reserve
Pukekura Scenic Res
Kennaway Hill 823
Mt Browne 1354
Healey Creek Hut
Mt Bowen 1985
Frews Hut
Frisco Hut
Bluff Hut
Poet Hut
Mt Park 2036

Wanganui Bluff
Wanganui River Flat Wildlife Management Area
Lake Ianthe Matatai
Lake Ianthe Scenic Reserve
Polluck Creek Hut
Dickie Spur Hut
Remarkable Peak 1790
Frew Bivvy
Mt Meta 1648
Sir Robert Hut
Mt Stout 2148
Mt Treadwell 2102

Pye Creek WMA
Lower Poerua Ecological Area
Mt Bonar 1076
Mt Allen 1524
Top Tuke Hut
Mt Beaumont 2118
Mt Tancred 1925
Mt Frieda 2130
Mt Bryce 2182
Mt Tregear 2042

D

Minehan SR
Herepo
6
25
Urquhart Knob 1228
Mt Hitchin 1720
Raged Peak 1943
Top Waitaha Hut
Mt Wylde Brown 1475
Ivory Lake Hut
Price Basin Hut
Price Flat Hut (Old Hut)
Price Flat Hut
Mt Marion 2119
Mt Young 2080
Urquhart Peak 2132
Canyon Crk Bivvy
Mt Williams 2300

Harihari
109
Lake Rotokino
Mt Ashmore 1463
Kiwi Flat Hut
Moonbeam Hut
Mt Bloomfield 2106
Mt Thorndike 2035
Park Dome 2340
Wilkinson Hut
Mt McWhirter 2111

The Exile 102
The Exiles SR
Poerua River SR
Te Taho
Mt Hercules 347
Mt Hercules Scenic Res
30
Scamper Torrent Hut
County Stream Hut
Mt Warner 2249
Neave Hut
Mt Neave 2290
Centennial Cabin
West Mathias Bivvy
Mistake Hill 2099

E

Wilberg Range Scenic Res
Bryan Hill 617
Mt Durward 1929
Mt Barry 2074
Mt Evans 2620
Hinge Peak 2184
Mathias Hut

Mt Willberg 1218
Mirage Knob 1780
Smyth Hut
The Amazons Breasts
Ragged Range
Mathias River

Mt Ferguson 1677
Avalon Peak 1796
Hunters Hut
Mueller Peak 2016
Smyth Hut
Mt Whitcombe 2650
Mt Roberts 2107
Lauper Peak 2485
Mt Butler 2103
Evans Hut
Totara Peak 1959
Manuka Peak 1686

Mt Tri 1815
Blue Lookout 1273
Lord Range
Mt Lord 2072
Louper Bivvy
Prospect Hill 889

F

Adams Wilderness Area
Mt Adams 2208
Mt Kensington 2444
Mt Hulka 2346
Mt Farrar 2424
Mt Lambert 2430
Blair Peak 2486
Mt Stoddart 2223
Mt Ramsay 2454
Mt Kinkel 2179
Reischek Hut
Bastion Peaks 2441
Cascade Hill 1546
Whaleback 670

Mt Barlow 2100
Guardian Peak 2218
Newton Peak 2543
Baker Peak 2259
Mt Goethe 2350
Malcolm Peak 2512
Prelude Peak 1946
Lyell Hut
North Peak 2628
Jagged Peak 2706
Palmer Range

The Great Unknown 2196
Outram Peak 2399
The Warrior 2580
Mt Renegade 2389
Lawrence Bivvy
Mt Arrowsmith 2781
Cameron Hut
Smite Peak 2003

Nolans Hut
Mt Moreton 1775
Sceptre Peak 2319
Amazon Peak 2486
McCoy Hut
Mt Johnstone 2320
South Peak 2276
Teddys Hill 1638
Shaggy Hill 922
Lagoon Peak 1988

G

ALPS
Scone Hut
Mt Edison 2337
Helmet Peak 2215
Veil Bivvy
Watchdog Hut
Mt Jollie 2241
Pito Peak 2401
Wild Mans Hill 1856
Middle Hill 1624
Staces Hill 1479

Bamford Knob 1845
Butler Ra
Mt Rangatira 2157
Ice Lake
Eric Twins 2123
St Winifred Hut
Watchdog Peak 2079
Lawrence Hut
Top Hut
Mt Sugarloaf 1238

Butler Junction Hut
McKinnon Peak 2504
Mt Petermann 2346
St Winifred Hut
Mt McRae 1737
Hakatere Conservation Park
Pyramid 1598

Top Butler Hut
Mt Victoire 2517
Mt Loughnan 2590
McClure Peak 2486
Mt McMillan 1883
Curtis Memorial Hut

H

SOUTHERN
Mt Wolseley 2558
Mt Fletcher 2467
Mistake Flats Hut
Murphy's Bivvy
Cloudy Peak 2403
Potts Hut
Red Mountain 1610
Lake Heron Nature Reserve

Cassino Peak 2450
Mt Moffat 2638
The Commander 2337
Forbes Bivvy
Mt D'Archiac 2875
Mt Earle 2410
Finlay Hill 2003
Mt Caroline 1384
Mt Potts 2184
The Pyramid 1748
Isolated Hill 802

Mt Huss 2502
Godley Hut
Mt Coates 2400
East Sentinel 2133
Carney's Bivvy
Boundary Creek Hut

Brodrick Peak 2669
Mt Mannering 2669
Pukewhero Peak 2006
Mt Forbes 2583

Murchison Hut
Mt Acland 2662
Eade Memorial Hut
Mt Sunday 611
"Edoras"
Mt Potts
Dogs Hill 1067
L Emily
Maori Lakes Nature Res

J

RANGE
Mt Richmond 2509
Red Stag Hut
SIBBALD RANGE
Mt Sibbald 2811
Exeter 2327
Alma 2510
Black Mountain 1809
Harpers Knob 841
Mt Guy 1319
Hakatere

The Ant-hill 2517
Mt Chevalier 2404
Low Peak 2450
Myrmidon 2474
Dog Kennel Bivvy

Mt Conrad 2598
Macaulay Hut
Ajax 2319
TWO THUMB RANGE
The Thumbs 2546
Mt Brabazon 1792
Lake Clearwater Wildlife Refuge
Dogs Hill
Lake Camp Rec Res

Mt Olaf 2641
Charlies Knob 1114
Mt Chevalier
Mt Ross 2366
Split Peaks 2345
Crooked Spur Hut
Lake Emma
Trinity Hill 1016
Mt Barrosa 1364

Mt Ronald Adair 2818
Paris 2175
Mt Pattisson 2313

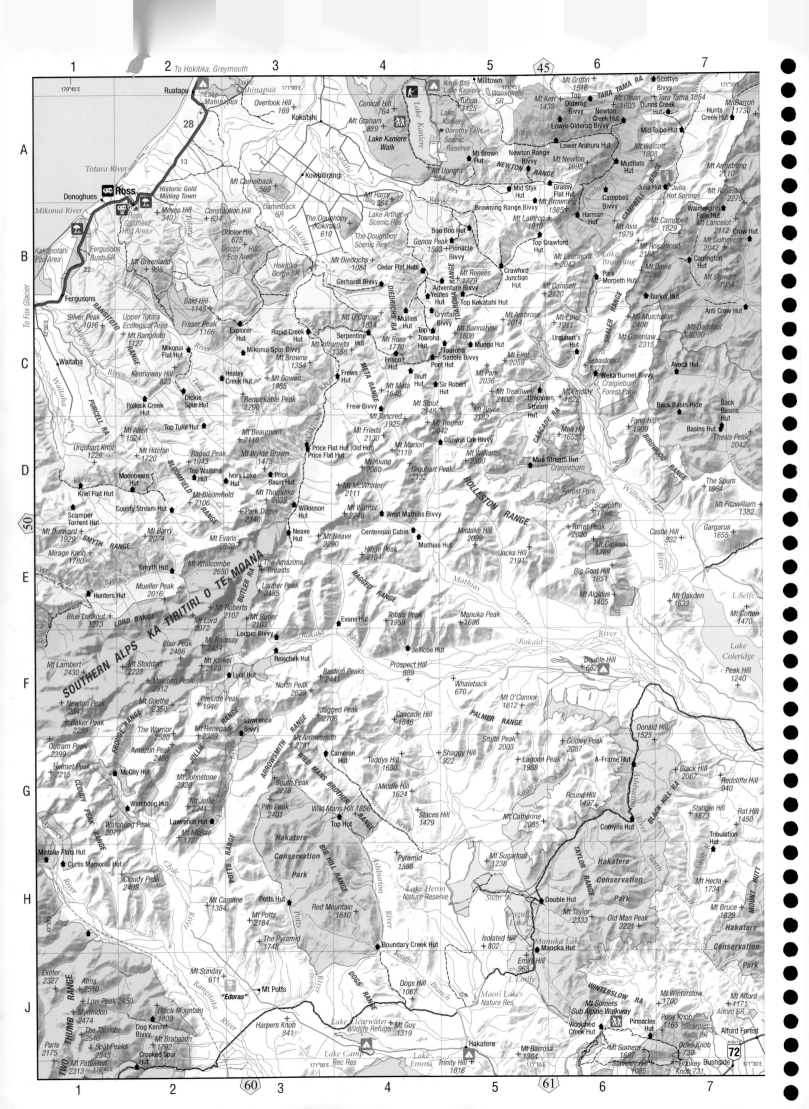

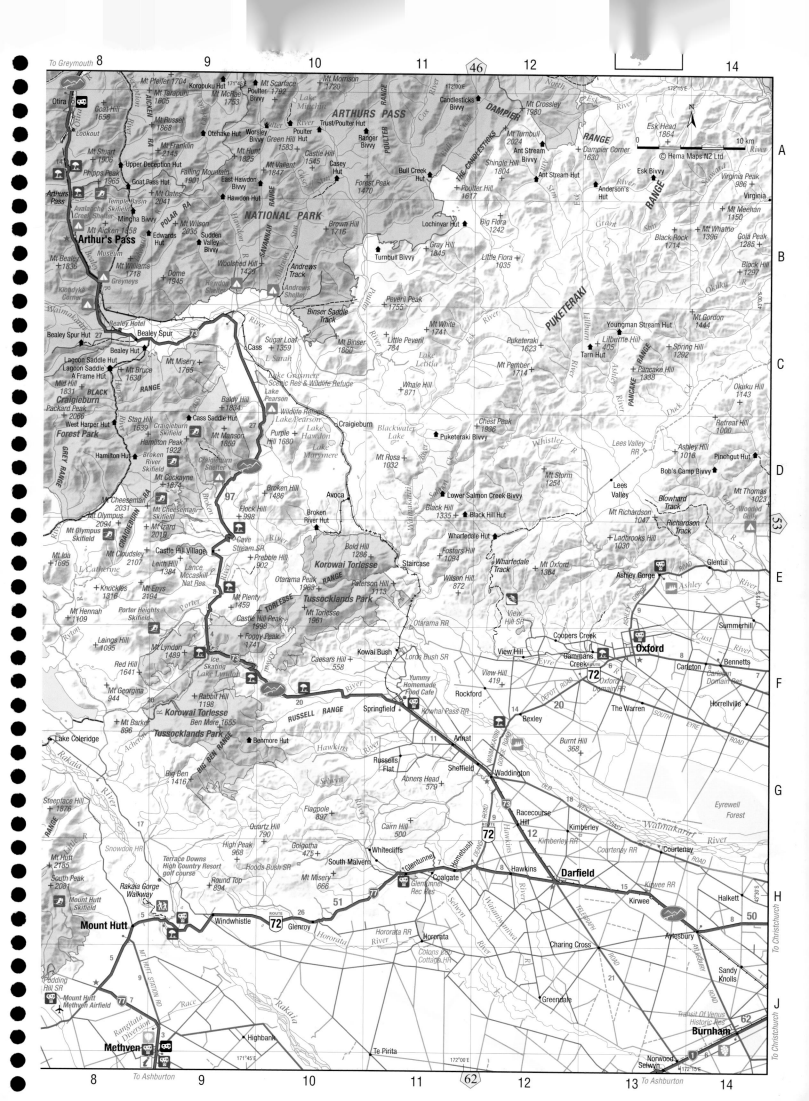

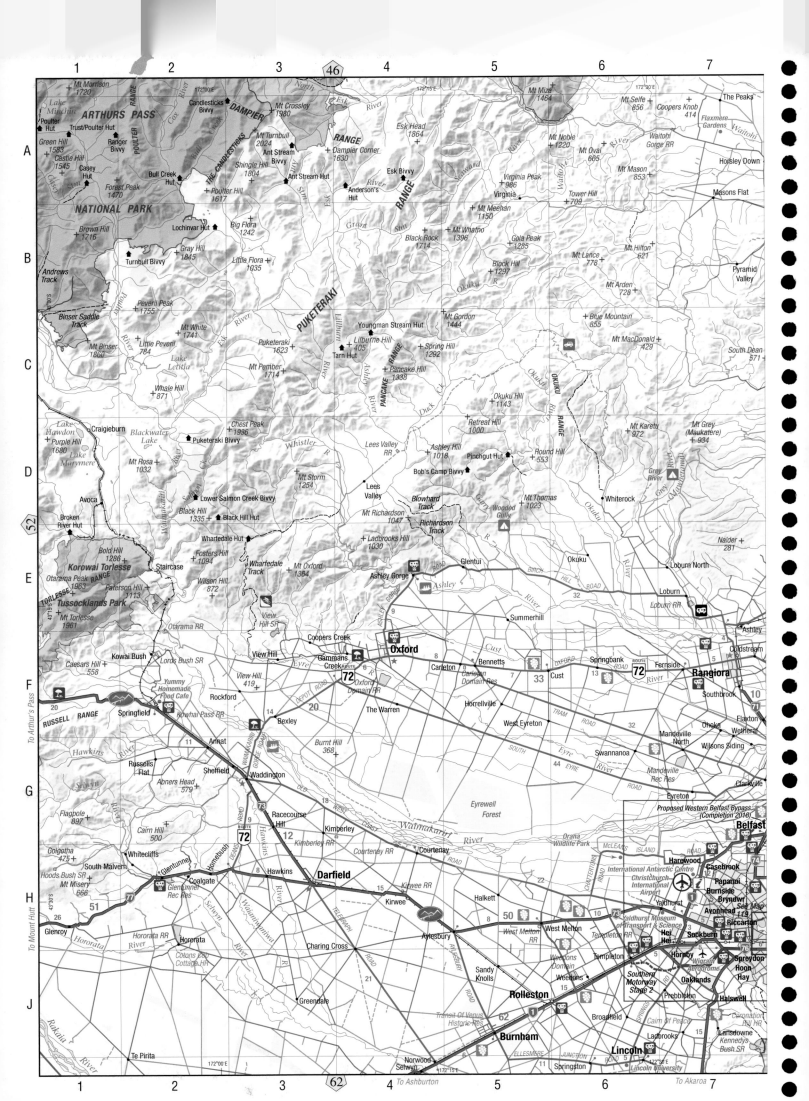

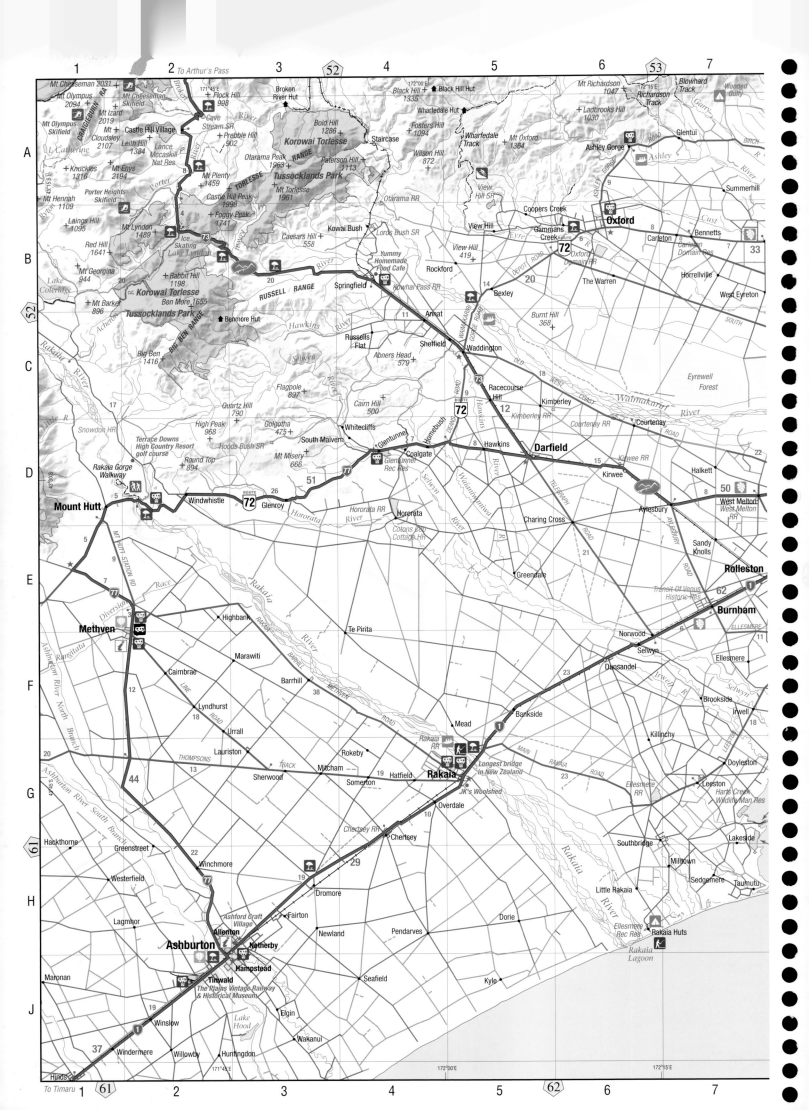

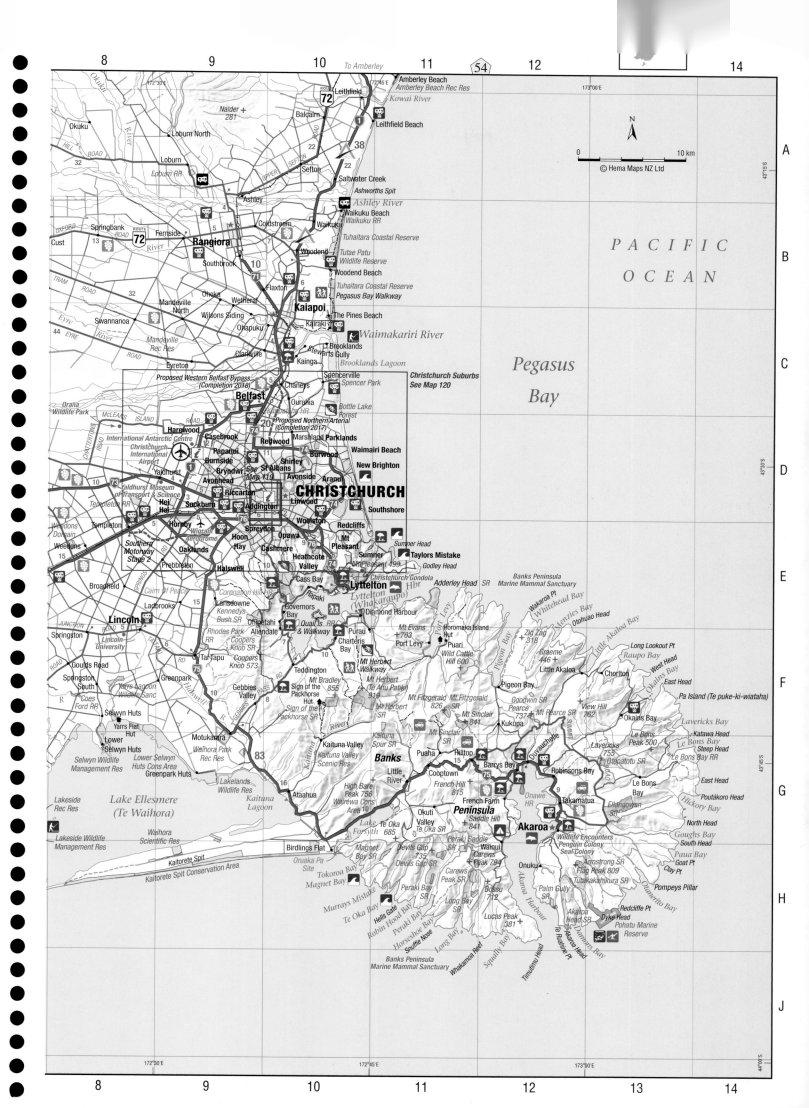

MAP
57
SOUTH ISLAND

N

0   10 km
© Hema Maps NZ Ltd

168°15'E
168°30'E
168°45'E
43°45'S
44°00'S
44°15'S

TASMAN SEA

Open Bay Islands
Wildlife Sanctuary
Taumaka Is

Mussel Pt

Hannahs Clearing

Jackson Bay

Penguins & Seals   Jackson Head
Smoothwater Pt   Waiatoto River
Smoothwater Bay   Jackson Bay
Stafford Bay   Neils Beach
Stafford Hut   Waiatoto
Gill Hill
+ 106
Mt McLean
671 +   Lake Nisson

Cascade Pt
Teer Hill   Arawhata
Teer Hill 340   Clarke Hill +
Cascade River   631
Mt Iota   Mt Ellery
146   793
Halfway Bluff   Mt Alpha
826   Lake Ellery
Watson Bluff   Mt Watney
Barn Bay   Martyr   Mt Beta   1503
993
Cascade Bay   Jackson   Mt Heveldt   Lake
Steep Head   Mt Eggeling   1416 +   Greaney
Sandrock Bluff   494   1136   Smiths   Mt Jackson   Mt Duncan
Browne Island   Ponds   1189   1753
Mt Delta   Lake Clarke   Mt Clio
Bonar Knob   1161   Mt Lindsay   1910
Spoon   Spoon Hut   1181   Lake Leeb   Rosy Peak
Rocky Pt   Mt Theta   Martyr Hill   2093
Gorge Islands   1137   1031   Distal Collyer   Sombre Peak
Gorge River Hut   1420   1643 Baal   2040
Longridge Pt   Mt Malcolm   River   Dagon 945   Datamos   Pegasus
+ 718   1683   1816   Flanagans Peak
Jerry R   Staircase Mountain   Summit   2160
MALCOLM RANGE   1660   Lucifer   2044
Theta Tarn   Mt Richards   1751 Fingals Head   Munro Peak
Junction Hill   1450   1986   2374
Mt Beck   1012   Mt Raddle Tararua Peak   Mt Bel   Canon Peak
1083   1297   1579   1618   Hyperia 2149
Bald Mountain   Mt Nob   1780   Mt Ragan
Awarua   1547   1279   2254
Pt   Mt McKenzie   Mt Barry   MOUNT ASPIRING
981 +   Joe Peak   The Pommel 1374   NATIONAL PARK
Telescope Hill   1927   1154   Corner Post   Mt Taurus
Big Bay   Pyke Big Bay   1117   1832   2009
Track   Snowden   Moonraker Pickelhaube
Big Bay Hut   The Knoll   Alfred Peak   1543   2054   2265
Penguin   Three Mile   407   Red Mountain 1781   Buncombe   Spike   Glacier Dome
Rock   Beach   Waiuna   1705   1918   Stargazer 2126   2367
Lagoon   Beacon   Tyler   2352   Fastness Peak
1531   Eros   1976   Colin Todd Rolling Pin   2383
Battlement Peak   Toreador Peak   2230   Mt Ionia Hut   + 2249   Sisyphus Peak
+ 1605   1951   Turks Head 2266   1859
1831

STAFFORD RANGE
HAAST RANGE
DRAKE
Waiatoto
RED HILLS RANGE
OLIVINE
RANGE
WAIRARA

168°15'E
168°30'E
168°45'E

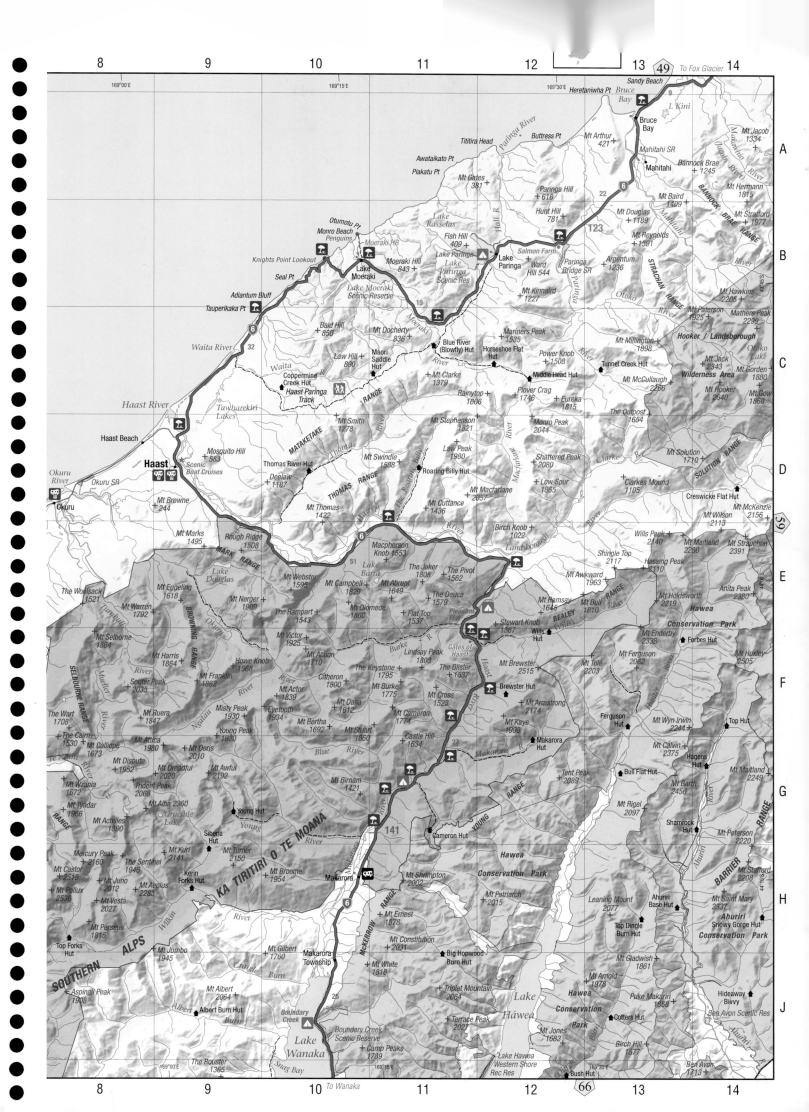

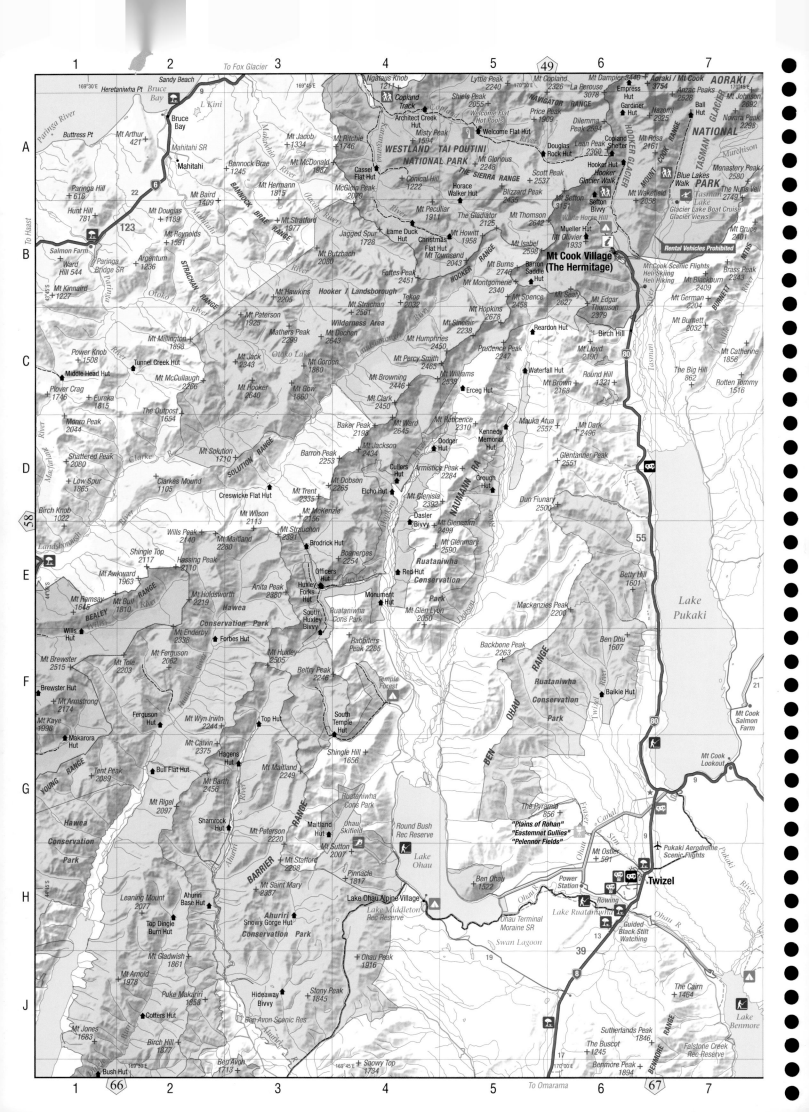

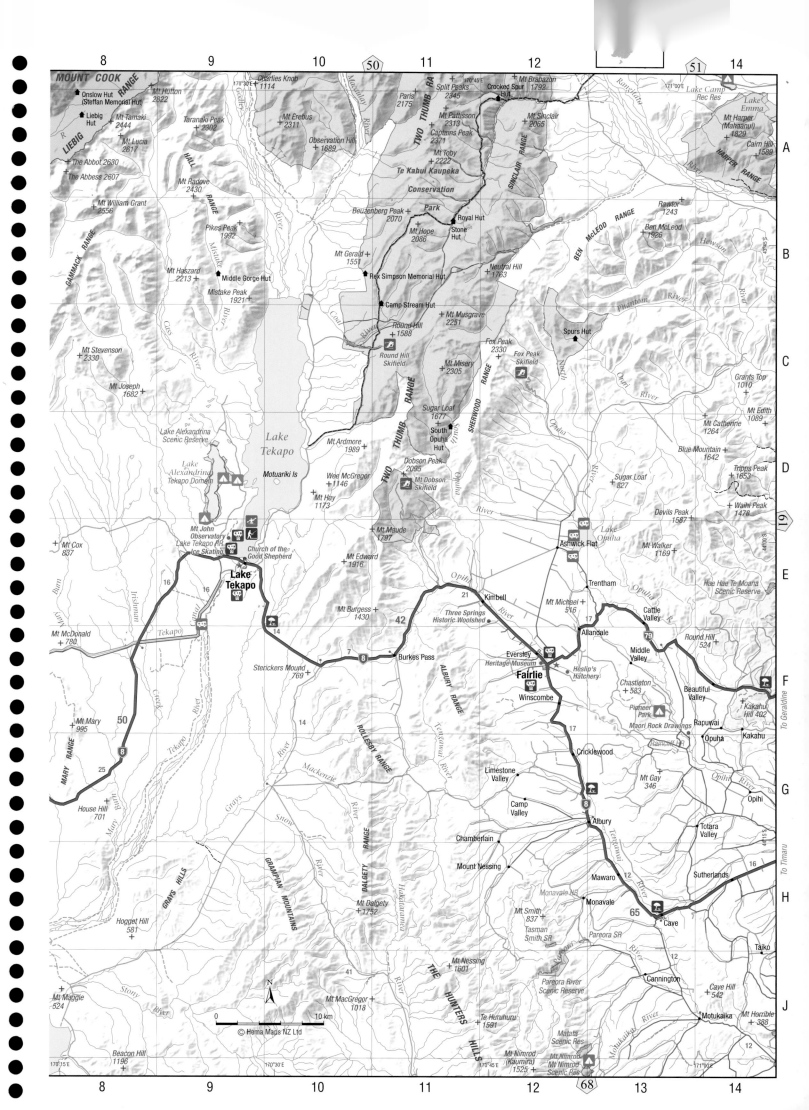

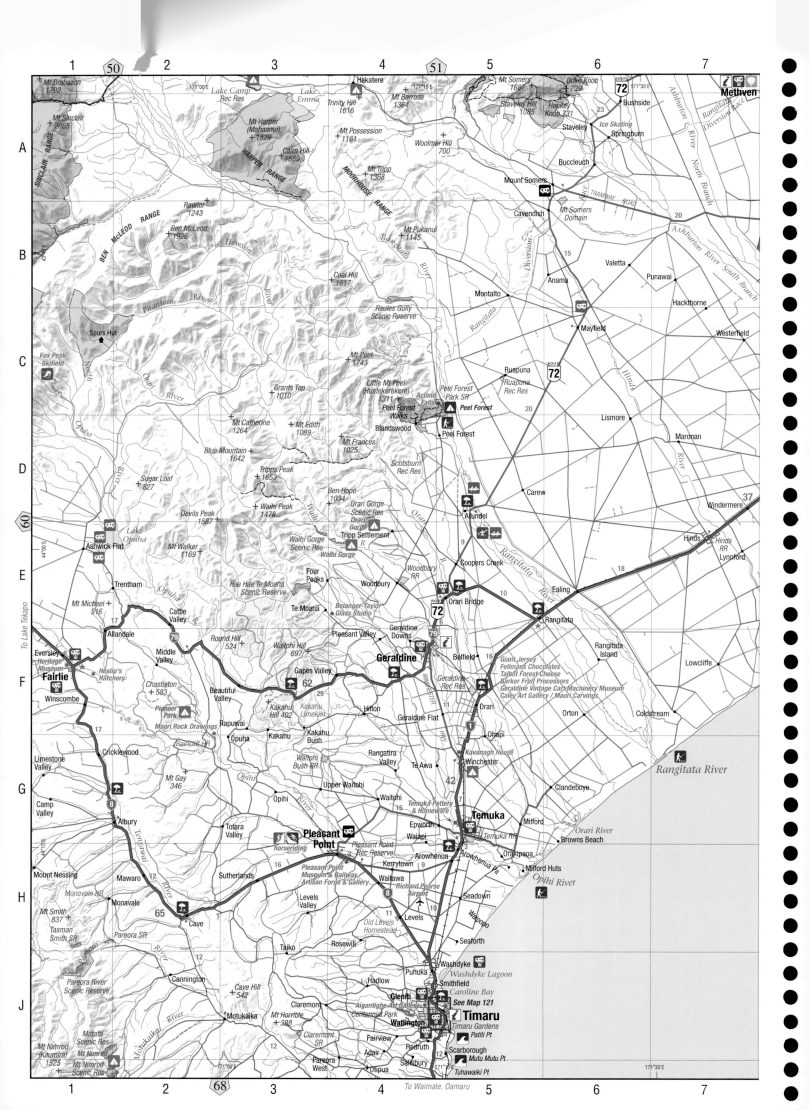

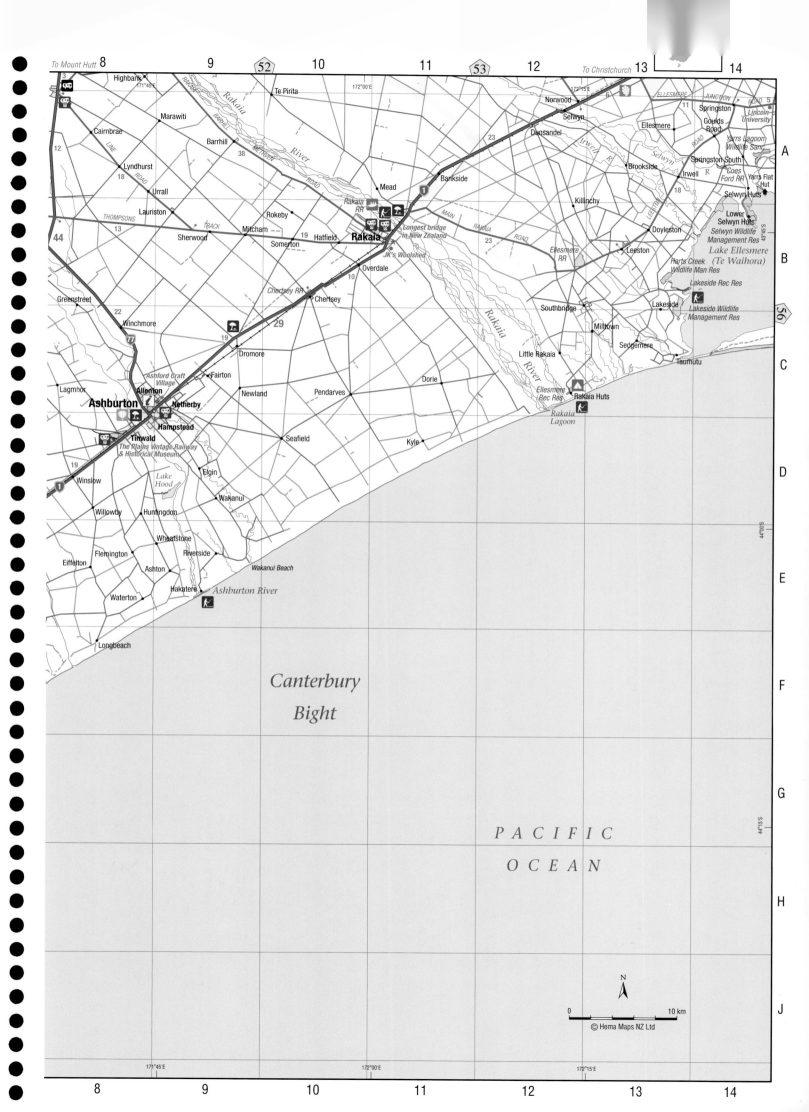

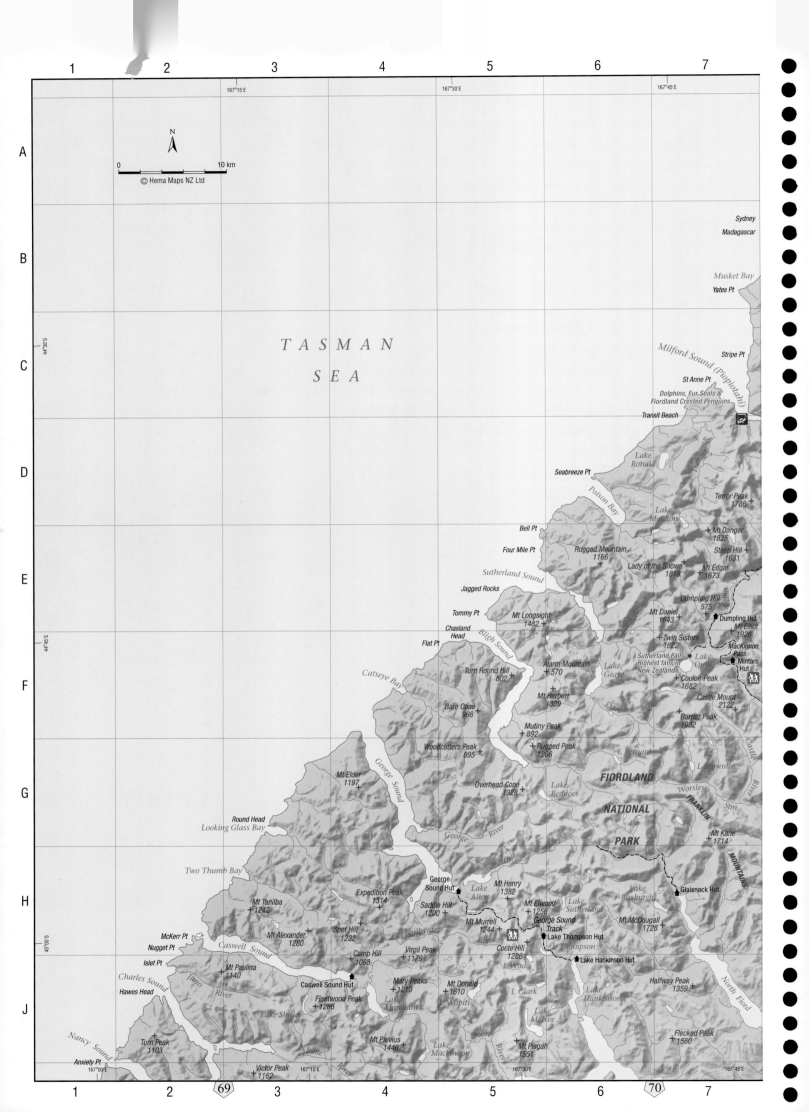

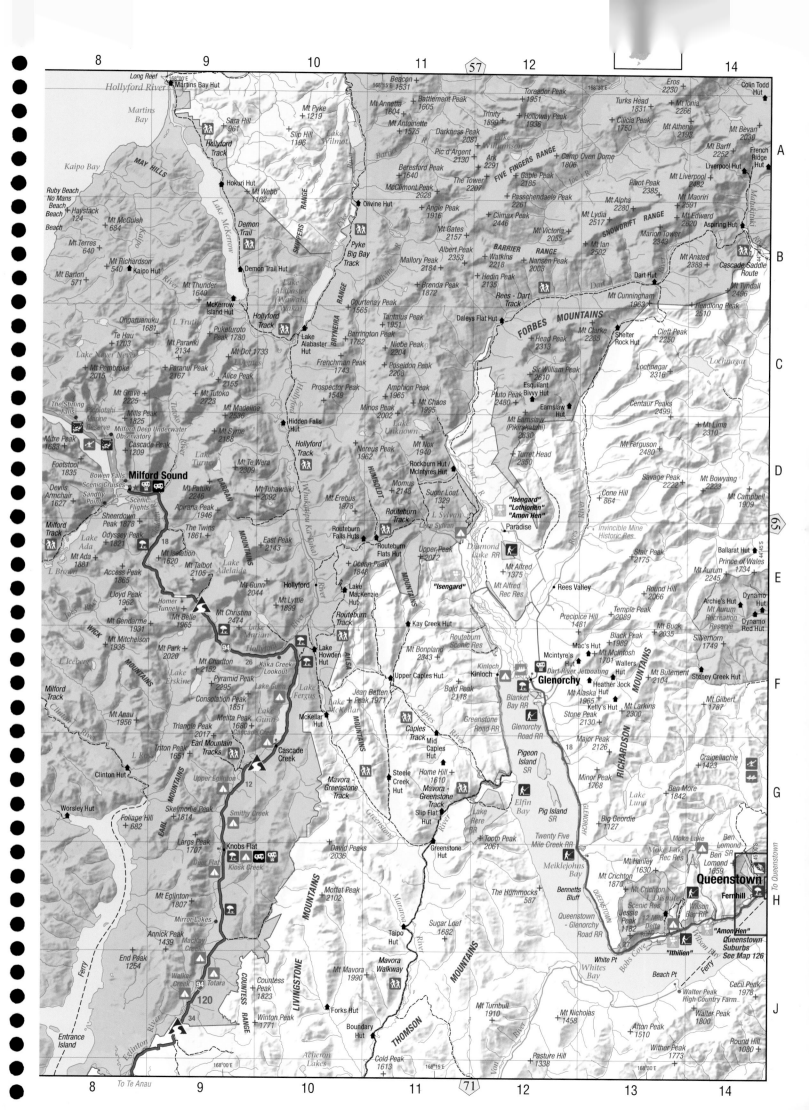

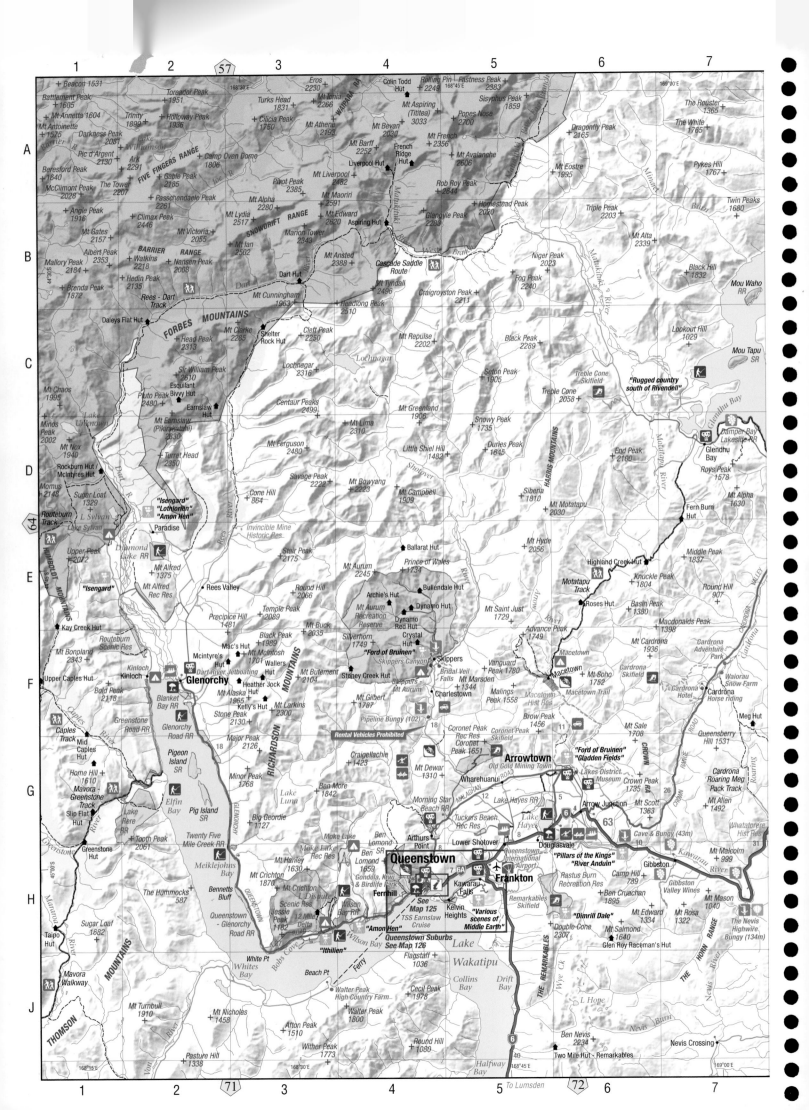

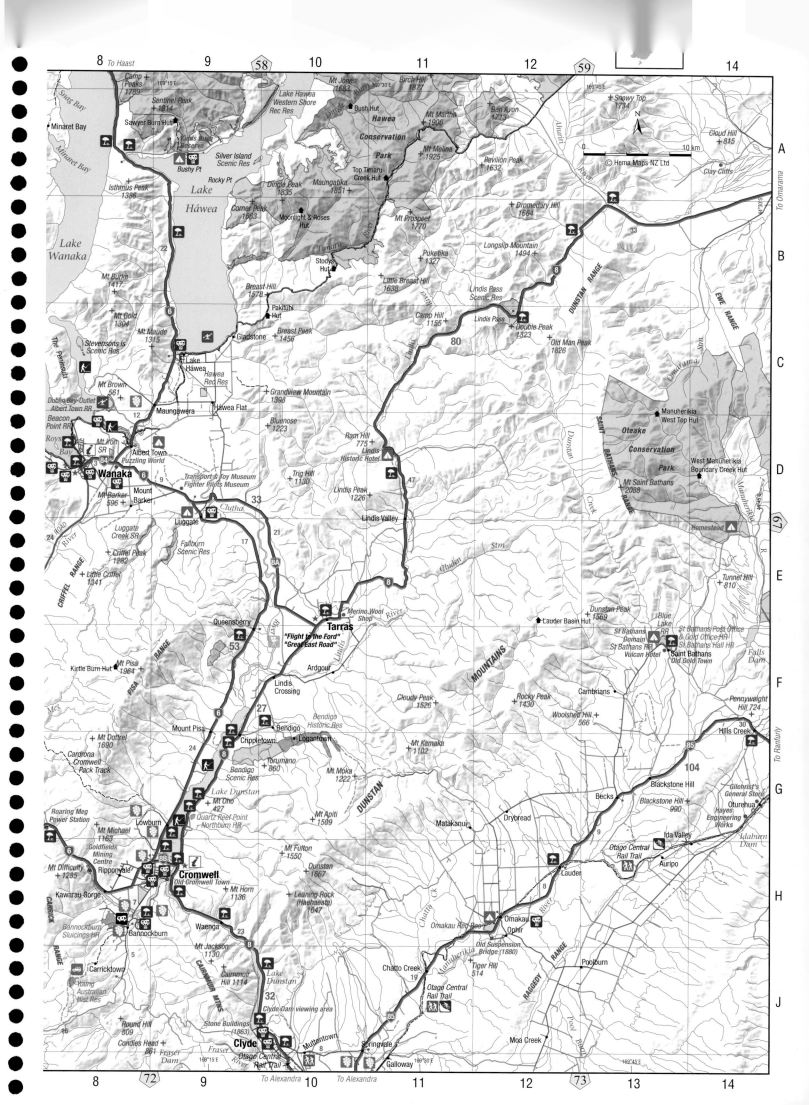

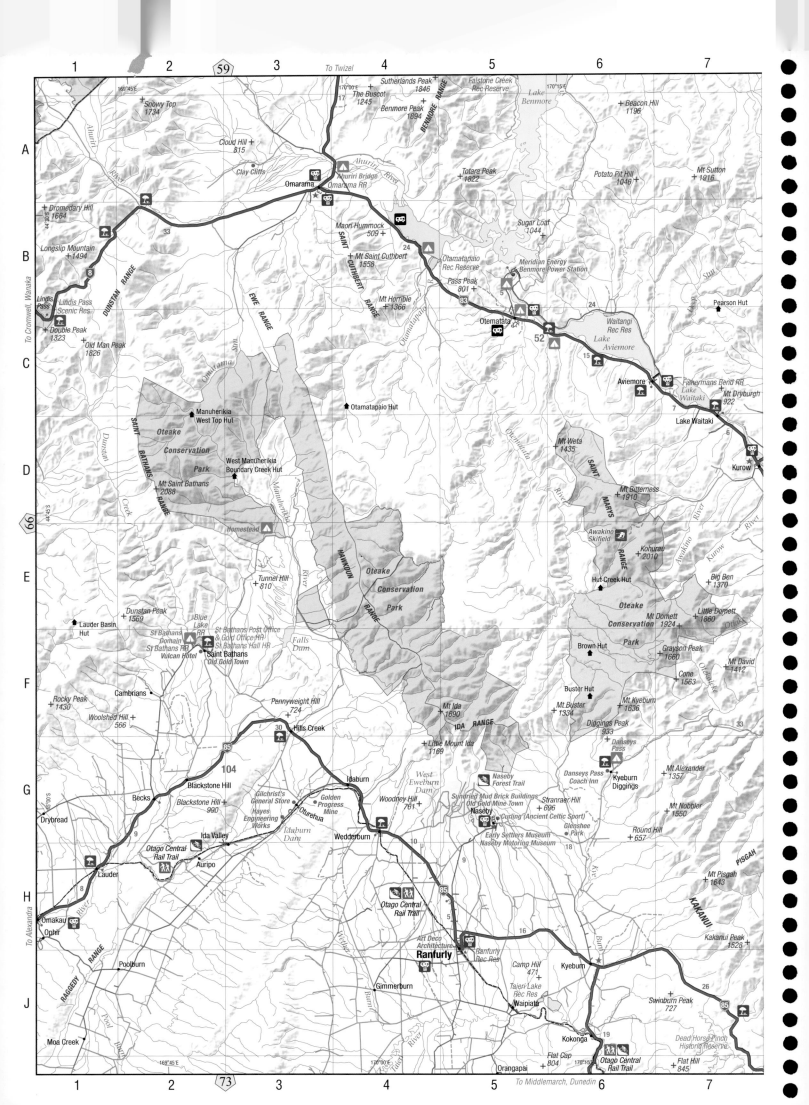

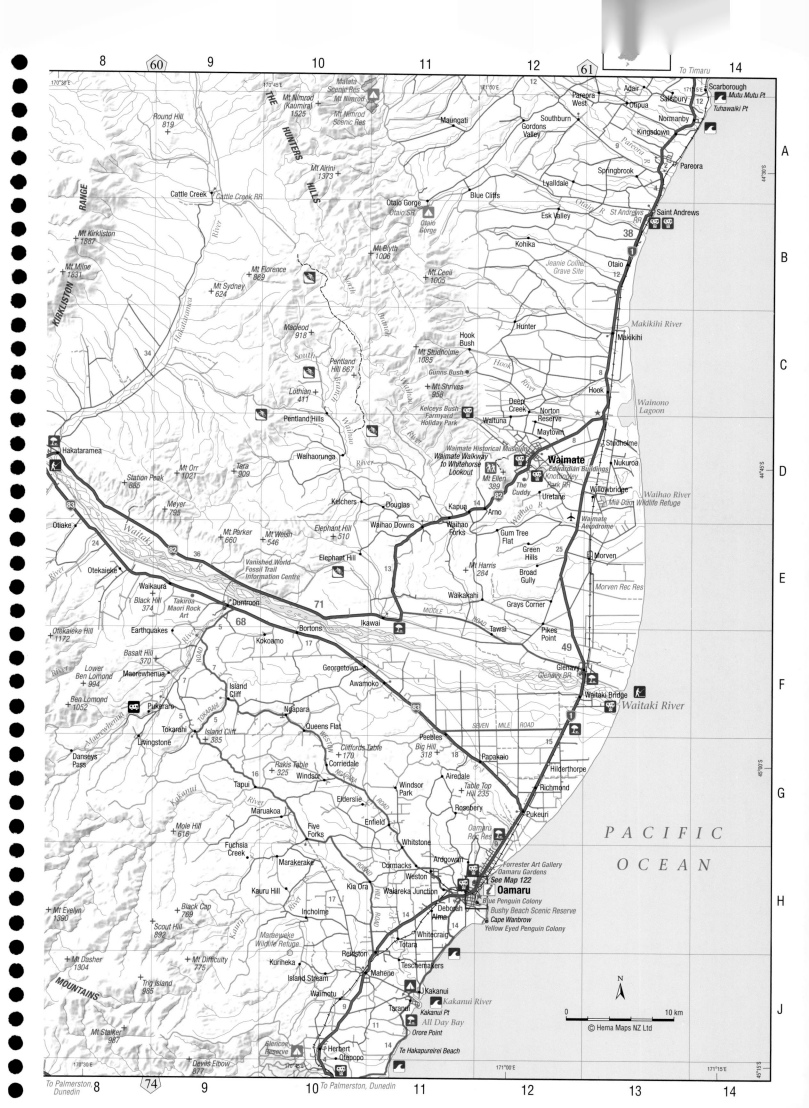

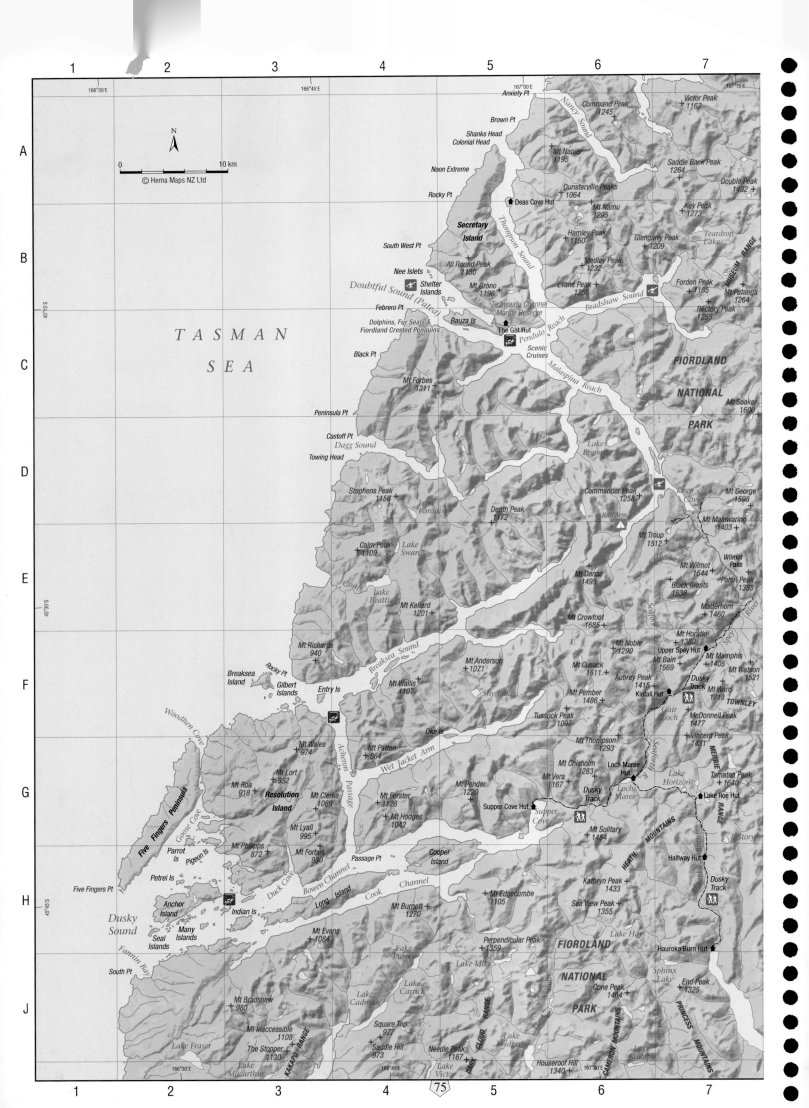

63 8 9 10 11 12 To Milford Sound 13 64 14

Mt Pluvius 1446
Lake Mackinnon
Irene River
Lake Bloxham
167°30'E
Middle Fiord
Rocky Pt
Boat Hbr
Bog Lake
Te Anau Downs
168°00'E
Acheron Lakes
River
DUNTON RANGE
Upukerora
A

Mt Irene 1859
Miller Peak 1503
Doubtful Island
Pleasant Bay
Dunton Peak 1412
Mt Richmond 1673
45°15'S

Coronation Peak 1769
Mt Wera 1435
L Wisely
Mt Max 1625
Aurora Pt
Centre Is
Henry Creek
Army Hut
Snowdon Peak 1573
B

Gerald Peak 1602
Lake Hilda
L Hall
L Duncan
L Eyles
MURCHISON MOUNTAINS
Ettrick Burn
South Burn
Lake Te Au
Lake Orbell
Lake Te Anau
Largest Lake in the South Island
Te Anau Caves Glow Worms
30
Te Anau Hill 504
The Dale
Dale Hill 747
Limestone Hill 678
Whitestone River
Kiwi Burn Hut
Bare Peak 1209

Mt Baird 1528
Mt Lyall 1892
Mt Owen 1763
Black Cone 1681
West Beach
Dome Islands
"Fangorn Forest"
94
Mt Scott 1523
Mt Kidd 1558
South Fiord
Mt Prospect 969
Little Hill 548
C
167°45'E

Mt Fannin 1569
Mt Maury 1658
Forward Peak 1354
Kepler Track
Lookout Hill 312
East Cove
Upukerora River
35

Lake Annie
KEPLER MOUNTAINS
Mt Pickering 1650
Mt Tinsley 1537
Luxmore Hut
Brod Bay
Patience Bay
Scenic Cruises
Wildlife Park
Danby Hill 724
D

"Rugged country south of Rivendell"
"Flight to the Ford"
Lake Herries
Spire Peak 1689
Iris Burn Hut
JACKSON PEAKS
Mt Luxmore 1472
Kepler Track
Te Anau
Ivon Wilson Park
Ramparts Scenic Res
15
95
45°30'S
71

Freeman Burn Hut
Lake Victoria
Iris Burn
Harts Hill 645
Kepler Track
Moturau Hut
"River Anduin"
Waiau River
20
ROAD
94
10
The Key
20
78
Lake Thomas
E

Norwest Lakes
CATHEDRAL PEAKS
North Arm
Beehive 587
Shallow Bay
Shallow Bay Hut
"Dead Marshes"
New Zealand's Second Deepest Lake
HILLSIDE
Mt York 406
Spear Peak 630
Centre Hill 818
To Lumsden

Steep Peak 1372
Leaning Peak 1477
West Arm Power Station
West Arm Hut
Mt Gray 1502
TURRET RANGE
West Arm
Lake Lois
Fairy Beach
Trinity Lakes
Precipice Peak 1381
Pomona Island
Rona Is
Lake Manapouri
Manapouri Scenic Cruises
5
Freestone Hill 336
Woodhen Hill 969
Lower Princhester Hut
Waterloo Peak 1077
Mt Hamilton 1487

Cone Peak 1495
South Arm
Hope Arm
Hope Arm Hut
Back Valley Hut
8
Upper Princhester Hut
Clare Peak 1490
Aparima Forks Hut
Becketts Hut
North Braxton 1080
F

WALL MOUNTAINS
HUNTER MOUNTAINS
Flat Mount 1748
Garnock Burn
Mt Crescent 1639
Pudding Hill 239
Lake Rakatu
Paddock Hill 905
WEIR ROAD
Cheviot Downs Hut
Brown Peak 1470
Excelsior Peak 1543
Gladstone Peak 1569
Aparima Peaks 1570
Spence Hut
South Braxton 1018
Aparima Huts
Aparima R
45°45'S

Mt Titiroa 1715
North Branch
Tower Peak 1425
White Hill 1398
Whare Creek Hut
Revelation Peaks 1560
Spence Peak 1634
TAKITIMU MOUNTAINS
McLean Peaks 1495
Upper Wairaki Hut
Coral Bluff 555
G

Mt Puteketeke 1563
North Borland Hut
Middle Branch
South Branch
Borland Burn
Waiau River
24
Redcliff Ck
Redcliff Hut
Brunel Peaks 1582
Telford Hut
Mackinnon Peaks 1502
Telford Peak 1577
Lower Wairaki Hut
Letham Hill 962
Etal Hill 931
Chimney 754

Borland Bivvy
Mt Burns 1645
Eldrig Peak 1595
Green Lake Hut
Black Mount 540
BLACKMOUNT
85
Corner Peaks 1414
The Pate 946
Nugget Hill 675
Beaumont Hill 841

Clark Hut (historic)
Clark Hut (A Frame)
Island Lake
Green Lake
Mt Cuthbert 1248
Monowai
Blackmount
The Knob 821
Mt Nichols 1007
Gibraltar Hill 704
Morley Hill 665
Wether Hill 676
H

Rocky Top 1450
Monowai Hut
Cleughearn Peak 1578
Rodgers Inlet Hut
White Hill 478
Diggers Hill 515
Løudon Hill 376
Mt Linton 500
Mt Franklin 418
Crawfords
The Nightcaps 345
Tinkertown

Electric River
KAHERKEKAU MOUNTAINS
Eel Creek Hut
White Peak 1574
Edge Peak 1082
Hindley Peak 1219
Knoll Peak 1057
Dean Hill 777
Bell Mount 406
28
Waiau River
Sharpridge 302
Birchwood
Lonekers Bush SR
Otahu Flat
Wairaki River
BLACKMOUNT ROAD
CLIFDEN HWY Ohai
168°00'E
Nightcaps 16
J

167°15'E
Caroline Hut
167°30'E
76
To Clifden
167°45'E
To Clifden
LONGAL ROAD
13
77
14 To Winton
To Winton

8 9 10 76 11 12 13 77 14

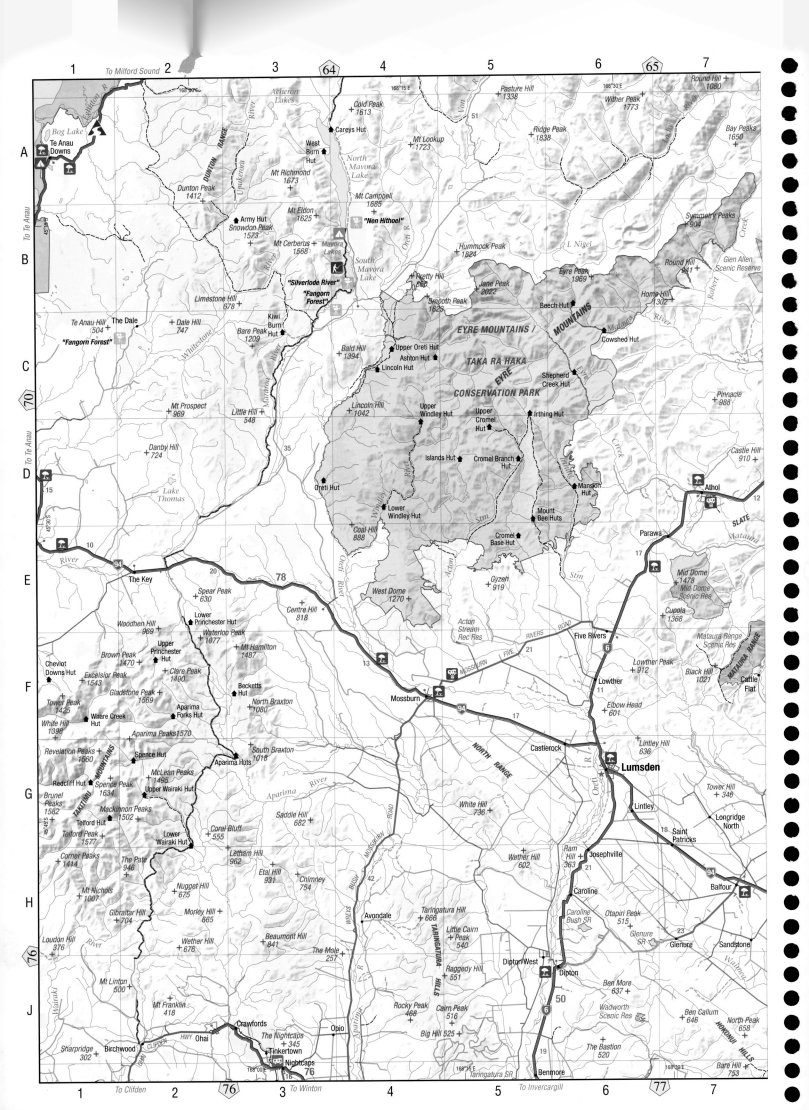

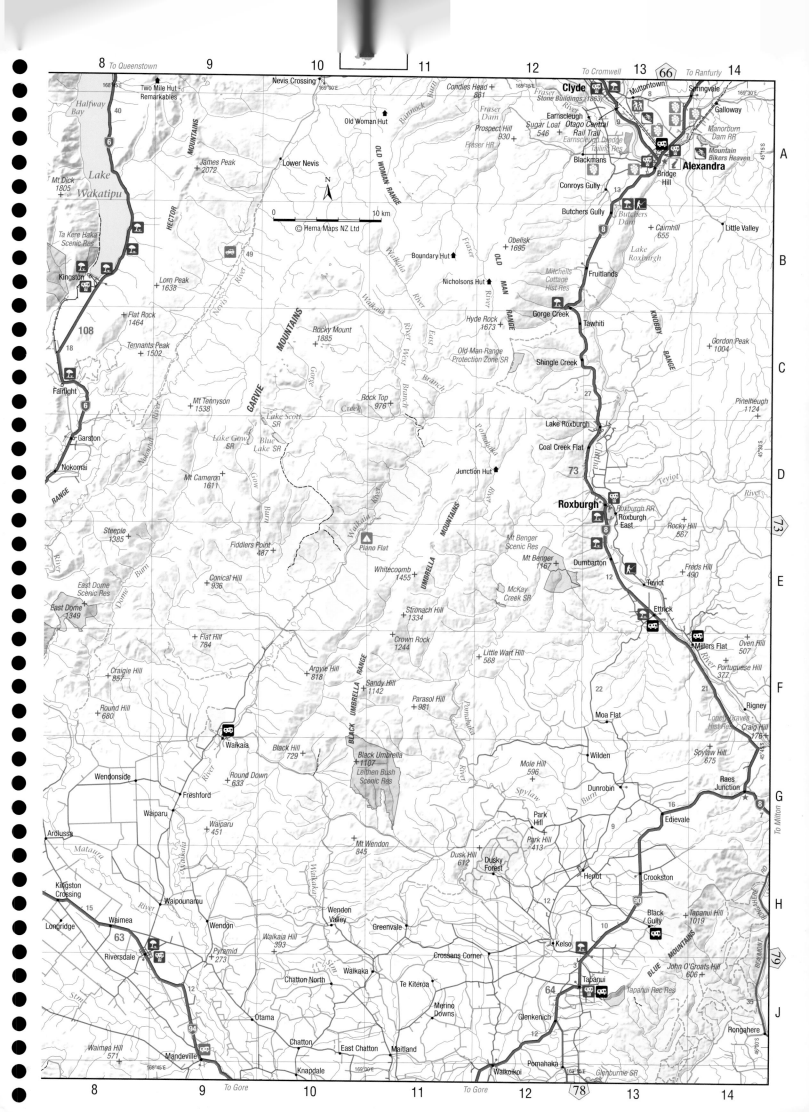

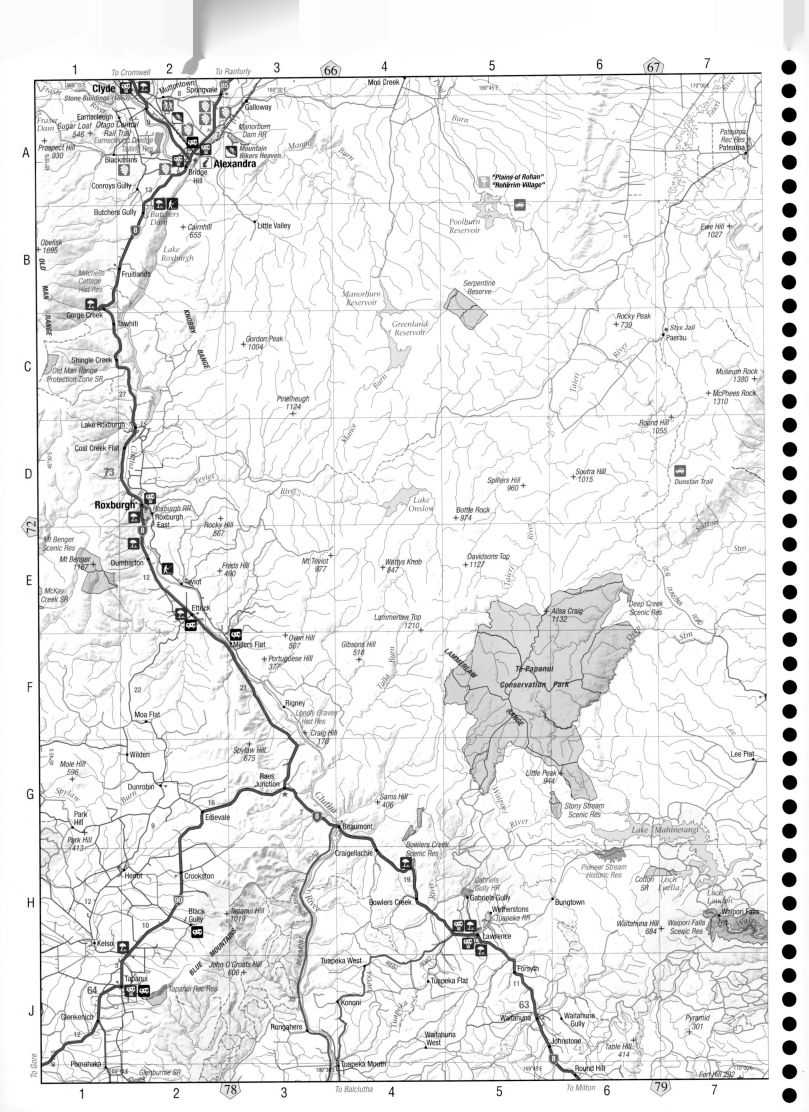

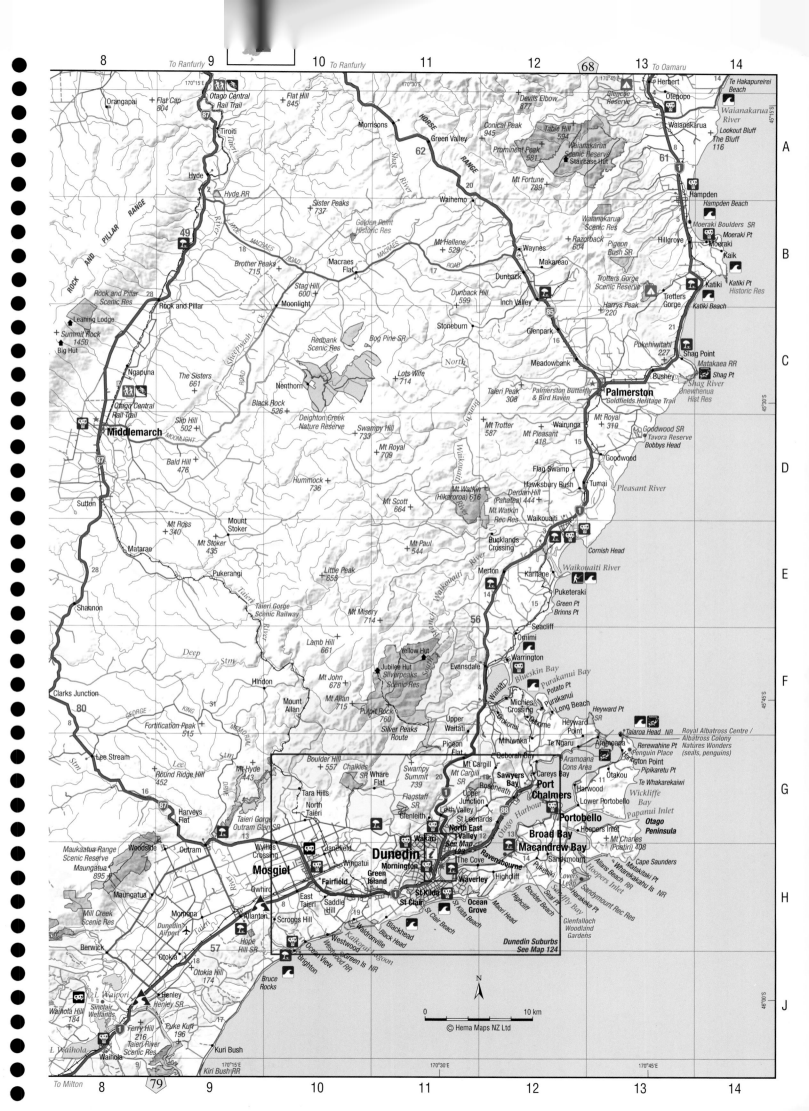

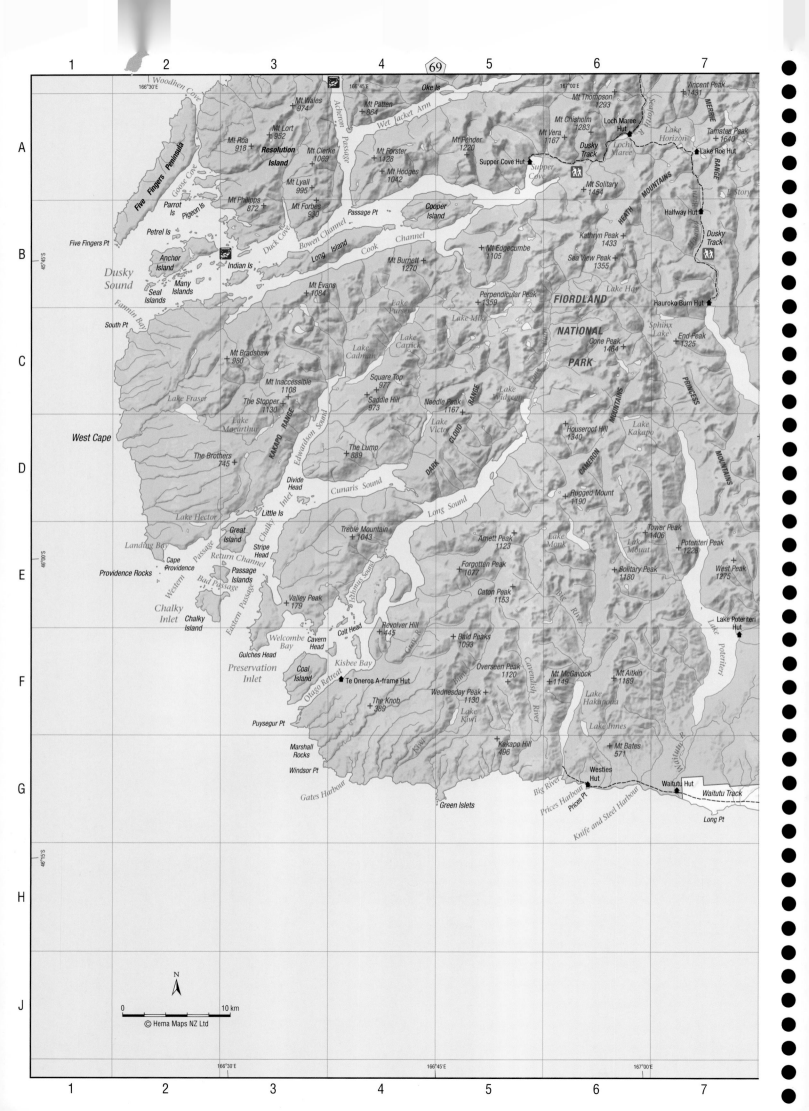

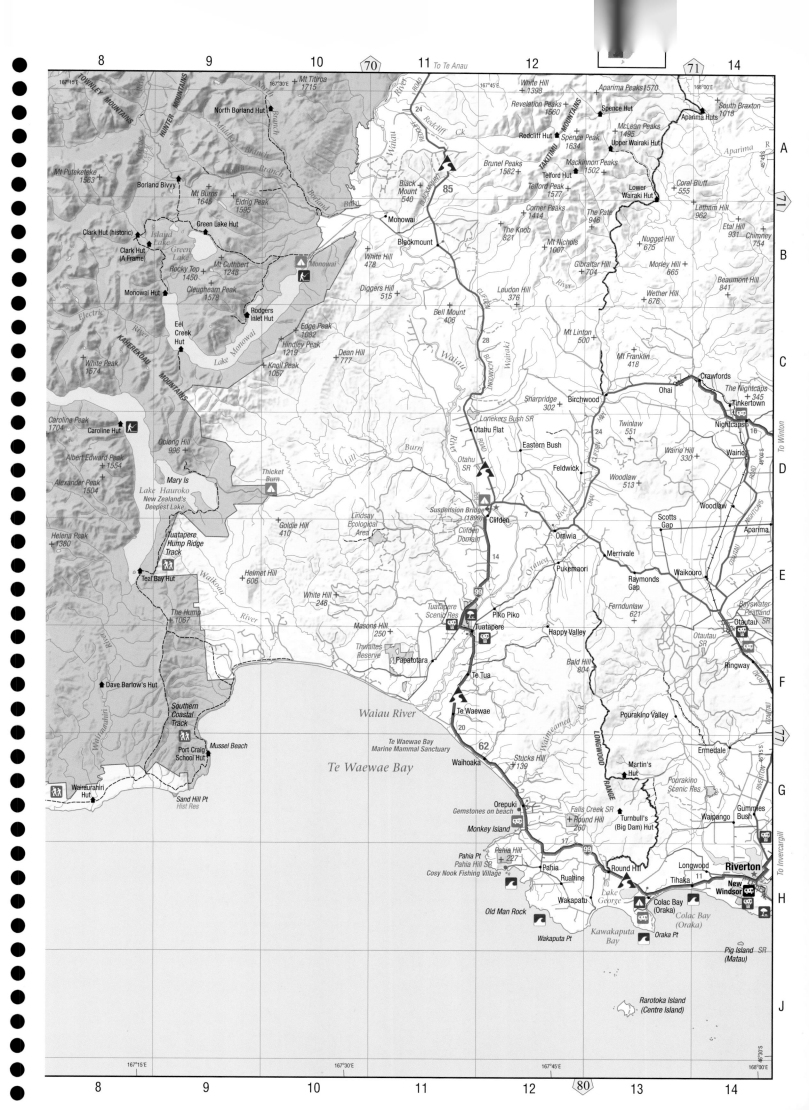

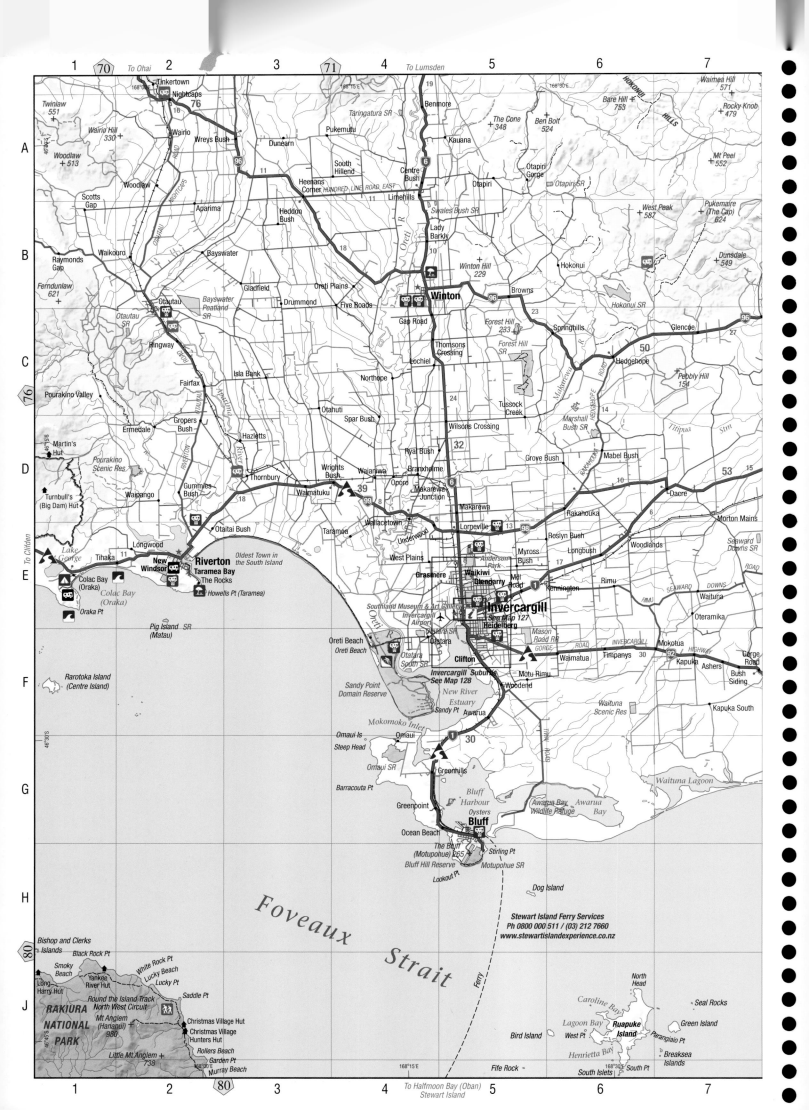

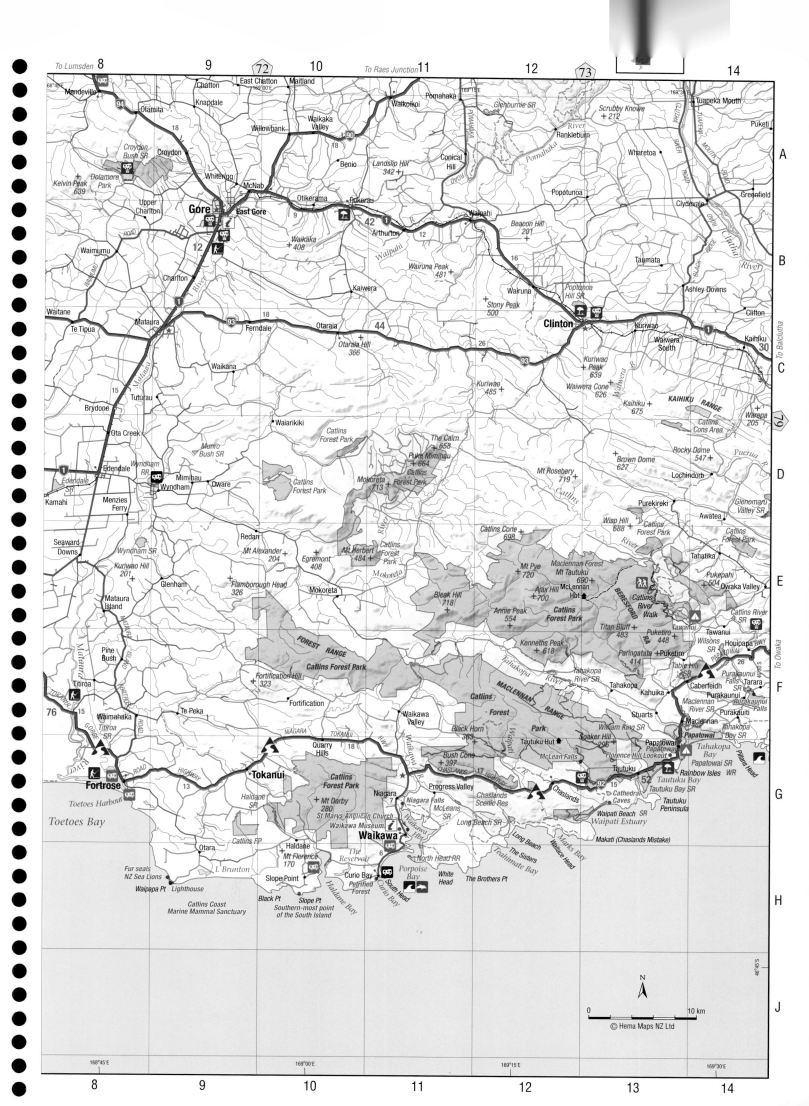

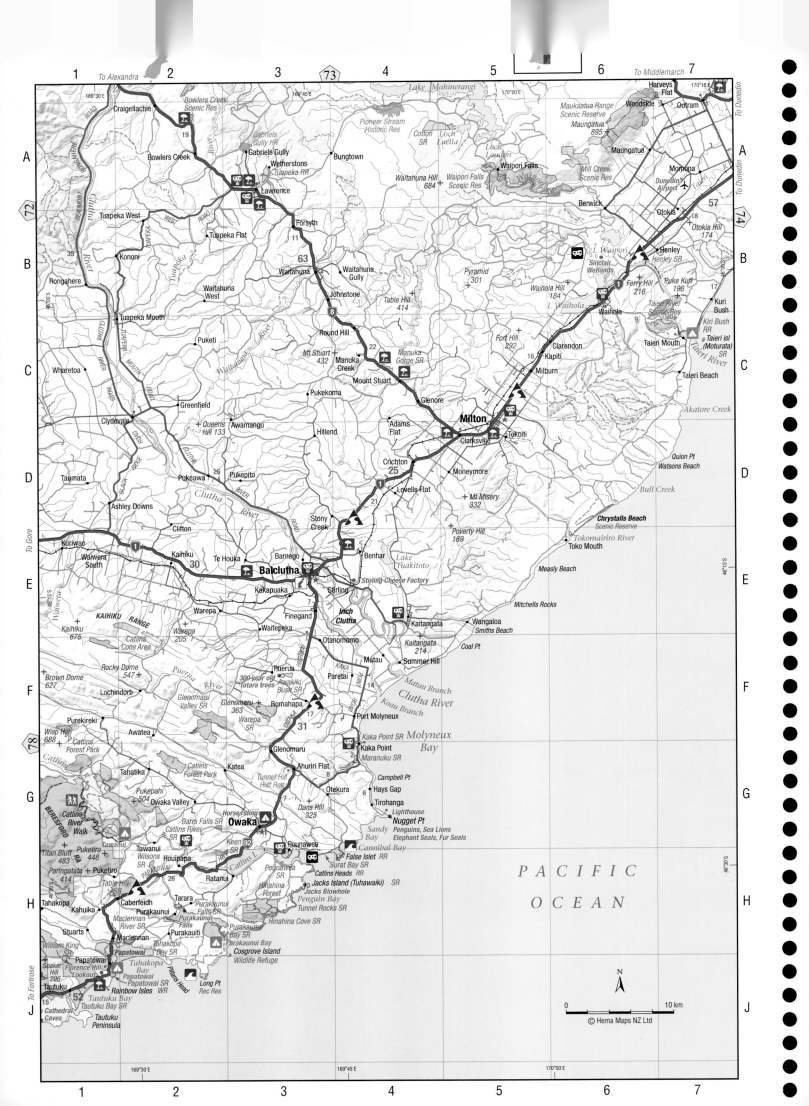

Legend

Motorway	
Urban Route	6
State Highway	1
Ring Road	R
Main Road	
Street	
Lane/Path	
Railway & Station	Auckland
City Tramway	
Road Tunnel	
Major Bridge/overpass	
Ferry Route	
Major Building	
Govt Building	
Accommodation	
Theatre/Cinema	
Shopping	
Mall/City Square	
School/Educational	
Park/Reserve	

Cemetery	✝ ✝
Hospital	✚
Postal Service	✉
Police Station	POLICE
Church	✝
One Way Street	→
Place of Interest	• Tui Brewery
Information Centre	i
To Airport	✈
Alpine Pacific Triangle Tourist Route	
Inland Scenic Tourist Route	ROUTE 72
Southern Scenic Tourist Route	
Twin Coast Tourist Route	
Thermal Explorer Tourist Route	
Pacific Coast Tourist Route	
Forgotten World Tourist Route	Forgotten World
Classic New Zealand Wine Trail	
The Great Alpine Highway	

Suburbs Legend

Motorway	
Motorway (proposed)	
Urban Ring Road	R
State Highway/Number	1
Main Rd/Regional Number	72
Secondary Road	
Minor Road	
Railway and Station	Rolleston
Busway	
Park, Reserve, Golf Course	Harewood
Special Use	Hospital
Mountain	▲ Mt Herbert
Ferry Route	
Tourist Point of Interest	• Christchurch Gondola
Major Shopping Centre	The Palms Mall
Information Centre	i

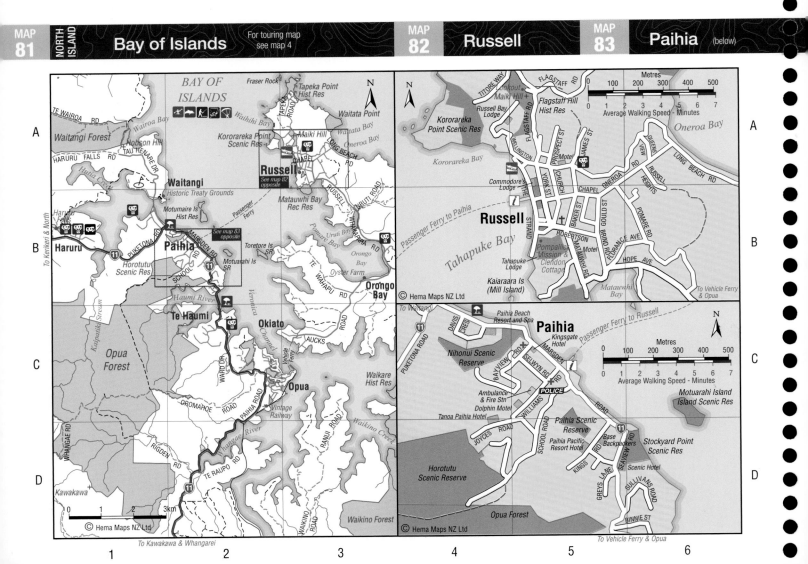

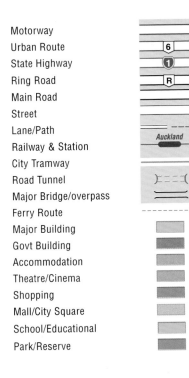

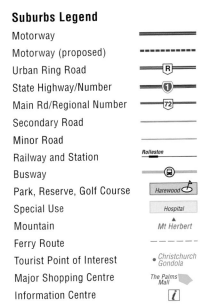

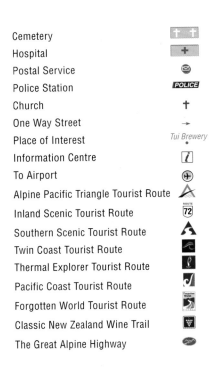

BAY OF ISLANDS

Fraser Rock
Tapeka Point Hist Res
Waitata Point
TE WAIROA RD
Waitangi Forest
Waihihi Bay
Waihihi Bay
Waitata Bay
Kororareka Point Scenic Res
Oneroa Bay
Waitangi Forest
Hobson Hill
TAU HENARE DR
HARURU FALLS RD
Hutia Creek
Russell — See map 82 opposite
LONG BEACH RD
Waitangi
Historic Treaty Grounds
Matauwhi Bay Rec Res
Motumaire Is Hist Res
Passenger Ferry
RUSSELL WHAKAPHARA ROAD
URUTI ROAD
Haruru Falls
Paihia — See map 83 opposite
Toretore Is SR
Uruti Bay
Pomare Bay
Orongo Bay
Oyster Farm
Haruru
PUKETONA RD
MARSDEN RD
Horotutu Scenic Res
SCHOOL RD
Motuarahi Is SR
TE WAHAPU RD
VERONICA Channel
Haumi River
Te Haumi
Okiato
Orongo Bay
WARD DR
AUCKS RD
Vehicle Ferry
Opua Forest
OROMAHOE ROAD
PAIHIA ROAD
Opua
Vintage Railway
Waikare Hist Res
Kaipatiki Stream
WHANGAE RD
RIGDEN RD
TE RAUPO RD
RANUI ROAD
Whangae River
Waikino Creek
Kawakawa
Waikino Forest
To Kawakawa & Whangarei
© Hema Maps NZ Ltd
0 1 2 3km

Russell

TITORE WAY
Lookout
Maiki Hill
Russell Bay Lodge
FLAGSTAFF RD
Flagstaff Hill Hist Res
Kororareka Point Scenic Res
Kororareka Bay
WELLINGTON
FLAGSTAFF RD
PROSPECT ST
JAMES ST
Motel
Oneroa Bay
QUEENS VIEW RD
RUSSELL HEIGHTS
LONG BEACH RD
Commodore's Lodge
YORK ST
CHURCH ST
CHAPEL
ONEROA ST
GOULD ST
POMARE RD
Passenger Ferry to Paihia
THE STRAND
BAKER ST
ROBERTSON
MATAUWHI RD
BRIND RD
FLORANCE AVE
HOPE AVE
Russell
Tahapuke Bay
Pompallier Mission & Clendon Cottage
Tahapuke Lodge
Motel
Kaiaraara Is (Mill Island)
Matauwhi Bay
To Vehicle Ferry & Opua
© Hema Maps NZ Ltd
Metres
0 100 200 300 400 500
Average Walking Speed - Minutes

Paihia

To Waitangi
PUKETONA ROAD
DAVIS CRES
Paihia Beach Resort and Spa
Kingsgate Hotel
Passenger Ferry to Russell
BAY VIEW RD
SELWYN RD
MARSDEN RD
Nihonui Scenic Reserve
Ambulance & Fire Stn
Dolphin Motel
Tanoa Paihia Hotel
WILLIAMS RD
POLICE
Paihia Scenic Reserve
JOYCES ROAD
SCHOOL ROAD
Paihia Pacific Resort Hotel
Base Backpackers
KINGS RD
SEAVIEW RD
Motuarahi Island Island Scenic Res
Stockyard Point Scenic Res
Horotutu Scenic Reserve
GREYS LANE
SULLIVANS ROAD
Scenic Hotel
BINNIE ST
Opua Forest
To Vehicle Ferry & Opua
© Hema Maps NZ Ltd
Metres
0 100 200 300 400 500
Average Walking Speed - Minutes

A   B   C   D

1   2   3   4   5   6

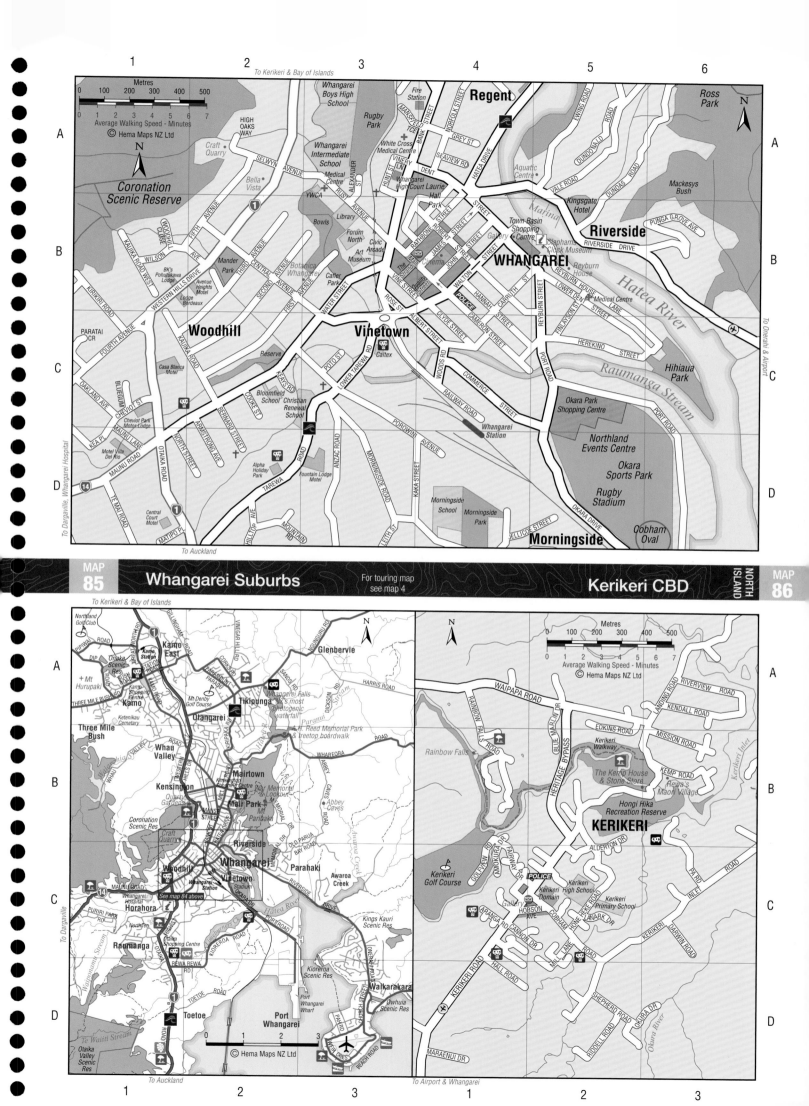

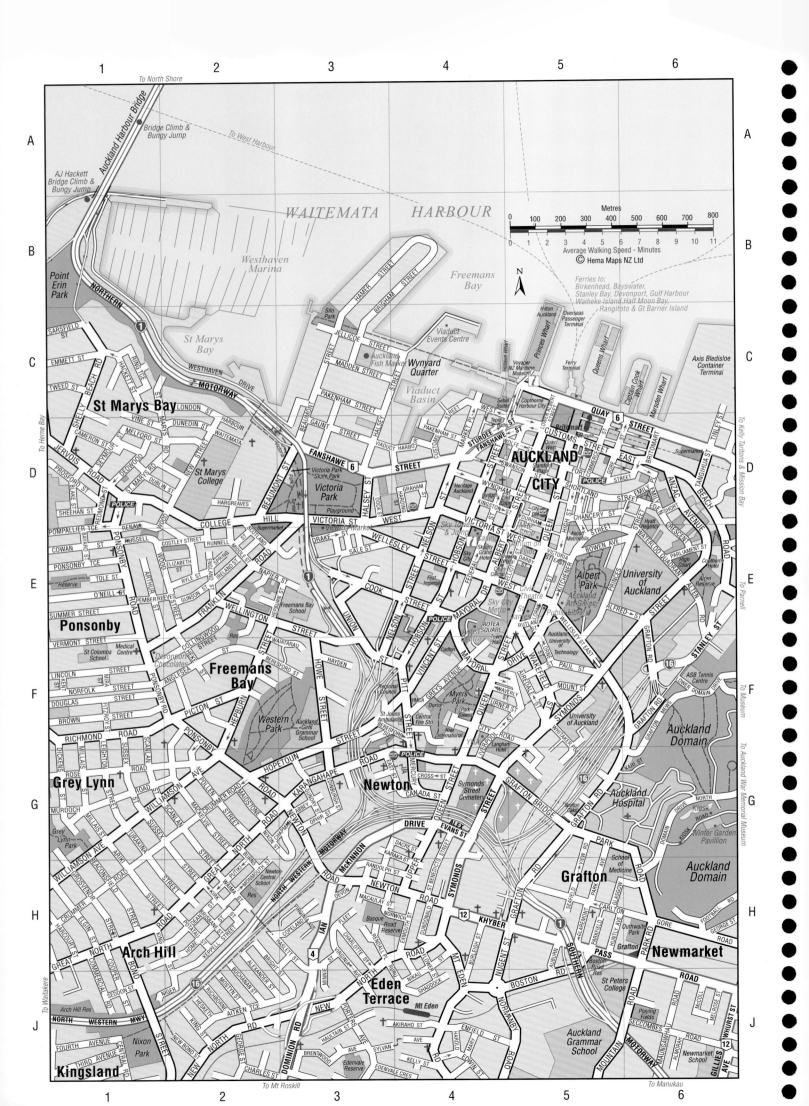

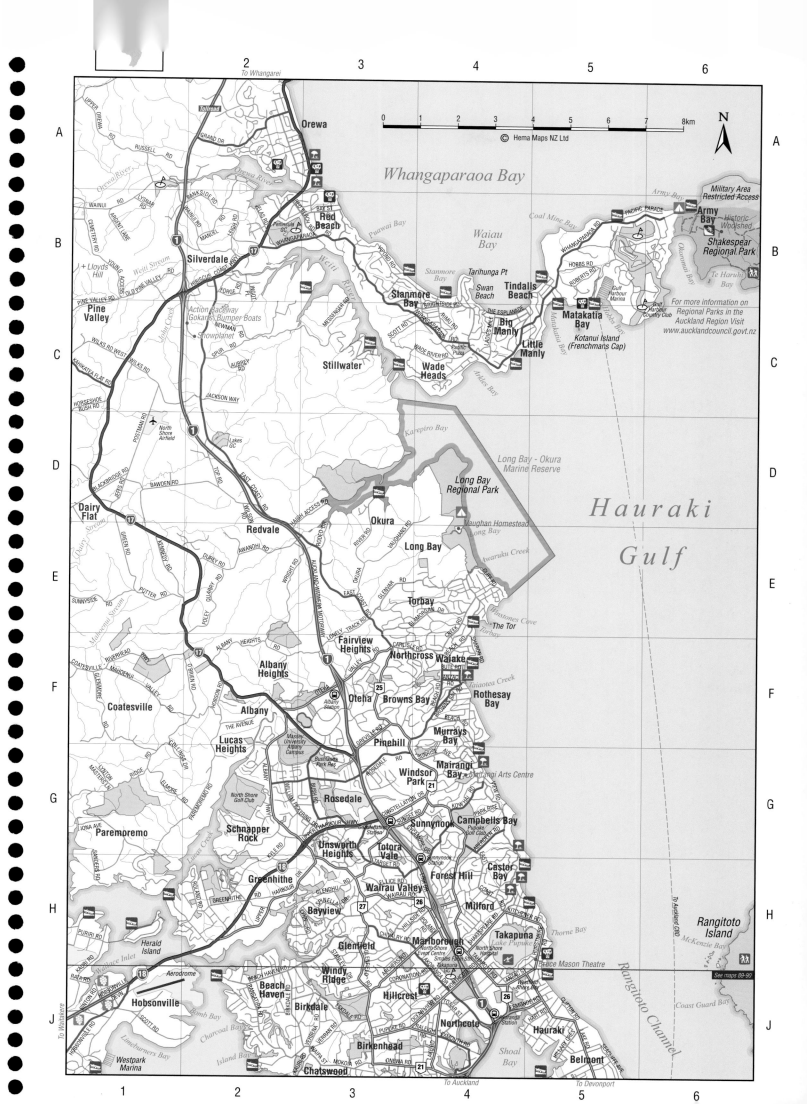

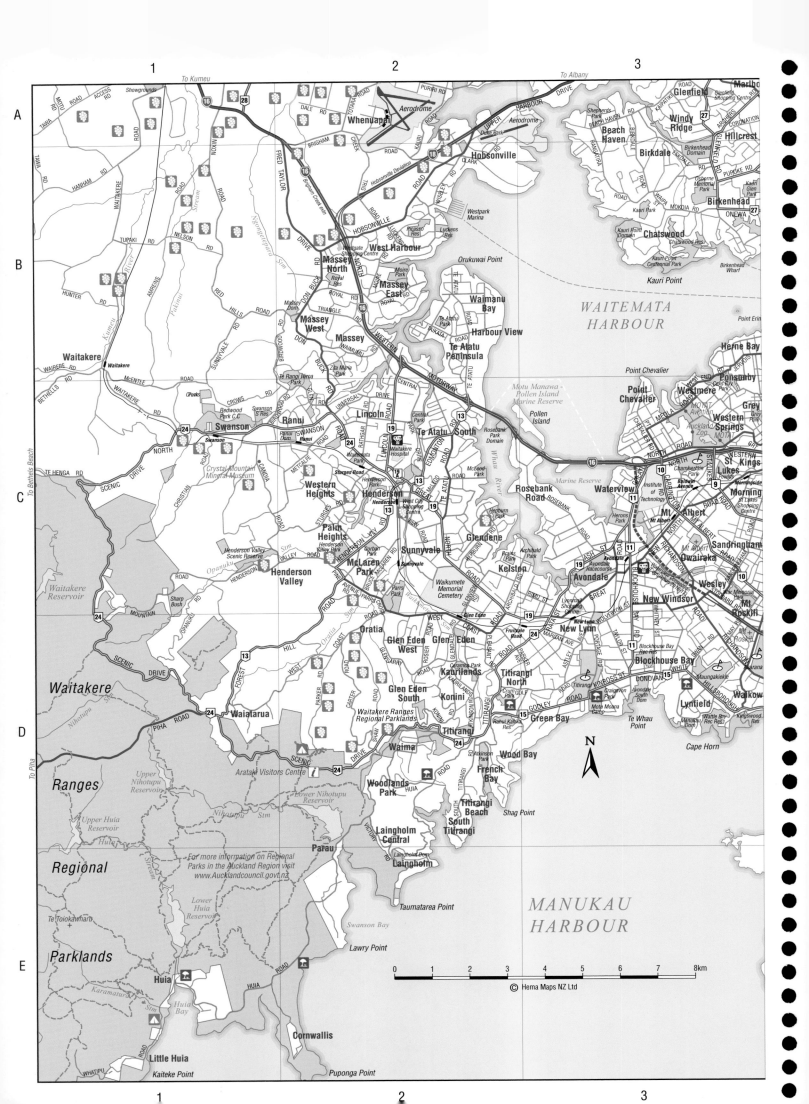

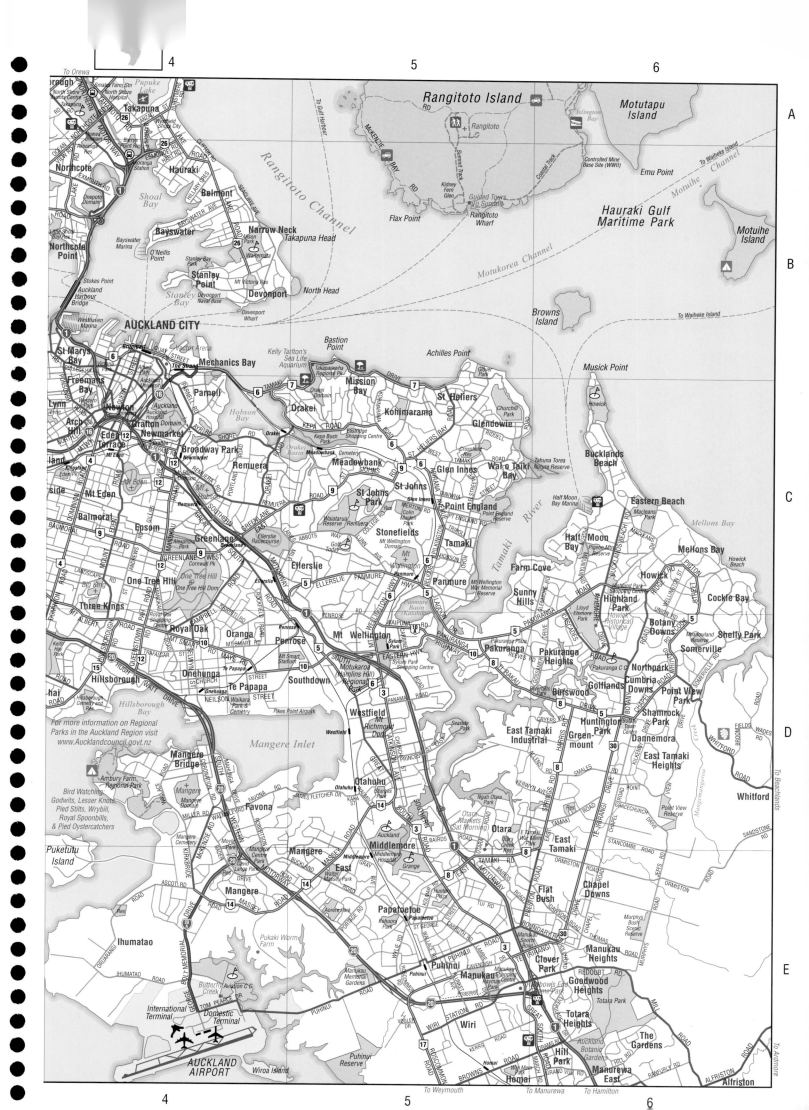

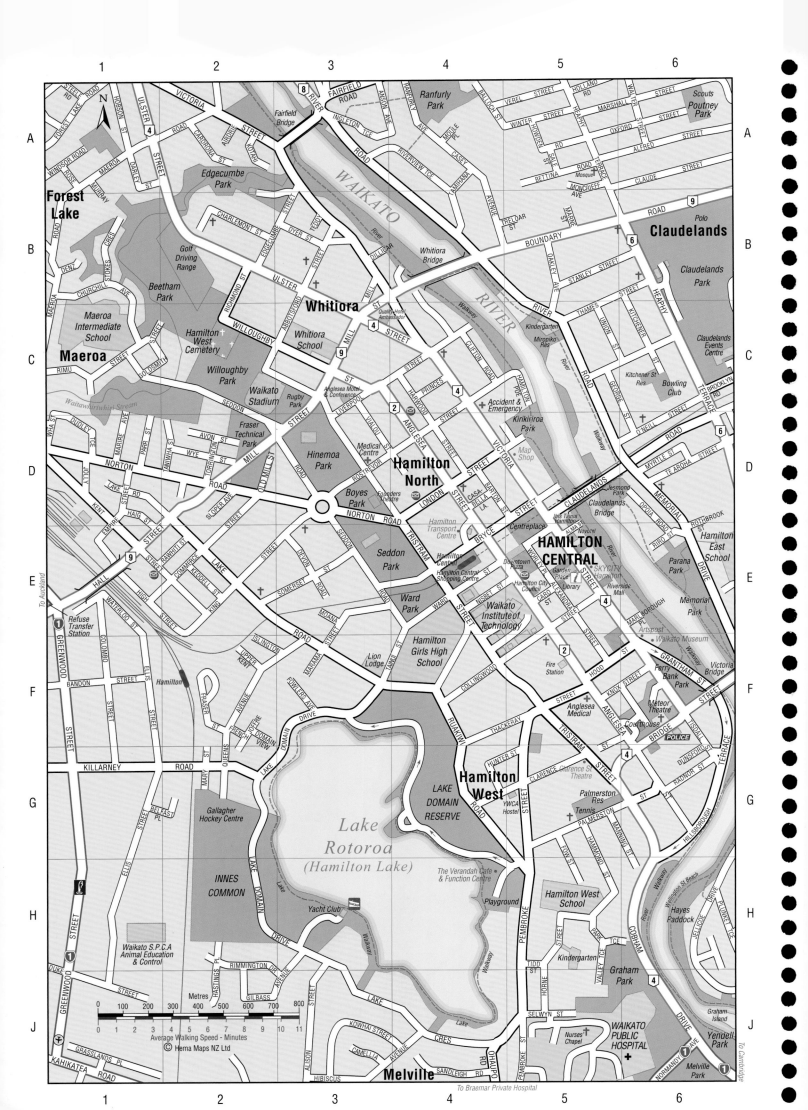

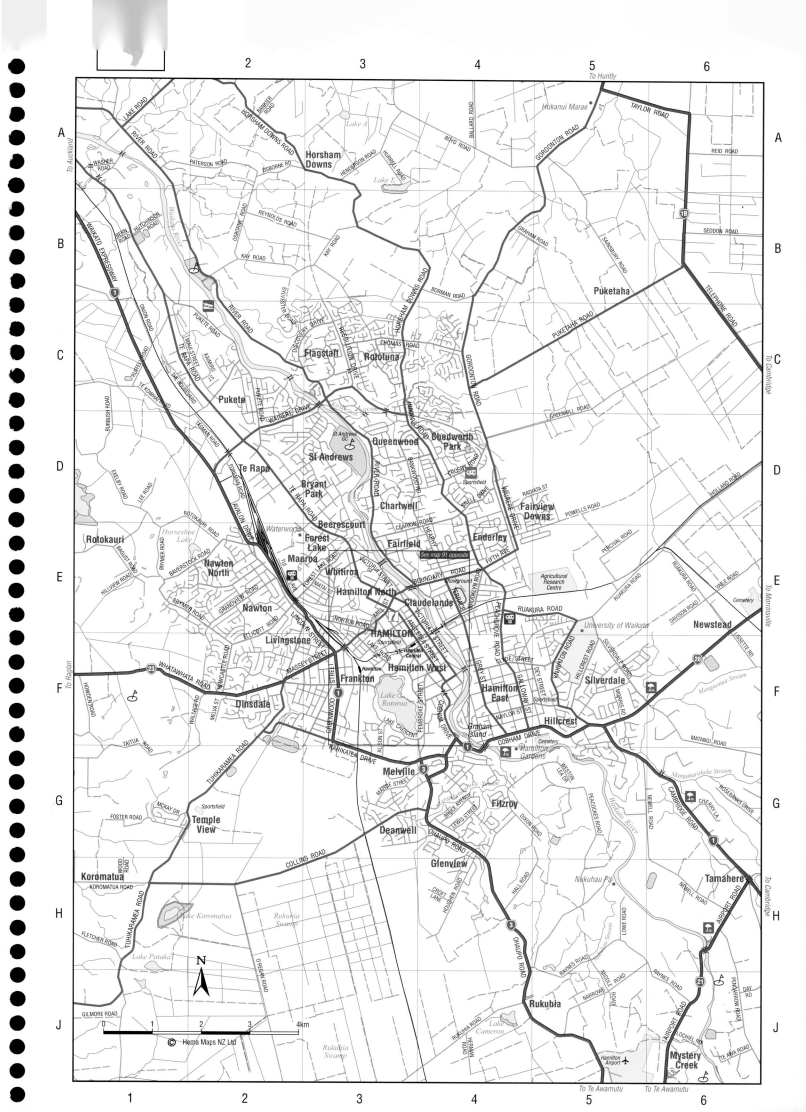

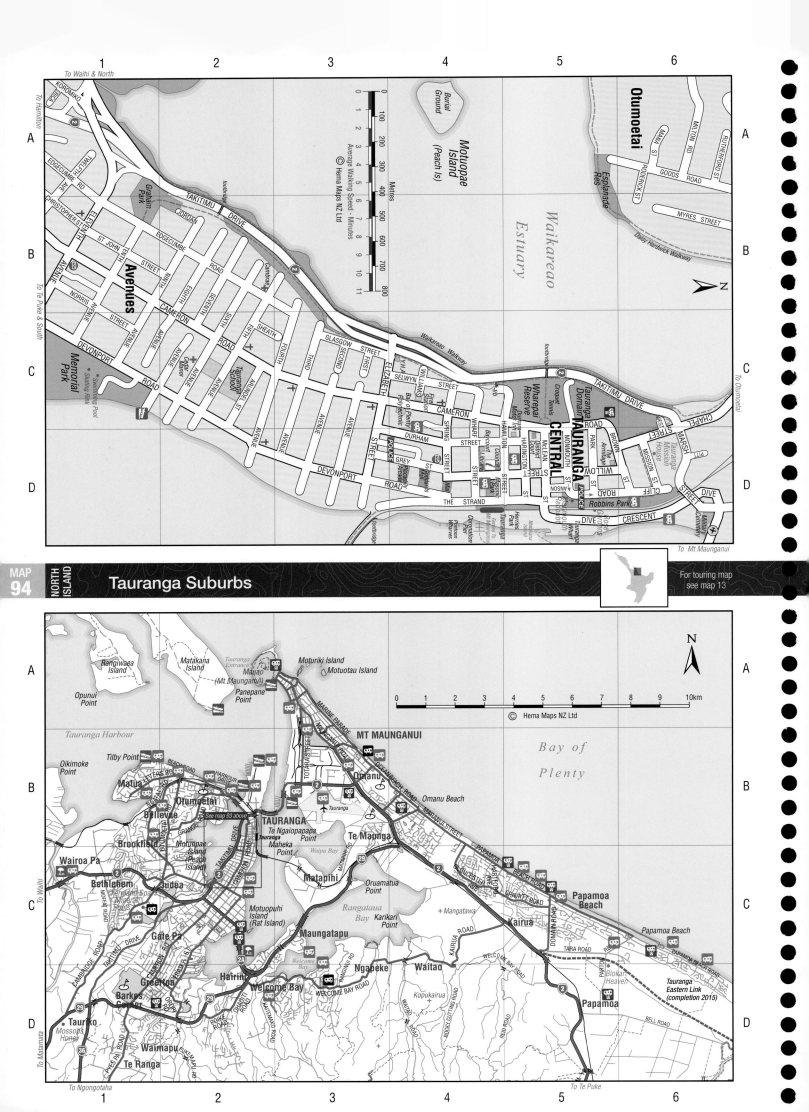

MAP
94
NORTH ISLAND
Tauranga Suburbs
For touring map
see map 13

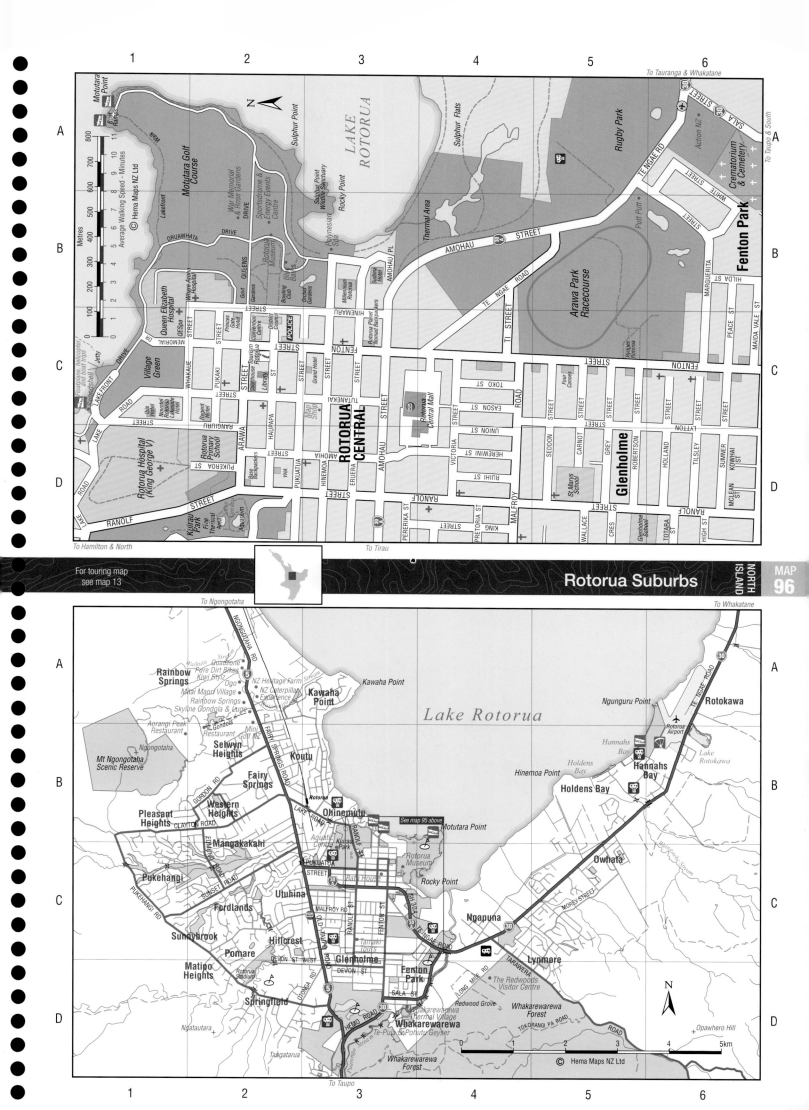

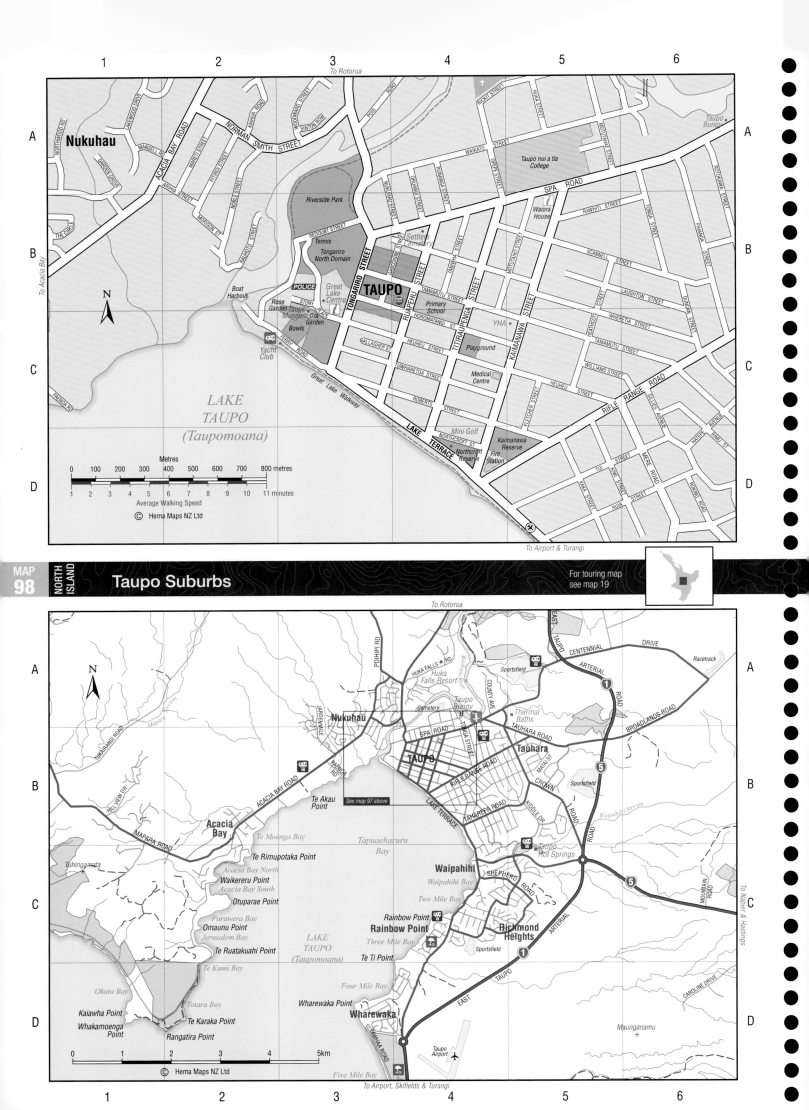

Top map (Taupo city centre):

Nukuhau

TAUPO

LAKE TAUPO
(Taupomoana)

Riverside Park

Tennis
Tongariro
North Domain

POLICE

Boat
Harbour

Rose
Garden
Taupo
Museum
Ora
Garden
Bowls

STORY
PLACE

Great
Lake
Centre

Yacht
Club

Settlers
Cemetery

Primary
School

YHA

Playground

Medical
Centre

Mini Golf

Kaimanawa
Reserve

Northcroft
Reserve

Fire
Station

Taupo nui a tia
College

Waiora
House

Taupo
Bungy

To Rotorua

To Acacia Bay

To Airport & Turangi

Streets (top map): NORTHWOOD RD, LAKEWOOD DRIVE, GARDEN GROVE, MANSELL RD, ACACIA BAY ROAD, KAHUIA ROAD, NORMAN SMITH STREET, MAFETI STREET, NOBLE STREET, PITIROI STREET, ARIHIA STREET, MORRISON ST, THE CIRCLE, RAINFORD STREET, SINTON ROW, WOODWARD STREET, PERU ROAD, REDOUBT STREET, TONGARIRO STREET, GASCOIGNE STREET, STREET, RUAPEHU STREET, TAMAMUTU STREET, HOROMATANGI STREET, TITIRAUPENGA STREET, KAIMANAWA, HEUHEU STREET, GALLAGHER STREET, TUWHARETOA STREET, ROBERTS STREET, NORTHCROFT ST, FLETCHER STREET, LAKE TERRACE, FERRY ROAD, Great Lake Walkway, WAIKATO STREET, ORUANUI STREET, NUKUHAU STREET, RUNANGA STREET, OPEPE STREET, RICKIT STREET, HUKA STREET, MOTUNUI STREET, MOTUTAIKO STREET, TAWIHA STREET, SPA ROAD, RAWHITI STREET, SCANNELL STREET, LAUGHTON STREET, WHERETIA STREET, HEATHCOTE, WILLIAMS STREET, HEUHEU STREET, TONGA STREET, PIHANGA STREET, DUNCAN STREET, RIFLE RANGE ROAD, GILLIES AVENUE, HATEPE STREET, RIMI ST, TUI STREET, KIRI STREET, MERE ROAD, KAKA STREET, HUIA, ROKINO ROAD, ROTOKAWA STREET

Scale (top map): Metres 0 100 200 300 400 500 600 700 800 metres
1 2 3 4 5 6 7 8 9 10 11 minutes
Average Walking Speed
© Hema Maps NZ Ltd

MAP
98
NORTH ISLAND
Taupo Suburbs
For touring map
see map 19

Bottom map (Taupo Suburbs):

Acacia Bay

Nukuhau

TAUPO

Tauhara

Waipahihi

Richmond Heights

Wharewaka

Tuhingamata

LAKE TAUPO
(Taupomoana)

Huka Falls Resort

Cemetery

Taupo Bungy

Thermal Baths

Taupo Hot Springs

Te Akau Point

Te Moenga Bay

Te Rimupotaka Point

Acacia Bay North
Waikereru Point
Acacia Bay South

Otuparae Point

Parawera Bay
Omaunu Point
Jerusalem Bay

Te Ruatakuahi Point

Te Kumi Bay

Okuta Bay

Kaiawha Point
Whakamoenga Point

Totara Bay
Te Karaka Point
Rangatira Point

Tapuaeharuru Bay

Rainbow Point
Three Mile Bay

Te Ti Point

Two Mile Bay

Waipahihi Bay

Four Mile Bay

Wharewaka Point

Sportsfield

Sportsfield

Sportsfield

Sportsfield

Racetrack

Taupo Airport

Maunganamu

Five Mile Bay

See map 97 above

To Rotorua

To Napier & Hastings

To Airport, Skifields & Turangi

Roads (bottom map): POIHIPI RD, HUKA FALLS RD, JARDEN MILE, RAEKOA RD, ACACIA BAY ROAD, MAPARA ROAD, TUKAIRANGI ROAD, HILL VIEW DR, COUNTY AVE, EAST TAUPO ARTERIAL, CENTENNIAL DRIVE, BROADLANDS ROAD, TAUHARA ROAD, SPA ROAD, TONGARIRO STREET, RIFLE RANGE ROAD, MATAI ST, CROWN ROAD, KIDDLE DR, TAHAREPA ROAD, SHEPHERD ROAD, LAKE TERRACE, MOUNTAIN ROAD, TAUPO EAST ARTERIAL, CAROLINE DRIVE, FAWHA ROAD, Mapara Stream, Waipahihi Stream

Scale (bottom map): 0 1 2 3 4 5km
© Hema Maps NZ Ltd

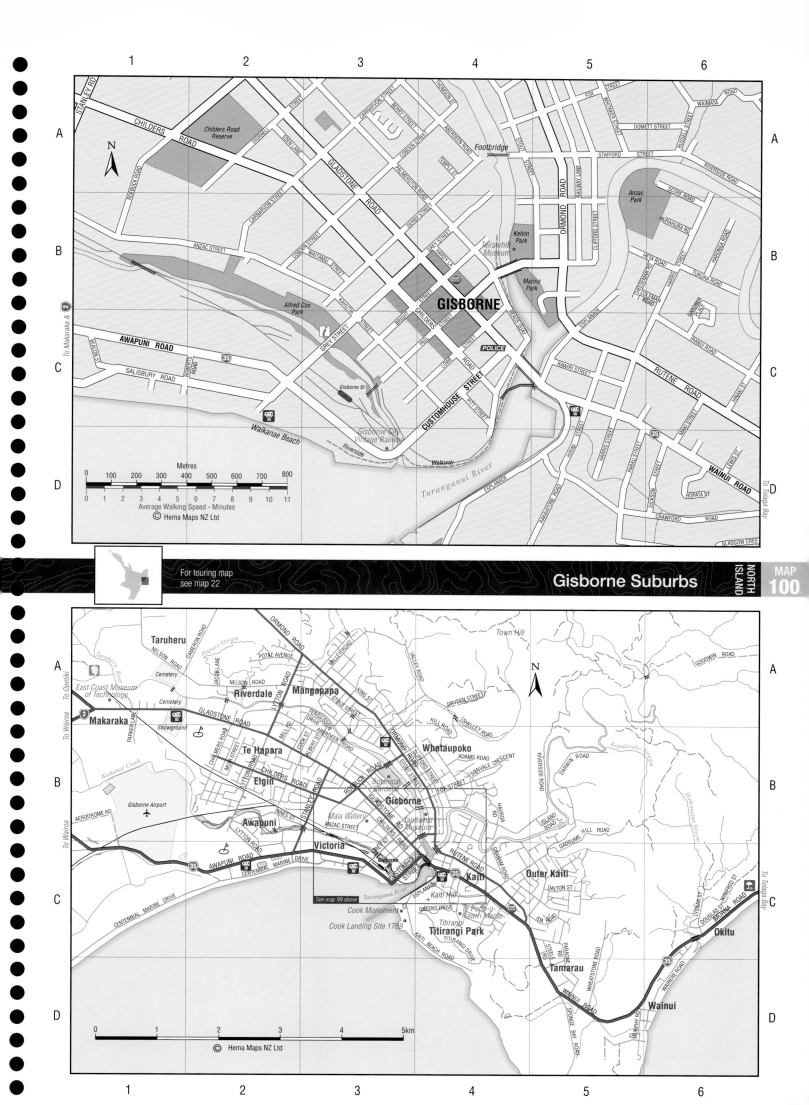

MAP 100

For touring map
see map 22

Map 99 (Gisborne City)

Grid columns: 1 2 3 4 5 6
Grid rows: A B C D

STANLEY RD
CHILDERS ROAD
Childers Road Reserve
DISRAELI STREET
EDEN LANE
CARNARVON STREET
GLADSTONE ROAD
PALMERSTON ROAD
CORDEN STREET
BERRY STREET
CARNARVON STREET
THOMSON ST
ABERDEEN STREET
TEMPLE ST
Footbridge
STOUT STREET
FOX STREET
WHITAKER STREET
RUSSELL STREET
WAIMATA ROAD
DOMETT STREET
STAFFORD STREET
RIVERSIDE ROAD
SCORE ROAD
Anzac Park
HURAHURA RD
HIRONGA ROAD
ROEBUCK ROAD
ANZAC STREET
CORDEN STREET
WAITANGI STREET
GREY STREET
GLADSTONE ROAD
DERBY STREET
GREY STREET
HARDY LA
Tairawhiti Museum
Kelvin Park
ORMOND ROAD
RAILWAY LANE
CLIFFORD STREET
HETA ROAD
TUKURA ROAD
GARDNER PLACE
Marina Park
GISBORNE
Alfred Cox Park
KAHUTIA STREET
BRIGHT STREET
CHILDERS STREET
PEEL STREET
READS QUAY
ESPLANADE
CHEESEMAN RD
COLEMAN ROAD
IRANUI ROAD
AWAPUNI ROAD
BEACON ROAD
SALISBURY ROAD
ROBERTS ROAD
35
GREY STREET
Gisborne St
LOWE ROAD
POLICE
CUSTOMHOUSE STREET
PITT STREET
RAWIRI STREET
RUTENE ROAD
HINAKI ST
MAKI STREET
HUBIN STREET
HARRIS STREET
PARAU STREET
35
WAINUI ROAD
LEWIS ST
Waikanae Beach
Gisborne City Vintage Railway
Riverside
Walkway
Turanganui River
RAKAIATANE ROAD
DICKSON STREET
ROPATA ST
CRAWFORD ROAD
GLASGOW CRES
To Makaraka & 2
AWAPUNI ROAD
BEACON ROAD
To Tolaga Bay
WAINUI ROAD

Metres
0 100 200 300 400 500 600 700 800
0 1 2 3 4 5 6 7 8 9 10 11
Average Walking Speed - Minutes
© Hema Maps NZ Ltd

Map 100 (Gisborne Suburbs)

Grid columns: 1 2 3 4 5 6
Grid rows: A B C D

Taruheru
Taruheru River
To Opotiki
East Coast Museum of Technology
Cemetery
NELSON ROAD
CAMERON ROAD
Hapara Stream
JACOB LANE
POTAE AVENUE
NELSON ROAD
ORMOND ROAD
VALLEY ROAD
Town Hill
GOODWIN ROAD
VALLEY ROAD
Riverdale
Mangapapa
KING ST
DRYDEN STREET
HILL ROAD
SHELLEY ROAD
To Wairoa
2
Makaraka
PARKER LANE
Cemetery
Showground
GLADSTONE ROAD
LYTTON ROAD
FERGUSSON DRIVE
STOUT STREET
ORMOND ROAD
CLIFFORD STREET
STOUT STREET
Whataupoko
ADAMS ROAD
SUNVALE CRESCENT
RIVERSIDE ROAD
DARWIN ROAD
Kopakiraho Stream
Te Hapara
CHALMERS ROAD
MUIR STREET
COOK ST
ALBERT ST
ABERDEEN ROAD
ROEBUCK ROAD
GLADSTONE RD
FOX STREET
Botanical Gardens
Gisborne
Tairawhiti Museum
HAUIRA RD
ISLAND ROAD
GADDUMS HILL ROAD
Hununahua Stream
Waikanae Creek
Gisborne Airport
Elgin
CHILDERS ROAD
STANLEY ROAD
LYTTON ROAD
INNES ST
Maia Gallery
ANZAC STREET
GLADSTONE ROAD
CHILDERS ROAD
GRAHAM ROAD
To Wairoa
AERODROME RD
Awapuni
LYTTON ROAD
35
AWAPUNI ROAD
CENTENNIAL MARINE DRIVE
Victoria
CUSTOMHOUSE STREET
Gisborne
RUTENE ROAD
35
Kaiti
Outer Kaiti
DALTON ST
See map 99 above
Turanganui River
ESPLANADE
Kaiti Hill
QUEENS DRIVE
Te Poho-o-Rawiri Marae
IDA ROAD
LYSNAR ST
DOUGLAS ST
WINIFRED ST
MOANA ROAD
To Tolaga Bay
CENTENNIAL MARINE DRIVE
Cook Monument
Cook Landing Site 1769
Titirangi Park
KAITI BEACH ROAD
TITIRANGI DRIVE
STEEL RD
PARAONE RD
WHEATSTONE ROAD
WAIRERE ROAD
Okitu
Tamarau
WAINUI ROAD
SPONGE BAY ROAD
MURPHY RD
Wainui
35

0 1 2 3 4 5km
© Hema Maps NZ Ltd

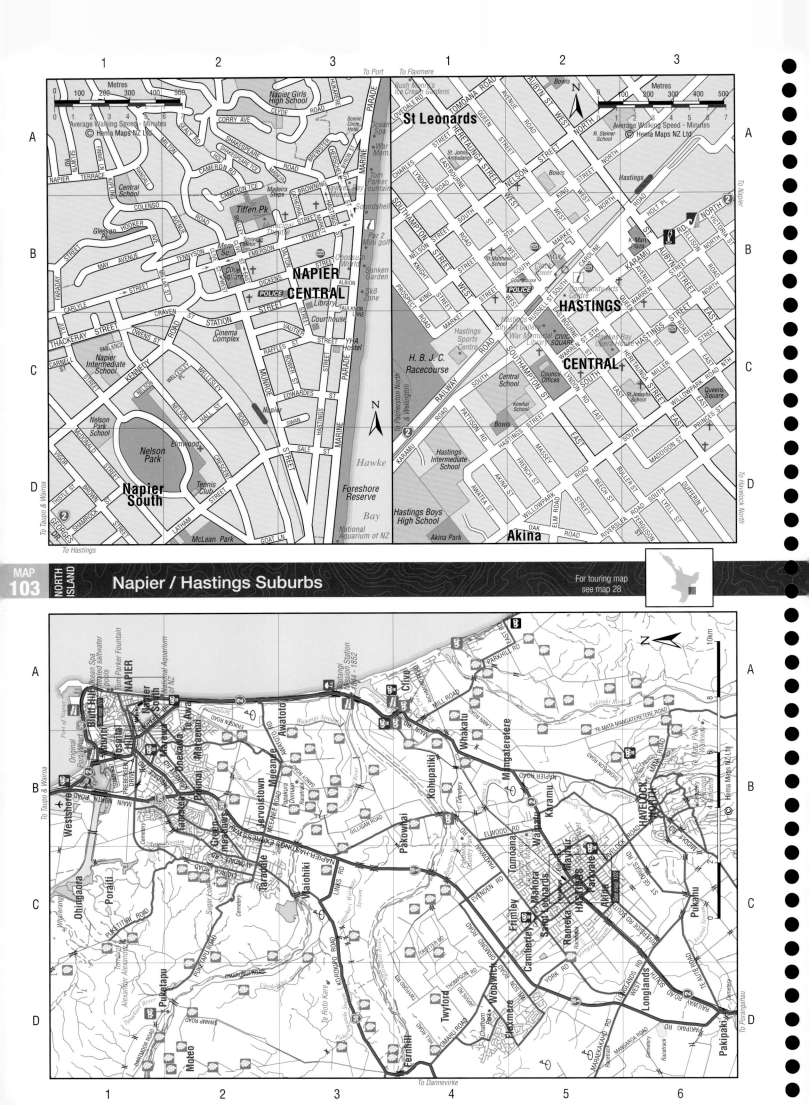

MAP
103
NORTH ISLAND

Napier / Hastings Suburbs

For touring map
see map 28

For touring map
see map 28

Palmerston North Suburbs

NORTH ISLAND

MAP
105

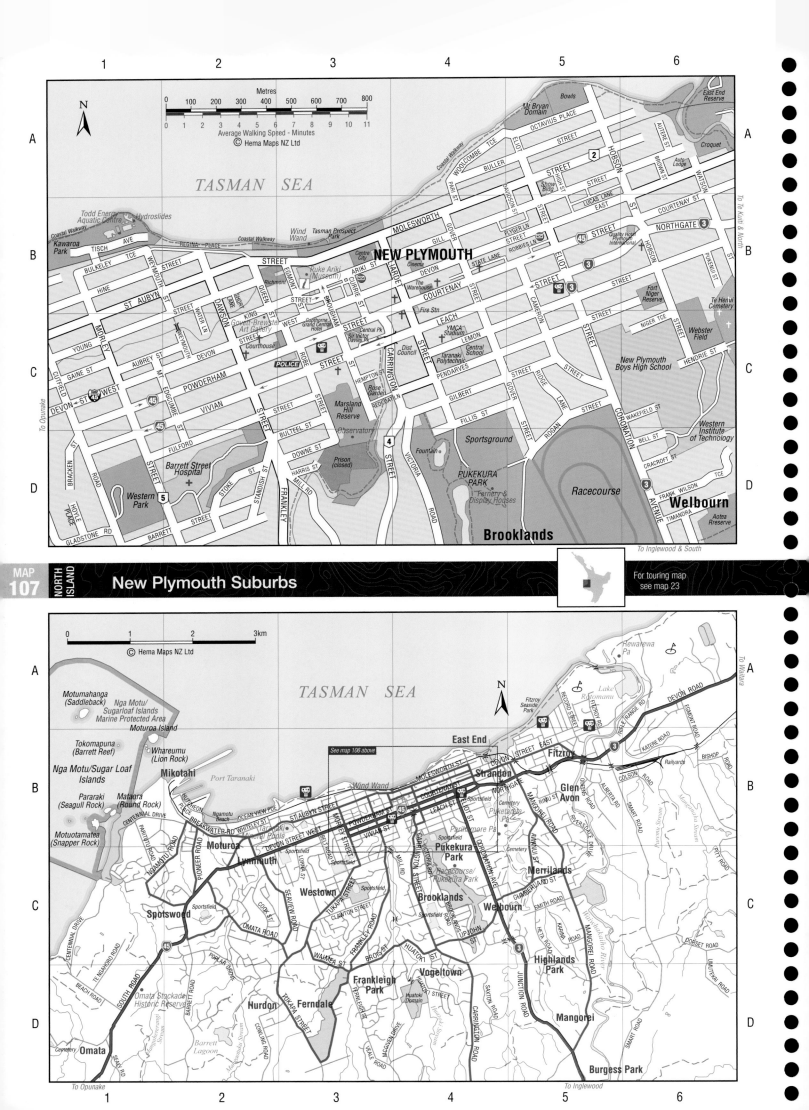

MAP
107
NORTH ISLAND
New Plymouth Suburbs
For touring map
see map 23

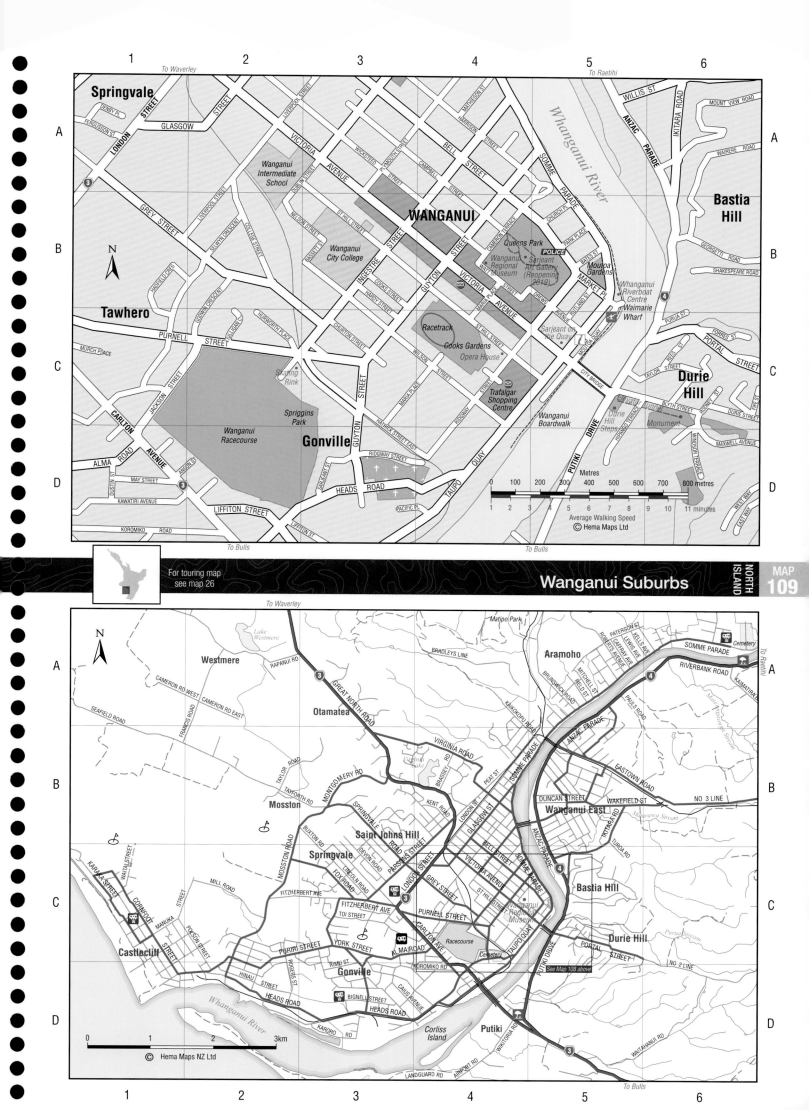

Wanganui Suburbs

For touring map see map 26

© Hema Maps Ltd

© Hema Maps NZ Ltd

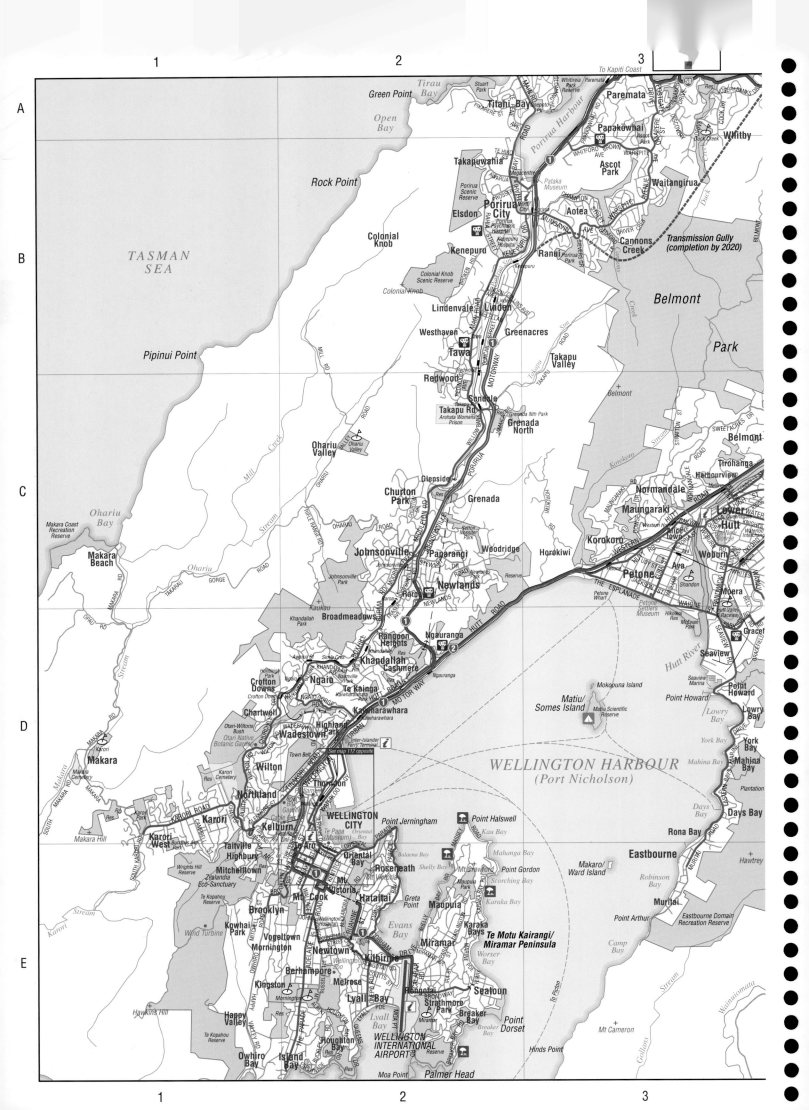

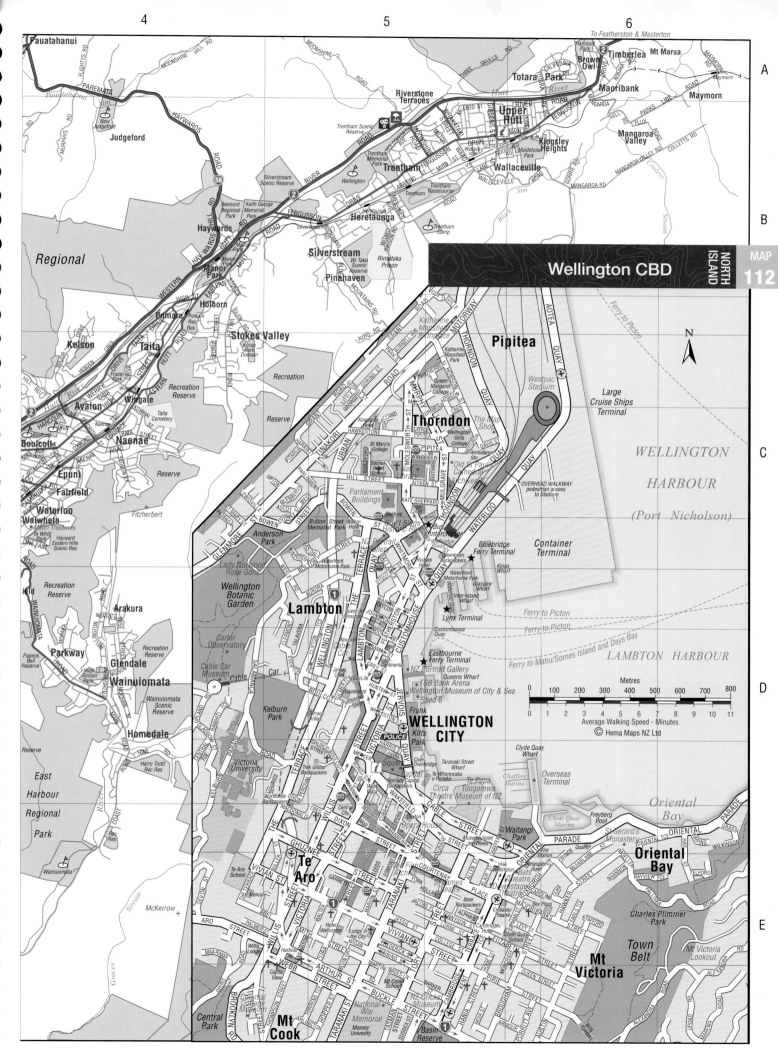

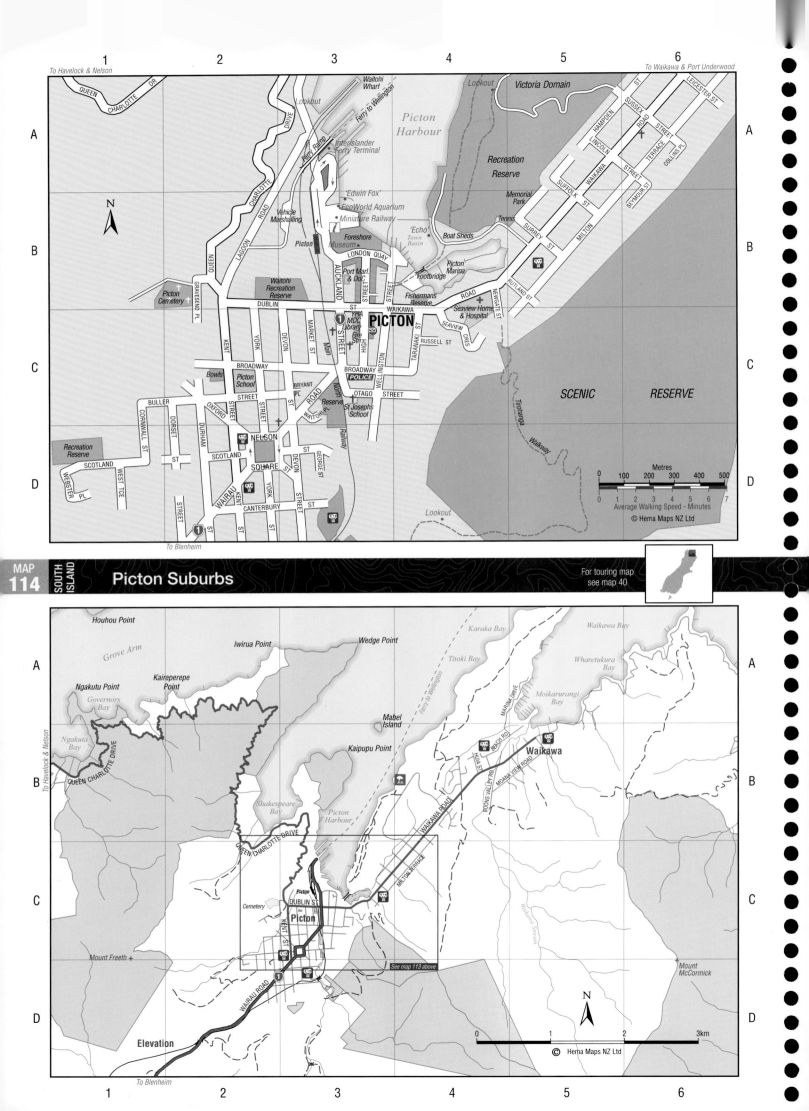

Picton Suburbs

MAP 114 SOUTH ISLAND

For touring map see map 40

Top Map (Picton – Map 113)

To Havelock & Nelson

To Waikawa & Port Underwood

Picton Harbour

Victoria Domain

Lookout

Recreation Reserve

Waitohi Wharf

Ferry to Wellington

Lookout

Interislander Ferry Terminal

Ferry Ramp

QUEEN CHARLOTTE DR

CHARLOTTE ROAD

LAGOON

QUEEN ST

GRAVESEND PL

Picton Cemetery

Vehicle Marshalling

Picton

'Edwin Fox'

EcoWorld Aquarium

Miniature Railway

Foreshore Museum

'Echo' Town Basin

Boat Sheds

Picton Marina

Footbridge

HAMPDEN ST

LINCOLN

SUSSEX ST

LEICESTER ST

ROAD

STREET

COLLINS PL

TERRACE

SEYMOUR ST

WAIKAWA

MILTON

SUFFOLK ST

SURREY ST

Memorial Park

Tennis

Waitohi Recreation Reserve

LONDON QUAY

AUCKLAND STREET

DUBLIN

KENT

YORK

DEVON

MARKET ST

Main STREET

HIGH

Port Marl. & DoC

YHA MDC Library Fire Stn

PICTON

WAIKAWA

Fishermans Reserve

Seaview Home & Hospital

NEWGATE ST

RUTLAND ST

ROAD

SEAVIEW CRES

TARANAKI ST

RUSSELL ST

WELLINGTON

BROADWAY

POLICE

BROADWAY STREET

SCENIC RESERVE

Tirohanga Walkway

Bowls

Picton School

BRYANT PL

ROAD

North

WAITOHI PL

Reserve

St Josephs School

OTAGO STREET

BULLER STREET

CORNWALL ST

DORSET

OXFORD STREET

DURHAM

GEORGE ST

DEVON ST

NELSON SQUARE

SCOTLAND

YORK ST

Recreation Reserve

SCOTLAND

WEBSTER PL

WEST TCE

WAIRAU STREET

KENT ST

CANTERBURY ST

Railway

Lookout

To Blenheim

Metres

0 100 200 300 400 500

Average Walking Speed - Minutes

0 1 2 3 4 5 6 7

© Hema Maps NZ Ltd

Bottom Map (Picton Suburbs)

Houhou Point

Iwirua Point

Wedge Point

Karaka Bay

Waikawa Bay

Grove Arm

Ngakutu Point

Kaireperepe Point

Governors Bay

Titoki Bay

Wharetukura Bay

Ngakuta Bay

QUEEN CHARLOTTE DRIVE

To Havelock & Nelson

Mabel Island

Ferry to Wellington

MARINA DRIVE

Moikarurangi Bay

BEACH RD

Waikawa

HUIA ST

BOONS VALLEY RD

MOANA VIEW ROAD

Kaipupu Point

Shakespeare Bay

Picton Harbour

WAIKAWA ROAD

MILTON TERRACE

Picton

DUBLIN ST

Cemetery

Picton

KENT ST

See map 113 above

Mount Freeth

WAIRAU ROAD

Hikinui Stream

Mount McCormick

Elevation

To Blenheim

0 1 2 3km

© Hema Maps NZ Ltd

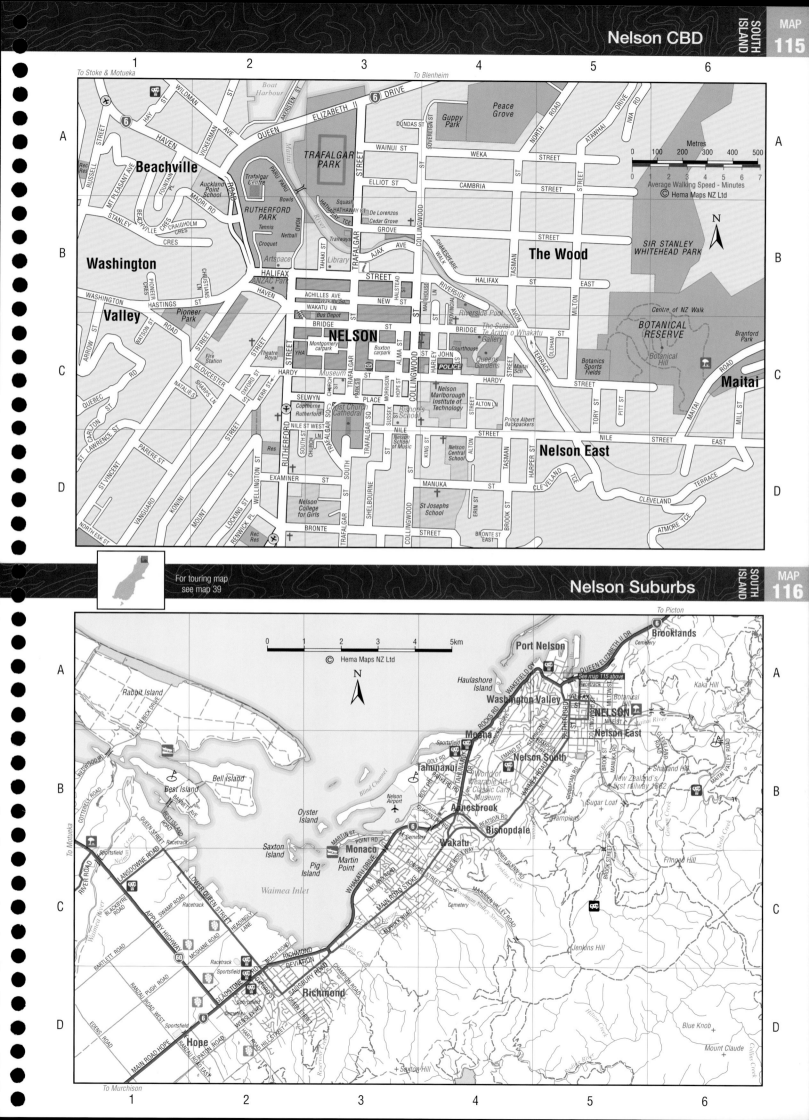

For touring map
see map 39

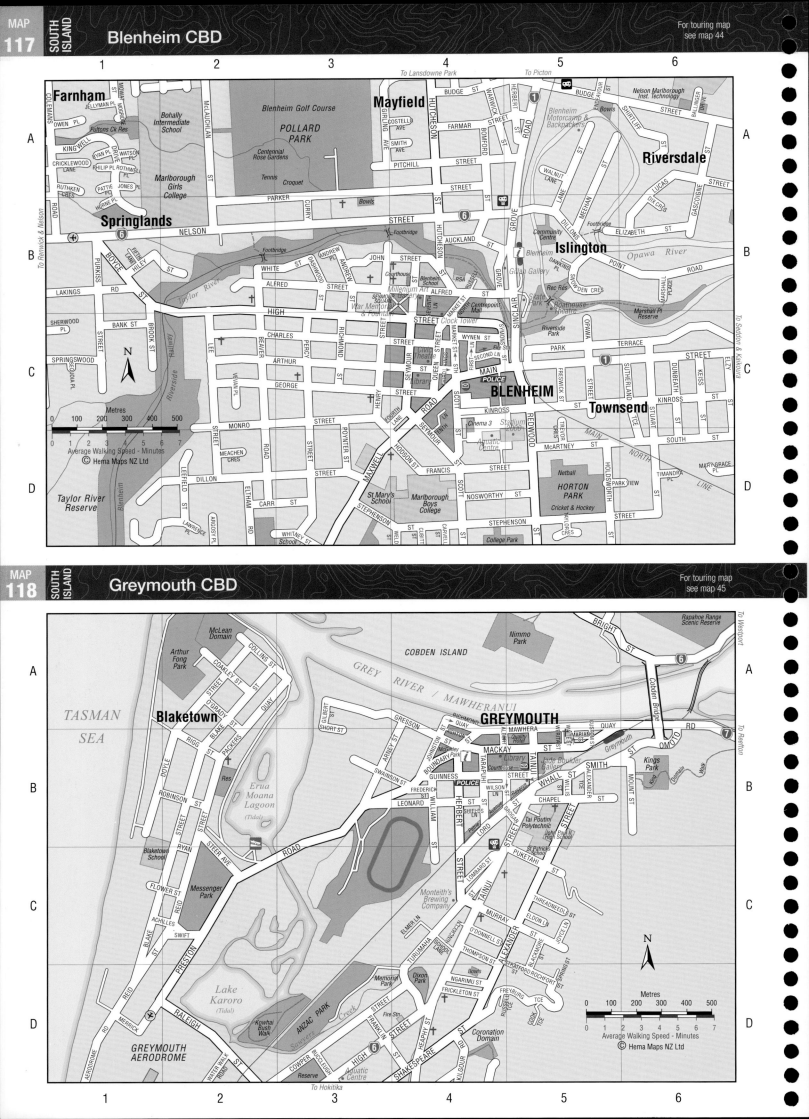

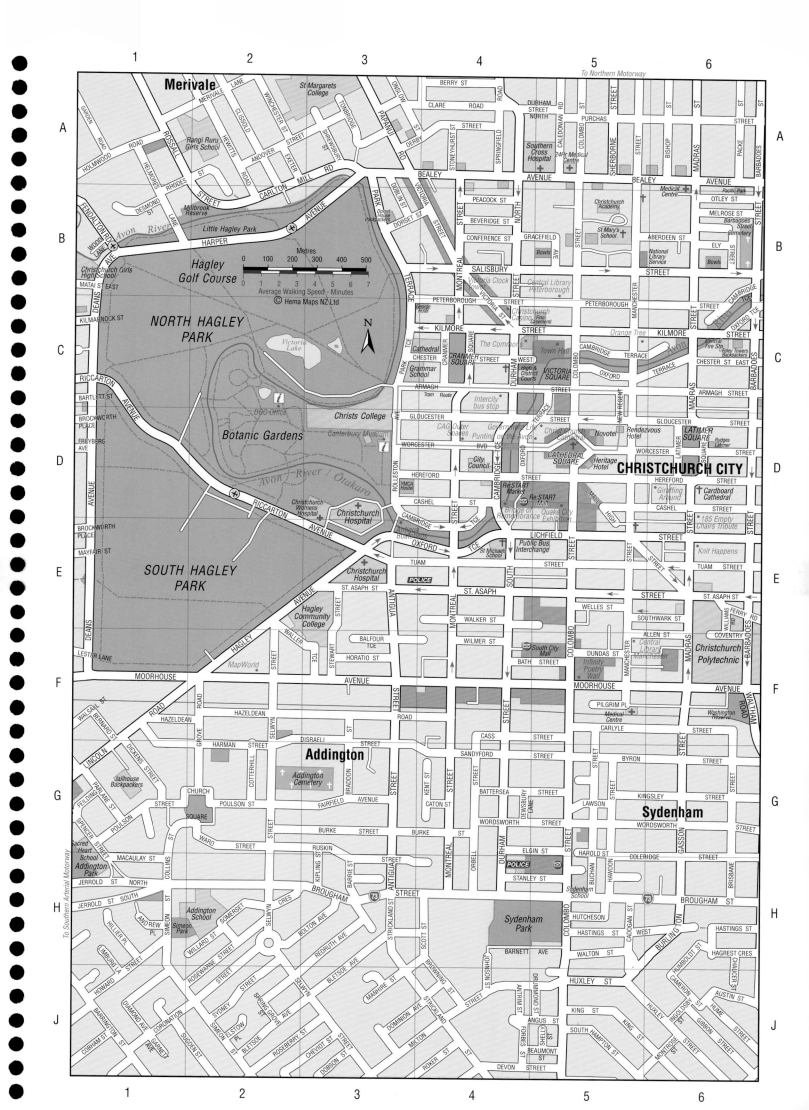

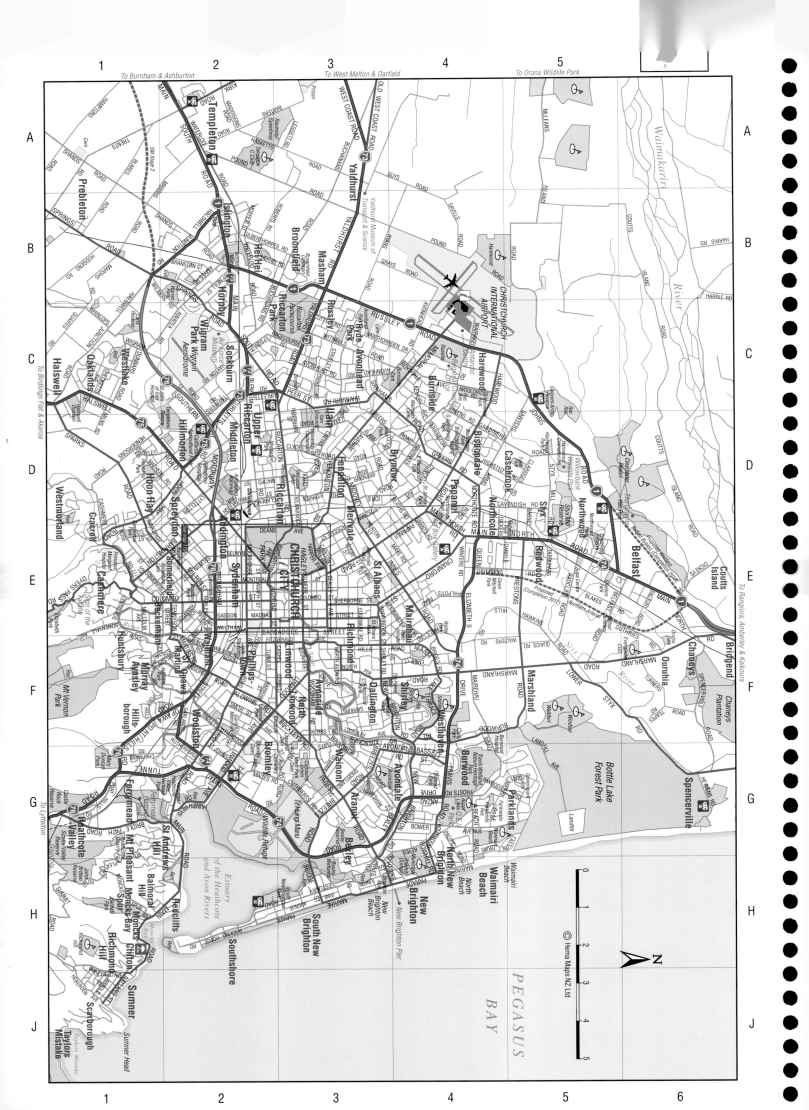

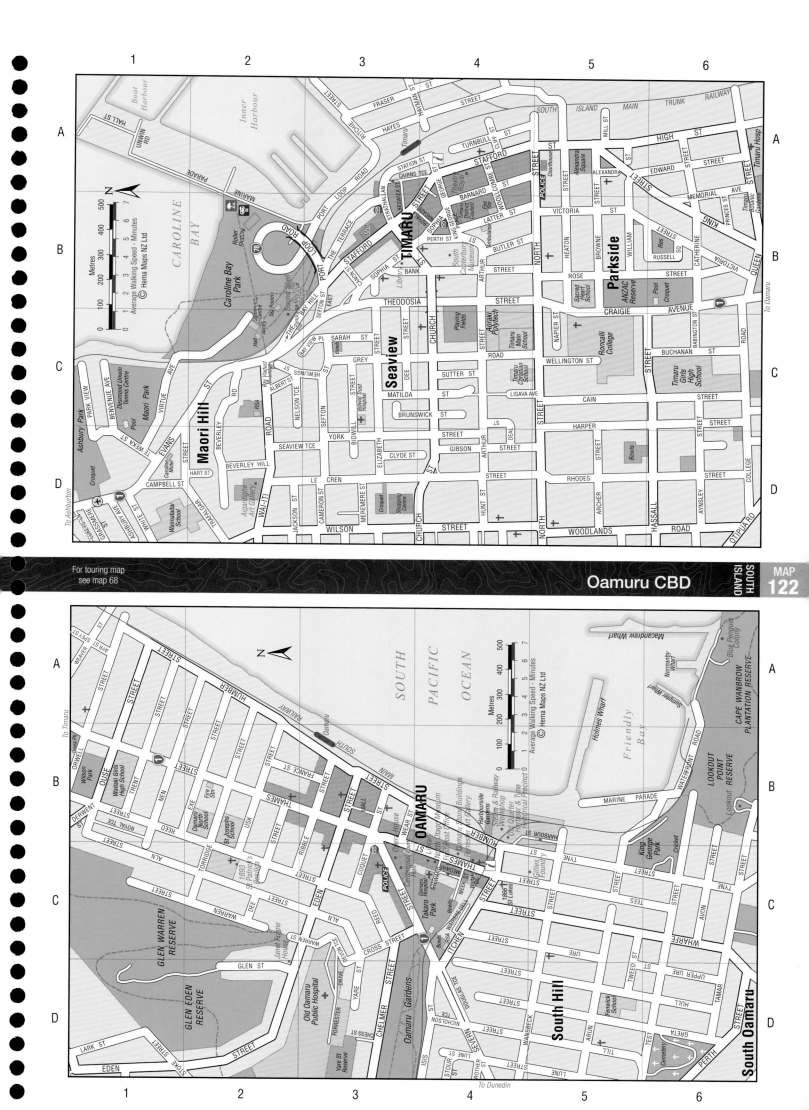

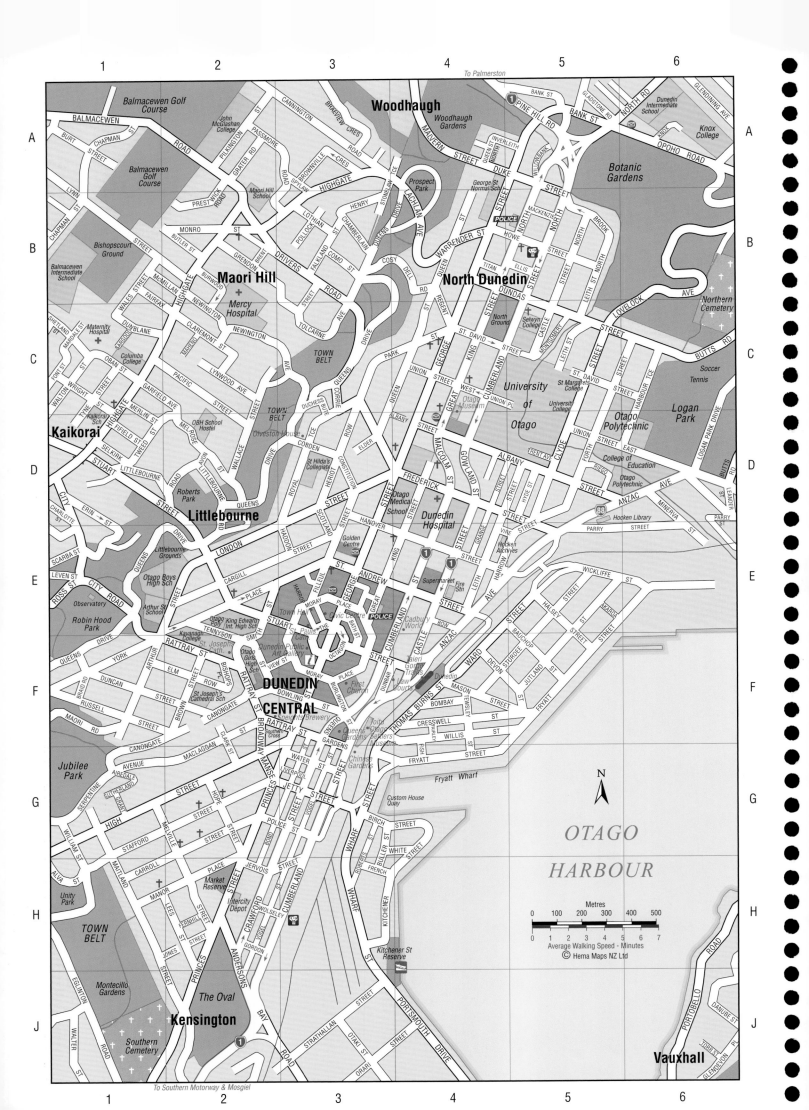

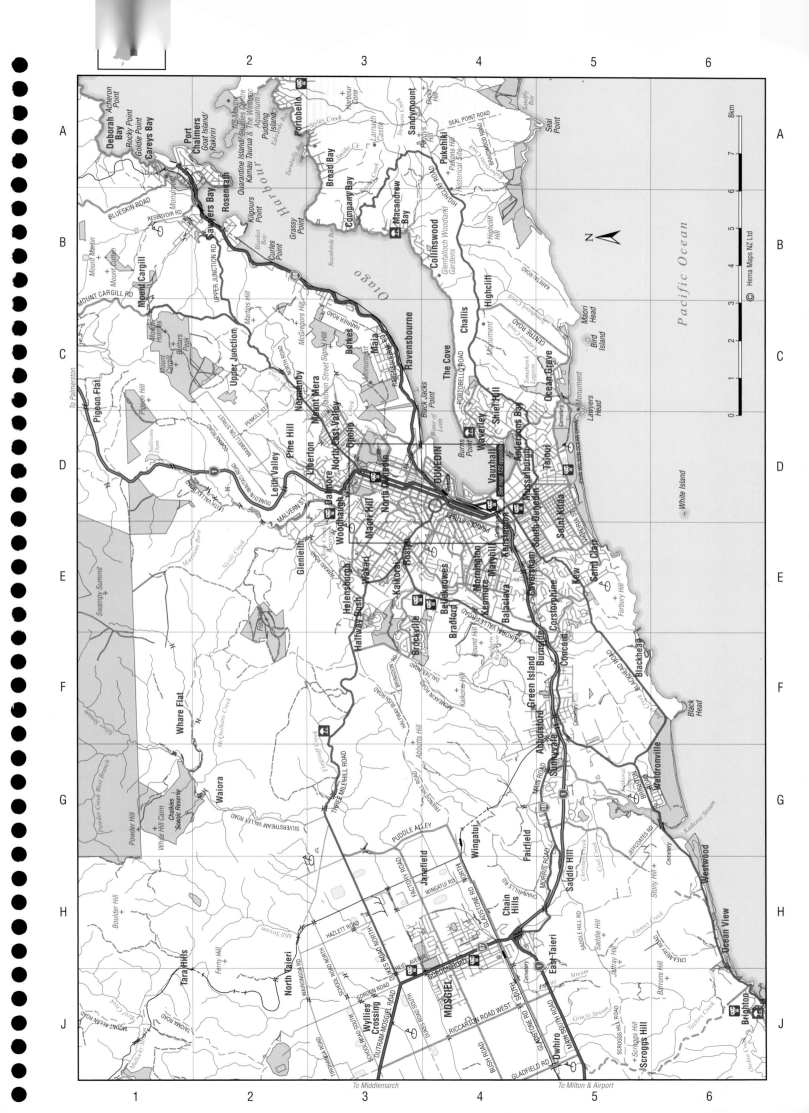

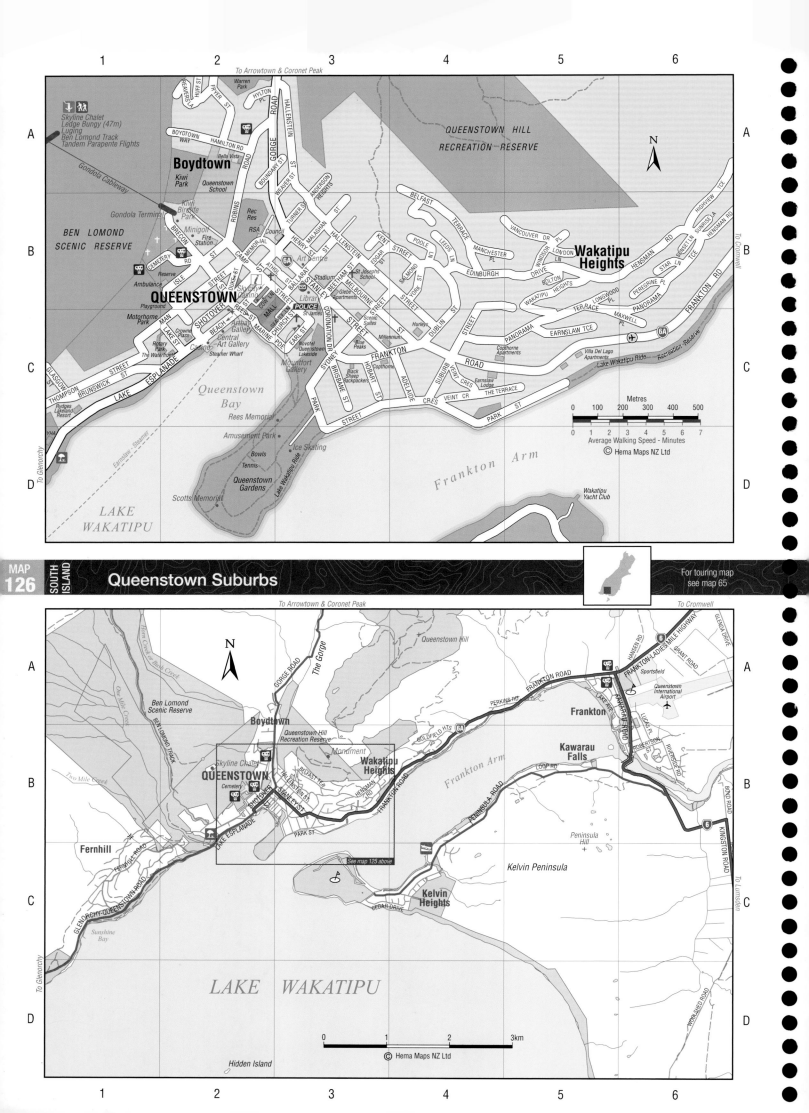

MAP 126 SOUTH ISLAND — **Queenstown Suburbs**

For touring map see map 65

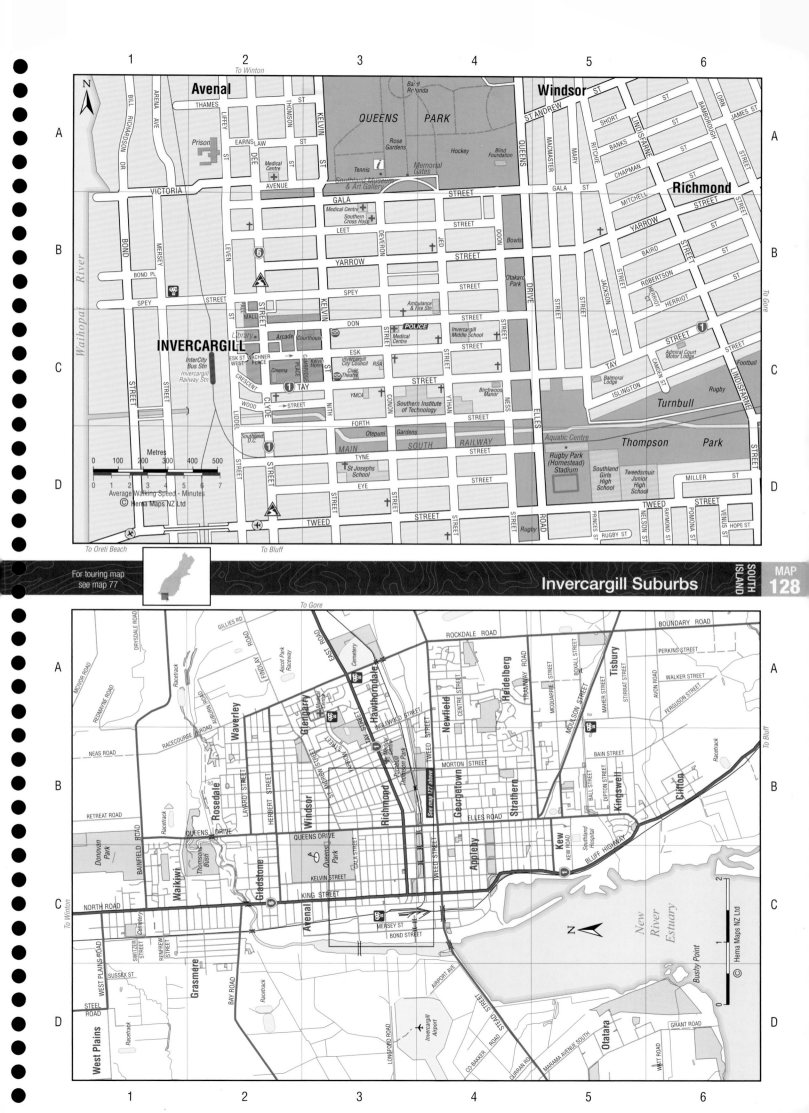

For touring map
see map 77

Invercargill Suburbs

SOUTH ISLAND

MAP
128

Map Labels (Top Map — Invercargill City)

Avenal · **Windsor** · **Richmond** · **INVERCARGILL** · **QUEENS PARK**

Bird Rotunda · Rose Gardens · Hockey · Tennis · Memorial Gates · Blind Foundation · Southland Museum & Art Gallery · Bowls · Otakaro Park · Ambulance & Fire Stn · POLICE · Invercargill Middle School · Medical Centre · Southern Cross Hosp · Kelvin Hotel · Invercargill City Council · RSA · Civic Theatre · YMCA · Courthouse · Cinema · Arcade · Library · InterCity Bus Stn · Invercargill Railway Stn · Prison · Medical Centre · Birchwood Manor · Southern Institute of Technology · Southland D.C. · St Josephs School · Rugby Park (Homestead) Stadium · Aquatic Centre · Southland Girls High School · Tweedsmuir Junior High School · Admiral Court Motor Lodge · Balmoral Lodge · Football · Rugby · Turnbull · Thompson Park · Richmond

Streets: THAMES ST · VICTORIA · GALA STREET · YARROW · SPEY · KELVIN · DON · ESK · TAY · FORTH · TYNE · EYE · TWEED · LEET · DEVERON · JED · DOON · NESS · CONON · YHAM · CAMBRIDGE · CLYDE · NITH · WOOD · LIDDEL · CRESCENT · WACHNER PLACE · TAY · MAIN SOUTH RAILWAY · ELLES · QUEENS DRIVE · ST ANDREW ST · MACMASTER · MARY · JACKSON · RITCHIE · CHAPMAN · SHORT · BANKS · LINDISFARNE · MITCHELL · YARROW · BAIRD · ROBERTSON · HERROT · HERRIOT · ISLINGTON · CAMDEN ST · TAY · LORN · BAMBOROUGH · JAMES ST · MILLER · TWEED · PRINCES ST · RUGBY ST · NELSON ST · RAYMOND ST · POMONA ST · VENUS ST · HOPE ST

To Winton · To Gore · To Oreti Beach · To Bluff

Metres
0 100 200 300 400 500
Average Walking Speed - Minutes
0 1 2 3 4 5 6 7
© Hema Maps NZ Ltd

Waihopai River · BILL RICHARDSON DR · ARENA AVE · BOND STREET · MERSEY · DEE · LEVEN · LIFFEY · EARNS LAW · THOMSON · KELVIN · PALL MALL · STREET · LAW · EARNS

Map Labels (Bottom Map — Invercargill Suburbs)

West Plains · **Waikiwi** · **Grasmere** · **Rosedale** · **Gladstone** · **Avenal** · **Waverley** · **Glengarry** · **Windsor** · **Hawthorndale** · **Richmond** · **Newfield** · **Heidelberg** · **Georgetown** · **Strathern** · **Appleby** · **Kew** · **Tisbury** · **Kingswell** · **Clifton** · **Otatara**

To Gore · To Winton · To Bluff

Roads: DRYSDALE ROAD · GILLIES RD · BOUNDARY ROAD · ROCKDALE ROAD · PERKINS STREET · MOIVOR ROAD · REDMAYNE ROAD · FINDLAY ROAD · AUBURN ROAD · EAST ROAD · TRAMWAY ROAD · WALKER STREET · AVON ROAD · FERGUSON STREET · NEAS ROAD · RACECOURSE ROAD · LAYARD STREET · HERBERT STREET · INGLEWOOD STREET · CENTRE STREET · MCQUARRIE STREET · BOXALL STREET · MAHER STREET · STIRRAT STREET · RETREAT ROAD · BAINFIELD ROAD · QUEENS DRIVE · LEETS STREET · TAY STREET · KARROW STREET · ST ANDREW ST · MORTON STREET · BAIN STREET · DIPTON STREET · BALL STREET · NORTH ROAD · KELVIN STREET · GALA STREET · ELLES ROAD · KEW ROAD · BLUFF HIGHWAY · SWITZER STREET · RENFREW STREET · SUSSEX ST · WEST PLAINS ROAD · STEEL ROAD · BAY ROAD · LONGFORD ROAD · AIRPORT AVE · CO-BAKER ROAD · STEAD STREET · CURRAN RD · MARAMA AVENUE SOUTH · GRANT ROAD · WATT ROAD · KING STREET · MERSEY ST · BOND STREET · MOULSON STREET

Cemetery · Racetrack · Ascot Park Raceway · Medical Centre · Donovan Park · Thomsons Bush · Queens Park · Pukehiki · Thompson Park · Southland Hospital · Invercargill Airport · Bushy Point · New River Estuary

© Hema Maps NZ Ltd

©ISTOCK.COM/KLAUS HOLLITZER

THE DISPOSAL OF WASTE from the sink, shower (grey) and toilet (black) is to be made at dump station/waste disposal sites. The locations listed here refer to most of the symbols shown on the maps. There may be a charge for using a dump station at holiday parks and camping grounds, unless you are staying there. Some dump stations on septic tanks may limit their availability during peak times.
Under no circumstances is it acceptable to dispose of wastewater in rubbish disposal facilities.

Motorhome Park / Caravan Park with Dump Station (Wastewater Disposal Site)

Motorhome Public Dump Station (Wastewater Disposal Site)

MOTORHOME TRAVELLING ALONG LAKE PUKAKI WITH THE SNOWCAPPED MT COOK/AORAKI MOUNTAIN RANGE IN THE BACKGROUND.

MOTORHOME PARK/CARAVAN PARK WITH DUMP STATION (WASTEWATER DISPOSAL SITE)

NORTH ISLAND

NORTHLAND

Pukenui Holiday Park (1 F5) – Lamb Rd, Pukenui; 45km north of Kaitaia; Opposite Pukenui School: (09) 409 8803
Wagener Holiday Park (1 F5) – On Houhora Heads Rd, Houhora; Opposite Wagener Museum: (09) 409 8564
Norfolk Motel & Campervan Park (1 H6) – Cnr SH1 & SH10; 300m from Awanui: (09) 406 7515
Ninety Mile Beach Holiday Park (1 H4) – 6 Matai Street, Awanui; 18km north of Kaitaia: (09) 406 7298
Ahipara Holiday Park (1 J5) – 164 Takahe St, Ahipara: (09) 409 4864
Whatuwhiwhi Top 10 Holiday Park (2 F7) – 17 Whatuwhiwhi Rd, Karikari Peninsula; RD 3, Kaitaia (09) 408 7202
Tokerau Beach Motor Camp (1 F7) – 13 Melissa Rd, Tokerau Beach: (09) 408 7150
Hihi Beach Holiday Camp (2 G9) – 58 Hihi Rd, Mangonui: (09) 406 0307
Whangaroa Harbour Holiday Park (2 H10) – Whangaroa Harbour, Kaeo: (09) 405 0306
Matauri Bay Holiday Park (2 H12) – Matauri Bay, Whangaroa: (09) 405 0525
Tauranga Bay Holiday Park (2 H11) – Tauranga Bay, Whangaroa; 17.5km from Kaeo: (09) 405 0436
Kerikeri Holiday Park & Motels (4 A8) – Aranga Drive, 500m south of town centre; Opposite BP Service Station, Kerikeri: (09) 407 9326
Gibby's Place (4 A8) – 331 Kerikeri Rd, Kerikeri: (09) 407 9024
Wagon Train RV Park (4 A9) – SH10, Kerikeri: (09) 407 7889
Waitangi Holiday Park (4 B9) – 21 Tahuna Rd, Waitangi: (09) 402 7866
Beachside Holiday Park (4 B10) – 1290 SH11 Paihia, 3km south of Paihia: (09) 402 7678
Bay of Islands Holiday Park (4 B9) – 678 Puketona Rd, Haruru: (09) 402 7646
Haruru Falls Resort, 'Panorama' (4 B9) – Old Wharf Rd, Haruru Falls; 5 min from Paihia: (09) 402 7525
Twin Pines Tourist Park (4 B9) – Puketona Rd, RD 1, Paihia: (09) 402 7322
Russell Top 10 Holiday Park (4 B10) – Long Beach Rd, Russell: (09) 403 7826
Orongo Bay Holiday Park (4 B10) – 5960 Russell Rd: (09) 403 7704
Oakura Motel & Holiday Park (4 C12) – 4 Te Kapua St, Oakura: (09) 433 6803
Bland Bay Motor Camp (4 B12) – Whangaruru North Head Road, Bland Bay: (09) 433 6759
Dargaville Holiday Park (3 J7) – 10 Onslow St, Dargaville: (09) 439 8296
Dargaville Campervan Park (3 J7) – 18 Gladstone St, Dargaville: (09) 439 8479
Kauri Coast Top 10 Holiday Park (3 G6) – Trounson Park Rd, Kaihu: (09) 439 0621
Baylys Beach Holiday Park (3 J6) – 22-24 Seaview Rd; 800m from beach: (09) 439 6349
Matakohe Top 10 Holiday Park (5 B5) – Church Rd, Matakohe: (09) 431 6431
Paparoa Motor Camp (5 B6) – Cnr SH12 &Pahi Rd, Paparoa: (09) 431 6515
Pahi Beach Motor Camp (5 B6) – Enter Pahi Domain and drive through to public toilets on right of wharf, Pahi: (09) 431 7322
Kellys Bay Reserve (5 D5) – Dale Rd, Kellys Bay, Pouto Peninsula: (09) 439 4204
Tutukaka Holiday Park (4 E13) – Matapour Rd, Tutukaka: (09) 434 3938
Whangarei Top 10 Holiday Park (4 G11) – 24 Mair St, Kensington, Whangarei: (09) 437 6856
Whangarei Central Holiday Park (4 F11) – 34 Tarewa Rd, Whangarei: (09) 438 6600
Blue Heron Waterfront Holiday Park (4 G12) – 85-87 Scott Rd, off Whangarei Heads Rd; Heading towards Parua Bay: (09) 436 2293
Ruakaka Beach Holiday Camp (4 J13) – 21 Beach Rd, Ruakaka: (09) 432 7590
Camp Waipu Cove (6 A8) – Cove Rd, Waipu Cove: (09) 432 0410
Waipu Cove Cottages & Camping (6 A8) – 685 Cove Rd, Waipu Cove: (09) 432 0851
Riverside Holiday Park (6 B9) – 41 Black Swamp Rd, Mangawhai: (09) 431 4825

AUCKLAND

Pakiri Beach Holiday Park (6 D10) – 261 Pakiri River Rd, RD 2 Wellsford, Pakiri: (09) 422 6199
Whangateau Holiday Park (6 D10) – 559 Leigh Rd, Whangateau: (09) 422 6305
Martin's Bay Holiday Park (6 E10) – 287 Martins Bay Rd, Warkworth: (09) 425 5655
Sandspit Holiday Park (6 E10) – 1334 Sandspit Rd, Sandspit Beach: (09) 425 8610
Orewa Beach Top 10 Holiday Park (7 A4) – 265 Hibiscus Coast Hwy, S end of Orewa Beach: (09) 426 5832
Pinewoods Motor Park Ltd (7 B4) – 23 Marie Ave, Red Beach: (09) 426 4526
Auckland North Shore Holiday Park (7 D4) – 52 Northcote Rd, Takapuna; Entrance next to Pizza Hut: (09) 418 2578
Takapuna Beach Holiday Park (7 D4) – 22 The Promenade, Takapuna: (09) 489 7909
Remuera Motor Lodge & Inner City Camping Ground – (7 E5) – 16 Minto Rd, Remuera: (09) 524 5126
Paradise Springs Camping Ground (5 H7) – Cnr Parkhurst & Springs Rd, Parakai; D/S is 7m from kerb: (09) 420 8998
Muriwai Beach Motorcamp (7 D1) – Beachfront at Muriwai: (09) 411 9262
Avondale Motor Park (7 E4) – 46 Bollard Ave, Avondale: (09) 828 7228
Campervan Park Auckland Airport (7 F4) – 15 Jimmy Ward Crescent, Auckland Airport: (09) 256 8527
Manukau Top 10 Holiday Park (7 F5) – 902 Great South Rd, Manukau: (09) 266 8016
Ramarama Country Caravan Park (7 H6) – Ararimu Rd, Ramarama: (09) 294 8903
Orere Point Top 10 Holiday Park (8 F9) – 2 Orere Point Rd, Clevedon: (09) 292 2774
Clarks Beach Holiday Park (7 H4) – Torkar Rd, Clarks Beach: (09) 232 1685
Sandspit Motor Camp (7 J4) – 15 Rangiwhea Rd, Waiuku; Jane Gifford Reserve: (09) 235 9913

HAURAKI/COROMANDEL

Miranda Holiday Park (8 H9) – Miranda Rd, Thames: (07) 867 3205
Dickson Holiday Park (8 G11) – 3km north of Thames on Coromandel Rd: (07) 868 7308
Te Puru Holiday Park (10 B8) – 473 Thames Coast Rd, TePuru: (07) 868 2879
Tapu Camp (8 F11) – SH25, Thames Coast: (07) 868 4837
Tapu Creek Campervan Park (8 F11) – Tapu-Coroglen Rd, Tapu: (07) 868 4560
River Glen Holiday Park & Campground (8 F12) – Tapu Rd, Coroglen; 3.5km from Coroglen Tavern: (07) 866 3130
Coromandel Top 10 Holiday Park (8 C11) – 636 Rings Rd, Coromandel: (07) 866 8830
Long Bay Motor Camp (8 C11) – 3200 Long Bay Rd, Coromandel: (07) 866 8720
Shelly Beach Top 10 Holiday Park (8 C11) – 243 Colville Rd, Coromandel: (07) 866 8988
Colville Bay Motel & Motor Camp (8 B11) – Wharf Rd, Colville, Coromandel: (07) 866 6814
Anglers Lodge Motels & Holiday Park (8 B10) – 1446 Colville Rd, Amodeo Bay: (07) 866 8584
Papa Aroha Holiday Park (8 C10) – Colville Rd, Coromandel: (07) 866 8818
Kuaotunu Motor Camp (8 C13) – 33 Bluff Rd, Kuaotunu: (07) 866 5628
Otama Beach Camping Ground (8 C13) – 400 Blackjack Rd, RD 2, Whitianga: (07) 866 2872
Flaxmill Bay Hideaway (8 D13) – 1019 Purangi Rd, Flaxmill Bay, Whitianga: (07) 866 2386
Mercury Bay Holiday Park (8 D13) – 121 Albert St, Whitianga: (07) 866 5579
Harbourside Holiday Park (8 D13) – 135 Albert St, Whitianga: (07) 866 5746
Mill Creek Bird & Campervan Park (8 E12) – 365 Mill Creek Rd, Whitianga: (07) 866 0166
Hahei Holiday Resort (8 D14) – Harsant Ave, Hahei, Whitianga: (07) 866 3889
Seabreeze Holiday Park (8 E13) – 1043 Tairua/Whitianga Rd, Whenuakite: (07) 866 3050
Hot Water Beach Top 10 Holiday Park (8 E14) – 790 Hot Water Beach Rd, Whitianga:(07) 866 3116
Pauanui Glade Holiday Park (8 G14) – 58 Vista Paku, Pauanui Beach: (07) 864 8559
Whangamata Motor Camp (8 J14) – 104 Barbara Ave, Whangamata: (07) 865 9128

WAIKATO

Port Waikato Holiday Park (9 E1) – Maunsell Rd, Port Waikato: (09) 232 9857
Te Aroha Holiday Park (10 G10) – 217 Stanley Rd, Te Aroha: (07) 884 9567
Waihi Motor Camp (10 F10) – 6 Waitete Rd, Waihi: (07) 863 7654
Opal Hot Springs Holiday Park (12 C11) – 257 Okauia Springs Rd, Matamata: (07) 888 8198
Waingaro Hot Springs (9 J3) – At Ngaruawahia turn west for 24km, Waingaro: (07) 825 4761
Hamilton City Holiday Park (11 C7) – 14 Ruakura Rd, Hamilton: (07) 855 8255
Roadrunner Motel and Holiday Park (11 E7) – 141 Bond Rd, Te Awamutu: (07) 871 7420
Cambridge Kiwi Motor Park (12 D8) – 32 Scott St, Leamington, Cambridge: (07) 827 5649
Lake Karapiro Camping Ground (12 D9) – Access from SH1, cross low level bridge at south end of Cambridge: (07) 827 4178
Raglan Kopua Holiday Park (11 C3) – Camp signposted from town centre: (07) 825 8283
Kawhia Beachside S-Cape (11 F3) – 225 Pouewe St, Kawhia: (07) 871 0727
Otorohanga Holiday Park (11 G6) – 20 Huiputea Drive, Otorohanga: (07) 873 7253
Camp Kiwi Holiday Park (11 G6) – Domain Drive, Otorohanga: (07) 873 7391
Waitomo Top 10 Holiday Park (11 H5) – Waitomo Caves Rd, Waitomo Village: (07) 878 7639
Forest View Motor Camp (11 F2) – 232 Waiwera St, Kawhia: (07) 871 0858

ROTORUA & CENTRAL PLATEAU

Rotorua Top 10 Holiday Park (13 G4) – 1495 Pukuatua St, Rotorua: (07) 348 1886
Holdens Bay Holiday Park & Conference Centre (13 G4) – 5-7 Stonebridge Park Drive, off Robinson Ave, Rotorua: (07) 345 9925
All Seasons Holiday Park (13 G5) – 50-58 Lee Rd, Hannahs Bay, Rotorua: 0800 422 674
Blue Lake Top 10 Holiday Park (13 H5) – 723 Tarawera Rd, on shores of Blue Lake, Rotorua: (07) 362 8120
Cosy Cottage Thermal Kiwi Holiday Park (13 G4) – 67 Whittaker Rd, Rotorua: (07) 348 3793
Rotorua Family Holiday Park (13 F4) – 22 Beaumonts Rd, Rotorua; near lake shore Ngongotaha: (07) 357 4289
Affordable Willowhaven Holiday Park (13 F4) – 31 Beaumonts Rd, Ngongotaha, Rotorua: (07) 357 4092
Waiteti Trout Stream Holiday Park (13 F4) – 14 Okona Cres, Ngongotaha, Rotorua: (07) 357 5255
Rotorua Thermal Holiday Park (13 G4) – 463 Old Taupo Rd (south end), Rotorua; Adjacent to golf course: (07) 346 3140
Lake Rotoiti Lakeside Holiday Park (13 F5) – On SH33, Okere Falls: (07) 362 4860
Kea Motel & Holiday Park (12 F11) – 95 Tirau St, SH1, Putaruru: (07) 882 1590
Tokoroa Motor Camp (12 H12) – 22 Sloss Rd, Tokoroa: (07) 886 6642
Tongariro Holiday Park (19 H1) – SH47, Tongariro: (07) 386 8062
Taupo De Bretts Spa Resort (19 D5) – 1.5km from Lake Taupo; SH5 Napier/Taupo Rd: (07) 378 8559
Lake Taupo Top 10 Holiday Resort (19 D5) – 28 Centennial Dr (off Spa Rd), Taupo: (07) 378 6860
Great Lake Holiday Park (19 D5) – 406 Acacia Bay Rd, Taupo: (07) 378 5159
Taupo All Seasons Kiwi Holiday Park (19 D5) – 16 Rangatira St, Taupo: (07) 378 4272
Oasis Motel & Holiday Park (19 G2) – SH41 Tokaanu: (07) 386 8569
Club Habitat (19 G3) – 25 Ohuanga Rd, Turangi: (07) 386 7492
Turangi Kiwi Holiday Park (19 G3) – Ohuanga Rd off SH41, Turangi: (07) 386 8754
Motutere Bay Holiday Park (19 F4) – On SH1, Motutere: (07) 386 8963
Ohakune Top 10 Holiday Park (26 C11) – 5 Moore St, Ohakune: (06) 385 8561
Motuoapa Motor Camp (19 G3) – 13 Parekarangaranga St, Motuoapa: (07 386 7162)
Wairakei Thermal Valley (19 C5) – SH1, Wairakei: (07) 374 8004
Whakapapa Holiday Park (18 J13) – Tongariro National Park, Mt Ruapehu: (07) 892 3897

BAY OF PLENTY

Waihi Beach Top 10 Holiday Park (10 F12) – 15 Beach Rd, Waihi Beach; Adjacent to Ocean Beach: (07) 863 5504

Beach Haven Holiday Camp (10 F12) – 21 Leo St, Waihi Beach: (07) 863 5505
Sea-Air Motel & Holiday Park (10 F12) – Emerton Rd, Waihi Beach South: (07) 863 5655
Athenree Hot Springs & Holiday Park (10 F12) – 1 Athenree Rd, Athenree: (07) 863 5600
Bowentown Beach Holiday Park (10 F12) – South end of Seaforth Rd, Bowentown: (07) 863 5381
Accommodation at Te Puna (10 J13) – Cnr Waihi Rd (SH2) & Minden Rd, Te Puna, Tauranga: (07) 552 5621
Tauranga Tourist Park (10 J13) – 9 Mayfair St, Tauranga: (07) 578 3323
Silver Birch Family Holiday Park (10 J13) – 101 Turret Rd, Tauranga: (07) 578 4603
Golden Grove Kiwi Holiday Park (13 B4) – 73 Girven Rd, Mt Maunganui: (07) 575 5821
Mount Maunganui Beachside Holiday Park (13 A4) – 1 Adams Ave, Mt Maunganui; at the base of the mountain: (07) 575 4471
Papamoa Village Park (13 B5) – 267 Parton Rd, Papamoa: (07) 542 1890
Papamoa Beach Top 10 Holiday Resort (13 B5) – 535 Papamoa Beach Rd, Papamoa: (07) 572 0816
Beach Grove Holiday Park (13 B5) – 386 Papamoa Beach Rd, Papamoa: (07) 572 1337
Pacific Park Christian Holiday Camp (13 B5) – 1110 Papamoa Beach Rd, Papamoa: (07) 542 0018
Maketu Hilltop Holiday Park (13 C6) – 195 Arawa Ave, Maketu: (07) 533 2222

EASTERN BAY OF PLENTY

Awakeri Hot Springs (14 F9) – On SH30, 16km south of Whakatane: (07) 304 9117
Whakatane Holiday Park (14 E11) – McGarvey Rd, Whakatane: (07) 308 8694
Thornton Beach Holiday Park (14 E110) – 163 Thornton Beach Rd off SH2; 14km NW of Whakatane: (07) 304 8296
Opotiki Holiday Park (14 F13) – Cnr of Grey St & Potts Ave, Opotiki: (07) 315 6050
Ohope Beach Top 10 Holiday Park (14 E12) – 367 Harbour Rd, east of Ohope: 0800 264 673
Ohiwa Beach Holiday Park (14 F12) – 380 Ohiwa Harbour Rd, Opotiki: (07) 315 4741
Waihau Bay Holiday Park (16 B8) – On SH35, 3km east of Waihau Bay: (07) 325 3844
Island View Holiday Park (14 F13) – 8 Appleton Rd, Waiotahi: (07) 315 7519
Te Kaha Holiday Park (15 C6) – SH35, Te Kaha: (07) 325 2894
Murphy's Holiday Camp (14 D8) – 174 SH2, Matata: (07) 322 2136

EASTLAND

Anaura Bay Motor Camp (16 J11) – Anaura Bay Rd, Anaura Bay: (06) 862 6380
Tolaga Bay Holiday Park (22 A13) – 167 Wharf Rd, Tolaga Bay: (06) 862 6716
Gisborne Showgrounds Park Motorcamp (22 D10) – 20 Main Rd, Gisborne: (06) 867 5299
Waikanae Beach Top 10 Holiday Park (22 E10) – Grey St, Gisborne: (06) 867 5634
Mahia Beach Holiday Park (22 J9) – 43 Moana Dr, Mahia Beach: (06) 837 5830
Riverside Motor Camp (21 H5) – 19 Marine Pde, Wairoa: (06) 838 6301
Waikaremoana Holiday Park (21 E2) – SH38, Lake Waikaremoana: (06) 837 3803

HAWKES BAY

Waipatiki Beach Holiday Park (28 B13) – 498 Waipatiki Beach Rd, Napier: (06) 836 6075
Bay View Snapper Holiday Park (28 D12) – 8 Gill Rd, Bayview: (06) 836 7084
Affordable Westshore Holiday Park (28 D12) – 88 Meeanee Quay, Westshore, Napier: (06) 835 9456
Kennedy Park Resort Napier (28 D12) – Storkey St, Napier: (06) 843 9126
Bay View Van Park (28 C12) – 10 Gill Rd, Bay View: (06) 836 7084
Hastings Top 10 Holiday Park (28 F12) – 610 Windsor Ave, Hastings: (06) 878 6692
Arataki Park (28 F12) – 139 Arataki Rd, Havelock North: (06) 877 7479
Clifton Beach Reserve Motor Camp (28 F13) – 495 Clifton Rd, R D 2 Hastings on east coast: (06) 875 0265
River's Edge Holiday Park (28 J9) – Harker St, Waipawa; Go to town clock, turn right travelling north: (06) 857 8976
Waipukurau Holiday Park (32 A10) – River Tce, Waipukurau off SH2, adjacent TukiTuki River: (06) 858 8184
Dannevirke Holiday Park (31 C6) – 29 George St, Dannevirke: (06) 374 7625
Beach Road Holiday Park (32 D11) – 566 Beach Rd, Porangahau Beach: (06) 855 5281

TARANAKI

Seaview Holiday Park (17 D5) – SH3, between Awakino and Mokau: (06) 752 9708
Taumarunui Holiday Park (18 F11) – SH4, Manunui: (07) 895 9345
Urenui Beach Camp Ground (17 G3) – 148 Beach Rd, Urenui: (06) 752 3838
Onaero Bay Holiday Park (17 G2) – SH3, North Taranaki: (06) 752 3643
Belt Rd Seaside Holiday Park (23 B5, 107 B3) – 2 Belt Rd, New Plymouth: (06) 758 0228
New Plymouth Top 10 Holiday Park (23 B5) – 29 Princes St, New Plymouth: (06) 758 2566
Marine Park Motor Camp (17 G1) – Centennial Ave, Waitara: (06) 754 7121
Fitzroy Beach Holiday Park (23 B5) – 1D Beach St, New Plymouth: (06) 758 2870
Sentry Hill Motel & Roadhouse (23 A6) – 56 Mountain Rd (SH3A): (06) 752 0696
Oakura Beach Holiday Park (23 B4) – 2 JansTce, Oakura: (06) 752 7861
Opunake Beach Holiday Park (23 F3) – Beach Rd, Opunake: (06) 761 7525
Stratford Top Town Holiday Park (25 B1) – 10 Page St, Stratford: (06) 765 6440
Hawera Holiday Park (25 E2) – 70 Waihi Rd, Hawera; SH3, adjacent to Park & gardens: (06) 278 8544
Patea Motor Camp (25 G3) – 9 Beach Rd, Patea: (06) 273 8620
Ashley Park Campground (25 G6) – 2924 State Highway 3, Waitotara: (06) 346 5917

WANGANUI

Raetihi Holiday Park (26 C10) – 10 Parapara Rd, Raetihi: (06) 385 4176
Mowhanau Holiday Park (25 H7) – Kai Iwi Beach: (06) 342 9658
Whanganui River Top 10 Holiday Park (26 H8) – 460 Somme Pde, Aramoho, Wanganui: (06) 343 8402
Whanganui Seaside Holiday Park (25 J7) – Cnr Karaka & Rangiora St, Wanganui; Adjacent to beach: (06) 344 2227
Bignell St Motel & Campervans (26 J8) – 86 Bignell St, Wanganui: 0800 244 635
Taihape Riverview Holiday Park (27 F2) – Old Abbattoir Rd, Taihape: (06) 388 0718

MANAWATU

Bridge Motor Lodge & Caravan Park (29 B6) – 2 Bridge St, Bulls: (06) 322 0894
Feilding Holiday Park (29 C7) – 5 Arnott St, Feilding: (06) 323 5623
Koitiata Camping Ground (29 A4) – Turakina Beach Rd, Koitiata: (06) 327 3770
Palmerston North Holiday Park (30 E8) – 133 Dittmer Dr, Palmerston North; Follow southern by-pass route to or from Woodville adjacent to swimming complex: (06) 358 0349
Foxton Beach Holiday Park (29 F4) – HolbenPde, Foxton: (06) 363 8211
Waitarere Beach Motor Camp (29 F4) – 133 Park Ave, Waitarere Beach: (06) 368 8732
Hydrabad Holiday Park (29 G4) – Forest Rd, Waitarere Beach: (06) 368 4941
Levin Holiday Camp (29 G5) – 38 Parker Ave, Levin: (06) 368 3549
Byron's Resort (29 J3) – 20 Tasman Rd, Otaki Beach; D/S at rear of camp: (06) 364 8121
Bridge Lodge (29 J4) – 3 Otaki Gorge Rd, Otaki: (06) 364 6667
Himatangi Beach Holiday Park (29 D4) – 30 Koputara Rd, Himatangi (06) 329 9575

WAIRARAPA

Carnival Park Campground (30 F9) – Glasgow St, Pahiatua: (06) 376 6340
Mawley Holiday Park (34 B9) – 15 Oxford St, Masterton: (06) 378 6454
Castlepoint Holiday Park & Motel (34 A13) – Jetty Road. D/S on roadway into camp: (06) 372 6705
Carterton Holiday Park (34 C8) – 196-8 Belvedere Rd, Carterton; 700m from main road, SH2: (06) 379 8267
Martinborough Top 10 Holiday Park (34 E7) – Cnr Princess & Dublin Sts, Martinborough: (06) 306 8946
Eketahuna Club (30 H8) – 30 Herbert Street, Eketahuna: (06) 375 8296

WELLINGTON

Lindale Motor Park (33 A3) – Ventnor Dr, Paraparaumu: (04) 298 8046
Paekakariki Holiday Park (33 B3) – 180 Wellington Rd, Paekakariki: (04) 292 8292
Camp Elsdon (33 D2) – 18 Raiha St, Porirua: (04) 237 8987
Aotea Camping Ground (33 D2) – 3 Whitford Brown Ave, Porirua: (04) 235 9599
Harcourt Holiday Park (33 C4) – 45 Akatarawa Rd, Upper Hutt; turn off SH2 just north of Caltex Service Station: (04) 526 7400
Capital Gateway Motor Inn (33 E2) – 1 Newlands Rd, Newlands: (04) 478 7812
Wellington Top 10 Holiday Park (33 E3) – 95 Hutt Park Rd, Lower Hutt: (04) 568 5913

SOUTH ISLAND

MARLBOROUGH

Okiwi Bay Holiday Park & Lodge (39 E7) – 15 Renata Rd, Rai Valley, Okiwi Bay: (03) 576 5006
Smiths Farm Holiday Park (40 G9) – 1419 Queen Charlotte Dr, Linkwater, Picton: (03) 574 2806
Havelock Motor Camp (40 G8) – 24 Inglis St, Havelock: (03) 574 2339
Alexanders Holiday Park (40 G10) – 2a Canterbury St, Picton: (03) 573 6378
Picton Top 10 Holiday Park (40 G10) – 70-78 Waikawa Rd, Picton: (03) 573 7212
Picton Campervan Park (40 G10) – 42 Kent St, Nelson Square, Picton: (03) 573 8875
Parklands Marina Holiday Park (40 G10) – 10 Beach Rd, Waikawa Marina, Picton: (03) 573 6343
Waikawa Bay Holiday Park (40 G10) – 5 Waimarama St, Waikawa Bay: (03) 573 7434
Spring Creek Holiday Park (44 B10) – 1199 Rapaura Rd: (03) 570 5893
Blenheim Top 10 Holiday Park (44 C11) – 78 Grove Rd, Blenheim: (03) 578 3667
Chartridge Park (40 H8) – SH6, 7km south of Havelock: (03) 574 2129

NELSON/TASMAN

Pohara Beach Top 10 Holiday Park (38 D8) – 809 Abel Tasman Dr, Takaka, Pohara: (03) 525 9500
Totaranui DOC camping ground (38 D10) – Totaranui Rd, Abel Tasman National Park: (03) 528 8083
Abel Tasman Marahau Beach Camp (39 D2) – 9 Franklin St, Marahau: (03) 527 8176
Kaiteriteri Beach Motor Camp (39 E2) – Sandy Bay Rd, Kaiteriteri: (03) 527 8010
Motueka Top 10 Holiday Park (39 E2) – 10 Fearon St, Motueka; north end of town: (03) 528 7189
Mapua Leisure Park (39 G2) – 33 Toru St, Mapua: (03) 540 2666
Greenwood Park (39 H3) – Cnr Lansdowne Rd & Coastal Hwy, Appleby, Richmond: (03) 544 4685
Richmond Motel & Top 10 Holiday Park (39 H3) – 29 Gladstone Rd, SH6, Richmond: (03) 544 5218
Club Waimea(39 H3) – 345 Lower Queen St, Richmond: (03) 543 9179
Maitai Valley Motor Camp (39 G4) – Maitai Valley, Nelson: (03) 548 7729
Nelson City Holiday Park & Motels (39 G4) – 230 Vanguard St, Nelson: (03) 548 1445
Tahuna Beach Holiday Park (39 G3) – 70 Beach Rd, Tahunanui, Nelson: (03) 548 5159
Quinney's Bush Camp & Caravan Park (42 C13) – SH6, Motupiko: (03) 522 4249
Tapawera Settle (42 B13) – 19 Tadmore Rd, Tapawera: (03) 522 4334
Kerr Bay DOC camp (42 G13) – St Arnaud; opposite kitchen shelter: (03) 521 1806
Kiwi Park Motel & Holiday Park (42 G9) – 170 Fairfax St, Murchison: (03) 523 9248
Collingwood Motor Camp (37 C7) – William Street, Collingwood: (03) 524 8149
Murchison Motorhome Park (42 F10) – 2595 Kawatiri-Murchison Hwy (SH6), Murchison: (03) 523 9666
Bethany Park Christian Camp (38 G10) – 88 Martin Farm Road, RD2, Kaiteriteri: (03) 527 8014

WEST COAST

Karamea Holiday Park (41 A7) – SH67; 3km south of Karamea: (03) 782 6758
Karamea Domain Camping Ground (41 A7) – Waverly St, Karamea, signposted W of township: (03) 782 6069
Westport Holiday Park & Motel (41 G3) – 31-37 Domett St, Westport: (03) 789 7043
Seal Colony Top 10 Tourist Park (41 G2) – Marine Pde, Carters Beach, Westport; adjacent to beach: (03) 789 8002
Punakaiki Beach Camp (45 B5) – SH6, Owen St, Punakaiki: (03) 731 1894
Rapahoe Beach Motor Camp (45 E4) – 10 Hawken St, Rapahoe: (03) 762 7025
Reefton Motor Camp (46 B9) – Main St, Reefton; on SH7: (03) 732 8477
Central Motor Home Park (45 E4) – 117-119 Tainui St, Greymouth: (03) 768 4924
Greymouth Seaside Top 10 Holiday Park (45 F4) – 2 Chesterfield St, Greymouth: 0800 867 104
Greymouth Kiwi Holiday Park & Motels (45 F3) – 318 Main South Rd, SH6, Greymouth: (03) 762 6768
Lake Brunner Motor Camp (45 G6) – 86 Ahau St, Moana: (03) 738 0600
Lake Brunner Country Motel & Holiday Park (45 G6) – 2014 Arnold Valley Rd, Moana: (03) 738 0144
Hokitika Kiwi Holiday Park (45 H2) – cnr Stafford St & Livingstone St, Hokitika: (03) 755 8172
Shining Star Beachfront Accommodation (45 H2) – 16 Richards Drive, Hokitika: (03) 755 8921
252 Beachside Motels & Holiday Park (45 H2) – 252 Revell St, Hokitika: (03) 755 8773
Jacksons Retreat Holiday Park(45 J6) – SH73, Great Alpine Hwy: (03) 738 0474
Rainforest Retreat Holiday Park (49 G6) – 46 Cron St, Franz Josef: (03) 752 0220
Franz Josef Top 10 Holiday Park (49 G6) – 2902 Franz Josef Hwy, SH6, Franz Josef: (03) 752 0735
Fox Glacier Top 10 Holiday Park (49 H4) – Kerrs Rd, Fox Glacier: (03) 751 0821
Fox Glacier Lodge & Campervan Park (49 H4) – 41 Sullivan Rd, Fox Glacier: (03) 751 0888
Haast Lodge (58 D9) – Marks Rd, Haast; 3km east of Haast Visitor Centre: (03) 750 0703
Haast Beach Holiday Park (58 D8) – Jacksons Bay Rd, Okuru: 0800 843 226
Harihari Motor Inn (50 D9) – Main Rd, Harihari: 0800 833 026
Glacier Country Campervan Park (49 G6) – 64 Cron Street, Franz Josef: (03) 752 0145

NORTH CANTERBURY

Hanmer Springs Top 10 Holiday Park (47 F5) – Cnr Bath St and Main St, Hanmer Springs: (03) 315 7113
Alpine Adventure Holiday Park (47 F5) – 200 Jacks Pass Rd, Hanmer Springs; 2km from village: (03) 315 7112
Hanmer River Holiday Park (47 G5) – 26 Medway Rd, Hanmer Springs: (03) 315 7111
Alpine Holiday Apartments & Campground (47 G5) – 9 Fowlers Lane, Hanmer Springs: (03) 315 7478
Pines Holiday Park (47 F5) – 158 Argelins Rd, Hanmer Springs: (03) 315 7152
Waiau Motor Camp (47 H7) – 9 Highfield St, Waiau: (03) 315 6672
Waipara Sleepers Motor Camp (54 C8) – 10 Glenmark Dr, 200m from junction of SH1 & SH7, Waipara: (03) 314 6003
Greta Valley Camping Ground (54 B10) – 7 Valley Rd, Greta Valley, SH1; halfway between Amberley and Cheviot: (03) 314 3340
Delhaven Motels & Caravan Park (54 D8) – 124 Carters Rd, Amberley; SH1: (03) 314 8550
Woodend Beach Holiday Park (56 B10) – 14 Beach Rd, Woodend Beach: (03) 312 7643
Leithfield Beach Motor Camp (56 A11) – 18 Lucas Dr, Leithfield Beach: (03) 314 8518
Rangiora Holiday Park (56 B9) – 337 Lehmans Rd, Rangiora: (03) 313 5759
Pineacres Holiday Park (56 B10) – 740 Main North Rd, Kaiapoi; on SH1: (03) 327 5022
Blue Skies (56 C10) – 12 Williams St, Kaiapoi; southern end of Old Main Rd: (03) 327 8007
Kairaki Beach Motor Camp (56 C10) – Featherstone Ave, Kaiapoi; at mouth of Waimakariri River: (03) 327 7335
Riverlands Holiday Park (56 C10) – 45 Doubledays Rd, Kaiapoi: (03) 327 5511
219 On Johns Motel & Holiday Park (56 C9, 120 D5) – 219 Johns Rd, Belfast: (03) 323 8640
Addington Accommodation Park (56 D9) – 47-51 Whiteleigh Ave, Addington, Christchurch: (03) 338 9770
Spencer Beach Holiday Park (54 G8) – 100 Heyders Rd, Spencerville, Christchurch: (03) 329 8721
Amber Kiwi Holiday Park (56 D9) – 308 Blenheim Rd, Riccarton, Christchurch: (03) 348 3327
Christchurch Top 10 Holiday Park (56 D9) – 39 Meadow St, Papanui, Christchurch: (03) 352 9176
Riccarton Park Holiday Park (56 D9) – 19 Main South Rd, Upper Riccarton, Christchurch: (03) 348 5690
South Brighton Holiday Park (56 D10) – 59 Halsey St, Christchurch: (03) 388 9844
All Seasons Kiwi Holiday Park (56 D10) – 5 Kidbrooke St, Bromley, Christchurch: (03) 384 9490
North South Holiday Park (56 D9) – Cnr Johns Rd & Sawyers Arms Rd, Harewood, Christchurch: (03) 359 5993
Alpine View Holiday Park (56 D8) – 650-678 Main South Rd, Templeton: (03) 349 7666
Akaroa Top 10 Holiday Park (56 G12) – 96 Morgans Rd, Banks Peninsula; off Old Coach Rd from SH75: (03) 304 7471
Duvauchelle Holiday Park (56 G12) – 19 Seafield Rd, Duvauchelle, Banks Peninsula: (03) 304 5777

Okains Bay Motor Camp (56 F13) – 1357 Okains Bay Rd, Banks Peninsula: (03) 304 8789
Kowai Pass Domain Camp (55 B4) – Domain Rd, Springfield; off SH73: (03) 318 4887
Glentunnel Holiday Park (55 D4) – SH77, Scenic Route 72, Homebush Rd, Glentunnel: (03) 318 2868
Ashley Gorge Holiday Park (55 A6) – 697 Ashley Gorge Rd, Ashley Gorge, Canterbury: (03) 312 4099
A1 Kaikoura Motels & Caravan Park (48 E12) – 11 Beach Rd, Kaikoura; on SH1: (03) 319 5999
Kaikoura Top 10 Holiday Park (48 E12) – 34 Beach Rd, Kaikoura: (03) 319 5362
Alpine-Pacific Holiday Park (48 E12) – 69 Beach Rd, Kaikoura: 0800 692 322
Kaikoura Peketa Beach Holiday Park (48 E11) – 665 State Highway 1, Peketa: (03) 319 6299
Kaikoura Coastal Campgrounds, Goose Bay (48 F11) – SH1, Kaikoura: (03) 319 5348
Awatere Motor Camp (44 E11) – Seddon Domain, Seymour St, Seddon: (03) 575 7285
Amberley Beach Reserve (54 D9) – Amberley Beach: (03) 314 8816

SOUTH CANTERBURY

Rakaia River Holiday Park & Motels (55 G5) – 16 Main South Rd, Raikaia; south end of Rakaia Bridge: (03) 302 7257
Coronation Holiday Park (55 J3) – 780 East St, Ashburton: (03) 308 6603
Abisko Campground (55 F2) – 74 Main St, Methven: (03) 302 8875
Ashburton Holiday Park (62 D8) – 86 Moronan Rd, Tinwald: (03) 308 6805
Grumpys Retreat (61 E5) – 7 Keen St, Orari Bridge: (03) 693 7453
Geraldine Kiwi Holiday Park (61 F4) – Cnr SH79 & Hislop St, Geraldine: (03) 693 8147
Fairlie Top 10 Holiday Park (61 F1) – 10 Allandale Rd, Fairlie: (03) 685 8375
Lake Tekapo Motels & Holiday Park (60 E9) – Lakeside Dr, Lake Tekapo: (03) 680 6825
Lake Ruataniwha Holiday Park (59 H6) – Max Smith Drive, Twizel: (03) 435 0613
Twizel Holiday Park (59 H6) – 122 Mackenzie Drive, Twizel: (03) 435 0507
Omarama Top 10 Holiday Park (67 A3) – 1 Omarama Ave, Omarama; junction of SH8 & SH83, closed in winter: (03) 438 9875
Ahuriri Motels (67 A3) – SH83, Omarama: (03) 438 9451
Temuka Holiday Park (61 G5) – 1 Fergusson Dr, Temuka: (03) 615 7241
Timaru Top 10 Holiday Park (61 J4) – 154a Selwyn St, Timaru: (03) 684 7690
Glenmark Holiday Park (61 J4) – 30 Beaconsfield Rd, Timaru: (03) 684 3682
Kurow Holiday Park (67 D7) – 76 Bledisloe St, Kurow; on SH83, west end of town: (03) 436 0725
Fisherman's Bend, Lake Aviemore(67 C7) – Nth side of Lake Aviemore (Oct to Apr only): (03) 689 8079
Knottingley Park (68 D12) – Waihoa Back Rd, Waimate; dump station at rear end of public toilets in camping area: (03) 689 8079
Victoria Park Camp and Cabins (68 D12) – Naylor St, Waimate: (03) 689 8079
Kelcey's Bush Farmyard Holiday Park (68 C11) – 677 Mill Rd, Waimate: (03) 689 8057
Waitaki Waters Holiday Park (68 F13) – 305 Kaik Rd, Waitaki: (03) 431 3880

OTAGO

Oamaru Top 10 Holiday Park (68 H11) – Chelmer St, Oamaru; off SH1 near railway: (03) 434 7666
Moeraki Boulders Kiwi Holiday Park (74 B13) – 2 Carlisle St, Hampden: (03) 439 4439
Moeraki Village Holiday Park (74 B14) – 114 Haven St, Moerake: (03) 439 4759
Olive Grove Lodge & Holiday Park (74 A13) – Waianakarua, adjacent SH1, 25km S of Oamaru: (03) 439 5830
Larchview Holiday Park (67 G5) – 8 Swimming Dam Rd, Naseby: (03) 444 9904
Ranfurly Holiday Park (67 H5) – 8 Reade St, Ranfurly: (03) 444 9144
Blind Billy's Holiday Camp (74 D8) – 28 Mold St, Middlemarch: (03) 464 3355
Waikouaiti Beach Motor Camp (74 E12) – 186 Beach St, Waikouaiti: (03) 465 7432
Leith Valley Touring Park (74 G11) – 103 Malvern St, Dunedin: 0800 555 331
Dunedin Holiday Park (74 H11) – 41 Victoria Rd, St Kilda, Dunedin: (03) 455 4690
Lake Waihola Holiday Park (79 B6) – Waihola Domain: (03) 417 8908
Brighton Motor Camp (74 H10) – 1044 Brighton Rd, Brighton, Dunedin: (03) 481 1404
Aaron Lodge Top 10 Holiday Park (74 H11) – 162 Kaikorai Valley Rd, Dunedin: (03) 476 4725
Portobello Village Tourist Park (74 G12) – 27 Hereweka St, Dunedin: (03) 478 0359
Taylor Park Motor Camp (79 C5) – 11 Park Rd, Milton: (03) 417 8109
Albert Town Tavern (66 D8) – 20 Alison Ave, Albert Town: (03) 443 4545
Balclutha Motor Camp (79 E3) – 56 Charlotte St, Balclutha: (03) 418 0088
Gold Park Motor Camp (79 A3) – Harrington St, Lawrence: (03) 485 9850
Otematata Holiday Park (67 C5) – East Road, Otematata: (03) 438 7826
Benmore Dam Recreation Reserve (67 C5) – SH83, Otematata: (03) 433 0300

CENTRAL OTAGO

Lake Hawea Holiday Park (66 C9) – 1208 Makarora Park Rd; 500m north of Lake Hawea turn-off: (03) 443 1767
Aspiring Holiday Park & Motels (66 D8) – Studholme Rd, Wanaka: (03) 443 6603
Lake Outlet Holiday Park (66 D8) – 197 Outlet Rd, Wanaka: (03) 443 7478
Glendhu Bay Motor Camp (65 D7) – 1128 Mt Aspiring Rd, Wanaka: (03) 443 7243
Wanaka Lakeview Holiday Park (66 D8) – 212 Brownston St, Wanaka; on right just before camp: (03) 443 7883
Arrowtown Holiday Park (65 G6) – 12 Centennial Ave, Arrowtown: (03) 442 1876
Glenorchy Holiday Park (65 F2) – 2 Oban St, Glenorchy; at the head of Lake Wakatipu: (03) 441 0303
Queenstown Top 10 Holiday Park (65 H4) – 54 Robins Rd, Queenstown: (03) 442 9447
Shotover Top 10 Holiday Park (65 G4) – 70 Arthurs Point Rd, Queenstown: (03) 442 9306
Frankton Motor Camp (65 H5) – Yewlett Cres, Frankton; in front of Remarkables Hotel, Queenstown: (03) 442 2079
Queenstown Lake View Holiday Park (65 H4) – 4 Cemetery Rd, Queenstown; 150m from Gondola: (03) 442 7252
Hectors (72 B8) – 16 Kent St, Kingston: (03) 248 8501
Cairnmuir Camping Ground (66 H8) – 219 Cairnmuir Rd, Bannockburn: (03) 445 1956
Cromwell Top 10 Holiday Park (66 H9) – 1 Alpha St, Cromwell: (03) 445 0164
The Chalets Holiday Park (66 H8) – 102 Barry Ave, Cromwell: (03) 445 1260
Alexandra Holiday Park (73 A2) – 44 Manuherikia Rd, Alexandra: (03) 448 8297
Clyde Holiday & Sporting Complex (66 J10) – Whitby St, Clyde: (03) 449 2713
Wanaka Top 10 Holiday Park (66 D8) – 217 Wanaka- Mt Aspiring Rd, Wanaka: (03) 443 7360
Glenquoich Caravan Park (71 D7) – Avon Street, Athol: (021) 184 5444

SOUTHLAND

Kaka Point Camping Ground (79 G4) – 39 Tarata St, Kaka Point; on coastal rd: (03) 412 8801
Keswick Park Camping Ground (79 H3) – 350 Pounawea Rd, Owaka: (03) 419 1110
Pounawea Motor Camp (79 H3) – Park Lane, Pounawea: (03) 415 8483
McLean Falls Holiday Park (78 G12) – 29 Rewcastle Rd, Owaka: (03) 415 8551
Mossburn Country Park (71 F5) – 333 Mossburn Five Rivers Rd, Mossburn: (03) 248 6444
Manapouri Motels & Holiday Park (70 E10) – 50 Manapouri-Te Anau Rd, Manapouri: (03) 249 6624
Te Anau Great Lakes Holiday Park (70 D11) – 15 Luxmore Dr, Te Anau: (03) 249 8538
Te Anau Top 10 Holiday Park (70 D11) – 128 Te Anau Tce & Mokonui St, Te Anau: (03) 249 7462
Te Anau Lakeview Kiwi Holiday Park (70 D11) – 1 Te Anau-Manapouri Rd, Te Anau; opposite DOC Visitor Centre: (03) 249 7457
Fiordland Great Views Holiday Park (70 C11) – 129 Milford Rd, Te Anau: (03) 249 7059
Tuatapere Motels, Backpackers & Holiday Park (76 F12) – 73 Main St, Tuatapere: 027 222 2612
Coachmans Inn Motor Lodge (77 E5) – 705 Tay St, Invercargill; east end: (03) 217 6046
Beach Road Holiday Park (77 F4) – 375 Dunns Rd, Otatara: (03) 213 0400
Invercargill Top 10 Holiday Park (77 E5) – 77 McIvor Rd, Invercargill: (03) 215 9032
Amble On Inn (77 F5) – 145 Chesney St, Kingswell: (03) 216 5214
Invercargill Kiwi Holiday Park (77 E5) – 352 Lorne Dancre Rd, Grove Bush, Invercargill: (03) 235 8031
Bluff Camping Ground (77 G5) – 2 Gregory St, Bluff; off SH1: (027) 626 2018
Gore Motor Camp (78 B9) – 35 Broughton St (SH1), Gore: (03) 208 4919
Dolamore Park (78 A8) – 70 Dolamore Park Rd, Upper Charlton: (03) 208 9080
Colac Bay Tavern & Camping Ground (77 E1) – 15 Colac Bay Rd, Colac Bay: (03) 234 8399
Last Light Lodge (76 E11) – 6 Clifden Rd, Tuatapere: (03) 226 6667
Kaitangata Riverside Motor Camp (79 E4) – 20 Water Street, Kaitangata: (03) 413 9219
Newhaven Holiday Park (79 H3) – 324 Newhaven Rd, Surat Bay: (03) 415 8834
Curio Bay Holiday Park (78 H11) – 601 Waikawa-Curio Bay Rd, Curio Bay: (03) 246 8897

MOTORHOME PUBLIC DUMP STATION (WASTEWATER DISPOSAL SITE)

NORTH ISLAND

NORTHLAND

Kaitaia Public D/S (1 J6) – A & P Showgrounds car park, South Rd, SH1 Kaitaia
Kaikohe Public D/S (3 C7) – Recreation Rd, Kaikohe; D/S on roadside at rear of Pioneer Village toilets
Mangonui Public D/S (2 H8) – Waterfront Drive, next to public toilets, 400m from SH10
Kerikeri Public D/S (4 A8, 86 C2) – 69 Cobham Rd, by memorial hall, Kerikeri
Kawakawa Public Toilets & D/S (4 C9) – Waimio St, off SH1, on the right hand side past entrance to bowling club, Kawakawa
Omapere Public D/S (3 E3) – SH12 on harbourside, between Omapere & Opononi
Dargaville Public D/S (3 J7) – Mobil Service Station, 69 Normanby St, Dargaville
Dargaville Public D/S (3 J7) – Caltex Service Station, 1 Normanby St, Dargaville
Dargaville Museum Public D/S (3 J7) – Dargaville Museum, Harding Park, Mt Wesley Coast Rd; In public car park, Dargaville
Kellys Bay Public Dump Station (5 D5) – Dale Rd, Kellys Bay, Pouto Peninsula
Ngunguru Public Toilets & D/S (4 F13) – Te Maika Rd, at North end of Ngunguru; opposite the school, near public toilets
Kamo Volunteer Fire Brigade (4 F11, 85 A1) – 589 Kamo Road, Kamo, Whangarei
Caltex Whangarei (4 F11, 84 C3) – 15 Lower Tarewa Rd, Whangarei
Whangarei Public D/S (4 G12, 85 C2) – at the Waste Water Treatment Plant; 28 Kioreroa Rd, Whangarei
Recreational Concepts (4 F11, 85 C1) – 8 South End Ave, Whangarei
Public D/S Tarewa Drive 15 Lower Tarewa Rd, Vinetown, Whangarei
Langs Beach / Waipu Public Toilet & D/S (6 A8) – Cove Road, Langs Beach

AUCKLAND

Wellsford Centennial Park D/S (6 D8) – Centennial Park Road, Wellsford
Te Arai Point Public Toilets & D/S (6 C9) – Beside public toilets, Te Arai
Warkworth Public D/S (6 E10) – Kowhai Park Scenic Reserve, cnr of SH1 & Sandspit Rds, Warkworth
Orewa Estuary Toilets & Public D/S (6 G10) – 214B Hibiscus Coast Highway, Orewa
Whangaparaoa Public D/S (6 H11, 88 B5) – Gulf Harbour adjacent to public toilet by public boat ramp, Whangaparaoa
Vipond Road Public D/S (6 H10) – 43 Vipond Road, Whangaparaoa
Shelly Beach (7 A1, 5 G7) – Kaipara Harbour, Helensville, beside public toilet
Henderson Public D/S (7 D2) – McLeod Rd extension, TeAtatu South, fenced area in McLeod Pk opposite Riverglade Parkway Road
Halfmoon Bay Marina Toilets & Dump Station (7 E5, 90 C6) – Half Moon Bay, Auckland
Mobil Wiri SS (7 F5, 90 E5) – 62 Wiri Station Road, Wiri, Manukau
Waharau Public D/S (8 G9) – Opposite Waharau Regional Park, Kaiaua Coast
Pukekohe Public D/S (7 H5) – Franklin Rd, Pukekohe; 400m past sports stadium
Tuakau Public D/S (7 J6) – In St Stephens Drive, Tuakau, opposite Police Station
Drury Public D/S (7 G6) – Tui St, behind shops, Pukekohe
Waiuku Public D/S (7 J4) – Jane Gifford Reserve, on bypass road to Manukau Heads, on right
Maraetai Public D/S (7 E7) – 188 Maraetai Drive, Maraetai
Claris Landfill D/S (36 E5) – Gray Rd, Great Barrier Island

HAURAKI/COROMANDEL

Ngatea Public D/S (8 J11) – On SH2 (Orchard West Rd) in village centre near public hall
Stuart Moore Motors Service Station (8 H11) – 100 Banks St, Thames
Coromandel Public Dump Station (8 C11) – Wharf Road Scenic Reserve, Coromandel; Turn left towards Long Bay, 300m over bridge, near public toilets
Whitianga Refuse Transfer Station & Public D/S (8 D13) – 237 South Highway, Whitianga
Pauanui Public D/S (8 F14) – Pleasant Point Boat Ramp (off Vista Paku)
Whangamata Public Toilets & D/S (8 J14) – Martyn Rd, Whangamata
Waihi Public D/S (10 F11) – Victoria Park, Seddon Avenue, Waihi
Paeroa Public D/S (10 E9) – Marshall St, Paeroa, near public toilet and information centre
Paeroa RV Centre (10 E9) – Coronation Rd, Paeroa
Tairua Public D/S (10 A11) – 175 Beach Road, Tairua
Cooks Beach Public D/S (8 D13) – Next to public toilets, Cooks Beach

WAIKATO

Hampton Downs Motorsport Park (9 E4) – 20 Hampton Downs Road, Meremere
Te Kauwhata Public D/S (9 F5) – Turn off Mahi Rd into Domain in township
Te Aroha Public D/S (10 G9) – Skate Park toilets on Terminus Street, Te Aroha
Matamata Public Toilets & D/S (12 C11) – 1 Hetana St (on SH27, turn off Broadway)
Ngaruawahia Public D/S (9 H4) – Lower Waikato Esplanade at the Domain (The Point), on riverbank between Rowing Club & Railway bridge
Tirau Public D/S (12 E11) – 54 Main Rd (near public toilets down service lane from SH1)
Mobil Te Awamutu Public D/S (11 E7) – 133 Arawhata St, Te Awamutu
Hamilton Public D/S (11 C6, 92 E2) – SH1, Minogue Park, Tui Ave, Forest Lake
Raglan Public D/S (11 C3) – Raglan Club, 22 Bow St, Raglan
Mighty River Domain (12 E9) – 601 Maungatautari Rd, Karapiro
Mangakino Public D/S (12 J11) – 44 Wairenga Rd, Mangakino
Waipapa Hydro Dam D/S (12 J10) – Waipapa Rd, Ngaroma

ROTORUA & CENTRAL PLATEAU

Rotorua Public D/S (13 G4) – at the Wastewater Treatment Plant, Te Ngae Rd
Okawa Bay Reserve Public D/S (13 F5) – Okawa Bay Rd, Lake Rotoiti (in reserve near trailer yacht club boat ramp)
Otaramarae Public D/S (13 F5) – Otaramarae boat ramp, Otaramarae Rd (SH33), Lake Rotoiti
Tokoroa Public D/S (12 H12) – Whakauru St, Tokoroa; Next to sewerage treatment station
Wairakei BP Connect (19 C5) – SH1, Wairakei; D/S in parking area at the rear on left side
Kinloch Marina D/S (19 D4) – In Marina Car Park, Mata Place, Kinloch
Taupo Domain Toilets & Public D/S (19 D5) – Rainbow Point, 2 Mile Bay, Taupo
Tokaanu Public D/S (19 G3) – At boat ramp, 379 Mangaroa St, Tokaanu
Putaruru Public D/S (12 F11) – Market St. Heading south on SH1, fi rst left turn after roundabout
Boatshed Bay Wastewater D/S (13 H5) – Near Boatshed Bay boat ramp, Spencer Rd, Lake Tarawera

BAY OF PLENTY

Katikati Public D/S (10 G11) – North side of Katikati shopping centre turn off SH2 into roadway beside the A&P showgrounds
Z Service Station (13 B4) – 81 Hewletts Rd, Omanu, Mt Maunganui
Tauranga Public D/S (13 B3, 93 C5) – Tauranga Domain, Cameron Rd, Tauranga
Te Puke Public D/S (13 C5) – Situated at public toilets
Tauranga Public D/S (10 J13, 94 D2) – Maleme Rd, can be reached from Oropi Rd or Cameron Rd, close to transfer station, Tauranga
Omokoroa Public D/S (10 H12) – Omokoroa Beach at west end of Peninsula in Omokoroa Domain Car and Trailer Park, Omokoroa
Mt Maunganui Public D/S (10 J14, 13 B4, 94 B3) – Seawind Lane, Tauranga Airport

EASTERN BAY OF PLENTY

Kawerau Public D/S (14 G8) – Plunket St, Kawerau
Whakatane Public D/S (14 E10) – Caltex Service Station, 149 Commerce St, next to fire station
Ohope Public D/S (14 E11) – Situated at public toilets, half-way along beach before bridge, in Maraetotara Reserve with play equipment
Waiotahi Beach Public D/S (14 F13) – Waiotahi Beach Domain; On SH35 at public toilets
Opotiki BP Service Station (14 F13) – Cnr Bridges St & Church St, past the last diesel pump
Opotiki Truckstop (14 F13) – 60 Bridge St, Opotiki
Murupara Public D/S (20 B11) – Behind BP Station, Pine Dr; off SH38, Murupara
Omaio Public D/S (15 D5) – Omaio Domain, off SH35
Te Kaha School House Bay (15 C6) – Toilet block, Te Kaha

EASTLAND

Gisborne Mobil Portside (22 D10, 99 C5) – 49 Wainui Rd, Kaiti, Gisborne; East end of main road across bridge
Foster & Tyler Service Station (22 D10, 100 B3) – Corner Ormond Rd & Sheridan St, Gisborne
Te Araroa Public D/S (16 B12) – Transfer Stn, 26 Te Arawapaia Rd, Te Araroa
Gisborne Public D/S (22 D10, 100 C3) – Watson Park, Awapuni Rd, Gisborne

HAWKES BAY

Napier Public D/S (28 D12) – Marine Parade by Ellison
Napier Public D/S (28 D12) – 104 Latham St, Napier; Beside Council Sewerage Pump Station
Clive BP 2GO S/S (28 E12) – 154 Main Rd, Clive
Hastings BP Connect S/S (28 F11, 103 C5) – Stortford Lodge; Corner Maraekakaho Rd & Heretaunga St, St Leonards, Hastings
Waipawa Public D/S, BP 2GO Service Station (28 J9) – 1 High St, Waipawa
Takapau Public D/S (16 F11) – 15 Nang St, Takapau

TARANAKI

New Plymouth Public D/S, Mobil Service Station (23 B5, 106 B5) – 82 Leach St, New Plymouth
New Plymouth Public D/S, BP 2GO Service Station (23 B5, 106 C3, 107 B4) – 71 Powderham St, New Plymouth
Opunake Public D/S (23 F3) – Beach Rd, Opunake
Whangamomona Domain (24 C11) – 32 Whangamomona Rd
Normanby Public D/S (25 D1) – On Main Hwy, North of Hawera, Normanby
Opunake Public D/S (23 F3) – Corner Napier and King Sts, Opunake
Stratford Public D/S (25 B1) – Esk Road

WANGANUI

Taihape Public D/S (27 F2) – Linnet St, Taihape
Wanganui Public D/S (26 J8, 109 C3) – Springvale Park, London St, Wanganui
Ohakune Public D/S (26 C11) – Ohakune Club, 72 Goldfinch Ave, Ohakune
Taihape BP Connect Connection (27 F2) – 86 Hautapu St, Taihape
Ruakawa Adventure Centre (26 F11) SH4, Kakatahi

MANAWATU

Feilding BP Connect Service Station (29 C7) – 134 Kimbolton Road, Feilding
Feilding Sewerage Treatment Plant (29 C7) – KawaKawa Rd, Feilding, past abattoir and Manfield Racetrack, on LHS down long drive, turn right at end of drive
Whitehorse Inn (29 E7) – 2180 State Highway 56, Longburn
Ashhurst Public D/S (30 D9) – Ashhurst Domain, SH3, Ashhurst
Palmerston North Caltex Service Station (29 E7, 104 D4) – 161 Fitzherbert Ave (Cnr Fitzherbert & College St)
BP Connect Palmerston North (29 E7, 105 B3) – 339 Rangitikei Street, Palmerston North
Palmerston North Public D/S, Totara Rd Wastewater Plant (29 E4, 105 D2) – 69 Totara Rd, Awapuni, Palmerston North
Foxton Public D/S (29 E5) – Inside the entrance to Victoria Park off Victoria St
Levin Public D/S (29 G5) – Sheffield St, Levin
BP Connect Levin (29 G5) – 59 Oxford St, Levin
Marty's Panel & Paint (29 G5) – 23 Coventry St, Levin
Otaki Public D/S (29 J4) – Riverbank Rd, Otaki; Off SH1 just north of the Otaki River bridge

WAIRARAPA

Pongaroa Public D/S (30 G13) – Behind public toilets on SH52; limited van access
Woodville Public D/S (30 D10) – Rear of swimming pool area, Pollen St, Woodville
Greytown Public D/S (34 C7) – At Arbor Reserve, Greytown; Rest/picnic area on SH2 opposite Kuranui College
Martinborough Public D/S (34 E7) – West end of Dublin St, Martinborough, close to Motor Camp & swimming pool
Carterton Public D/S (34 C7) – Dalefield Rd, Carterton
Eketahuna Club D/S (30 H8) – 30 Herbert Street, Eketahuna
Dannevirke Caltex Westlow D/S (31 C6) – 166 High Street, Dannevirke (at the rear of the station)
Woodville & Community Centre (31 D4) – 64 Ross Street, Woodville
Pahiatua D/S (30 F10) – Tararua Club, 15 Tararua Street, Pahiatua (by Albert Street gate)

WELLINGTON

Upper Hutt Public D/S (33 D4, 111 B5) – On SH2 (River Rd), Upper Hutt; 500m north of Moonshine Bridge at Rest Area sign, beside toilets on gravel road by river
Tawa Public D/S (33 D2) – Tawa Swimming Pool, Davis St; D/S opposite pool entrance
Wellington Public D/S (33 F1, 110 D2) – Ngauranga Gorge, Hutt Rd, Wellington
Paraparaumu Public D/S (33 B4) – Mobil Service Station, corner SH1 and Kapiti Rd, Paraparaumu
Porirua Public D/S (33 D2) – Prosser St, Porirua
Lower Hutt Public D/S (33 E3, 110 D3) – Seaview Marina, Port Road, Lower Hutt

SOUTH ISLAND

MARLBOROUGH

Blenheim Public D/S (44 C10) – 33 Grove Road, Blenheim
Picton D/S (35 J3, 40 G10, 44 A11, 113 C3) – Challenge Service Station, 30 Wairau Rd (Corner Wairau Rd and Kent St), Picton
Picton Auto Services D/S (44 E11) – 4 Clifford St, Seddon

NELSON/TASMAN

Takaka Mobil Service Station (38 E8) – Cnr Commercial St & Motupipi Rd, Takaka
Takaka Fuels & Fishing (38 E8) – 2 Commercial St, Takaka
Takaka Public D/S (38 E8) – Golden Bay i-Site Visitor Centre in the car park, 8 Willow Street, Takaka
Motueka Public D/S (38 G10) – Follow sign from High St into Tudor St to Hickmott Pl
Richmond Public D/S (43 A4) – Jubilee Park, Gladstone Rd, Richmond
Nelson Public D/S (38 J12) – BP Truck Stop, Hay St, Port Nelson
Murchison Public D/S (42 G9) – On SH6 by entry to TNL Freight Yard, between Mobil Service Station and Matakitaki Bridge
Murchison Public D/S (42 G9) – Mobil Service Station, 41 Waller St, Murchison; on back fence past the truck diesel pump
Tahunanui Mobil D/S (38 J11) – 28 Tahunanui Drive, Tahunanui
Quinney's Bush D/S (42 C13) – SH6, Tapawera

WEST COAST

Greymouth Public D/S (45 F4) – Challenge S/S 119 Tainui St, Greymouth
New World Supermarket Greymouth (45 F4) – 128 High St, Greymouth
Hokitika Public D/S (45 H2) – SH6; north end of town, 1km from centre at 215 Kumara Junction Highway, adjacent to sewage ponds
Glacier Motors Mobil Service Station (49 G6) – Franz Josef, on SH6
Haast Public D/S (58 D9) – In front of public toilets on Marks Rd, Haast
Westport Public D/S (41 G3) – Countdown car park, 18 Fonblanque St, Westport. Enter via Russell St.
New World Supermarket - Westport Public D/S (41 G3) – New World car park, 244 Palmerston St, Westport
Nelson Creek Public D/S (45 E6) – Nelson Creek Domain, Nelson Creek
Blackball Public D/S (45 D5) – 144 Main Road, Blackball; adjacent to Sports Domain
Runanga Public D/S (45 E4) – Runanga Workingmen's Club, 15 Pitt St, Runanga
Ross Information and Heritage Centre (50 B11, 51 B2) – 4 Aylmer St, Ross
Greymouth Public D/S (45 F3) – New World car park, cnr High and Marlborough St
Greymouth Public D/S (45 F3) – Cobden Bridge rest area, north side of bridge
Charming Creek Tavern D/S (41 F4) – 31 Main Road, Waimangaroa

CHRISTCHURCH

Styx Mill Road Eco Dept Public D/S (53 H7, 56 D9, 120 E5) – 76 Styx Mill Rd, Casebrook, Christchurch
Canterbury A&P Association D/S (120 C2) – 71 Wigram Road, Wigram Park, Christchurch
A & P Showgrounds (53 J6) – Curletts Rd, Christchurch; between motorway corridor and Lincoln/Halswell Rd intersection
Lincoln Club (53 J6) – 24 Edward St, Lincoln
Templeton Public D/S (56 D8, 120 A2) – 784 Main South Road, Templeton
Rolleston BP Connect (56 E8) – Cnr Main South Rd & Tennyson St, Rolleston

CANTERBURY

Cheviot Public D/S (48 J9) – Centre of village, accessed from service lane (key at Mobil service station)
Waikari Public D/S (54 B8) – in domain, Princess St; signposted off SH7 at Waikari (Key held by Mary Booker, 20 Princes St or Roger Mander, 18 Princes St)
Oxford Public D/S (53 F4) – High St, Oxford; approximately 800m from the cnr of Oxford Rd & Main St
Amberley Public D/S (54 D8) – Mobil S/S Carters Rd, Amberley
Kaiapoi Public D/S (54 G8, 56 B10) – Charles St, Kaiapoi
Rangiora Public D/S (53 F7, 56 B9) – 22 Railway Rd, Rangiora
Kaikoura BP 2GO (48 E12) – 84 Beach Rd, north side of Kaikoura
Kaikoura Public D/S (48 E12) – South Bay Domain, Kaikoura
Washdyke Public D/S (61 J5) – Allied Truck Stop site, Sheffield St, Timaru
Fairlie Public D/S (60 F12, 61 F1) – Gladstone Grand Hotel, 43 Main St, Fairlie
Lake Tekapo Public D/S 1 (60 E9) – Alexander Terrace, Tekapo village; on roadside, 400m from village centre on SH8 towards Fairlie
Lake Tekapo Public D/S 2 (60 E9) – On road in Lakeside Drive, follow Motor Camp sign for 200m.
Rakaia Public D/S (55 G5) – Rolleston St, Rakaia; off SH1, beside public toilet
Rakaia Gorge Public D/S (55 D2) – SH72; at public toilet, north side of river
Methven Public D/S (55 F1) – Mobil Service Station Hall St, Methven
Methven Motor Services (55 F1) – 170 Main St, Methven
Twizel Public D/S (59 H6) – Turn off SH8 to town centre, adjacent to petrol station
Timaru Public D/S (61 J4) – Marine Parade, Caroline Bay
Lake Benmore (67 C5) – At Otematata Boat Harbour Campground, and at Wildlife Camping Ground
Oamaru Public D/S (68 H12) – SH1 on northern boundary of town, outside Waitaki Transport yard
Wanaka Public D/S (66 D8) – Brownston St, S of McDougall St

OTAGO

DK Auto Services (74 E12) – 175 Main Rd, Waikouaiti, at rear
Warrington Public D/S (74 F12) – Warrington Domain; off SH1 at Evansdale, follow signs to beach, at public toilet
Mosgiel Public D/S (74 H10) – BP 2GO, Alco Motors, 72 Gordon Rd, Mosgiel
Dunedin North (74 H11) – BP 2GO, 867 Cumberland St North, one way system, south near gardens
Dunedin Shell Service Station (74 H11) – Andersons Bay Rd, Dunedin
Z Service Station (74 H11, 124 E4) – 248 Kaikorai Valley Rd, Belleknowes, Dunedin
Ranfurly Public D/S (67 H5) – Reade St, Ranfurly
Dunedin Public D/S (74 H11, 123 H3) – BP Connect Southern, 50 Cumberland St, Dunedin Central

CENTRAL OTAGO

Arrowtown Public D/S (65 G6) – Behind the Lakes District Museum at the public toilets, Ramshaw Lane
Queenstown BP Connect Public D/S (65 H4, 126 A5) – Cnr SH6 & Frankton Rd, Frankton
Caltex Cromwell (66 H8) – 9 Murray Tce, Cromwell
Caltex Alexandra (72 A13) – 50 Centennial Ave, Alexandra
Roxburgh Council Depot (72 D13) – Teviot St, close to motorcamp
Lawrence Public D/S (79 A3) – SH8; on west side of town beside rest area
Clinton Public D/S (78 C13) – On the roadside adjacent to park, from SH1 turn at petrol station and War Memorial
Albion Cricket Club (66 D9) – SH6, Main Rd, Luggate
Omakau Public D/S (66 H12, 67 H1) – Omakau Recreation Reserve, 13 Alton St, Omakau
Cromwell Public D/S (66 H9) – BP 2GO, 2 Iles Street, Cromwell
Queenstown Public D/S (65 H5, 125 B2, 126 B2) – Cemetery Rd
Clyde (66 J10) – Clyde Recreation Reserve, 7 Whitby St

SOUTHLAND

Milford Sound Public D/S (64 D8) – In car park Milford Village
Knobs Flat Public D/S (64 H9) – SH 94, Te Anau, Council operated
Te Anau Public D/S (70 D11) – Lake Front Dr, Te Anau; at boat harbour, adjacent to public toilets
Manapouri Public D/S (70 E11) – 45 Hillside Rd, Manapouri
Otautau Public D/S (76 F14) – At public toilet, behind Plunket Rooms in Hulme St, just off Main St
Riverton BP Service Station (77 E2) – Bay Rd, towards Riverton Rocks
Riverton Race Course Public D/S (77 E2) – 2236 Riverton-Wallacetown Highway, Riverton
Invercargill Public D/S (77 E5, 128 C3) – Rockgas Invercargill, 20 Spey St, Invercargill
Glengarry Public Toilets & D/S (77 E5, 128 A3) – Yarrow Road, Glengarry, Invercargill
Challenge Service Station (72 J9) – 94 Newcastle St, Riversdale
Gore Public D/S (78 B9) – Gore A&P Showgrounds; down first entry
Gore Public D/S (78 B9) – Richmond Rd, Gore; at kerbside, 750m upstream from SH1 Bridge and Trout Monument
Winton Public D/S (77 B4) – Great North Road; behind Mobil Service Station, Winton

A

1849 Dansey Pass Hotel - Kyeburn Diggings 67 G6
Abbotsford 124 F5
Abbotslee Historic Home - Waipawa 28 J9
Abel Tasman Coastal Track - Great Walk 38 E10 39 C2
Abel Tasman Memorial 38 D9
Abel Tasman National Park 38 E9 39 C1
Acacia Bay 19 D5
Acheron Hut 43 J4 48 B8
Acheron Lakes 64 J10 70 A14 71 A3
Acland Falls 61 C5
Ada Pass Hut 46 D14 47 D2
Adair 61 J4 68 A13
Adams Flat 79 C4
Adams Wilderness Area 50 F9
Addington 53 H7 56 D9 119 G3 120 D2
Adelaide Tarn 37 F6
Adelaide Tarn Hut 37 F6
Adele Island 38 F10 39 D2
Agrodome - Rotorua 13 F4
Ahaura 45 D6
Ahikiwi 3 G6
Ahikouka 34 C7
Ahipara 1 J5 3 A1
Ahititi 17 F4
Ahuriri 103 B1
Ahuriri Base Hut 58 H13 59 H2
Ahuriri Conservation Park 58 H14 59 H3
Ahuriri Flat 79 G3
Ahuroa 6 F9
Aickens 45 J7
Aiguilles Island 36 B4
Airedale 68 G11
Airim Basin Hut 64 E14 65 E4
Aka Aka 7 J4 9 D1
Akaroa, NI 30 G13 31 G7
Akaroa, SI 56 G12
Akarua 111 D4
Akatere 2 G9
Akerama 4 D10
Akina 102 D2 103 C5
Akitio 32 G8
Albany Heights 6 J9 7 C3 88 F2
Albany Village 88 F2
Albert Town 66 D8
Albury 60 G13 61 G2
Aldermen Islands 10 A13
Alexandra 72 A13 73 A2
Alford Forest 51 J7
Alfred Track 23 D5
Alfredton 30 H10 31 H4
Alfriston 7 F6 9 A3 90 E6
Algies Bay 6 F10
Alicetown 110 C3
Allandale 60 F12 61 F1
Allanton 74 H9
Allendale 54 J8 56 F10
Allenton 55 H2 62 C8
Allports Island 35 J3 40 G10
Alma 68 H11
Almadale 30 B8 31 B2
Almer Hut 49 H6
Alpha Hut 33 B6
Alpine Lake / Ata Puai 49 F5
Alton 24 H8 25 E3
Amberley 54 D8
Amberley Beach 54 D9 56 A11
Amodeo Bay 8 B10 36 J4
Amuri Skifield 47 E4
Anakiwa 35 K3 40 G9
Anama 61 B6
Anatimo 38 D9 39 B1
Anatoki Forks Hut 37 F6
Anatoki Track 37 E6
Anawhata 7 E2
Anchor Island 69 H2 75 B2
Anchorage Hut 38 F10 39 D2
Anchorage Island 80 H2
Ancient Kauri Kingdom - Awanui 1 H6
Anderson Memorial Hut 33 A6
Andersons Bay 124 D4
Anderson's Hut 52 A13 53 A4
Andrews Track 52 B10 53 B1
Angelus Hut 42 H12
Aniwaniwa 21 E3
Annat 52 G11 53 G2 55 C4
Anne River Hut 47 D3
Annesbrook 116 B4
Ant Stream Hut 52 A12 53 A3
Anti Crow Hut 51 C7

Aokautere 30 D8 31 D2 105 C6
Aongatete 10 H12 12 A13 13 A2
Aoraki/Mt Cook 59 B6
Aoraki/Mt Cook National Park 49 J6 59 A7
Aorangi (East Cape, NI) 16 F10
Aorangi (Manawatu) 29 C7 31 C1
Aorangi Forest Park 33 G6
Aorere 37 C6
Aorere Historic Goldfields 37 C6
Aorere Hut 37 E5
Aoroa 4 J8 5 A3
Aotea 11 E2
Aotea – Wellington 110 B3
Aotuhia 24 D11 25 A6
Apanui 14 F13 15 F2
Aparima 76 E14 77 B2
Aparima Forks Hut 70 F13 71 F2 76 A13
Aparima Huts 70 G14 71 G3 76 A14
Apata 10 H12 12 A13 13 A2
Apiti 27 J3
Apiti Hut 14 J10
Aponga 4 F9
Appleby 128 C5
Aputerewa 2 H8
Arahiwi 12 F13 13 F2
Arahura 45 H2
Arakura 33 E3 35 A3
Aramiro 11 D4
Aramoana, NI 32 B12
Aramoana, SI 74 G13
Aramoho 26 H8 109 A5
Aranga 3 G5
Aranga Beach 3 G5
Aranui 54 H8 56 D10 120 G3
Arapae 18 A9
Arapaoa 5 C5
Araparera 6 F8 7 A2
Arapawa Island 35 G2 40 F12
Arapito 37 J2 41 A7
Arapohue 4 J8 5 A3
Arapuni 12 F10
Ararata 23 G7 25 D2
Ararimu 7 H7 9 C4
Ararua 5 A5
Arataki 19 B3
Aratapu 5 A3
Aratiatia 19 C6
Aratika 45 G6
Aratoro 18 B10
Arawhata 57 F6
Arch Hill 87 H1 90 C4
Archway Islands 37 A7
Ardgour 66 F10
Ardgowan 68 H11
Ardkeen 21 G3
Ardlussa 72 G8
Ardmore 7 F6 9 A3
Ardmore Airport 7 F6 9 A3
Arero 16 J11
Arete Forks Hut 29 J6
Argyll East 28 H9
Aria 18 B8
Ariki 42 G8
Army Bay 88 B6
Arno 68 D12
Aroha Island 2 K13 4 A9
Arohena 12 G9
Around the Mount Circuit 23 E4
Arowhenua 61 H5
Arowhenua Pa 61 H5
Arrow Junction 65 G6
Arrowtown 65 G6
Arthur's Pass 52 B8
Arthur's Pass National Park 52 A10 53 A1
Arthurs Point 65 G4
Arthurstown 45 J2
Arthurton 78 B11
Arundel 61 D5
Asbestos Cottage 37 H7
Ashburton 55 H2 62 C8
Ashcott 27 J7
Ashers 77 F7
Ashhurst 30 D9 31 D3
Ashley 53 E7 56 A9
Ashley Clinton 27 J6 30 A13 31 A7
Ashley Downs 78 B13 79 D1
Ashley Gorge 52 E13 53 E4 55 A6
Ashton 62 E9
Ashton Hut 71 C4
Ashwick Flat 60 E12 61 E1
Aspiring Hut 64 B14 65 B4
Ataahua 56 G10

Atapo 42 E13
Atarau 45 D6
Atau Paparua 40 C9
Atawhai 38 J12 39 G4
Atea 29 G7 31 G1
Atene 24 J14 26 F9
Athenree 10 F12
Athenree Hot Springs 10 F12
Athol 71 D7
Atiamuri 19 A5
Atiwhakatu Hut 34 A7
Auckland 7 D4
Auckland City 87 D5
Auckland International Airport 7 F4 9 A1 90 E4
Auckland Zoo 7 D4
Aukopae 18 F9 24 A14
Aurere 2 G7
Auripo 66 H13 67 H2
Auroa 23 F4
Ava 110 C3
Avalon 33 E3 35 A3 111 C4
Avenal 127 A2 128 C3
Avenues 93 B1
Aviemore 67 C6
Avoca Hut 51 C7
Avoca, NI 4 H8
Avoca, SI 52 D10 53 D1
Avondale (Auckland) 89 C3
Avondale (Christchurch) 120 G4
Avondale (Southland) 71 H4
Avonhead 53 H7 56 D9 120 C3
Avonside 54 H8 56 D10 120 F3
Awahou 13 F4
Awahou North 30 B9 31 B3
Awahou South 30 C9 31 C3
Awahuri 29 C7 31 C1
Awaiti 10 E9
Awakaponga 14 E9
Awakeri 14 F10
Awakeri Hot Springs 14 F9
Awakeri Springs 14 F9
Awakino 17 C5
Awakino Point 4 J8
Awakino Ski Huts 67 E6
Awakino Skifield 67 E6
Awamangu 79 C3
Awamarino 11 H2
Awamoko 68 F11
Awanui (Bay of Plenty) 15 D6
Awanui (Northland) 1 H6
Awapoto Hut 38 E9 39 C1
Awapuni (Gisborne) 100 B2
Awapuni (Manawatu) 29 E7 31 E1
Awapuni (Palmerston North) 105 D2
Awariki 30 C13 31 C7
Awaroa 3 B2
Awaroa Creek 85 C3
Awaroa Hut 38 E10 39 C2
Awarua, NI 3 E7
Awarua, SI 77 F5
Awatane 11 G7
Awatea 78 D14 79 F2
Awatere 16 C12
Awatere Hut 27 J5
Awatoitoi 34 B11
Awatoto 28 E12 103 A3
Awatuna, NI 23 F5
Awatuna, SI 45 H3
Awhitu 7 G3
Awhitu Central 7 G3
Aylesbury 52 H14 53 H5 55 D7

B

Back Ridge Hut 27 B7
Back River 2 H8
Back Valley Hut 70 F10
Bainesse 29 E6
Bainham 37 D6
Balaclava 124 E4
Balcairn 54 E8 56 A10
Balclutha 79 E3
Balfour 71 H7
Ballance 30 E9 31 E3
Ballarat Hut 64 E14 65 E4
Ballard Hut 28 A8
Balloon Hut 37 H6
Balmoral 90 C4
Balmoral Hill 120 H1
Balmoral Huts 68 G8
Balmoral, SI 47 J4 54 A8
Bankside 55 F5 62 A11

Bannockburn 66 H8
Bare Island / Motu o Kura 28 H13
Bark Bay Hut 38 E10 39 C2
Barker Hut 51 B6
Barkes Corner 94 B1
Barlow Hut 27 F6
Barnego 79 E3
Barra Track 34 A7
Barrhill 55 F3 62 A9
Barron Saddle Hut 59 B5
Barrys Bay 56 G12
Barrytown 45 C5
Barryville 18 B13 19 B1
Bartletts 22 F9
Basins Hut 51 D7
Bastia Hill 108 B6 109 C5
Batley 5 C6
Battersea 33 D7
Bauza Island 69 C5
Bay of Islands Airport 4 A8
Bay View (Auckland) 88 H3
Bay View (Hawkes Bay) 28 C12
Baylys Beach 3 J6
Bayswater 90 B4
Bayswater, SI 77 B2
Beach Haven 88 J2
Beachlands 7 E6
Beachville 115 A1 116 A4
Beaconsfield 30 B8 31 B2
Bealey Hut 52 C8
Bealey Spur 52 C8
Bealey Spur Hut 52 C8
Beaumont 73 G4
Beautiful Valley 60 F14 61 F3
Beckenham 120 E1
Becketts Hut 70 F14 71 F3
Becks 66 G13 67 G2
Beebys Hut 42 F14 43 E2
Beerescourt 92 E3
Belfast 54 G8 56 C10 120 E6
Belfield 61 F5
Belgrove 39 J1 42 C14 43 B2
Bell Block 23 A5
Bell Hill 45 G7
Bell Island 38 J11 39 G3 43 A4
Belleknowes 124 E4
Bells Junction 26 D12
Bellvue 94 B1
Belmont (Auckland) 90 B4
Belmont (Wellington) 33 D3 35 A2 110 C3
Bench Island 80 E6
Bendigo 66 F10
Benhar 79 E4
Benio 78 A10
Benmore 71 J5 77 A4
Benmore Hut 52 G9 55 C2
Bennetts 52 F14 53 F5 55 B7
Bennetts Siding 27 F2
Benneydale 18 B11
Berhampore 110 E2
Berlins 41 H5
Berwick 74 J8 79 B6
Bethlehem 10 J13 12 B14 13 B3 94 C1
Bexley 52 F12 53 F3 55 B5 120 G3
Bideford 34 A11
Big Bay 7 F3
Big Bay Hut 57 J2
Big Hellfire Hut 80 D2
Big Island 80 H1
Big Lagoon 35 H6 44 C12
Big Manly 88 C5
Big Omaha 6 D10
Big River 46 C9
Big River Hut 46 C9
Billy Goat Track 8 G12 10 B10
Binser Saddle Track 52 C10 53 C1
Birch Hill 59 C6
Birchfield 41 F4
Birchville 33 C4
Birchwood 70 J13 71 J2 76 C13
Bird Island 77 J6
Birdlings Flat 56 H10
Birkdale 88 J2
Birkenhead 7 D4 6 J10 89 B3
Bishop and Clerks Islands 77 H1 80 B3
Bishopdale (Christchurch) 120 D4
Bishopdale (Nelson) 116 B4
Black Gully 72 H13 73 H2
Black Hill Hut 52 D11 53 D2 55 A4
Black Reef 41 F2
Black Rock 80 H4
Blackball 45 D5
Blackburn 27 H7

Blackhead, NI 32 C12
Blackhead, SI 74 H11 124 F5
Blackmans 72 A12 73 A1
Blackmount 70 H11 76 B11
Blacks Point 46 B9
Blackstone Hill 66 G13 67 G2
Blackwater 46 C8
Blackwater Lake 52 D11 53 D2
Blackwater River Ecological Area 41 H4
Blairlogie 34 B12
Blaketown 118 A2
Blandswood 61 D4
Blenheim 35 J6 44 C11 117 C4
Blind River 44 E12
Blockhouse Bay 7 E4 89 D3
Blowhard Track 52 D13 53 D4
Blue Cliffs 68 A11
Blue Lake Hut 47 A4
Blue Lake, NI 18 J14 19 J2
Blue Lake, SI 72 D10
Blue Lakes Walk 59 A7
Blue Range Hut 29 J7 31 J1
Blue River (Blowfly) Hut 58 C11
Blue Spur 45 H2
The Bluff/Motupohue 77 H5
Bluff Damp Hut 48 C10
Bluff Hill 103 A1
Bluff Hut 50 C13 51 C4
Blumine Island 35 G2 40 F12
Blyth Hut 26 B12
Blyth Track 26 B12
Blythe Valley 54 B12
Boat Group 80 H1
Bobs Hut 46 C14 47 C2
Boddytown 45 F4
Bog Inn Hut 18 C13 19 C1
Bog Lake 70 A12 71 A1
Bombay 7 H6 9 C3
Bonny Glen 29 A5
Bortons 68 F10
Botany Downs 90 D6
Bouldcott 111 C4
Boulder Lake 37 E6
Boundary Stream Track 20 J12
Bowen Falls 64 D8
Bowentown 10 F12
Bowlers Creek 73 H4 79 A2
Bowscale Tarn 47 B6
Boyd Hut 19 J6
Boydtown 125 A2 126 A2
Boyle Flat Hut 46 E14 47 E2
Boyle Village 46 F13 47 F1
Bradford 124 E4
Braeburn 38 H9 39 F1
Braigh 5 A7
Brames Falls Track 23 E4
Branch Creek Hut 42 D10
Branxholme 77 D4
Breaker Bay 110 E2
Breaksea Island 69 F3
Breaksea Islands (North Stewart Is) 77 J7
Breaksea Islands (South Stewart Is) 80 G6
Bream Islands 4 H14
Brewster Hut 58 F12 59 F1
Bridal Veil Falls, NI - Raglan 11 D3
Bridal Veil Falls, SI 65 F4
Bridge Hill 72 A13 73 A2
Bridge Pa 28 F11
Bridgend 120 F6
Brighton 74 J10 124 J6
Brightwater 39 H2 43 A3
Brixton 17 G1 23 A6
Broad Bay 74 G12
Broad Gully 68 E12
Broadfield 53 J6 56 E8
Broadlands 20 B8
Broadmeadows 110 D2
Broadway Park 90 C4
Broadwood 3 A3
Brockville 124 F3
Brodrick Hut 59 E3
Broken Hills 8 G13 10 B10
Broken Islands 36 E3
Broken River Hut 52 E10 53 E1 55 A3
Broken River Skifield 52 D9
Bromley 120 G2
Bronte 38 J10 39 G2
Brookby 7 F6 9 A3
Brookfield 94 B1
Brooklands (New Plymouth) 106 D4 107 C4
Brooklands Lagoon 54 G8 56 C10
Brooklands, SI (Christchurch) 54 G8 56 C10
Brooklands, SI (Nelson) 38 J12 39 G4 116 A6

Brooklyn 110 E1
Brooklyn, SI 38 G9 39 E1
Brookside 55 F7 62 A13
Broomfield 54 D8 120 B3
Brown Hut 37 E5
Brown Owl 33 D4 111 A4
Browne Island 57 G3
Browns 77 B5
Browns Bay 6 J10 7 C4
Browns Beach 61 G6
Browns Island 7 D5
Bruce Bay 58 A13 59 A2
Brunner 45 E5
Brunswick 26 H8
Bruntwood 12 C8
Bryant Park 92 D3
Brydone 78 C8
Brynavon 4 F13
Brynderwyn 5 B7
Brynderwyn Hills Walkway 6 B8
Bryndwr 53 H7 56 D9 120 D4
Buccleuch 61 A6
Buckland (Auckland) 7 J6 9 D3
Buckland (Waikato) 12 D10
Buckland Peaks Hut 41 H3
Bucklands Beach 7 D6 90 C6
Bucklands Crossing 74 E12
Buckleton Beach 6 E10
Bull Creek Hut 52 A11 53 A2
Bull Flat Hut 58 G13 59 G2
Bulls 29 B6
Bulwer 40 D9
Bungaree Hut 80 D5
Bungtown 73 H6 79 A4
Bunker Islets 80 D6
Bunnythorpe 30 D8 31 D2
Burgess Island 36 A2
Burgess Park 107 D5
Buried Village - Rotorua 13 H5
Burkes 124 C2
Burkes Pass 60 F11
Burn Creek Hut 46 B14 47 B2
Burn Hut 29 G7 31 G1
Burnbrae 46 A12
Burnetts Face 41 G5
Burnham 52 J14 53 J5 55 E7
Burnside (Christchurch) 53 H7 56 D9 120 C4
Burnside (Dunedin) 124 F5
Burnt Bush Hut 66 B11
Burswood 90 D6
Burwood 54 H8 56 D10 120 G4
Bush Hut 58 J12 59 J1 66 A10
Bush Siding 77 F7
Bushey 74 C13
Bushline Hut 42 H13 43 G1
Bushline Hut (Sylvester) 37 G6
Bushside 51 J7 61 A6
Butchers Dam 72 B13 73 B2
Butchers Gully 72 B13 73 B2
Butler Junction Hut 50 G8

C

Caberfeidh 78 F13 79 H1
Cabin Hut 65 D5
Cable Bay 2 H8
Cable Bay Walkway 38 H13 39 F5
Cairnbrae 55 F2 62 A8
Caldervale 37 H2
Callaghans 45 H3
Camberley 103 C5
Camborne 33 C2
Cambrians 66 F13 67 F2
Cambridge 12 D8
Cameron Hut (Lake Sumner) 46 H10
Cameron Hut (Ruahine FP) 27 C7
Cameron Hut (Westland) 50 G12 51 G3
Camerons 45 G3
Camp Valley 60 G12 61 G1
Campbells Bay 88 G4
Candlesticks Bivvy 52 A12
Cannibal Gorge Hut 46 D14 47 D2
Cannington 60 J13 61 J2
Cannons Creek 110 B3
Canvastown 39 G7 44 A8
Cape Brett Track 4 A12
Cape Foulwind 41 G2
Cape Palliser Lighthouse 33 J6
Cape Reinga 1 A1
Cape Reinga Lighthouse 1 A1
Caples Track 64 F11 65 F1
Capleston 46 A10

Captains Creek Hut 39 H5 43 A6
Cardiff 23 E6 25 B1
Cardrona 65 F7
Cardrona Cromwell Pack Track 66 G8
Cardrona Hotel 65 F7
Cardrona Roaring Meg Pack Track 65 G7
Cardrona Skifield 65 F6
Carew 61 D5
Careys Bay 74 G12 124 A1
Carkeek Hut 29 J6
Carleton 52 F14 53 F5 55 B7
Carlton 34 B8
Carluke 39 G7
Carlyle Hut 47 F2
Carnarvon 29 D6
Caroline 71 H6
Caroline Creek Hut 47 B4
Caroline Hut 70 J8 76 D8
Carricktown 66 J8
Carrington 34 B8
Carrington Estate Golf Course 2 F7
Carrington Hut 51 B7
Carroll Hut 45 J7
Carswell 34 B11
Carters Beach 41 G3
Carterton 34 C8
Cascade Creek 64 G10
Cascade Hut (Kaimanawa FP) 19 H5
Cascade Hut (Mt Aspiring NP) 64 B14 65 B4
Cascade Saddle Route 65 B4
Cascade Track 42 H13
Casebrook 53 H7 56 D9 120 D5
Casey Hut 52 A10 53 A1
Cashmere (Christchurch) 120 E1
Cashmere (Wellington) 110 D2
Cashmere, SI 54 J8 56 E10
Casnell Island 6 F10
Cass 52 C9
Cass Bay 54 J8 56 E10
Cass Saddle Hut 52 D9
Cassel Flat Hut 59 A4
Castle Hill Village 52 E9 55 A2
Castle Rock Hut 38 F9 39 D1
Castle Rocks Hut 49 H6
Castlecliff 25 J7 109 C1
Castlehill 30 J10 31 J4
Castlepoint 34 B13
Castlerock 71 G6
Castor Bay 6 J10 7 C4 88 H5
Cathedral Caves 78 G13 79 J1
Cathedral Cliffs - Gore Bay 54 A13
Cathedral Cove - Haihei 8 D13
Catlins Forest Park 78 E12
Catlins Lake 79 H3
Catlins River Walk 78 E13 79 G1
Cattle Creek 68 A9
Cattle Creek Hut 30 A12 31 A6
Cattle Flat 71 F7
Cattle Ridge Hut 29 J7
Cattle Valley 60 E13 61 E2
Cavalli Islands 2 H12
Cave 60 H13 61 H2
Cavendish 61 B6
Caverhill 48 J9
Caversham 124 E4
Cayenne Hut 68 J8
Cecil Kings Hut 42 C10
Cedar Flat Hut 50 B13 51 B4
Centennial Hut 49 H6
Central Te Hoe Hut 20 F11
Central Waiau Hut 20 E12
Central Whirinaki Hut 20 E10
Centre Bush 77 A4
Centre Island 70 B11
Chain Hills 124 H4
Chalky Island 75 E2
Challis 124 C4
Chamberlain 60 G12
Chancellor Hut 49 H5
Chancet Rocks 44 G12
Chaneys 54 G8 56 C10 120 F6
Chapel Downs 90 E6
Charing Cross 52 H13 53 H4 55 D6
Charleston 41 H2
Charlestown 65 F4
Charlton 78 B9
Charming Creek Walkway 41 E6
Charteris Bay 54 J8 56 F10
Chartwell (Hamilton) 92 D3
Chartwell (Wellington) 110 D1
Chaslands 78 G12
Chasm Creek Walkway 41 D7
Chatswood 88 J3
Chatto Creek 66 J11

Chatton 72 J10 78 A9
Chatton North 72 J10
Cheddar Valley 14 F12
Chedworth Park 92 D4
Cheltenham (Auckland) 90 B4
Cheltenham (Manawatu) 30 B8 31 B2
Chertsey 55 G4 62 B10
Chesterfield 45 G3
Chetwode Islands 40 C10
Cheviot 48 J9 54 A13
Cheviot Museum 48 J9 54 A13
Chorlton 56 F13
Christchurch 54 H8 56 D10
Christchurch City 119 C5 120 E4
Christchurch International Airport 53 H7 56 D9
Christmas Village Hut 77 J2 80 C4
Christopher Hut 47 D3
Chrystalls Beach 79 D6
Chummies Track 42 C11
Churchill 9 F4
Churton Park 110 C2
Clandeboye 61 G6
Claremont 61 J3
Clarence 48 B14
Clarendon 79 C6
Clareville 34 C8
Claris 36 E5
Clark Hut 70 H8 76 B8
Clarks Beach 7 G4 9 B1
Clarks Junction 74 F8
Clarksville 79 D5
Clarkville 53 G7 56 C9
Claudelands 91 B6 92 E4
Claverley 48 G10
Clay Cliffs 66 A14 67 A3
Clendon House - Rawene 3 C4
Clevedon 7 F7 9 A4
Clifden 76 D12
Clifton (Christchurch) 120 H1
Clifton (Hawkes Bay) 28 F13
Clifton, SI (Clutha) 78 B14 79 D2
Clifton, SI (Invercargill) 77 F5 128 B6
Clifton, SI (Tasman) 38 D8
Clinton 78 C12
Clinton Forks Hut 64 G8
Clive 28 E12 103 A4
Cloustonville 33 B4
Clover Park 90 E6
Cloverlea 29 D7 31 D1 105 B2
Clyde 66 J10 72 A13 73 A2
Clydesdale 29 C5
Clydevale 78 A14 79 C2
Coal Creek Flat 72 D13 73 D2
Coal Island 75 F3
Coalgate 52 H11 53 H2 55 D4
Coatesville 6 J9 7 C3 88 F1
Cobb Hut 37 G6
Cobb Reservoir 37 H7
Cobb Track 37 G6
Cobden 45 E4
Codfish Is (Whenua Hou) Nature Res 80 D1
Codfish Island (Whenuahou) 80 D1
Colac Bay/Oraka (township) 76 H13 77 E1
Cold Stream Hut 46 J13 47 J1
Coldstream (Ashburton) 61 F7
Coldstream (Waimakariri) 53 F7 56 B9
Coldwater Hut 42 H13 43 G1
Colenso Hut 27 F5
Colin Todd Hut 57 J6 64 A14 65 A4
Colliers Junction 26 E13
Collingwood 37 C7
Collinswood 124 B4
Colonial Knob Walkway 33 D2 35 B2
Colville 8 B11 36 J5
Colyton 30 C8 31 C2
Comet Hut 27 D7
Company Bay 124 B3
Concord 124 F5
Cone Hut 33 B6
Conical Hill 78 A11
Conroys Gully 72 A13 73 A2
Conway Flat 48 G10
Cooks Beach 8 D13
Coombe Rocks 35 H4 40 H11 44 A12
Coonoor 30 E12 31 E6
Cooper Island 69 H5 75 B5
Coopers Beach 2 H8
Coopers Creek (Timaru) 61 E5
Coopers Creek (Waimakariri) 52 F12
53 F3 55 B5
Cooptown 56 G11
Copland Shelter 59 A6
Copland Track 49 J3 59 A4

Corbyvale 41 D7
Cormacks 68 H11
Cornwallis (Te Karanga-a-Hape) 7 F3 89 E2
Coroglen 8 E13
Coromandel 8 C11
Coromandel Forest Park 8 A10 36 H4 10 D10
Coromandel Walkway 8 A10 36 G4
Coronet Peak Skifield 65 G5
Corriedale 68 G10
Corstorphine 124 E5
Cosgrove Island 79 H3
Cosseys - Wairoa Track 7 G7 9 B4
Cosseys Reservoir 7 G7 9 B4
Cotters Hut 58 J13 59 J2
County Stream Hut 50 D11 51 D2
Courtenay 52 H13 53 H4 55 D6
Coutts Island 120 E6
Cove, The 74 H11 124 C4
Cow Creek Hut 29 J6
Cowes 8 D8
Cowins Track 37 J6 42 B11
Cracroft 120 D1
Craigellachie 73 H4 79 A2
Craigieburn (Buller) 45 D7
Craigieburn (Selwyn) 52 D10 53 D1
Craigieburn Conservation Park 52 C8
Craigieburn Skifield 52 D9
Crail Bay 35 J2 40 F10
Crater Lake 26 A13
Crawford Junction Huts 50 B14 51 B5
Crawfords 70 J14 71 J3 76 C14
Crichton 79 D4
Cricklewood 60 G12 61 G1
Crippletown 66 G9
Croesus Track 45 C5
Crofton 29 A6
Crofton Downs 110 D1
Cromel Base Hut 71 E5
Cromel Branch Hut 71 D5
Cromwell 66 H9
Cronadun 46 A9
Crookston 72 H13 73 H2
Crossans Corner 72 H12
Crow Hut (Arthur's Pass NP) 51 B7
Crow Hut (Kahurangi NP) 37 J5 42 A10
Crow Hut (Ruahine FP) 27 G5
Crown Hill 88 H4
Croydon 78 A9
Crucible Lake 58 G9
Crumb Hut 67 H7
Crushington 46 B9
Cullers Hut 59 D4
Culverden 47 J5
Cumbria Downs 90 D6
Cupola Hut 42 J12
Curio Bay 78 H11
Curtis Memorial Hut 50 H10 51 H1
Cust 53 F5 55 B7
Cuthill 6 J10 7 C4 88 G3

D

Dacre 77 D7
Dairy Flat 6 H9 7 B3 88 D1
Dairy Flat Airport 6 H9 7 B3
Dale, The 70 C13 71 C2
Dalefield 34 C7
Daleys Flat Hut 64 C12 65 C2
Dallington 120 F3
Dalmore 124 D3
Dannemora 90 D6
Dannevirke 30 C12 31 C6
Danseys Pass 68 G8
Daphne Hut 27 J5
Darfield 52 H12 53 H3 55 D5
Dargaville 4 J8
Dart Hut 64 B13 65 B3
Dashwood 44 D11
Davies Track 23 C4
Dawson Falls 23 E5
Days Bay 33 E2 35 B3 110 D3
Dead Dog Hut 27 E7
Deanwell 92 G3
Deas Cove Hut 69 A5
Deborah 68 H11
Deborah Bay 74 G12 124 A1
Deep Creek 68 C12
Demon Trail 64 B9
Demon Trail Hut 64 B9
Denniston 41 F5
Denniston Walkway 41 F4
Devonport 7 D5 90 B4

De La Beche Hut 49 J6
Diamond Harbour 54 J8 56 E10
Diamond Lake 64 E12 65 E2
Dianes Hut 27 E7
Dickie Spur Hut 50 C11 51 C2
Diggers Hut 30 B11 31 B5
Diggers Valley 1 K6 3 A2
Dillmanstown 45 H4
Dinsdale 92 F2
Dip Flat 42 H14 43 G2
Dipton 71 J6
Dipton West 71 J5
Dobson 45 E5
Dodger Hut 59 D4
Dodson Valley 38 J12 39 G4
Dog Island 77 H5
Dome Islands 70 C11
Dome Valley 6 E9
Dome Valley Forest Track 6 E9
Domett 54 A12
Donnellys Crossing 3 F5
Donoghues 50 A10 51 A1
Dora Track 29 J6
Dorie 55 H5 62 C11
Dorothy Falls 50 A14 51 A5
Dorset Ridge Hut 29 J6 33 A7
Doubtful Hut 46 F13
Doubtful Island 70 A11
Doubtful Sound 69 B4
Doubtless Hut 46 F12
Douglas Corner 13 D4
Douglas Rock Hut 59 A5
Douglas, NI 24 D8 25 A3
Douglas, SI 68 D11
Douglasvale 65 G5
Dovedale 38 J9 42 A14 43 A2
Dover Track 23 D4
Downes Hut 24 J14 26 F9
Downie Hut 47 B3
Doyleston 55 G7 62 B13
Dreyers Rock 30 J9 31 J3
Dromore 55 H3 62 C9
Drummond 77 B3
Drury 7 G6 9 B3
Drybread 66 G12 67 G1
Duckville Hut 14 J9 20 A12
Dumbarton 72 E13 73 E2
Dumpling Hut 63 E7
Dun Mountain Walkway 39 H4 43 A5
Dunback 74 B12
Dundas Hut 29 H6
Dunearn 77 A3
Dunedin 74 H11 124 D4
Dunedin Airport 74 H9 79 A7
Dunedin Central 123 F3
Dunganville 45 G5
Dunmore 9 H3 11 A4
Dunns Creek Hut 51 A7
Dunollie 45 E4
Dunolly 30 A8 31 A2
Dunrobin 72 G13 73 G2
Dunsandel 55 F6 62 A12
Duntroon 68 E9
Durie Hill 108 C6 109 C5
D'Urville Hut 42 H12
D'Urville Island / Rangitoto ki te Tonga 40 B8
D'Urville Track 42 J11 47 A3
Dusky Forest 72 H12
Dusky Sound 69 H1 75 B1
Dusky Track 69 F7
Duvauchelle 56 G12
Dyerville 33 E7

E

Eade Memorial Hut 50 H8
Ealing 61 E6
Earl Mountain Tracks 64 G9
Earnscleugh 72 A13 73 A2
Earnslaw Hut 64 C12 65 C2
Earthquake Flat 13 H5
Earthquake Lakes 37 H5 42 A10
Earthquakes 68 F9
East Cape Lighthouse 16 C13
East Chatton 72 J10 78 A9
East Egmont 23 D5
East End 107 B4
East Gore 78 B9
East Hawdon Bivvy 52 A10
East Island / Whangaokeno Island 16 C14
East Matakitaki Hut 47 B3
East Ruggedy Hut 80 C2

East Taieri 74 H10 124 H5
East Takaka 38 E8
East Tamaki 7 E5 90 D6
East Tamaki Industrial 90 D6
Eastbourne 33 F2 35 B4 110 E3
Eastern Beach 90 C6
Eastern Bush 76 D12
Echo Cliffs - Turangi 19 G3
Echolands 18 F11
Eden Terrace 87 J3 90 C4
Edendale 78 D8
Edgecumbe 14 E9
Edievale 72 G13 73 G2
Edwards Hut 52 B8
Edwards Island (Motunui) 80 D6
Egmont National Park 23 D5
Egmont Village 23 C5
Eiffelton 62 E8
Eight Mile Hut 65 F6
Eight Mile Junction 18 A9
Eketahuna 30 H8 31 H2
Elaine Bay 40 E8
Elcho Hut 59 D4
Elderslie 68 B10
Elephant Hill 68 E10
Elgin (Canterbury) 55 J3 62 D9
Elgin (Gisborne) 100 B2
Elizabeth Hut 46 H9
Ella Hut 47 A3
Ellerslie 90 C5
Ellesmere 55 F7 62 A13
Elletts Beach 7 G5 9 B2
Ellis Hut (Kahurangi NP) 37 J7 42 A12
Ellis Hut (Ruahine FP) 27 F7
Elsdon 110 B2
Elsthorpe 28 J11
Elstow 10 G9
Eltham 23 F7 25 C2
Empress Hut 49 J5 59 A6
Endeavour Inlet 35 H1 40 E11
Enderley 92 E4
Enfield 68 G11
Engineers Camp 46 G13 47 G1
Enner Glynn 38 J12 39 H4 43 A5
Enner Island 63 J1 69 A5
Entry Island 69 H2 75 B2
Epsom 90 C4
Epuni 33 E3 35 A3 111 C4
Epworth 61 G5
Erceg Hut 59 C5
Ermedale 76 G14 77 D2
Ernest Island 80 J2
Ernest Islands 80 F2
Erua 26 A11
Esk Valley 68 B12
Eskdale 28 C11
Ettrick 72 E13 73 E2
Eureka 9 J7 12 B8
Evans Hut 50 E13 51 E4
Evansdale 74 F12
Eversley 60 F12 61 F1
Explorer Hut 50 C12 51 C3
Eyre Mountains/Taka Ra Haka
Conservation Park 71 C5
Eyreton 53 G7 56 C9

F

Fairburn 2 J7
Fairdown 41 F4
Fairfax 77 C2
Fairfield (Dunedin) 74 H10 124 G4
Fairfield (Hamilton) 92 E3
Fairfield (Wellington) 111 C4
Fairhall 35 K6 44 C10
Fairlie 60 F12 61 F1
Fairlight 72 C8
Fairton 55 H3 62 C9
Fairview 61 J4
Fairview Downs 92 D4
Falls Dam 66 F14 67 F3
Fanal Island 36 A2
Farewell Spit Nature Reserve 38 A9
Farm Cove 90 C5
Farnham 117 A1
Favona 90 D4
Featherston 33 D6
Featherston Heritage Museum 33 D6
Feilding 29 C7 31 C1
Feldwick 76 D12
Fencourt 12 D8
Fendalton 120 D3

Fenella Hut 37 G6
Fenton Park 95 B6 96 D3
Ferguson Hut 58 F13 59 F2
Fergusons 50 B10 51 B1
Fern Flat, NI (Northland) 2 J8
Fern Flat, NI (Wanganui) 29 A6
Fern Flat, SI 42 G8
Ferndale (New Plymouth) 107 D3
Ferndale (Southland) 78 C9
Fernhill, NI 28 E11 103 B4
Fernhill, SI 64 H14 65 H4 126 C1
Ferniehurst 48 G9
Fernland Spa Mineral Pools - Tauranga 10 J13
12 B14 13 B3
Fernside, NI 33 C6
Fernside, SI 53 F7 56 B9
Ferntown 37 B7
Ferry landing 8 D13
Ferrymead 120 G1
Field Hut 33 A6
Fields Track 33 B6
Fife Rock 77 J5
Finegand 79 E3
Finlay Face Hut 50 H10 51 H1
Fiordland National Park 69 A7
Fisherman Island 38 F10 39 D2
Fitzroy (Hamilton) 92 G4
Fitzroy (New Plymouth) 23 A5 107 B5
Five Bridges, The 22 A12
Five Forks 68 G10
Five Mile Lagoon 49 F5
Five Rivers 71 F6
Five Roads 77 B4
Flag Swamp 74 D12
Flagstaff 92 C3
Flanagans Hut 37 J6 42 A11
Flat Bush 90 E6
Flat Island 2 G11
Flaxmere 28 F11 103 D5
Flaxton 53 F7 56 B9
Flemington, NI 32 B9
Flemington, SI 62 E8
Flora Hut 37 H7
Forbes Hut 58 F13 59 F2
Fordell 26 J9
Fordlands 96 C2
Forest Lake 91 B1 92 E2
Forks Hut 30 B11 31 B5
Forks, The 49 F6
Forsyth 73 J5 79 B3
Forsyth Island / Te Paruparu 40 D10
Fortification 78 F10
Fortrose 78 G8
Four Peaks 61 E3
Four Rivers Plain 42 G9
Fox Glacier 49 H4
Foxhill 39 J1 43 B2
Foxton 29 F5
Foxton Beach 29 E4
Frankleigh Park 107 D3
Frankton (Hamilton) 92 F3
Frankton (Queenstown) 65 H5 126 A5
Franz Josef Glacier 49 G6
Fraser Dam 66 J9 72 A12 73 A1
Frasertown 21 H5
Freds Camp Hut 80 E4
Freemans Bay 87 F2 90 C4
French Bay 89 D2
French Farm 56 G12
French Pass, SI 40 C9
French Pass, NI 12 D9
French Ridge Hut 64 A14 65 A4
Frenchmans Swamp 4 B10
Freshford 72 G9
Frews Hut 50 C13 51 C4
Frimley 103 C5
Frisco Hut 50 C13 51 C4
Fruitlands 72 B13 73 B2
Fuchsia Creek 68 H9

G

Gable Islet 22 C13
Gabriel Hut 46 H13
Gabriels Gully 73 H5 79 A3
Gair Loch 69 F7
Galatea 20 A11
Galloway 66 J11 72 A14 73 A3
Gammans Creek 52 F13 53 F4 55 B6
Gap Road 77 C4
Gapes Valley 61 F4
Gardens, The 90 E6

Gardiner Hut 59 A6
Garston 72 D8
Gate Pa 10 J13 94 C2 13 B3
Gebbies Valley 56 F9
George Lyon Hut 47 A3
George Sound Track 63 H5
Georgetown (Invercargill) 128 B4
Georgetown (Oamaru) 68 F10
Geraldine 61 F4
Geraldine Downs 61 F4
Geraldine Flat 61 F5
Gibbs Track 42 C11
Gibbston 65 H7
Gibbstown 37 C7
Gilbert Islands 69 F3
Gillespies Beach 49 H3
Gillows Dam 41 G3
Gimmerburn 67 J4
Gisborne 22 D10 99 B4 100 B3
Gisborne Point 13 F6
Gladfield 77 B3
Gladstone, NI (Manawatu) 29 H5
Gladstone, NI (Wellington) 34 C9
Gladstone, SI (Grey) 45 F3
Gladstone, SI (Invercargill) 128 C2
Gladstone, SI (Queenstown) 66 C9
Glasnevin 54 D8
Glen Afton 9 H3 11 A4
Glen Avon 107 B5
Glen Eden 7 E3 89 D2
Glen Eden South 89 D2
Glen Eden West 89 D2
Glen Innes 7 E5 90 C5
Glen Massey 9 H4 11 A5
Glen Murray 9 F3
Glen Oroua 29 D6
Glenavy 68 F13
Glenbervie 4 F12 85 A3
Glenbrook 7 H4 9 C1
Glenbrook Beach 7 H4 9 C1
Glencoe 77 C7
Glendale 111 D4
Glendene 89 C2
Glendhu 34 G9
Glendhu Bay 65 D7
Glendowie 90 C5
Glenduan 38 H13 39 F5
Glenfield 6 J10 7 C4 88 H3
Glengarry (Invercargill) 77 E5 128 B2
Glengarry (Tasman) 42 H8
Glenham 78 E9
Glenholme 95 D5 96 C3
Glenhope 42 E11
Gleniti 61 J4
Glenkenich 72 J12 73 J1
Glenleith 74 G11 124 E2
Glenomaru 79 G3
Glenorchy 64 F12 65 F2
Glenore 79 C4
Glenpark 74 C12
Glenrae Hut 46 J14 47 J2
Glenroy 52 H10 53 H1 55 D3
Glenside 53 E2 35 B3 110 C2
Glentui 52 E14 53 E5 55 A7
Glentunnel 52 H11 53 H2 55 D4
Glenure 71 H7
Glenvar 6 J10 7 C4 88 E3
Glenview 92 H4
Glinks Gully 5 B2
Glorit 6 F8
Goat Creek Hut 42 E8
Goat Island 6 D11
Goat Pass Hut 52 A8
Godley Hut 50 H8
Gold Creek Hut 27 G6
Golden Cross 10 E10
Golden Downs 42 D14 43 C2
Golden Springs 19 B7
Golden Stairs Walkway 3 C2
Golden Valley 10 E11
Goldsborough / Waimea 45 H3
Golflands 90 D6
Gomorrah Track 42 C11
Gonville 108 D3 109 D3
Goodwood 74 D13
Goodwood Heights 90 E6
Goose Bay 48 F10
Gordon 10 J10 12 B11
Gordons Valley 68 A12
Gordonton 9 J6 11 B7
Gore 78 B9
Gore Bay 54 A13
Gorge Creek 72 B12 73 B1

Gorge Islands 57 H2
Gorge Road 77 F7
Gouland Downs Hut 37 E4
Goulds Road 56 F8 62 A14
Governors Bay 54 J8 56 E10
Gowanbridge 42 F11
Gracefield 33 E3 35 A3 110 D3
Grafton 87 H5 90 C4
Grahams Beach 7 G3 9 B1
Granity 41 E5
Granity Pass Hut 42 D11
Grasmere 77 E5 128 D2
Grassy Flat Hut 51 A6
Grays Corner 68 E12
Grays Hut 68 J8
Great Barrier Island Aotea 36 D4
Great Island 75 E3
Great Mercury Island 8 B14
Greatford 29 B6
Green Bay 89 D3
Green Gate Huts 65 F5
Green Hills 68 E12
Green Island, SI (Dunedin) 74 H11 124 F4
Green Island, SI (Foveaux Strait) 77 J7
Green Island, SI (Pacific Ocean) 74 J10
Green Islets 75 G5
Green Lake 70 H9 76 B9
Green Lake Hut 70 H9 76 B9
Green Meadows 103 B2
Green Valley 74 A11
Greenacres 110 B2
Greendale 52 J12 53 J3 55 E5
Greenfield 78 A14 79 C2
Greenhills 77 G4 80 A6
Greenhithe 89 A2
Greenland Reservoir 73 C4
Greenlane 90 C4
Greenmount 90 D6
Greenpark 56 F9
Greenpark Huts 56 G9
Greenpoint 77 G4 80 A6
Greenstone / Pounamu 45 H4
Greenstreet 55 G2 62 B8
Greenvale 72 H11
Greerton 10 J13 12 B14 13 B3 94 D1
Greigs 45 D4
Grenada 110 C2
Grenada North 110 C2
Greneys Road 54 D8
Greta Valley 54 B10
Greta Valley Walkway 54 B10
Grey Group Islands 36 D3
Grey Lynn 7 D4 87 G1
Greymouth 45 F4 118 A4
Greys Hut 37 J3 42 A8
Greytown 33 C7
Griffin Creek Hut 45 J5
Groper Island 36 A1
Gropers Bush 77 D2
Grough Hut 59 D5
Grove Bush 77 D6
Grove, The 35 K3 40 G9
Grovetown 35 J6 40 J10 44 C11
Gulf Harbour 6 H11 7 B5
Gum Tree Flat 68 E12
Gumdiggers Park 1 G6
Gummies Bush 76 G14 77 D2
Gumtown 4 F10
Guthrie 12 J14 13 J3

H

Haast 58 D9
Haast Beach 58 D8
Haast Hut 49 J6
Haast Paringa Track 58 C10
Hackthorne 55 H1 61 C7
Hadlow 61 J4
Hagens Hut 58 G14 59 G3
Hahei 8 D14
Hairini (Bay of Plenty) 10 J13 13 B4
Hairini (Waikato) 11 E7
Hakarimata Walkway 9 H4 11 A5
Hakaru 6 B8
Hakataramea 68 D8
Hakatere Conservation Park 51 H3 51 H6 51 H7
Hakatere (Ashburton Coast) 62 E9
Hakatere (Ashburton) 50 J14 51 J5 61 A4
Haku 11 J3 17 A7
Halcombe 29 B7 31 B1
Haldane 78 G10

Half Moon Bay 7 E6 90 C6
Half Moon Hut 68 H8
Halfmoon Bay / Oban 80 E5
Halfway Bush 124 E3
Halfway Hut 69 H7 75 B7
Halkett 52 H14 53 H5 55 D7
Halswell 53 J7 56 E9 120 C1
Hamama 38 E8
Hamilton 9 J6 11 B7 92 E3
Hamilton Airport 11 D7
Hamilton Central 91 E5
Hamilton East 92 F4
Hamilton Gardens 11 C7
Hamilton Hut 52 D8
Hamilton North 91 D4 92 E3
Hamilton West 91 G4 92 F3
Hampden 74 A13
Hampstead 55 J3 62 D9
Hamua 30 G9 31 G3
Hamurana 13 F4
Hanamahihi Hut 20 A13 21 A1
Hangaroa 21 E7
Hangatiki 11 H6
Hanmer Conservation Park 47 F4
Hanmer Springs 47 F5
Hanmer Springs Thermal Resort 47 F5
Hannahs Bay 13 G5 96 B5
Hannahs Clearing 57 E7
Happy Daze Hut 27 J5 30 A12 31 A6
Happy Valley (Auckland) 7 H7 9 C4
Happy Valley (Wellington) 110 E1
Happy Valley, SI 76 E12
Hapuakohe Track 9 E6
Hapuku 48 D13
Harakeke 38 J10 39 G2
Harapepe 11 D5
Harbour View (Auckland) 89 B2
Harbour View (Wellington) 110 C3
Haretaunga 111 B5
Harewood 53 H7 56 D9 120 C4
Harihari 50 D9
Hariki Beach 15 C6
Harington Point 74 G13
Harini 94 D2
Harkness Hut 27 A6
Harman Hut 51 B6
Haroto Bay 11 C4
Harper Pass Bivvy 46 H9
Harper Pass Track 46 H11
Harrisville 7 J6 9 D3
Haruru 4 B9 81 B1
Haruru Falls - Paihia 4 B9
Harveys Flat 74 G9 79 A7
Harwood 74 G12
Hastings 28 F11 103 C5
Hastings Central 102 B2
Hastwell 30 H8 31 H2
Hataitai 110 E2
Hatepe 19 F5
Hatfield 55 G4 62 B10
Hatfields Beach 6 G10 7 A4
Hatuma 32 A9
Hatuma Lake 32 A10
Hauiti 22 A13
Haukawakawa 40 C9
Haumoana 28 E12
Haunui 30 G11 31 G5
Hauparu Bay 13 F5
Haupiri 46 G9
Hauraki 90 B4
Hautanoa 16 G11
Hautapu 12 D8
Hautu Village 19 G3
Hauturu 11 F3
Hauturu / Little Barrier Island 36 D1 6 C13
Hauwai 44 E12
Havelock 40 G8
Havelock North 28 F12 103 B6
Hawai 15 E4
Hawarden 54 B8
Hawdon Hut 52 B9
Hawea Conservation Park 58 H12 59 E3
Hawea Flat 66 C9
Hawera 23 H7 25 E2
Hawkes Bay Museum - Napier 28 D12
Hawkins 52 H12 53 H3 55 D5
Hawksbury Bush 74 D12
Hawkswood 48 H9
Hawthorndale 128 B3
Hays Gap 79 G4
Haystack Hut 42 D9
Haystack, The 40 C11
Haywards 33 D3 35 A2 111 B4

Hazletts 77 D3
Healey Creek Hut 50 C11 51 C2
Heao 18 G8 24 A13
Heaphy Hut 37 F2
Heaphy Track - Great Walk 37 E3
Heathcote Valley 54 J8 56 E10 120 G1
Heatherlea 29 G5
Hector 41 E5
Heddon Bush 77 B3
Hedgehope 77 C6
Heenans Corner 77 A3
Hei Hei 53 H7 56 D9 120 B2
Heidelberg 77 E5 128 B4
Heipipi 20 D12
Helena Bay 4 C12
Helensburgh 124 E3
Helensville 6 H8 7 B2
Helicopter Flat Hut 42 C9
Hells Gate - Rotorua 13 F5
Helvetia 7 H5 9 C2
Hen and Chickens Islands 6 A10
Hen and Chickens Islands Nature Reserve 6 A10
Henderson 7 E3 89 C2
Henderson Valley 89 C2
Henley 74 J9 79 B7
Hepburn Creek 6 F10
Herbert 68 J10 74 A13
Herbertville 32 F10
Herekino 3 B1
Herekino Forest 1 K6 3 A2
Herekopare Island / Te Marama 80 D6
Herepai Hut 29 H7 31 H1
Herepo 50 D9
Heriot 72 H13 73 H2
Herne Bay 89 B3
Herricks Hut 27 E7
Hexton 22 D10
Heyward Point 74 G12
Hicks Bay 16 B11
Hidden Falls Hut 64 D10
Highbank 52 J9 55 E2 62 A8
Highbury (Auckland) 88 J3
Highbury (Wellington) 110 E1
Highcliff 74 H12 124 B5
Highland Park 90 C6
Highland Park (Wellington) 110 D2
Highlands Park 107 C5
Hihi 2 G9
Hihitahi 26 E14 27 E2
Hikawera 34 F8
Hikuai 8 G13 10 B10
Hikumutu 18 G10
Hikurangi 4 E11
Hikutaia 8 J12 10 D9
Hikuwai 16 H11
Hilderthorpe 68 G12
Hill Park 90 E6
Hillcrest (Auckland) 88 J3
Hillcrest (Hamilton) 92 F5
Hillcrest (Rotorua) 96 C2
Hillend 79 D3
Hillersden 43 D6
Hillgrove 74 B13
Hills Creek 66 F14 67 F3
Hillsborough (Auckland) 90 D4
Hillsborough (Christchurch) 120 F2
Hillsborough, NI (Taranaki) 23 B5
Hilltop 56 G11
Hilmorton 120 D2
Hilton 61 F4
Himatangi 29 E5
Himatangi Beach 29 D4
Hinakura 34 F9
Hinau, NI 27 H3
Hinau, SI 46 B8
Hindon 74 F10
Hinds 55 J1 61 E7
Hinehopu 13 F6
Hinemoa 30 G10 31 G4
Hinerua Hut 27 H6
Hinuera 12 D11
Hira 38 J13 39 G5
Hiruharama 16 E11
Hiwinui 30 C8 31 C2
Hiwipango 42 D14 43 C2
Hoanga 4 J8
Hobsonville 7 D3 88 J1
Hodderville 12 G11
Hoe-O-Tainui 9 G7
Hohonu 45 H4
Hokianga - Kai Iwi Coastal Track 3 E3
Hokio Beach 29 G4
Hokitika 45 H2

Hokonui 77 B6
Hokowhitu 104 D6 105 C4
Hokuri Hut 64 A9
Holborn 111 B4
Holdens Bay 13 G4 96 B5
Holly Hut 23 D5
Hollyford 64 E10
Hollyford Track 64 A9
Homai 90 E5
Home Point 4 H13
Homebush, NI 34 B9
Homebush, SI 52 H11 53 H2 55 D4
Homedale 111 D4
Homer Tunnel 64 E9
Hone Heke Monument - Kaikohe 3 C7
Honeymoon Valley 2 J8
Honikiwi 11 G5
Hook 68 C13
Hook Bush 68 C11
Hooker / Landsborough Wilderness Area 59 B4
Hooker Glacier Walk 59 A6
Hooker Hut 59 A6
Hoon Hay 53 J7 56 E9 120 D2
Hoopers Inlet 74 G12
Hope 39 H3 43 A4 116 D2
Hope Kiwi Hut 46 G12
Hope shelter 46 G13
Hopelands 30 D11 31 D5
Hopeless Hut 42 J12
Hopeone 21 A3
Hopuhopu 9 H5 11 A6
Horace Walker Hut 59 B5
Horahia 8 J11 10 D8
Horahora 85 C1
Horahora (Northland) 4 F13
Horahora (Waikato) 12 E10
Horeke 3 C5
Hornby 53 J7 56 E9 120 B2
Hornby Hut 44 J9 48 A13
Horoeka 30 F13 31 F7
Horoera 16 B13
Horohoro 12 H14 13 H3
Horokino 18 A12
Horokiwi 110 C3
Horomanga 14 J8 20 A11
Horopito 26 B11
Hororata 52 H11 53 H2 55 D4
Horotiu 9 J5 11 B6
Horrellville 52 F14 53 F5 55 B7
Horseshoe Flat Hut 58 C12
Horseshoe Lake 28 J11
Horsham Downs 9 J5 11 B6 92 A3
Horsley Down 54 A8
Hospital Hill (Napier) 103 B1
Hospital Hill (Opotiki) 14 F13 15 F2 103 B1
Hot Water Beach 8 E14
Hot Water Beach Hot Springs 8 E14
Hoteo 6 E8
Hoteo North 6 D8
Houghton Bay 110 E2
Houhora 1 E5
Houhora Heads 1 F5
Houhou 45 H2
Houipapa 78 F14 79 H2
Houpoto 15 E5
Houto 4 G9
Howard 42 G12
Howard Junction 42 F12
Howard Track 42 H12
Howick 7 E6 90 C6
Howletts Hut 27 J5
Huapai 6 J8 7 C2
Huarau 5 B6
Huia 7 F2 89 E1
Huiakama 24 D9 25 A4
Huiarua 16 G9
Huinga 24 E8 25 B3
Huirangi 17 H1 23 B6
Huiroa 24 D8 25 A3
Huka Falls - Taupo 19 D5
Huka Village 98 A4
Hukanui 30 G8 31 G2
Hukapapa 18 H11
Hukarere 46 C8
Hukatere (Northland - Far North) 1 F4
Hukatere (Northland) 5 C5
Hukawai 46 D8
Hukerenui 4 D10
Humphreys 45 J3
Hundalee 48 G10
Hungahunga 10 J10 12 B11
Hunter 68 C12
Hunterville 26 J13

Huntingdon 55 J2 62 D8
Huntington Park 90 D6
Huntly 9 G5
Hunts Creek Hut 51 A7
Huntsbury 120 F1
Hunua 7 G7 9 B4
Hunua Falls - Auckland 7 G7 9 B4
Hunua Ranges Regional Park 8 G8 9 B5
Hupara 4 C9
Hurdon 107 D2
Hurford 23 B4
Hurleyville 24 H8 25 E3
Hurricane Hut 42 D9
Hurunui 54 A9
Hurunui Hot Springs 46 H11
Hurunui Hut 46 H11
Hurunui Mouth 54 A13
Hurworth 23 C5
Hutnters Hut 50 E10 51 E1
Hutxley Forks Hut 59 E3
Hyde 74 A9
Hyde Park 120 C3

I

Ice Lake 50 G8
Ida Valley 66 H14 67 H3
Idaburn 67 G4
Idaburn Dam 66 G14 67 G3
Ihaia Track 23 E4
Ihakara 29 G5
Ihumatao 90 E4
Ihungia 16 G10
Ihuraua 30 J9 31 J3
Ikamatua 46 C8
Ikawai 68 E11
Ikawatea Forks Hut 27 E6
Ilam 120 F11
Inaha 23 G6
Inangahua 41 H6
Inangahua Junction 41 H6
Inangahua Landing 41 H5
Inch Clutha 79 E4
Inch Valley 74 B12
Inchbonnie 45 H6
Incholme 68 H10
Indian Island 69 H3 75 B3
Inglewood 17 J1 23 C6
Inland Track 38 E9 39 C1
Invercargill 77 E5 127 C2
Invercargill Airport 77 E4
Irirangi 26 D14 27 D2
Iris Burn Hut 70 C10
Iron Bark Hut 27 F5
Iron Gate Hut 27 J5
Iron Whare Hut 28 A8
Irwell 55 F7 62 A13
Isla Bank 77 C3
Island Bay 33 F1 35 C4 110 E2
Island Block 7 J7 9 D4
Island Cliff 68 F9
Island Gully Hut 47 B5
Island Lake (Buller) 38 G5
Island Lake (Southland) 70 H9 76 B9
Island Lake (Tasman) 47 B6
Island Stream 68 J10
Island View 10 F12
Islands Hut 71 D5
Islington (Blenheim) 117 B5
Islington (Christchurch) 120 B2
Ivory Lake Hut 50 D12 51 D3
Ivydale 3 C5
Iwikau Village 26 A13
Iwitahi 19 F7

J

Jackett Island 38 H10 39 F2
Jacks Blowhole 79 H3
Jacks Island / Tuhawaiki 79 H3
Jackson Bay 57 E5
Jacksons 45 J6
Jacky Lee Island / Pukeokaoka 80 D6
Jacobs River 49 J2
Jam Hut 44 J8 48 A12
James Mackay Hut 37 E3
Jameson Ridge Track 42 J11
Janefield 74 H10 124 H4
Jerusalem 24 G13 26 D8
Jervois Hut 47 E3
Jervoistown 103 B2

John Coull Hut 24 D12 25 A7
John Reid Hut 42 C11
John Tait Hut 42 J13
Johnson Hut 42 C8
Johnson Track 42 C8
Johnsonville 33 E2 35 B3 110 C2
Johnstone 73 J5 79 B3
Jollie Brook Hut 46 H13 47 H1
Josephville 71 H6
Jubilee Hut 74 F11
Judea 94 C2
Judgeford 33 D3 35 A2 111 B4
Julia Hot Springs 51 A7
Julia Hut 51 A7
Jumbo Hut 34 A7
Junction Burn Hut 70 A9
Junction Hut 66 B10
Junction Islands 36 E3

K

Ka Whata Tu o Rakihouia Conservation Park 48 C11
Kaawa 9 G2
Kaeo 2 J11
Kaharoa 13 E4
Kahika 28 A12
Kahikatoa 3 B5
Kahoe 2 H10
Kahotea 11 G6
Kahui Hut 23 D4
Kahui Track 23 D4
Kahuika 78 F13 79 H1
Kahunui Hut 21 B4
Kahurangi National Park 37 F5
Kahutara 33 E6
Kai Iwi 25 H7
Kai Iwi Beach 25 H7
Kaiaka 2 J8
Kaiapoi 54 G8 56 C10
Kaiata 45 F4
Kaiate Falls 13 C4
Kaiatea 4 F13
Kaiaua 8 G9 9 B6
Kaiewe Junction 27 F3
Kaihere 9 E7
Kaihiku 78 C14 79 E2
Kaihinu 45 H2
Kaihu 3 G6
Kaihu Forest 3 G7
Kaiiwi Lakes 3 H6
Kaik 74 B14
Kaikarangi 26 H13
Kaikohe 3 C7
Kaikorai 123 D1 124 E3
Kaikou 4 E8
Kaikoura 48 E12
Kaikoura Island 36 D3
Kaikoura Peninsula Walkway 48 E12
Kaimai-Mamaku Conservation Park 10 G10 12 E12 13 E1
Kaimamaku 4 D11
Kaimanawa Forest Park 19 H4 27 A3
Kaimarama 8 E12
Kaimata, NI 17 J2 23 C7
Kaimata, SI 45 F5
Kaimaumau 1 G6
Kaimiro 23 C5
Kainga 54 G8 56 C10
Kaingaroa 1 H7
Kaingaroa Forest 20 A10
Kainui 9 H5 11 A6
Kaipaki 11 D7
Kaipara Flats 6 E8
Kaipara Flats Airfield 6 E9
Kaipara Lighthouse 5 E5
Kaiparoro 30 H8 31 H2
Kaipikari 17 G3 24 A8
Kairakau Beach 28 J12
Kairaki 54 G8 56 C10
Kairanga 29 D7 31 D1
Kairangi 12 E9
Kairara 3 G7
Kairua 13 B4 94 C5
Kaitaia 1 J6
Kaitaia Airport - Awanui 1 H6
Kaitangata 79 E4
Kaitaratahi 22 C9
Kaitawa (Hawke's Bay) 21 F2
Kaitawa (Manawatu) 30 F10 31 F4
Kaite 100 C4
Kaitemako 13 C4
Kaiteriteri 38 G10 39 E2

Kaitieke 18 H10
Kaitoke (Manawatu) 30 C12 31 C6
Kaitoke (Waikato) 8 E13
Kaitoke (Wanganui) 26 J8
Kaitoke (Wellington) 33 C5
Kaitoke Hot Springs 36 D4
Kaitoke Lake 26 J8
Kaitui 3 F5
Kaituna Lagoon 56 G9
Kaituna Track 37 B6
Kaituna Valley 56 G10
Kaituna, NI 34 A8
Kaituna, SI 40 J8 44 B9
Kaiwaiwai 33 D7
Kaiwaka 6 C8
Kaiwera 78 B10
Kaiwhaiki 26 G8
Kaiwharawhara 110 D2
Kaka 42 D12
Kaka Point 79 G4
Kakahi 18 G11
Kakahu 60 F14 61 F3
Kakahu Bush 61 F3
Kakanui, NI 6 G8 7 A2
Kakanui, SI 68 J11
Kakapo Hut 42 B9
Kakapo Track 42 B8
Kakapotahi 50 B10
Kakapuaka 79 E3
Kakaramea 24 J8 25 F3
Kakariki (Gisborne) 16 D12
Kakariki (Manawatu) 30 G8 31 G2
Kakariki (Wanganui) 29 B6
Kakatahi 26 F11
Kamahi 78 D8
Kamaka 45 E5
Kambton 112 D5
Kamo 4 F11 85 A1
Kamo East 85 A1
Kanakanaia 22 B10
Kangaroo Lake 45 G7
Kaniere 45 J2
Kaniwhaniwha 11 D5
Kanohi 6 G8 7 A2
Kanohirua Hut 20 C14 21 C2
Kapakapanui Hut 33 A5
Kapenga 13 H4
Kapiro 2 K12 4 A8
Kapitea Reservoir 45 H4
Kapiti 79 C5
Kapiti Island 33 A3
Kapiti Island Nature Reserve 29 J2 33 A3
Kaponga 23 F5
Kapowairua 1 A2
Kapua 68 D11
Kapuka 77 F7
Kapuka South 77 F7
Kapuni 23 F5
Karahaki 24 J9 25 F4
Karaka 7 G5 9 B2
Karakariki 9 J4 11 C5
Karamea / Red Island, NI 28 H13
Karamea Bend Hut 37 J5 42 A10
Karamea Centennial Museum 37 J2 41 A7
Karamea, SI 37 J2 41 A7
Karamu (Hawke's Bay) 28 F12 103 B5
Karamu (Waikato) 11 D5
Karangahake 10 F10
Karangahake Gorge 10 F10
Karangarua 49 J3
Karapiro 12 D9
Karatia (Thoms Landing) 1 C2
Karehana Bay 33 C2 35 B1
Karekare 7 F2
Karekare Falls 7 F2
Kareponia 1 H6
Karere 29 E7 31 E1
Karetu 4 C10
Karewarewa 27 H3
Karioi 26 C12
Karioitahi 7 J3 9 D1
Karitane 74 E12
Karori 33 F1 35 C4 110 D1
Karori West 110 D1
Karoro 45 F4
Karuhiruhi 3 D4
Katea 79 G2
Katikati 10 G11
Katiki 74 B14
Katipo Creek Shelter 37 G2
Kauaeranga 8 H12 10 C9
Kauana 77 A5
Kauangaroa 26 J10

Kaukapakapa 6 H8 7 B2
Kaupokonui 23 G5
Kauri 4 F11
Kauri Flat 9 J2 11 B3
Kaurilands 89 D2
Kauroa 11 C3
Kauru Hill 68 H10
Kauwhata 29 D7 31 D1
Kawa 36 C4
Kawaha Point 96 A3
Kawakawa (Northland - Far North) 1 G7
Kawakawa (Northland) 4 C9
Kawakawa Bay 8 E8 9 A5
Kawakawa Hut 33 H6
Kawarau Falls 65 H5 126 B5
Kawarau Gorge 66 H8
Kawatiri 42 F11
Kawatiri Walkway 42 F12
Kawau Island 6 F11
Kawautahi 18 H10
Kaweka Forest Park 19 J6 27 C7
Kaweka Hut 27 B7
Kawerau 14 G8
Kawerua 3 F4
Kawhia 11 F2
Kawhia Museum 11 F2
Kawiti 4 C8
Kawiti Caves - Kawakawa 4 C9
Kekerengu 44 H11
Kelburn 110 D1
Kelchers 68 D10
Kelly Knight Hut 27 H5
Kelly Tarltons Underwater World - Auckland 7 D5 90 B4
Kellys Bay 5 D4
Kellyville 7 J7 9 D4
Kelman Hut 49 J7
Kelso 72 H12 73 H1
Kelson 33 D3 35 A2 111 C4
Kelston 89 C2
Kelvin Grove 30 D8 31 D2 105 A5
Kelvin Heights 65 H5
Kenana 2 H9
Kenepuru 110 B2
Kenepuru Head 35 H2 40 F11
Kenepuru Sound 35 K2 40 F9
Kenmure 124 E4
Kennedy Bay 8 C11 36 J5
Kennedy Memorial Hut 59 D5
Kennington 77 E5
Kensington 123 J2
Kensington (Dunedin) 124 E4
Kensington (Whangarei) 85 B1
Kepler Track - Great Walk 70 C10
Kereone 10 J9 12 B10
Kerepehi 8 J11 10 D8
Kereru 28 F8
Kererutahi 14 F12
Kereta 8 E10
Keretu 21 B6
Kerikeri 4 A8 86 B2
Kerikeri Inlet 2 K13 4 A9
Kerin Forks Hut 58 H9
Kerosene Creek Thermal Area - Waiotapu 13 J5
Kerrytown 61 H4
Ketetahi 18 H13
Ketetahi Hot Springs - Tongariro National Park 18 J13 19 J1
Ketetahi Hut 18 J13 19 J1
Kew (Dunedin) 124 E5
Kew (Invercargill) 128 B5
Key, The 70 E13 71 E2
Khandallah 33 E1 35 C3 110 D2
Kia Ora 68 H11
Kihikihi 11 F7
Kikiwa 42 F13 43 E1
Kilburnie 110 E2
Killinchy 55 G6 62 B12
Kimbell 60 E12
Kimberley 52 G12 53 G3 55 C5
Kimbolton 30 A9 31 A3
Kime Hut 33 B6
Kimihia 9 G5
Kina 38 H10 39 F2
Kings Creek Hut 42 C10
Kingsdown 68 A13
Kingseat 7 G5 9 B2
Kingsland 87 J1 89 D2 90 C4
Kingsley Heights 111 B6
Kingston (Wellington) 110 E1
Kingston Crossing 72 H8
Kingston, SI 72 B8
Kingswell 128 B5

Kinleith 12 H12 13 H1
Kinloch, NI 19 D4
Kinloch, SI 64 F12 65 F2
Kinohaku 11 G2
Kintail Hut 69 F7
Kiokio 11 G6
Kirikau 18 G9 24 A14
Kirikopuni 4 H9
Kirioke 3 D7
Kiripaka 4 F13
Kiritaki 30 C11 31 C5
Kiritaki Hut 30 C10 31 C4
Kiritehere 11 J2
Kiriwhakapapa 29 J7 31 J1 34 A8
Kirwans Track 46 A10
Kirwee 52 H13 53 H4 55 D6
Kiwi 42 D12
Kiwi Hut 46 J8
Kiwi Mouth Hut 27 B7
Kiwi Saddle Hut (Kahurangi FP) 42 C10
Kiwi Saddle Hut (Kaweka FP) 27 B7
Kiwi Track 42 C10
Kiwitahi 10 J8 12 B9
Kiwitahi Station 10 J8 12 B9
Kiwitea 30 B9 31 B3
Klondyke Track 46 C11
Knapdale 72 J10 78 A9
Knights Track 27 J4 30 A11 31 A5
Knobbies, The 80 C1
Knobs Flat 64 H9
Koaunui Hut 14 J12 15 J1 21 A3
Koeke Junction 26 F13
Kohaihai Shelter 37 G2
Kohatu 42 C13 43 B1
Kohe 3 B2
Kohekohe 7 H3
Kohi 24 J9 25 F4
Kohika 68 B12
Kohiku 30 G12 31 G6
Kohinui 30 E11 31 E5
Kohukohu 3 C5
Kohumaru 2 J9
Kohupatiki 103 B4
Kohuratahi 17 H6 24 B11
Koiro 18 G9 24 A14
Koitiata 29 A4
Kokako 21 F3
Kokatahi 50 A12 51 A3
Kokiri 45 F5
Kokoamo 68 F10
Kokonga 67 J6
Kokopu 4 G10
Kokowai Track 23 D5
Komako 30 B10 31 B4
Komakorau 9 H5 11 A6
Komata 10 E9
Komata Reefs 10 E10
Komokoriki 6 F8
Kongahu 37 J2 41 A7
Konini (Auckland) 89 D2
Konini (Manawatu) 30 F9 31 F3
Kononi 73 J4 79 B2
Kopaki 18 A10
Kopane 29 D7
Kopara 46 G8
Kopikopiko 30 F8 31 F2
Kopu 8 H11 10 C8
Kopua 30 B14 32 B8
Kopuaranga 34 A9
Kopuaroa 16 F11
Kopuawhara 22 J8 22 AA1
Kopuku 8 J8 9 D5
Kopuriki 14 J9 20 A12
Koputaroa 29 G5
Korakonui 12 G8
Koranga 21 B5
Koranga Forks Hut 21 A4
Korapuki Island 8 B14
Koremoa 5 B3
Korere 42 D13 43 C1
Koriniti 24 J14 26 F9
Korito 23 C5
Korokoro 110 C3
Koromatua 11 C6 92 H1
Koromiko 35 J4 40 F10 44 A11
Koropuku Hut 46 J8 52 A9
Korora 30 F12 31 F6
Korowai/Torlesse Tussocklands Park 52 E10 52 F9
Koru 23 B4
Kotare 17 F5
Kotemaori 20 J13 21 J1

Kotepato Hut 14 J13 15 J2 21 A4
Kotinga 38 E8
Kotuku 45 F6
Kourawhero 6 F9
Koutu (Kauri Coast) 3 D3
Koutu (Rotorua) 13 G4 96 B2
Kowai Bush 52 F11 53 F2 55 B4
Kowhai Park 110 E1
Kowhitirangi 50 A12 51 A3
Kuaotunu 8 C13
Kuku 29 H4
Kukumoa 14 F13 15 F2
Kukupa 56 F12
Kumara 45 G4
Kumara Junction 45 G3
Kumara Reservoir 45 H4
Kumeroa 30 D11 31 D5
Kumeti Hut 30 B11 31 B5
Kumeu 6 J8 7 C2
Kundy Station 80 H1
Kupe 23 D7 25 A2
Kuranui 10 H8 12 A9
Kuratau 19 F3
Kuratau Junction 18 F14 19 F2
Kuri Bush 74 J9 79 B7
Kuriheka 68 J10
Kuripapango 27 C7
Kuriwao 78 C13 79 E1
Kurow 67 D7
Kutarere 14 F12 15 F1
Kyeburn 67 J6
Kyeburn Diggings 67 G6
Kyle 55 J5 62 D11

L

Ladbrooks 53 J7 56 E9
Lady Barkly 77 B4
Lady Knox Geyser - Waiotapu 13 J5 20 A8
Lady Lake 45 G7
Lagmhor 55 H2 62 C8
Laingholm 7 F3 89 E2
Laingholm Central 89 D2
Lairdvale 18 F10
Lakehead Hut 42 H13
Lake Ada 64 E8
Lake Adelaide 64 E9
Lake Agnes 64 C9
Lake Ahaura 46 F8
Lake Alabaster/Wawahi Waka 64 B10
Lake Alabaster Hut 64 C10
Lake Alexandrina 60 D9
Lake Alice, NI 29 B5
Lake Alice, NI (locality) 29 B5
Lake Alice, SI 63 H5
Lake Angelus 42 H12
Lake Aniwhenua 14 J9
Lake Annie 70 C8
Lake Aorere 37 G4
Lake Arapuni 12 G10
Lake Aratiatia 19 C6
Lake Areare 9 H5 11 A6
Lake Atiamuri 12 J13 13 J2 19 A5
Lake Aviemore 67 C6
Lake Barfoot 37 H4
Lake Barra 58 E11
Lake Beattie 69 E4
Lake Beddoes 63 G5
Lake Benmore 67 A5
Lake Bernard, NI 29 B5
Lake Bernard, SI 63 G6
Lake Bloxham 70 A9
Lake Brown 64 E8
Lake Browne 69 D6
Lake Browning 51 B6
Lake Brownlee 63 G7
Lake Brunner 45 G6
Lake Brunton 78 H9
Lake Cadman 69 J4 75 C4
Lake Camp 50 J13 51 J4 60 A13 61 A3
Lake Carrick 69 J4 75 C4
Lake Catherine 52 E8 55 A1
Lake Chalice 43 D5
Lake Chalice Track 43 D4
Lake Christabel 46 E12
Lake Christabel Hut 46 E12
Lake Christabel Track 46 E12
Lake Clark 63 J5
Lake Clarke 57 G6
Lake Clearwater 50 J13 51 J4
Lake Cobb 37 G5
Lake Coleridge 51 F7

Lake Coleridge (locality) 52 G8
Lake Constance 47 A4
Lake Daniell 46 D13
Lake Dispute 64 H13 65 H3
Lake Dive Hut 23 E5
Lake Dive Track 23 E5
Lake Douglas 58 E9
Lake Dudding 29 A5
Lake Duncan 70 B8
Lake Dunstan 66 H9
Lake Ella 47 A3
Lake Ellery 57 F6
Lake Ellesmere / Te Waihora 56 G8
Lake Elmer 37 G4
Lake Elterwater 44 F12
Lake Emily 50 J14 51 J5
Lake Emma 50 J13 51 J4 60 A13 61 A3
Lake Erskine 64 F9
Lake Eyles 70 B9
Lake Fergus 64 F10
Lake Ferry 33 G4
Lake Forsyth 56 G10
Lake Fraser 69 J2 75 C2
Lake Gault 49 H4
Lake George 76 H13 77 E1
Lake Gow 72 D9
Lake Grasmere 52 C10
Lake Grassmere 44 E12
Lake Grassmere (locality) 44 E12
Lake Grave 63 F6
Lake Greaney 57 F7
Lake Gunn 64 F10
Lake Guyon 47 D4
Lake Guyon Hut 47 C4
Lake Hakanoa 9 G5
Lake Hakapoua 75 F6
Lake Half 1 E4
Lake Hall 70 B8
Lake Hankinson 63 J6
Lake Hankinson Hut 63 J6
Lake Hanlon 41 C7
Lake Harihari 11 G2
Lake Haupiri 46 G8
Lake Hauroko -
New Zealand's deepest lake 76 D8
Lake Hawdon 52 D10 53 D1
Lake Hawea 66 A9
Lake Hawea (locality) 66 C9
Lake Hay 69 H6 75 B6
Lake Hayes 65 G5
Lake Head Hut 42 H13 43 G1
Lake Head Track 42 H13 43 G1
Lake Heaton 29 B5
Lake Hector 75 E2
Lake Herbert 29 B5
Lake Herengawe 25 G5
Lake Heron 50 H14 51 H5
Lake Herries 70 C9
Lake Hilda 70 B9
Lake Hochstetter 45 E7
Lake Hope 65 J6
Lake Horizon 69 G7 75 A7
Lake Horowhenua 29 G5
Lake Howden Hut 64 F10
Lake Humuhumu 5 D5
Lake Ianthe 50 C9
Lake Iceberg 64 F8
Lake Innes 75 F6
Lake Jasper 44 E11
Lake Jeanette 42 D9
Lake Jewell 37 H4
Lake Kaiiwi 3 H5
Lake Kaikokopu 29 E5
Lake Kakapo 69 J6 75 D6
Lake Kaniere 50 A13 51 A4
Lake Kaniere Walk 50 A13 51 A4
Lake Kanono 5 E5
Lake Karaka 5 D4
Lake Karapiro 12 E9
Lake Kaurapataka 46 J8
Lake Kereta 5 G6
Lake Kimihia 9 G5
Lake Kini 49 J1 58 A13 59 A2
Lake Kiwi 75 F5
Lake Koitiata 29 B4
Lake Koputara 29 E5
Lake Kuratau 18 F14 19 F2
Lake Kuwakakai 5 G6
Lake Leeb 57 G6
Lake Letitia 52 C11 53 C2
Lake Lockett 37 G6
Lake Lois 70 E8
Lake Luna 64 G13 65 G3

Lake Lyndon 52 F9 55 B2
Lake Macarthur 69 J3 75 D3
Lake Mackinnon 63 J4 70 A8
Lake Mahinapua 45 J1 50 A11 51 A2
Lake Mahinerangi 73 G7 79 A5
Lake Man 46 F12
Lake Mangakaware 11 D6
Lake Mangawhio 24 H11 25 E6
Lake Manuwai 2 K11 3 A7
Lake Mapourika 49 F6
Lake Maraetai 12 J11 19 A3
Lake Marahau 25 H6
Lake Maratoto 11 D7
Lake Marchant 63 J4
Lake Marian 64 E10
Lake Marina 42 C8
Lake Marion 46 H12
Lake Marymere 52 D10 53 D1
Lake Mason 46 J12
Lake Matahina 14 G9
Lake Matheson 49 H4
Lake Matiri 42 F9
Lake Matiri Hut 42 F9
Lake Maungarataiti 26 H12
Lake Maungaratanui 26 H12
Lake McIvor 63 J5
Lake McKellar 64 F10
Lake McKerrow 64 B9
Lake McRae 48 B9
Lake Middleton 59 H4
Lake Mike 69 J5 75 C5
Lake Minchin 46 J9 52 A10 53 A1
Lake Moananui 12 H11
Lake Moawhango 26 C14 27 C2
Lake Moeraki 58 B11
Lake Moeraki (locality) 58 B10
Lake Mokeno 5 E4
Lake Monk 75 E6
Lake Monowai 70 J9 76 C9
Lake Morehurehu 1 D4
Lake Moreton 63 E7
Lake Morgan 46 H8
Lake Mouat 75 E6
Lake Moumahaki 24 J10 25 F5
Lake Mudgie 45 H4
Lake Mueller 49 H4
Lake Namunamu 26 H12
Lake Never-never 64 C8
Lake Ngaroto 11 E7
Lake Ngaruru 26 H11
Lake Ngatu 1 H5
Lake Nigel 71 B6
Lake Nisson 57 F7
Lake Norwest 70 D8
Lake Ohakuri 19 A6
Lake Ohau 59 H4
Lake Ohau Alpine Village 59 H4
Lake Ohia (locality) 1 H7
Lake Okareka 13 G5
Lake Okareka (locality) 13 G5
Lake Okataina 13 G5
Lake Okoia 25 G5
Lake Omapere 3 B7
Lake Omapere (locality) 3 B7
Lake Onoke 33 G4
Lake Onslow 73 D4
Lake Opuha 60 E12 61 E1
Lake Orbell 70 B11
Lake Otamangakau 18 G13 19 G1
Lake Otamatearoa 7 J3 9 D1
Lake Ototoa 5 F6
Lake Otuhie 37 C5
Lake Oturi 25 G4
Lake Owhareiti 4 C8
Lake Papaitonga 29 G4
Lake Paradise 69 D4
Lake Parangi 11 E2
Lake Paringa 58 B11
Lake Paringa (locality) 58 B12 59 B1
Lake Pearson 52 D10
Lake Perrine 42 D8
Lake Phyllis 42 C8
Lake Poerua 45 H6
Lake Pokorua 7 H3
Lake Poteriteri 75 E7
Lake Poteriteri Hut 75 F7
Lake Pouarua 20 G8
Lake Poukawa 28 G10
Lake Pounui 33 F4
Lake Pukaki 59 F7
Lake Pupuke 6 J10 7 D4
Lake Purser 69 J4 75 C4
Lake Quill 63 F7

Lake Rahui 41 G5
Lake Rakatu 70 F10
Lake Rasselas 58 B11
Lake Ratapiko 17 J2 23 C7 25 A2
Lake Repongaere 22 D9
Lake Rerewhakaaitu 13 J6
Lake Roe Hut 69 G7 75 A7
Lake Ronald 63 D7
Lake Ross 64 G9
Lake Rotoaira 18 H14 19 H2
Lake Rotoehu 13 F7
Lake Rotoiti, NI 13 F6
Lake Rotoiti, SI 42 G13 43 F1
Lake Rotokakahi 13 H5
Lake Rotokare 24 F8 25 C3
Lake Rotokauri 9 J5 11 B6
Lake Rotokauwau 26 J9
Lake Rotokawa 19 C6
Lake Rotokawau (Northland - Far North) 1 F6
Lake Rotokawau (Northland) 5 E5
Lake Rotokino 50 E8
Lake Rotoma 13 F7
Lake Rotoma (locality) 13 F7
Lake Rotomahana 13 H6
Lake Rotongaro 9 F4
Lake Rotonuiaha 20 G14 21 G2
Lake Rotopounamu 19 H2
Lake Rotorangi 24 G9 25 D4
Lake Rotoroa, NI (Northland) 1 H5
Lake Rotoroa, NI (Waikato) 11 C7
Lake Rotoroa, SI 42 H12
Lake Rotorua, NI 13 F4
Lake Rotorua, SI 48 E11
Lake Rototuna 5 D4
Lake Roxburgh (Central Otago) 72 C13 73 C2
Lake Roxburgh (locality) 72 D13 73 D2
Lake Roxburgh (Southland) 63 H7
Lake Ruapapa 21 G3
Lake Ruataniwha 59 H6
Lake Sarah 52 C10
Lake Scott 72 D10
Lake Selfe 51 E7
Lake Serpentine 11 E7
Lake Sheila 80 D3
Lake Sheppard 46 J12
Lake Shirley 63 J3
Lake Stanley 37 F6
Lake Story 69 G7 75 A7
Lake Sumner 46 H12
Lake Sumner Conservation Park 46 F14 47 F2
Lake Sutherland 63 H6
Lake Swan 69 E4
Lake Sylvan 64 D11 65 D1
Lake Sylvester 37 G6
Lake Taeore 1 D4
Lake Taharoa (Northland) 3 H5
Lake Taharoa (Waikato) 11 G2
Lake Tarawera 13 H6
Lake Tauanui 3 D7
Lake Taupo / Taupomoana 19 E4
Lake Taylor 46 J12
Lake Te Anau 70 A11
Lake Te Au 70 B8
Lake Te Kahika 1 C4
Lake Tekapo 60 D10
Lake Tekapo (locality) 60 E9
Lake Tennyson 47 C4
Lake Thomas 75 E2
Lake Thompson (Southland) 63 H5
Lake Thompson (Tasman) 47 B4
Lake Tikitapu 13 H5
Lake Track 20 E13 21 E1
Lake Truth 64 C9
Lake Tuakitoto 79 E4
Lake Turner 64 D9
Lake Tutira 28 A12
Lake Unknown 64 D11 65 D1
Lake Victor 69 J4 75 D4
Lake Victoria 70 D9
Lake Vipan 29 A5
Lake Waahi 9 G4
Lake Wade 63 J5
Lake Wahakari 1 D3
Lake Wahapo 49 F6
Lake Waiau 25 G5
Lake Waihola 74 J8 79 B6
Lake Waikare (Taranaki) 24 J11 25 F6
Lake Waikare (Waikato) 9 F5
Lake Waikareiti 21 E3
Lake Waikareiti Track 21 D3
Lake Waikaremoana 20 E14 21 E2
Lake Waikere 3 G5
Lake Waimimiha 1 J5

Lake Waipapa 12 J10
Lake Waiparera 1 G5
Lake Waipori 74 J8 79 B6
Lake Waipu 29 A4
Lake Wairarapa 33 E5
Lake Waitaki 67 C7
Lake Waitaki (locality) 67 D7
Lake Waitawa 29 H4
Lake Wakatipu 64 H14 65 H4
Lake Wanaka 66 B8
Lake Whakamaru 19 A4
Lake Whakaneke 5 E4
Lake Whangape 9 F4
Lake Widgeon 69 J5 75 C5
Lake Williamson 64 A12 65 A2
Lake Wilmot 64 A10
Lake Wiritoa 26 J8
Lake Wisely 70 A9
Lakeside 55 G7 62 B13
Lakeside Track 42 H13 43 G1
Lame Duck Hut 59 B4
Langdale 34 B12
Langs Beach 6 A8
Lansdowne 53 J7 56 E9
Larrikin Creek Hut 42 D9
Larrys Creek 41 J5 46 A9
Lauder 66 H12 67 H1
Lauriston 55 G3 62 B9
Lawrence 73 H5 79 A3
Lawrence Hut 50 G11 51 G2
Lawyers Delight Hut 50 A13 51 A4
Le Bons Bay 56 F12
Le Crens Hut 59 E5
Leamington, NI 12 D8
Leamington, SI 48 J8
Lee Flat 73 G7
Lee Stream 74 G8
Lees Valley 52 D13 53 D4
Leeston 55 G7 62 B13
Leigh 6 D11
Leith Valley 74 G11 124 D2
Leithfield 54 E8 56 A10
Leithfield Beach 54 E8 56 A10
Leon Kinvig Hut 27 J5 30 A12 31 A6
Lepperton 17 H1 23 B6
Leslie - Karamea Track 37 J5 42 A10
Levels 61 H4
Levels Valley 61 H3
Levin 29 G5
Lewis Hut 37 F2
Lewis Pass Scenic Res 46 D13 47 D1
Liberton 124 D3
Lichfield 12 F11
Liebig Hut 60 A8
Limehills 77 A4
Limestone Downs 9 F1
Limestone Valley 60 G12 61 G1
Lincoln 89 C2
Lincoln University 53 J6 56 F8 62 A14
Lincoln, SI 53 J6 56 F8
Linden 33 D2 35 B2 110 B2
Lindenvale 110 B2
Lindis Crossing 66 F10
Lindis Hut 66 B11
Lindis Valley 66 D11
Linkwater 40 G9 44 A10
Lintley 71 G6
Linton 29 E7 31 E1
Linwood 54 H8 56 D10 120 F3
Lismore 61 D6
Little Akaloa 56 F12
Little Barrier Island 6 C13 36 D1
Little Barrier Island Nature Reserve
6 C13 36 D1
Little Bay 8 B11 36 J5
Little Huia 7 F2 89 E1
Little Island 75 D3
Little Manly 88 C5
Little Rakaia 55 H6 62 C12
Little River 56 G11
Little Valley 72 B14 73 B3
Little Waihi 13 C6
Little Wanganui 41 B7
Littlebourne 123 D2
Liverpool Hut 64 A14 65 A4
Livingstone (Hamilton) 92 F2
Livingstone (Wanganui, NI) 26 J13 27 J1
Livingstone, SI 68 G8
Loburn 53 E7 56 A9
Loburn North 53 E7 56 A9
Loch Katrine 46 H12
Loch Loudon 73 H7 79 A5

Loch Luella 73 H7 79 A5
Loch Maree 69 G6 75 A6
Loch Maree Hut 69 G6 75 A6
Loch Norrie 6 H8 7 B2
Lochiel 77 C4
Lochindorb 78 D14 79 F2
Lochinvar Hut 52 B11 53 B2
Lochnagar 64 C14 65 C4
Locke Stream Hut 46 J9
Logantown 66 G10
Lonely Lake Hut 37 F6
Long Bay 6 H10 7 B4 88 E4
Long Beach 74 F12
Long Harry Hut 77 J1 80 C3
Long Island (Marlborough) 35 G2 40 F12
Long Island (Southland) 69 H3 75 B3
Long Range Lake 32 B12
Longbeach 62 F8
Longburn 29 E7 31 E1
Longbush, NI 34 D8
Longbush, SI 77 E6
Longford 42 G9
Longlands 28 F11 103 D6
Longridge 72 H8
Longridge North 71 G7
Longview Hut 27 J5
Longwood 76 H14 77 E2
Lorneville 77 E5
Lovells Flat 79 D4
Loveridge Hut 37 J6 42 A11
Lowburn 66 G9
Lowcliffe 61 F7
Lower Arahura Hut 51 A6
Lower Goulter Hut 43 D4
Lower Hutt 33 E3 35 A3 110 C3
Lower Kaimai 12 C13 13 C2
Lower Kawhatau 27 G3
Lower Matakuhia Hut 20 G10
Lower Moutere 38 H9 39 F1
Lower Nevis 72 A10
Lower Portobello 74 G12
Lower Princhester Hut 70 E13 71 E2
Lower Selwyn Huts 56 G8 62 B14
Lower Shotover 65 H5
Lower Tama Lake 19 J1 26 A13 27 A1
Lower Waihou 3 C3
Lower Waiohine Track 33 B7
Lower Wairaki Hut 70 H13 71 H2 76 B13
Lower Windley Hut 71 D4
Lowgarth 23 E6 25 B1
Lowry Bay 33 E3 35 A3 110 D3
Lowther 71 F6
Lucretia Hut 46 E13 47 E1
Luggate 66 D9
Lumsden 71 G6
Luna Hut 42 C9
Lupton Hut 26 B12
Luxmoore Hut 70 C10
Lyall Bay 33 F2 35 B4 110 E2
Lyalldale 68 A12
Lyell 41 G7
Lyell Hut 50 F12 51 F3
Lyell Walkway 41 G7
Lyndhurst 55 F2 62 A8
Lynfield 89 D3
Lynmore 13 G4 96 C5
Lynmouth 107 C2
Lynnford 61 E7
Lyttelton 54 J8 56 E10
Lyttelton Harbour/Whakaraupo 54 J9

M

Maata 23 F7 25 C2
Mabel Bush 77 D6
Macandrew Bay 74 H12 124 B3
Macetown 65 F5
Mackaytown 10 F10
Mackenzie Hut 46 H10
Mackford 17 D5
Mackintosh Hut 28 B8
Maclennan 78 F13 79 H1
Macraes Flat 74 B10
Maerewhenua 68 F9
Maeroa 91 C1 92 E2
Maewa 29 C7 31 C1
Magdalen Hut 46 F14 47 F2
Mahakirau 8 E12
Mahana 38 J10 39 G2
Mahanga 22 H9 22 AA2
Maharahara 30 C11 31 C5
Maharahara West 30 C10 31 C4

Maharakeke 32 A9
Maheno 68 J10
Mahia 22 J9 22 AA2
Mahia Beach 22 J9 22 AA2
Mahina Bay 110 D3
Mahinepua 2 H11
Mahitahi 58 A13 59 A2
Mahoe 23 E6
Mahoenui 17 B7
Mahora (Bay of Plenty) 16 E12
Mahora (Hastings) 103 C5
Mahurangi 6 F10
Mahurangi West 6 F10 7 A4
Mahuta (Northland) 5 A2
Mahuta (Waikato) 9 G4 11 A5
Maia 124 C3
Maihiihi 11 H7
Maimai 46 B8
Maioro 7 J4 9 D1
Maioro Sands 9 E1
Mairangi Bay 6 J10 7 C4
Mairehau 120 E4
Mairetahi 5 G7
Mairoa 11 J4
Mairtown 85 B2
Maitahi 3 H6
Maitai 115 C6
Maitai Dam 38 J13 39 G5 43 A6
Maitland 72 J11 78 A10
Makahika 29 G6
Makahu 24 D10 25 A5
Makahu Saddle Hut 28 B8
Makaka (Taranaki) 23 F5
Makaka (Waikato) 11 D2
Makakaho 24 G12 25 D7
Makakaho Junction 24 H11 25 E6
Makara 33 E1 35 C3 110 D1
Makara Beach 33 E1 35 C3 110 C1
Makaraka 22 D10 100 A1
Makaranui 26 C11
Makarau 6 G8 7 A2
Makareao 74 B12
Makaretu 27 J6 30 A13 31 A7
Makaretu Hut 27 J5 30 A12 31 A6
Makarewa 77 D5
Makarewa Junction 77 D5
Makaro / Ward Island 110 E3
Makarora 58 H10
Makarora Township 58 J10
Makarora Hut 58 G12 59 G1
Makauri 22 D10
Makerua 29 F6
Maketawa Track 23 D5
Maketu 13 C6
Maketu Pa 11 F2
Makikihi 68 C13
Makino 30 B8 31 B2
Makirikiri 30 C12 31 C6
Makirikiri South 29 A5
Makohine Valley 26 G14 27 G2
Makomako (Manawatu) 30 F9 31 F3
Makomako (Waikato) 11 E3
Makomako Hut 21 C3
Makorori 22 D11
Makotuku 30 B13 31 B7
Makuri 30 F11 31 F5
Mamaku 12 F14 13 F3
Mamaranui 3 H6
Mana 33 C2 35 B1
Mana Island 33 C1 35 C1
Manaia (Taranaki) 23 G5
Manaia (Waikato) 8 D11
Manakau 29 H4
Mananui 45 J1
Manaohau Right Branch Hut 20 A13
Manapouri 70 E10
Manaroa 35 J2 40 F10
Manawahe 13 F7
Manawaora 4 B11
Manawaru 10 H10 12 A11
Manawatawhi/Great Island (75 E3)
Manawatu River Estuary Wetland 29 F4
Mandeville 72 J9 78 A8
Mandeville North 53 G7 56 C9
Mangaehuehu Hut 26 B12
Mangaeteroa 26 C10
Mangahao 30 E9 31 E3
Mangahao Flats Hut 29 H6
Mangahei 30 C13 31 C7
Mangahouhou 18 G13 19 G1
Mangaiti 10 G9
Mangakahika Hut 20 F11

Mangakahu Valley 18 D11
Mangakakahi 96 C2
Mangakino 12 J11 19 A3
Mangakino Track 10 G10
Mangakirikiri Hut 15 F6
Mangakura 6 F8
Mangakuri Beach 28 J12 32 A13
Mangamahu 26 G11
Mangamaire 30 F9 31 F3
Mangamako Hut 14 J9
Mangamate Hut 20 E11
Mangamaunu 48 D13
Mangamingi 24 F8 25 C3
Mangamuka 2 K9 3 A5
Mangamuka Bridge 3 A5
Mangamuka Gorge Walkway 2 K7 3 A3
Mangamutu 30 E9 31 E3
Manganui Skifield -
Mt Taranaki / Mt Egmont 23 D5
Manganuku Hut 15 J3
Mangaohae 11 J3
Mangaokewa 18 A11
Mangaone Walkway 33 A5
Mangaonoho 26 H13 27 H1
Mangaoranga 30 H9 31 H3
Mangaorapa 32 D9
Mangaore 29 G6
Mangaorongo 11 G7
Mangaotaki 17 A7
Mangapa 2 J9 3 A5
Mangapai 4 H11
Mangapakeha 34 B12
Mangapapa 100 A3
Mangaparo 18 F8
Mangapehi 18 B11
Mangapiko 11 E6
Mangapiko Valley 9 F6
Mangapouri Hut 20 C12
Mangarakau 37 B5
Mangarawa 30 D10 31 D4
Mangarimu 27 J3
Mangaroa 33 D4
Mangaroa Valley 111 B6
Mangatainoka 30 E10 31 E4
Mangatainoka Hot Springs -
Tarawera 20 J8 28 A8
Mangatainoka Hut 19 J7
Mangataiore 2 J8 3 A4
Mangatangi 8 H8 9 C5
Mangatangi Reservoir 8 G8 9 B5
Mangatara 3 J7
Mangataraire 3 C6
Mangatarata 8 J10 9 D7
Mangatawhiri 7 H7 9 C4
Mangatea 11 J5
Mangateparu 10 H8 12 A9
Mangatepopo Hut 18 J13 19 J1
Mangatera 30 C12 31 C6
Mangateretere 28 F12 103 B4
Mangati 11 F5
Mangatiti 30 G12 31 G6
Mangatoatoa Hut 21 C3
Mangatoetoe 2 J7
Mangatoetoe Hut 33 J5
Mangatoi 13 D4
Mangatoki 23 F6 25 C1
Mangatoro 30 D13 31 D7
Mangatu 3 F5
Mangatuna (Gisborne) 16 J11 22 A13
Mangatuna (Manawatu) 30 D14 32 D8
Mangatupoto 18 D10
Mangaturuturu Hut 27 A7
Mangaturuturu Hut 26 B12
Mangatutara Hut 15 E7
Mangatutu 12 H8
Mangawara 9 G5
Mangaweka 27 G2
Mangawhai Cliffs Walkway 6 B9
Mangawhai Golf Course 6 B9
Mangawhai Heads 6 B9
Mangawhai Point 6 B9
Mangawhata 29 E6
Mangawhere 3 J7
Mangawhero (Northland) 3 D4
Mangawhero (Taranaki) 23 F5
Mangawhero (Waikato) 11 H6
Mangawhero Hut 20 A12
Mangawhio 24 J10 25 F5
Mangere 7 F5 9 A2 90 E4
Mangere Bridge 90 D4
Mangere East 90 E5
Mangitaipa 3 A4
Mangles Valley 42 G9

Mangonui 2 H8
Mangonui Whaling Museum 2 G8
Mangorei 23 B5 107 D5
Mangorei Track 23 C4
Mangungu 3 C5
Mangungu Mission House 3 C5
Maniatutu 13 D6
Manoeka 13 C5
Manor Park 33 D3 35 A2 111 B4
Manorburn Reservoir 73 B4
Mansion Hut 71 D6
Manson Hut 27 B7
Manson Nicholls Memorial Hut 46 D13
Mansons Siding 18 H11
Manui 27 G2
Manuka Creek 79 C4
Manuka Lake 51 H5
Manukau - Auckland 7 F5 9 A2 90 E5
Manukau - Northland 3 A2
Manukau Heights 90 E6
Manunui 18 F11
Manuoha Track 20 D14 21 D2
Manurewa 7 F5 9 A2
Manurewa East 90 E6
Manutahi 23 H7 25 E2
Manutuke 22 E9
Many Islands 69 H2 75 B2
Maori Hill (Dunedin) 123 B2 124 D3
Maori Hill (Timaru) 121 D2
Maori Lakes 50 J14 51 J5
Maori Rocks 36 A2
Maoribank 111 A6
Mapau 5 B4
Mapiu 18 C10
Mapua 38 J10 39 G2
Mara 30 H13 31 H7
Maraehara 16 D12
Maraekakaho 28 F10
Maraenui 103 B2
Maraeroa (Northland) 3 B5
Maraeroa (Waikato) 18 B13
Maraetaha 22 F9
Maraetai (Auckland) 7 E7
Maraetai (Waikato) 12 J10
Marahau 38 F10 39 D2
Marakerake 68 H10
Maramarua 8 J8 9 D5
Mararewa 42 C13 43 B1
Maratoto 8 J13 10 E10
Marauiti Hut 20 E13 21 E1
Marawiti 55 F3 62 A9
Marco 17 H6 24 B11
Mareretu 5 A6
Marewa 28 D12 103 B2
Marima 30 F8 31 F2
Mariri 38 H10 39 F2
Market Cross 37 J2 41 A7
Marlborough 88 H3
Marlborough Forest 3 F6
Marlow 4 E10
Marohemo 5 B6
Marokopa 11 H2
Marokopa Falls 11 H3
Maromaku 4 D10
Maronan 55 J1 61 D7
Maropea Forks Hut 27 G5
Maropiu 3 H6
Marsden 45 G4
Marsden Bay 4 H13
Marsden Point Oil Refinery 4 H13
Marshland 54 H8 56 D10 120 F5
Marshlands 35 J5 40 J10 44 B11
Martha Gold & Silver Mine - Waihi 10 E11
Martinborough 34 E7
Marton 29 A6
Marton Block 27 J4
Marua 4 E12
Maruakoa 68 G10
Maruia 46 B12
Maruia Springs 46 E13 47 E1
Maruia Springs Thermal Resort 46 E13 47 E1
Marumaru 21 G5
Mary Island 76 D9
Marybank, NI 26 J8
Marybank, SI 38 J12 39 G4
Maryhill 124 E4
Masham 120 B3
Mason Bay Hut 80 E3
Masons Flat 53 A7
Massey 7 D3 89 B2
Massey East 89 B2
Massey North 89 B2
Massey West 89 B2

Masterton 34 B9
Mata (Northland - Far North) 3 B4
Mata (Northland) 4 H12
Matahanea 14 G13 15 G2
Matahapa 14 G12 15 G1
Matahi 14 J11
Matahina 14 G9
Matahiwi (Wanganui) 24 H14 26 E9
Matahiwi (Wellington) 34 A8
Matahuru 9 F6
Matai, NI 12 C11
Matai, SI 45 D6
Mataikona 30 J13 31 J7
Matakana 6 E10
Matakana Island 10 H13 12 A14 13 A3 94 A2
Matakanui 66 G11
Matakatia Bay 88 C5
Matakawau 7 G3
Matakitaki 42 J9
Matakohe 5 B5
Matamata 12 C11
Matamata Aerodrome 10 J10 12 B11
Matamau 30 B12 31 B6
Matangi 12 C8
Matangirau 2 H11
Matapihi 13 B4 94 C3
Matapouri 4 E13
Matapu 23 F6 25 C1
Matarae 74 E8
Matarangi 8 C12
Mataraua 3 E6
Mataraua Forest 3 E5
Matarawa 34 C7
Matarau 4 F11
Matariki 42 C12
Mataroa 26 F14 27 F2
Matata 14 D9
Matatoki 8 H12 10 C9
Matau, NI 17 J4 24 C9
Matau, SI 79 F4
Mataura 78 C9
Mataura Island 78 E8
Matauri Bay 2 H12
Matawai 21 A6
Matawaia 4 D8
Matawhera 3 C4
Matawhero 22 D10
Matea 20 E9
Matemateaonga 24 F9 25 C4
Matemateaonga Track 24 E12 25 B7
Matiere 18 E9
Matihetihe 3 C2
Matingarahi 8 F9 9 A6
Matipo Heights 96 D2
Matira 9 G2 11 A3
Matua 94 B1
Maud Island 35 K1 40 E9
Maude Track 23 C5
Mauao/Mt Maunganui 94 A2
Mauku 7 H5 9 C2
Maungahuka hut 33 A6
Maungakaramea 4 H10
Maungapohatu 20 C14 21 C2
Maungapohatu Track 20 C14 21 C2
Maungaraki 110 C3
Maungarau Hut 24 F12 25 C7
Maungaroa 18 J9 24 C14
Maungatapere 4 G10
Maungatapu 13 B4 94 C3
Maungatautari 12 E9
Maungati 68 A11
Maungatua 74 H8 79 A6
Maungaturoto 5 B7
Maungawera 66 C9
Maungawhio Lagoon 22 J9 22 AA2
Maunu 4 G11
Maupuia 110 E2
Mauriceville 30 J8 31 J2
Mauriceville West 30 J8 31 J2
Mavora - Greenstone Track 64 G10
Mavora Walkway 64 J11 65 J1
Mawaro 60 H13 61 H2
Mawheraiti 46 C8
Maxwell 25 G6
Mayfair 103 C5
Mayfield 117 A3
Mayfield (Ashburton) 61 C6
Maymorn 33 D4 111 A6
Mayor Island / Tuhua 10 E13
Maytown 68 D12
McConchies Hut 42 E9
McCoy Hut 50 G10 51 G1
McKellar Hut 64 F10

McKerrow Island Hut 64 B9
McKerrow Track 33 F3 35 A4
McKinnon Hut 27 G5
McLaren Falls - Tauranga 12 C13 13 C2
McLaren Park 89 C2
McLean Falls (SI) 78 G12
McLeod Bay 4 H13
McNab 78 A9
Mead 55 F5 62 A11
Meadowbank 90 C5
Meadowbank, SI 74 C12
Mechanics Bay 90 B4
Medbury 54 A8
Meeanee 28 E12 103 B2
Meg Hut 65 F7
Mellons Bay 90 C6
Melrose 110 E2
Melville 91 J4 92 G3
Menzies Ferry 78 D8
Mercer 7 J7 9 D4
Mercury Islands / Iles d'Haussez 8 B13
Meremere (Taranaki) 24 G8 25 D3
Meremere (Waikato) 7 J7 9 E4
Meringa 18 F12
Merino Downs 72 J11
Merita 2 F7
Merivale 119 A1 120 D3
Mermaid Pods - Matapouri 4 E13
Merrijigs 46 C9
Merrilands 107 C5
Merrivale 76 E13
Merton 74 E12
Methven 52 J9 55 F2 62 A8
Michies Crossing 74 F12
Mid Flat Hut 58 F13 59 F2
Mid Glenroy Hut 46 B13 47 B1
Mid Goulter Hut 43 D4
Mid Greenstone Hut 64 G11 65 G1
Mid Okahu Hut 20 D12
Mid Pohangina Hut 30 A11 31 A5
Mid Robinson Hut 46 F11
Mid Styx Hut 50 A14 51 A5
Mid Taipo Hut 51 A7
Mid Trent Hut 46 H9
Mid Waiohine Hut 33 A7
Mid Wairoa Hut 43 D4
Middle Head Hut 58 C12 59 C1
Middle Hill Hut 28 A8
Middle Hut 68 H8
Middle Stream Hut 27 H6
Middle Valley 60 F13 61 F2
Middlemarch 74 D8
Middlemore 90 D5
Middleton 120 D2
Middy Creek Hut 39 J5 43 B6
Midhirst 23 D6 25 A1
Midway Hut 20 B12
Mihi 19 B7
Mihiwaka 74 G12
Mikimiki 34 A9
Miko 41 D5
Mikonui Flat Hut 50 C11 51 C2
Mikotahi 107 B2
Milburn 79 C5
Milford Huts 61 H5
Milford Sound (Piopiotahi) 63 C7
Milford Sound (locality) 64 D8
Milford Track - Great Walk 64 E8
Milford, NI 6 J10 7 C4
Milford, SI 61 G5
Mill Creek 8 E12
Mill Road 77 E5
Millers Flat 72 F14 73 F3
Millerton 41 E5
Milltown (Selwyn) 55 H7 62 C13
Milltown (Westland) 45 J4 50 A14 51 A5
Milnthorpe 37 C7
Milson 30 D8 31 D2 105 A4
Milton 79 C5
Mimihau 78 D9
Mina 48 J8
Minaret Bay 66 A8
Minchin Bivvy 46 J9
Minden 10 J12 12 B13 13 B2
Minehaha 42 H8
Mingha Bivvy 52 B8
Minginui 20 D11
Mintaro Hut 63 F7
Miramar 33 F2 35 B4 110 E2
Miranda 8 H9 9 C6
Miranda Hot Springs 8 H9 9 C6
Mirror Lakes 64 H9
Mission Bay 7 D5 90 C5

Mission Bush 7 H4 9 C1
Mistake Flats Hut 50 H10 51 H1
Mitcham 55 G3 62 B9
Mitchells 45 H5
Mitchells Hut 68 J8
Mitchelltown 110 E1
Mitikarukaru 40 C8
Mitimiti 3 C2
Mititai 5 A3
Mitre Flats Hut 29 J6 34 A7
Moa Creek 66 J12 67 J1 73 A4
Moa Flat 72 F13 73 F2
Moa Park Hut 38 F9 39 D1
Moana (Nelson) 116 B4
Moana (Westland) 45 G6
Moana Roa Beach 29 C5
Moawhango 27 E3
Moeatoa 11 J2
Moeawatea 24 G10 25 D5
Moehau 3 D5
Moengawahine 4 F9
Moenui 40 G8 44 A9
Moera 110 C3
Moeraki 74 B14
Moeraki Boulders 74 B13
Moerangi (Waikato) 11 E4
Moerangi (Wanganui) 18 F13 19 F1
Moerangi Hut 20 E11
Moerewa 4 C9
Moeroa 24 F10 25 C5
Moewhare 4 H11
Mohaka 21 J3
Mohuiti 3 B4
Moirs Hill Walkway 6 F9
Mokai 19 B4
Mokaikai Scenic Reserve 1 B3
Mokau (Northland) 4 C12
Mokau (Waikato) 17 D5
Mokau Tarns Track 20 E14 21 E2
Mokauiti 18 C9
Moke Lake 64 H14 65 H4
Mokihinui 41 D6
Mokihinui Forks Ecological Area 42 E8
Mokihinui Forks Hut 42 D8
Mokohinau Islands (Flax Islands)
Nature Reserve 36 A2
Mokohinau Islands / Flax Islands 36 A2
Mokoia 23 H7 25 E2
Mokoia Island 13 F4
Mokoreta 78 E10
Mokotua 77 F7
Mole Hut 42 J11
Mole Track 42 J11
Molesworth Recreation Reserve 48 B8
Momona 74 H9 79 A7
Monaco 116 C3
Monavale, NI 12 D8
Monavale, SI 60 H12 61 H1
Moncks Bay 120 H1
Moncks Spur 120 H1
Moneymore 79 D5
Monowai 70 H11 76 B11
Monowai Hut 70 H9 76 B9
Montalto 61 B5
Montgomerie Hut 46 B10
Monument Hut 59 E4
Moonbeam Hut 50 D11 51 D2
Moonlight 74 C10
Moonlight Hut 66 B10
Moonstone Lake 42 B10
Morere 22 H8
Morere Hot Springs 22 H8
Morgan Hut 42 J12
Morningside (Auckland) 89 C3
Morningside (Whangarei) 84 D5
Mornington 110 E1
Mornington (Dunedin) 74 H11 124 E4
Morrinsville 10 H8 12 A9
Morrisons 74 A11
Morrisons Bush 33 D7
Morton Mains 77 D7
Morven 68 E13
Mosgiel 74 H10 124 J4
Mossburn 71 F4
Mosston 109 B2
Motairehe 36 C4
Motakotako 11 D3
Motatau 4 D9
Motea 30 D13 31 D7
Moteo 28 D11 103 D2
Motiti Island 13 A6
Motu 15 J4
Motu Rimu 77 F5

Motuanauru Island 39 E7
Motuara Island 35 G1 40 E12
Motuariki Island 60 D10
Motuarohia Island 4 A10
Motueka 38 G10 39 E2
Motueka Aerodrome 38 G9 39 E1
Motuhaku Island 13 A7
Motuhaku Island / Schooner Rocks 13 A7
Motuhina Island 16 J11
Motuihe Island 7 D6 90 B6
Motukahaua Island 8 B10 36 J4
Motukaika 60 J14 61 J3
Motukaraka 3 C4
Motukaramarama Island 8 C10 36 J4
Motukarara 56 G9
Motukauri 3 C3
Motukawaiti Island 2 H12
Motukawanui Island 2 H12
Motukawao Group 8 C10 36 J4
Motuketekete Island 6 F11
Motukiekie Island 4 A11
Motukiore 3 C5
Motumakareta Island 8 B10 36 J4
Motumaoho 10 J7 12 B8
Motunau Beach 54 C11
Motunau Island / Plate Island, NI 13 B7
Motunau Island, SI 54 C11
Motunui 17 G2 23 A7
Motuoapa 19 G3
Motuora Island 6 F11 7 A5
Motuoroi Island 16 J11
Motuoruhi Island 8 C10
Motupapa Island 2 K13 4 A9
Motupiko 42 C13 43 B1
Moturau Hut 70 D10
Moturekareka Island 6 F11
Moturoa 107 B2
Moturoa Island (Northland - Far North) 1 E7
Moturoa Islands 1 E7
Moturua Island (Northland) 4 A10
Moturua Island (Waikato) 8 C10
Motutaiko Island (Auckland) 36 D3
Motutaiko Island (Taupo) 19 F4
Motutangi 1 F5
Motutangi Swamp 1 F5
Motutapere Island 8 D10
Motutapu Island 6 J12 7 C6 90 A6
Motutapu Island Recreation Reserve 6 J12 7 C6
Motutere 19 F4
Motuti 3 C3
Motutoa 3 D3
Motuwi Island 8 B10 36 J4
Mou Tapu 65 C7
Mou Waho 65 B7
Moumahaki 25 G5
Moumoukai 8 G8 9 B5
Mount Albert 7 E4
Mount Albert 89 C3
Mount Allan 74 F10
Mount Arthur Hut 37 H7 42 A12
Mount Aspiring National Park 57 H7
Mount Auckland Walkway 6 F8
Mount Barker 66 D8
Mount Bee Huts 71 D5
Mount Biggs 29 C7
Mount Brown Hut 50 A14 51 A5
Mount Bruce 29 J7 31 J1
Mount Bruce National Wildlife Centre
- Eketahuna 30 H8 31 H2
Mount Cargill 74 G12 124 B1
Mount Cheeseman Skifield 52 D9
Mount Cook Village (The Hermitage) 59 B6
Mount Cook (Wellington) 110 E2 112 E5
Mount Cook / Aoraki, SI 59 B6
Mount Cook / Aoraki National Park 49 J6 59 A7
Mount Curl 26 J12
Mount Eden 7 E4 90 C4
Mount Eggeling 57 G4
Mount Herbert Walkway 56 F10
Mount Holdsworth Track 34 A7
Mount Hut 68 J9
Mount Hutt 52 H8 55 D1
Mount Hutt Methven Airfield 52 J8
Mount Hutt Skifield 52 H8
Mount Lyford Skifield 48 F8
Mount Marua 111 A6
Mount Matthews Track 33 F3
Mount Maunganui 13 A4 94 B3
Mount Misery Hut 42 J12
Mount Nessing 60 H12 61 H1
Mount Olympus 37 E5
Mount Olympus Skifield 52 E8 55 A1

Mount Owen 42 D11
Mount Parahaki 4 G12
Mount Pickering 70 C9
Mount Pisa 66 F9
Mount Pleasant 54 J8 56 E10 120 G1
Mount Pleasant (Marlborough) 35 J4
40 H10 44 A11
Mount Pleasant (mountain) 54 J8 56 E10
Mount Potts 50 J12 51 J3
Mount Richards 30 B10 31 B4
Mount Richmond Conservation Park 39 F7 40 H8
43 B7 44 A9
Mount Robert Skifield 42 H13 43 G1
Mount Roskill 7 E4
Mount Roskill 89 C3
Mount Somers 61 A6
Mount Stoker 74 E9
Mount Stuart 79 C4
Mount Tinsley 70 C10
Mount Victoria 33 F1 35 C4 110 E2 112 E6
Mount Wellington 7 E5 90 D5
Mount Wesley 3 J7
Mount William Walkway 7 H7 9 C4
Mountain House Hut 33 A7
Mourea 13 F5
Mouse Point 47 H5
Moutahiauru Island 16 G12
Moutoa 29 F6
Moutohora 15 J4
Moutohora Island 14 D10
Moutoki Island 14 D10
Mud Spa - Rotorua 13 F5
Mudflats Hut 51 A6
Mueller Hut 59 B6
Muhunoa 29 H4
Muhunoa East 29 H5
Mukahanga 40 B9
Mullins Hut 50 C13 51 C4
Mungo Hut 50 C14 51 C5
Mungoven Gardens - Marton 29 A6
Murchison 42 G9
Murchison Hut 49 H7
Muri 33 C2
Muritai 110 E3
Muriwai 22 E9
Muriwai Beach 7 D1
Murray Aynsley 120 F2
Murray Bay 88 F4
Murupara 20 B11
Musselburgh 124 D4
Muttontown 66 J10 72 A13 73 A2
Myross Bush 77 E5
Mystery Creek 11 D7
Myttons Hut 37 H6

N

Naenae 33 E3 35 A3 111 C4
Naike 9 G3
Napenape 54 B13
Napier 28 D12 103 A1
Napier Central 101 B3
Napier South 101 D1 103 A1
Nardoo Hut 47 A2
Narrow Neck 90 B4
Naseby 67 G5
National Aquarium - Napier 28 D12
National Park 18 J11
Native Island 80 E6
Naumai 5 B3
Nawton 92 E2
Nawton North 92 E2
Neave Hut 50 E12 51 E3
Neavesville 8 H13 10 C10
Nee Islets 69 B4
Neill Forks Hut 33 B6
Neils Beach 57 E6
Nelson 38 J12 39 G4 115 C3 116 A5
Nelson Airport 38 J11 39 H3 43 A4
Nelson Creek 45 E6
Nelson East 115 D5 116 B5
Nelson Island 36 D3
Nelson Lakes National Park 47 A3
Nelson South 38 J12 39 G4 43 A5 116 B4
Nenthorn 74 C10
Ness Valley 8 F8 9 A5
Netherby, NI 9 H6 11 A7
Netherby, SI 55 H3 62 C9
Netherton 10 E9
Nevis Crossing 65 J7 72 A10
New Brighton 54 H8 56 D10 120 H4
New Creek 41 G6

New Lynn 7 E4 89 D3
New Plymouth 23 B5 106 B3
New Windsor 89 C3
New Windsor, SI 76 H14 77 E2
Newall 23 D3
Newbury 29 D7 31 D1
Newfield 128 A4
Newland 55 H3 62 C9
Newlands 110 C2
Newman 30 G8 31 G2
Newmarket 87 H6 90 C4
Newstead 11 C7 92 E6
Newton 87 G4 90 C4
Newton Creek Hut 51 A6
Newton Flat 42 G8
Newtown 33 F1 35 C4 110 E2
Nga Kiore / Jag Rocks 40 B10
Nga Manu Wildlife Sanctuary - Waikanae 33 A4
Nga Motu/Sugar Loaf Islands 23 B5
Ngaawapurua Hut 27 A7
Ngaere 23 E7 25 B2
Ngahape (Waikato) 11 G7
Ngahape (Wellington) 34 D11
Ngaheramai Hut 20 B13 21 B1
Ngahere 45 E6
Ngahinapouri 11 D6
Ngaio 33 E1 35 C3 110 D2
Ngaiotonga 4 B11
Ngaiotonga - Russell Forest Track 4 C11
Ngakawau 41 E5
Ngakonui 18 E11
Ngakuru 13 J3
Ngamatapouri 24 H11 25 E6
Ngamoko 30 A12 31 A6
Ngamoko Hut 30 A12 31 A6
Ngamoko Track 21 E3
Ngapaenga 11 J3
Ngapaeruru 30 C13 31 C7
Ngapara 68 F10
Ngapeke 13 B4 94 D3
Ngapipito 4 C8
Ngapuhi 3 D7
Ngapuke 18 F11
Ngapuna (Otago) 74 C8
Ngapuna (Rotorua) 96 C4
Ngaputahi 20 C12
Ngararatunua 4 F11
Ngarimu Bay 8 G11 10 B8
Ngaroma 12 J9
Ngaroto 11 E7
Ngarua 10 J9 12 B10
Ngaruawahia 9 H5 11 A6
Ngataki 1 E4
Ngatamahine 18 B9
Ngatapa 22 D8
Ngatea 8 J11 10 D8
Ngatimoti 38 H9 42 A14
Ngatira 12 F12 13 F1
Ngatiwhetu 1 D3
Ngaturi 30 F10 31 F4
Ngauranga 33 E2 35 B3 110 D2
Ngawaka 27 E2
Ngawapurua 30 E10 31 E4
Ngawaro 12 E14 13 E3
Ngawha 3 C7
Ngawha Springs - Kaikohe 3 C7
Ngawi 33 J5
Ngongotaha 13 F4
Ngongotaha Valley 12 G14 13 G3
Ngunguru 4 F13
Ngutunui 11 F5
Ngutuwera 25 G5
Niagara 78 G11
Niagara Falls 78 G11
Nichols Hut 29 J6 33 A7
Nightcaps 70 J14 71 J3 76 D14 77 A2
Nihoniho 18 E8
Nikau Caves - Waikaretu 9 G2
Nikau Flat Hut 21 A4
Nikau, NI 30 F9 31 F3
Nikau, SI 41 D6
Nina Hut 46 E13 47 E1
Nireaha 30 G8 31 G2
Noble Island 80 J2
Nobles 46 D8
Nokomai 72 D8
Nolans Hut 50 G8
Nonoti 48 J8 54 A12
Nopera 35 J2 40 F10
Norfolk 17 J1 23 C6
Normanby (Dunedin) 124 C2
Normanby, NI 23 G6 25 D1
Normanby, SI 68 A13

Normandale 33 E2 35 B3 110 C3
Norsewood 30 A13 31 A7
Norsewood Pioneer Museum 30 A13 31 A7
North Arm Hut 80 E5
North Cape -
Northernmost point of New Zealand 1 A4
North Clyde 21 H5
North Dunedin 123 B4 124 D3
North East Valley 74 G11 124 D3
North Egmont 23 D5
North Harbour 88 G3
North Harbour Stadium 6 J10 7 C4
North Island 80 D6
North Linwood 120 F3
North Mavora Lake 71 A4
North New Brighton 120 H4
North River 4 J12 5 A7
North Taieri 74 G10 124 J2
Northcote (Auckland) 7 D4 88 J4
Northcote (Christchurch) 120 D4
Northcote Central 90 B4
Northcote Point 90 B4
Northcross 88 F3
Northland 33 E1 35 C3 110 D1
Northope 77 C4
Northpark 90 D6
North-west Nelson Conservation Park 37 C5
Northwood 120 D5
Norton Reserve 68 D12
Norwest Lakes 70 D8
Norwood 52 J13 53 J4 55 F6 62 A12
Notown 45 E6
Nuhaka 22 J8
Nukuhau 19 D5 97 A1 98 A3
Nukuhou North 14 G12
Nukumaru 25 G6
Nukuroa 68 D13
Nukutaunga Island 2 G12
Nukutawhiti 3 F7
Nukuwaiata Island 40 C11
Nydia Track 40 F8

O

Oaklands 53 J7 56 E9 120 C1
Oakleigh 4 H11
Oaks Hut 33 F3 35 A4
Oakura (Northland) 4 C12
Oakura (Taranaki) 23 B4
Oamaru 68 H12 122 B4
Oamaru Hut 19 H7
Oaonui 23 E2
Oaro 48 F11
Oban / Halfmoon Bay 80 E5
Ocean Beach, NI (Hawke's Bay) 28 G13
Ocean Beach, NI (Northland) 4 H14
Ocean Beach, SI 77 G5 80 A6
Ocean Grove 74 H11 124 C5
Ocean Spa heated saltwater pools -
Napier 28 D12
Ocean View 74 H10 124 H6
Oeo 23 G4
Ohaaki 19 B7
Ohaeawai 4 C8
Ohai 70 J13 71 J2 76 C13
Ohakea Wing RNZAF Museum - Bulls 29 C6
Ohakune 26 C11
Ohakuri 19 A5
Ohana 40 D8
Ohane Hut 20 A14 21 A2
Ohangai 23 H7 25 E2
Ohapi 61 G5
Ohapuku 54 G8 56 C10
Ohariu Valley 110 C2
Ohau 29 H5
Ohau Skifield 59 G4
Ohaua 20 C13 21 C1
Ohauiti 13 C4
Ohaupo 11 D7
Ohautira 9 J3 11 C4
Ohawe 23 H6 25 E1
Ohineakai 16 F11
Ohinemutu 13 G4 96 B3
Ohinepaka 21 H4
Ohinepanea 13 D7
Ohinetahi 54 J8 56 E10
Ohinewai 9 F5
Ohingaiti 26 H14 27 H2
Ohingaroa 103 C1
Ohiwa 14 F12 15 F1
Ohiwa Oyster Farm 14 F11
Ohoka 53 F7 56 B9

Ohope 14 E11
Ohora Hut 14 J11
Ohotu 27 F3
Ohui 8 G14 10 B11
Ohura 18 F8
Ohurakura 28 A11
Ohuri 3 C4
Oingo Lake 28 E11
Oio 18 H11
Okaeria 9 E6
Okahu (Northland - Far North) 1 J6
Okahu (Northland) 5 A4
Okahu Island 4 A11
Okahukura 18 E10
Okaiawa 23 G6 25 D1
Okaihau 3 B7
Okains Bay 56 F13
Okaka 3 B6
Okapu 11 E3
Okarae 30 C13 31 C7
Okaramio 40 J8 44 B9
Okari Lagoon 41 H2
Okarito 49 E5
Okarito Lagoon 49 E6
Okato 23 C3
Okau 17 F5
Okauia 12 C12
Okauia Pa 12 C12 13 C1
Oke Island 69 G5 75 A5
Okere Falls 13 F5
Okete 11 C4
Okiato 81 C2 4 B10
Okiore 14 H13 15 H2
Okitu 22 E11 100 C6
Okiwa 88 D3
Okiwi 36 D4
Okiwi Bay 39 E7
Okoia 26 H9
Okokewa Island 36 D3
Okoki 17 G3 24 A8
Okoroire 12 E11
Okui Hut 20 B12
Okuku 53 E6 56 A8
Okuku Reservoir 45 J4
Okupu 36 E4
Okura 88 D3
Okura, NI 6 H10 7 B4
Okuru, SI 58 D8
Okuti Valley 56 G11
Old Man Rock 76 H12
Old Powell Hut 33 A7
Olivine Hut 64 B10
Omaha 6 E10
Omaha Flats 6 E10
Omahu (Hawke's Bay) 28 E11
Omahu (Waikato) 8 J12 10 D9
Omahuta Forest 2 K9 3 A5
Omaio 15 D5
Omakau 66 H12 67 H1
Omakere 32 A12
Omamari 3 H6
Omana 4 J9
Omana Beach 7 E7
Omanaia 3 D4
Omanawa 12 C14 13 C3
Omanawa Falls 12 D14 13 D3
Omanu 13 B4 92 B3
Omanu Beach 13 B4
Omanuka Lagoon 29 D5
Omapere 3 E3
Omarama 67 A3
Omaru Hut 24 D11 25 A6
Omarumutu 14 F14 15 F3
Omata 23 B4 107 D1
Omatane 27 F4
Omaui 77 G4 80 A6
Omaui Island 77 G4 80 A6
Omaunu 2 J10
Omiha 7 D7
Omihi 54 C9
Omimi 74 F12
Omoana 24 F9 25 C4
Omokoroa 10 J12 12 B13 13 B2
Omokoroa Beach 10 H12 12 A13 13 A2
Omori 19 F2
Omoto 45 F4
Onaero 17 G2 23 A7
One Tree Hill 7 E5 90 C4
Onehunga 7 E4 90 D4
Onekaka 37 D7
Onekawa 103 B2
Onemana 8 H14 10 C11
Onepoto 21 F2
Onepu 14 F8

Onepu Hut 14 J11
Onerahi 4 G12
Oneriri 5 D7
Oneroa 6 J13 7 D7
Onetangi 7 D7
Onewhero 7 J5 9 E2
Ongaonga 28 J8
Ongarue 18 D10
Ongaruru 16 H11
Onoke 3 C3
Onslow Hut 60 A8
Onuku 56 H12
Opaea 27 E3
Opaheke 7 G6 9 B3
Opahi 4 D9
Opakau Island 36 D3
Opaki 34 A9
Opaku 24 J9 25 F4
Opal Hot Springs - Matamata 12 C12
Opape 15 F3
Opara 3 C4
Oparara 37 J2 41 A7
Oparau 11 F3
Oparure 11 J5
Opatu 18 G8 24 A13
Opawa 54 J8 56 E10 120 F2
Opawe Hut 30 B10 31 B4
Open Bay Islands 57 D7
Ophir 66 H12 67 H1
Opihi 60 G14 61 G3
Opiki 29 E6
Opio 71 J3
Opito 8 C13
Opoho 124 D3
Oponae 14 J13 15 J2
Opononi 3 D3
Oporo 77 D4
Opotiki 14 F13 15 F2
Opou 37 B7
Opouriao 14 G11
Opoutama 22 J8 22 AA1
Opouteke 3 F7
Opoutere 8 G14 10 B11
Opua 4 B10 81 C3
Opuatia 9 E3
Opuawhanga 4 D12
Opuha 60 G14 61 G3
Opunake 23 F3
Opureke Track 20 G9
Oraka Beach 22 J9 22 AA2
Orakau 12 F8
Orakei 90 C5
Orakei Korako 19 B6
Orakipaoa 61 H5
Oranga 90 D4
Orangapai 67 J5 74 A8
Orangimea 24 J11 25 F6
Orangipongo 26 H13 27 H1
Oranoa 3 F5
Oraora 3 E4
Orapiu 8 D8
Orari 61 F5
Orari Bridge 61 E5
Oratia 7 E3 89 D2
Orauta 4 C8
Orautoha 26 B10
Orawau 3 B4
Orawia 76 E12
Oreore 26 D10
Orepuki 76 G12
Orere 8 F8 9 A5
Orere Point 8 F8 9 A5
Oreti Beach 77 F4
Oreti Plains 77 B4
Orewa 6 G10 7 A4 88 A3
Oriental Bay 110 E2 112 E6
Orikaka Ecological Area 41 F6
Oringi 30 C11 31 C5
Orini 9 G6
Orinoco 38 J9 42 A14
Orira 3 B5
Ormond 22 C9
Ormondville 30 B13 31 B7
Orokonui 74 F12
Oromahoe 4 B8
Orongo 8 H11 10 C8
Orongo Bay 4 B10 81 B3
Orongorongo Track 33 F3 35 A4
Oronui Hut, 16 E8
Oropi 13 D3
Orotere 2 J11
Oroua Downs 29 D5
Orton, NI 9 E4

Orton, SI 61 F6
Orua Bay 7 G3
Oruaiti 2 H9
Oruaiti Beach 16 B8
Oruaiwi 18 E12
Oruanui 19 C5
Oruatua 19 F4
Oruawharo 5 D7
Oruhia 120 F6
Oruru 2 H8
Osborne 74 F12
Ostend 7 D7
Ota Creek 78 D8
Otago Central Rail Trail 66 H13 67 H2 74 C8
Otaha 2 J12
Otahu Flat 70 J11 76 D11
Otahuhu 7 E5 90 D5
Otahuti 77 C3
Otaihanga 33 A3
Otaika 4 G11
Otaika Valley 4 G11
Otaio 68 B13
Otaio Gorge 68 B11
Otaitai Bush 77 E2
Otakairangi 4 F10
Otakeho 23 G4
Otaki 29 J4
Otaki Beach 29 J3
Otaki Forks 33 A5
Otakiri 14 E9
Otakou 74 G13
Otama, NI 8 C13
Otama, SI 72 J9
Otamakapua 26 H14 27 H2
Otamaraoa 16 B8
Otamatea 26 H8 109 A3
Otamatuna Ridge Track 14 J12 15 J1 21 A3
Otamauri 28 D9
Otamita 78 A8
Otane (Bay of Plenty) 21 A2
Otane (Wairarapa) 28 J10
Otanetea Hut 20 B14 21 B2
Otangarei 85 A2
Otangaroa 2 J9
Otangiwai 18 D9
Otanomomo 79 F3
Otao 4 B9
Otapiri 77 A5
Otapiri Gorge 77 A5
Otapukawa Hut 21 A3
Otara, NI 14 F13 15 F2
Otara, NI - Auckland 7 F5 9 A2 90 D5
Otara, SI 78 H9
Otaraia 78 C10
Otaramarae 13 F5
Otarawhata Island 16 A9
Otatara 77 F4
Otatara – Invercargill 128 D5
Otaua (Northland) 3 D6
Otaua (Waikato) 7 J4 9 D1
Otautau 76 F14 77 C2
Otawhao 30 A13 31 A7
Oteake Conservation Park 67 E4
Otehake Hut 52 A9
Otehirinaki 15 D5
Otekaieke 68 E8
Otekura 79 G3
Otematata 67 C5
Otepopo 68 J10 74 A13
Oteramika 77 E7
Otewa 11 H7
Otiake 68 E8
Otikerama 78 B10
Otipua 61 J4 68 A13
Otira 45 J7 52 A8
Otiria 4 C9
Otokia 74 J9 79 B7
Otoko 21 B7
Otoko Lake 58 C14 59 C3
Otonga 4 E11
Otoroa 2 H11
Otorohanga 11 G6
Otuhaereroa Island 39 E7
Otuhi 4 H10
Otukota Hut 27 F5
Otukou 18 H13 19 H1
Otumatu Rock 48 F11
Otumoetai 10 J13 13 B3 93 A6 94 B2
Otunui 18 F9
Oturehua 66 G14 67 G3
Oturere Hut 18 J14 19 J2
Oturoa 13 F3
Oturu 1 J6

Otutu Hut 27 B6
Otuwhare 15 D5
Otway 10 G9
Oue 3 D4
Oueroa 32 B11
Ouruhia 54 G8 56 C10
Outer Island 38 G10 39 E2
Outer Kaiti 100 C5
Outram 74 H9 79 A7
Overdale 55 G4 62 B10
Owahanga 30 H14 32 H8
Owairaka 89 C3
Owairaka Valley 12 F8
Owaka 79 G3
Owaka Valley 78 E14 79 G2
Oware 78 D9
Oweka 41 H5
Owen Island 80 G6
Owen Junction 42 F10
Owen River 42 F10
Owhango 18 G11
Owhata, NI (Bay of Plenty) 13 G4 96 C5
Owhata, NI (Northland) 3 B1
Owhata, SI 40 C8
Owhiro Bay 110 E1
Owhiro, NI 11 G3
Owhiro, SI 74 H10 124 J5
Owhiwa 4 G13
Oxford 52 F13 53 F4 55 B6

P

Pa Island / Te puke-ki-wiataha 56 F13
Pack Horse Hut 56 F10
Paekakariki 33 B3
Paemako 18 B8
Paenga 42 J8
Paengaroa 13 D6
Paepaerahi 12 F8
Paerata 7 H5 9 C2
Paerata Ridge 14 F13 15 F2
Paerau 73 C7
Paeroa 10 E9
Paetawa Track 20 B14 21 B2
Paewhenua 12 H8
Pahaoa 34 G9
Pahau 47 J5
Pahautane 45 A5
Pahautea 33 E6
Pahi 5 C6
Pahia 76 H12
Pahiatua 30 F10 31 F4
Pahoia 10 H12 12 A13 13 A2
Pahou 14 F10
Paiaka 4 D10
Paihia 4 B10 81 B2
Pakanae 3 D3
Pakaraka 4 C8
Pakatoa Island 8 D8
Pakawau 37 B7
Pakiaka Hut (Parahaki) 20 E12
Pakihi Heads Hut 15 H4
Pakihi Hut 15 H4
Pakihi Island 8 E8
Pakihikura 26 J14 27 J2
Pakipaki 28 F11 103 D6
Pakiri 6 D10
Pakotai 4 F8
Pakowhai 28 E12 103 B4
Pakuranga 7 E5 90 D5
Pakuranga Heights 90 D6
Pakuratahi 33 C5
Palm Beach 6 J13 7 D7
Palm Heights 89 C2
Palmerston 74 C13
Palmerston North 30 D8 31 D2
Palmerston North Central 104 B3
Palmerston North International Airport 105 A4
Pamapuria 1 J7
Panaki Island 2 G12
Pancake Rocks & Blowhole - Punakaiki 45 B5
Pandora 1 B2
Panekiri Hut 20 F14 21 F2
Panetapu 12 G8
Pangatotara 38 H9 39 F1
Panguru 3 C3
Panmure 7 E5
Papaaroha 8 C10
Papakai 18 H13 19 H1
Papakaio 68 G12
Papakowhai 110 A3
Papakura 7 G6 9 B3

Papamoa 13 B5 94 D5
Papamoa Beach 13 B5 94 C5
Papanui 53 H7 56 D9 120 D4
Papanui Junction 26 F12
Paparangi - Wellington 33 E2 35 B3
Paparangi (Taranaki) 24 J12 25 F7
Paparangi (Wellington) 110 C2
Paparata 7 H7 9 C4
Paparimu 7 H7 9 C4
Paparoa 5 B6
Paparoa National Park 45 A6
Paparore 1 G6
Papatawa 30 D10 31 D4
Papatea 15 B7
Papatoetoe 7 F5 9 A2 90 E5
Papatotara 76 F11
Papatowai 78 G13 79 J1
Papawai 34 D7
Papawera 16 E11
Paponga 3 B4
Papua 3 C4
Papueru 20 D12
Para 35 K4 40 H9 44 A10
Paradise 64 D12 65 D2
Paradise Valley Springs - Rotorua 12 G14 13 G3
Parahaka 4 J11
Parahaki 85 C3
Parahi 5 H7 7 B1
Parakai 5 H7 7 B1
Parakai Hot Springs 5 H7 7 B1
Parakao 4 G8
Parakiwai 8 J14 10 D11
Paranui 2 H8
Paraoanui Pa 14 J11
Parapara, NI 2 H7
Parapara, SI 37 C7
Paraparaumu 33 A3
Paraparaumu Beach 33 A3
Pararaki Hut 33 H6
Parau 7 F3 89 E2
Parawa 71 E7
Parawai 8 H11 10 C8
Parawera 12 F8
Parekarangi 19 A7
Parekura Bay 4 B11
Paremata (East Cape) 22 B12
Paremata (Wellington) 33 D2 35 B2
Paremoremo 6 J9 7 C3 88 G1
Pareora 68 A13
Pareora West 61 J4 68 A13
Paretai 79 F4
Parewanui 29 C5
Parihaka Pa (Cape Egmont) 23 D3
Parikino 26 G9
Parinui 24 E13 26 B8
Pariokara 15 D6
Park Hill 72 G12 73 G1
Park Morpeth Hut 51 B6
Parkhurst 5 H7 7 B1
Parklands 54 H8 56 D10 120 G5
Parks Peak Hut 27 F6
Parkside 121 B5
Parkvale 103 C5
Parkville 30 H8 31 H2
Parkway 111 D4
Parnassus 48 H9
Parnell 90 C4
Paroa Bay 4 B10
Paroa, NI 14 E10
Paroa, SI 45 F3
Paroanui 2 H9
Parore 3 J7
Parrot Island 69 G2 75 A2
Parua Bay 4 G13
Paske Hut 47 B4
Passage Islands 75 E3
Patangata 28 J10
Pataua 4 G13
Patea 24 J8 25 F3
Patearoa 73 A7
Paterangi 11 E6
Patetonga 10 F7
Patoka 28 B10
Patons Rock 37 D7
Patuki 40 A10
Patumahoe 7 H5 9 C2
Paturau River 37 B5
Patutahi 22 D9
Paua 1 C3
Pauanui 8 G14 10 B11
Pauatahanui 33 D3 35 A2 111 A4
Pauri Village 26 J8
Pawarenga 3 B2

Pea Viner Corner 38 J11 39 H3 43 A4
Peaks, The 47 J3 53 A7
Pearl Island 80 H2
Peats Hut 65 F5
Peebles 68 F11
Peel Forest 61 D5
Peel Forest Walks 61 C4
Peep-o-Day 27 J3
Pegasus Bay Walkway 54 F8 56 B10
Pehiri 21 D7
Pekerau 1 H7
Peketa 48 E11
Pelorus Bridge 39 H6 43 A7
Pelorus Sound 40 F9
Pelorus Track 39 H5 43 A6
Pemberton 27 H3
Pembroke 23 E6 25 B1
Pendarves 55 H4 62 C10
Penn Creek Hut 33 A6
Penn Creek Track 33 A6
Penrose 90 D5
Pentland Hills 68 C10
Pepepe 9 H3 11 A4
Pepin Island 38 H13 39 F5
Peria (Northland) 2 J8
Peria (Waikato) 12 C10
Perry Saddle Hut 37 E4
Petone 33 E2 35 B3 110 C3
Petrel Island 69 H2 75 B2
Pfeifer Bivvy 46 J8
Phillipstown 120 F2
Phoebe 48 J8
Piarere 12 E10
Pickersgill Island 35 G2 40 F12
Picton 35 J3 40 G10 44 A11 113 C3
Picton Museum & Historical Society 35 J4 40 H10 44 A11
Pig Island (Queenstown) 64 G12 65 G2
Pig Island / Matau (Southland) 76 H14 77 E2
Pigeon Bay 56 F12
Pigeon Bush 33 D6
Pigeon Flat 74 G11 124 D1
Pigeon Island (Queenstown) 64 G12 65 G2
Pigeon Island (Southland) 69 G2 75 A2
Piha 7 E2
Pihama 23 G4
Pikes Point 68 E12
Pikiwahine 4 J10
Piko Piko 76 E12
Pikowai 14 D8
Pine Bush 78 F8
Pine Hill (Auckland) 88 F3
Pine Hill (Dunedin) 124 D2
Pine Valley 88 C1
Pinedale 12 F11
Pinehaven 33 D3 111 B5
Pines Beach, The 54 G8 56 C10
Pioneer Hut 49 J6
Piopio 18 A8
Piopiotahi Marine Res 64 D8
Pios Beach 10 F12
Pipiriki 24 G13 26 D8
Pipiroa 8 J11 10 B8
Pipitea 35 J5 40 J10 44 B11
Pipiwai 4 F9
Piriaka 18 F11
Pirimai 103 B2
Pirinoa 33 F5
Piripai 14 E10
Piripaua 21 F3
Piripiri (Manawatu) 30 B12 31 B6
Piripiri (Waikato) 11 H3
Piripiri Caves 11 H3
Pirongia 11 E6
Pirongia Forest Park 11 E4
Piropiro 18 C11
Pitokuku Island 36 E5
Plateau Hut 49 J6
Plateau, The 33 C4
Pleasant Heights 96 B1
Pleasant Point 61 H4
Pleasant Point Museum & Railway 61 H4
Pleasant Valley 61 F4
Pleckville 30 H9 31 H3
Plimmerton 33 C2 35 B1
Poerua 45 H6
Poet Hut 50 C13 51 C4
Pohangina 30 B9 31 B3
Pohara 38 D8
Pohatu Marine Reserve 56 H13
Pohatukura 16 E11
Pohokura (Hawke's Bay) 20 G9
Pohokura (Taranaki) 17 J5 24 C10

Pohonui 26 G13
Pohuehue 6 F9
Point Chevalier 89 C3
Point Elizabeth Walkway 45 E4
Point England 90 C5
Point Howard 110 D3
Point View Park 90 D6
Point Wells 6 D10
Pokaka 26 B11
Pokapu 4 C8
Pokeno 7 J6 9 D3
Pokere 4 D9
Pokororo 38 J8 42 A13
Pokuru 11 F6
Pollock 7 G3
Polluck Creek Hut 50 C11 51 C2
Polnoon Hut 65 D5
Pomahaka 72 J12 73 J1 78 A11
Pomarangai 11 J2
Pomare (Rotorua) 96 C2
Pomare (Wellington) 33 D3 35 A2 111 B4
Pomona Island 70 E9
Pompeys Pillar 56 H13
Ponatahi 34 D8
Ponga 7 G6 9 B3
Pongakawa 13 D6
Pongakawa Valley 13 D6
Pongaroa 30 G13 31 G7
Ponsonby 87 E1
Ponui Island 8 E8
Poolburn 66 J13 67 J2
Poolburn Reservoir 73 B5
Poor Pete's Hut 42 E9
Popotunoa 78 A13
Poraiti 28 D12
Porangahau 32 D10
Porati 103 C1
Porewa 29 A7
Pori 30 G10 31 G4
Porirua 33 D2 35 B2 110 B2
Porootarao 18 B11
Poroporo 14 E10
Poroti 4 G10
Poroutawhao 29 F5
Port Albert 5 D7
Port Chalmers 74 G12
Port Charles 8 A11 36 H5
Port Craig School 76 G9
Port Fitzroy 36 D4
Port Jackson 8 A10 36 G4
Port Levy 54 J9 56 F11
Port Molyneux 79 F4
Port Motueka 38 H10 39 F2
Port Nelson 38 J12 39 G4 116 A5
Port Ohope 14 F12
Port Puponga 37 A7
Port Robinson 54 A13
Port Robinson Walkway 54 A13
Port Waikato 9 E1
Port Whangarei 4 G12 85 D2
Port William Hut 80 D5
Portage 35 J2 40 F10
Porter Heights Skifield 52 F9 55 B2
Porters Creek Hut 43 D2
Portland 4 H12
Portland Island 22 AC1
Portobello 74 G12 124 A2
Possum Hut 74 F11
Potaka 16 A10
Pouakai Hut 23 D4
Poukawa 28 G10
Poukiore 26 H13 27 H1
Poukura Pa 19 F3
Poulson's Hut 66 D12
Poulter Bivvy 46 J8
Poulter Hut 52 A10
Pounawea 79 H3
Pourakino Valley 76 F13 77 C1
Pourangaki Hut 27 H5
Pourerere 32 B12
Pourewa Island 22 B13
Pouri Hut 24 E11 25 B6
Pouto Point 5 E5
Pouwhakaura 26 H14 27 H2
Prebbleton 53 J7 56 E9
Prebelton 120 A2
Price Basin Hut 50 D12 51 D3
Price Flat Hut 50 D12 51 D3
Price Flat Hut (Old Hut) 50 D12 51 D3
Prices Corner 38 J10 39 G2
Progress Junction 46 B9
Progress Valley 78 G11
Providence Rocks 75 E2

Puaha 56 G11
Puahue 12 F8
Puangiangi Island 40 B10
Puari 54 J9 56 F11
Puau 24 J11 25 F6
Puerua 79 F3
Puha 22 B9
Puhata 3 B2
Puhinui 90 E5
Puhipuhi 4 D11
Puhoi 6 G9 7 A3
Puhuka 61 J4
Pukahu 28 F11 103 C6
Pukaki Aerodrome 59 H7
Pukapuka 6 F10
Pukaroro Rock 48 F11
Pukawa 19 F2
Pukearuhe 17 F4
Pukeatua 12 F9
Pukeawa 79 D2
Pukehangi 96 C1
Pukehiki 74 H12 124 A4
Pukehina 13 C7
Pukehou 28 H10
Pukeinoi 11 F3
Pukekapia 9 G4
Pukekaroro 5 B7
Pukekawa 9 E3
Pukekohe 7 H5 9 C2
Pukekohe East 7 H6 9 C3
Pukekoma 79 C3
Pukekura, NI 12 D8
Pukekura, SI 50 C10
Pukemaori 76 E12
Pukemiro (Northland) 3 B3
Pukemiro (Waikato) 9 H3 11 A4
Pukemoremore 12 C8
Pukemutu 77 A3
Pukengahu 24 E8 25 B3
Pukenui 1 F5
Pukeokahu 27 E4
Pukeoware 7 J4 9 D1
Pukepito 79 D3
Pukepoto 1 J6
Pukepuke Lagoon 29 D5
Pukerangi 74 E9
Pukeraro 68 F8
Pukerau 78 B10
Pukerimu 12 D8
Pukeroro 12 D8
Pukerua Bay 33 C2 35 B1
Puketaha 9 J6 11 B7 92 C5
Puketapu 28 D11 103 D1
Pukete 92 D2
Puketeraki 74 E12
Puketi Forest 2 K10 3 A6
Puketi, NI 3 A7
Puketi, SI 78 A14 79 C2
Puketiro 78 F13 79 H1
Puketitiri 28 B9
Puketoi 30 F12 31 F6
Puketona 4 B8
Puketotara 11 F6
Puketotara Hut 24 E13 26 B8
Puketui 8 G13 10 B10
Puketurua 12 F10
Puketurua Track 29 G7
Puketutu 18 A10
Puketutu Island 7 F4 9 A1
Pukeuri 68 G12
Pukio 33 E6
Punakaiki 45 B5
Punakitere 3 D6
Punakitere Valley 4 D8
Punaromia 13 H5
Punaruku 4 C12
Punawai 61 B7
Punehu 3 C3
Pungaere 2 K11 3 A7
Pungapunga 18 F11
Pungarehu (Taranaki) 23 D2
Pungarehu (Wanganui) 26 G9
Pungataua 27 E3
Puni 7 J5 9 D2
Puniho 23 C3
Puniho Track 23 D4
Puniwhakau 24 E9 25 B4
Puponga 37 A7
Pupu Springs Walking Track 37 E7
Pupuke 2 J10
Purakauiti 78 F14 79 H2
Purakanui (Dunedin) 74 F12

Purakanui Bay 74 F12
Purakaunui (Clutha) 78 F14 79 H2
Purakaunui Bay 79 H2
Purakaunui Falls 79 H2
Puramahoi 37 D7
Purangi (Taranaki) 17 J4 24 C9
Purangi (Waikato) 8 E13
Purau 54 J8 56 F10
Purekireki 78 D13 79 F1
Pureora 18 B13 19 B1
Pureora Forest Park 12 J9 18 A13 19 A1
Purerua 2 J13 4 A9
Purimu Lake 32 B9
Puriri 8 J12 10 D9
Purity Hut 27 H5
Purua 4 F10
Pururu 11 J7
Putangirua Pinnacles -
Aorangi Forest Park 33 G5
Putara 29 H7 31 H1
Putaruru 12 F11
Puteore Hut 24 E11 25 B6
Putiki 26 J8
Putorino (Hawke's Bay) 20 J13 21 J1
Putorino (Wanganui) 26 J13
Puwera 4 H11
Pyes Pa 12 C14 13 C3
Pyke Big Bay Track 57 J2
Pyramid Valley 53 B7

Q

Quail Island 54 J8 56 E10
Quail Island Walkway 54 J8 56 E10
Quarry Hills 78 G10
Queen Charlotte Sound 35 J3 40 G10
Queen Charlotte Walking Track 35 H2 40 F11
Queens Flat 68 F10
Queensberry 66 F9
Queenstown 65 H4 125 B2 126 B2
Queenstown Airport 65 H5
Queenwood 92 D3
Quigleys Track 46 C9

R

Rabbit Island 38 J11 39 G3
Racecourse Hill 52 G12 53 D2 55 C5
Raekohua Falls - Tahora 17 G6 24 A11
Raes Junction 72 G14 73 G3
Raetea Forest 2 K7 3 A3
Raetihi 26 C10
Raglan 11 C3
Rahanui 11 D2
Rahiri 3 B6
Rahotu 23 E2
Rai Valley 39 G6
Rainbow Falls - Kerikeri 2 K12 4 A8
Rainbow Hut 43 J1 47 A5
Rainbow Isles 78 G13 79 J1
Rainbow Point 98 C4
Rainbow Springs 96 A2
Rainbow Springs & Farm - Rotorua 13 G4 96 A2
Rainbow Valley Skifield 42 H13 43 G1
Rainbow Warrior wreck - Cavalli Islands 2 G12
Rainbows End Adventure Park -
Auckland 7 F5 9 A2
Raio 1 F5
Rakahouka 77 D6
Rakaia 55 G5 62 B11
Rakaia Gorge Walkway 52 H9 55 D2
Rakaia Huts 55 H6 62 C12
Rakaia Lagoon 55 H6 62 C12
Rakau 42 C13 43 B1
Rakaumanga 9 G4
Rakaunui (Manawatu) 30 G12 31 G6
Rakaunui (Waikato) 11 F3
Rakauroa 21 B6
Rakautao 3 D7
Rakautara 48 C13
Rakautatahi 30 A13 31 A7
Rakino Island 6 J12 7 C6
Rakitu Island 36 C5
Rakiura National Park 80 D3
Rakiura Track - Great Walk 80 D5
Ramanui 24 E13 26 B8
Ramarama 7 H6 9 C3
Rameka Track 38 E8
Ranana 24 H14 26 E9
Ranfurly 67 H5
Rangaiika 28 F14

Rangataua 26 C12
Rangatira Beach 5 G5
Rangatira Valley 61 G4
Ranger Bivvy 52 A10
Rangi Point 3 D3
Rangiahua (Hawke's Bay) 21 G4
Rangiahua (Northland) 3 B5
Rangiahua Island 36 D3
Rangiaowhia 11 E7
Rangiatea 11 H7
Rangihaeata 38 D8
Rangiora, NI 3 C4
Rangiora, SI 53 F7 56 B9
Rangiotu 29 E6
Rangipo 19 H3
Rangipo Hut 26 B13 27 B1
Rangipu 11 C3
Rangipukea Island 8 D10
Rangiputa 1 F6
Rangiriri 9 F4
Rangitaiki 20 F8
Rangitata 61 E5
Rangitata Island 61 F6
Rangitatau 25 G6
Rangitihi 1 J7
Rangitoto 11 J6
Rangitoto Island 6 J11 7 D5 90 A5
Rangitoto Island Scenic Reserve 6 J11 7 C5
Rangitoto Islands 40 B10
Rangitoto ki te Tonga / D'Urville Island 40 B8
Rangitukia 16 D13
Rangitumau 34 A9
Rangiuru 13 C5
Rangiwaea Island 10 H13 12 A14 13 A3
Rangiwaea Junction 26 D13
Rangiwahia 27 H3
Rangiwahia Hut 27 H4
Rangoon Heights 110 D2
Rankleburn 78 A12
Ranui 11 C4 89 C2
Ranui - Auckland 7 D3
Ranui - Wellington 110 B3
Rapahoe 45 E4
Rapaki 54 J8 56 E10
Rapanui 25 H7
Rapaura 35 K5 40 J9 44 B10
Rapid Creek Hut 50 C12 51 C3
Rapuwai 60 F14 61 F3
Rarangi 35 J5 40 J10 44 B11
Raroa 110 C2
Raroa Track 14 H11
Rarotoka Island / Centre Island 76 J13 77 F1
Raspberry Creek Hut 65 B5
Rata 26 J12 29 A7 31 A1
Rataiti 26 H12
Ratana 29 A4
Ratanui 79 H3
Ratapiko 17 J2 23 C7
Raukawa Falls 26 E10
Raukawa Rock 35 F3 40 G13
Raukokore 16 B8
Raukumara Forest Park 16 E8
Raumai 30 C9 31 C3
Raumanga 85 C1
Raumati 30 C12 31 C6
Raumati Beach 33 A3
Raumati South 33 B3
Raupo, NI 5 B3
Raupo, SI 45 D7
Raupunga 21 J2
Raureka 103 C5
Raurimu 18 J11
Ravensbourne 74 H12 124 C3
Rawene 3 C4
Rawhia 3 B5
Rawhiti 4 A11
Rawhitiroa 23 F7 25 C2
Raymonds Gap 76 E13 77 B1
Reardon Hut 59 C5
Red Beach 6 H10 7 B4
Red Hill 7 G6 9 B3
Red Hills Hut 43 E2
Red Hut 59 E4
Red Jacks 45 E6
Red Stag Hut 50 J8
Redan 78 E9
Redcliffs 54 J8 56 E10 120 H2
Redhill 5 A2
Redruth 61 J4 68 A13
Redvale 6 H10 7 B4 88 E2
Redwood Valley 38 J10 39 H2 43 A3
Redwood, NI 33 D2 35 B2 110 C2
Redwood, SI 53 H7 56 D9 120 E5

Redwoodtown 35 K6 44 C10
Reefton 46 B9
Reena 3 C3
Rees - Dart Track 64 B12 65 B2
Rees Valley 64 E12 65 E2
Regent 84 A4
Rehia 5 A4
Rehutai 3 J7 5 A2
Reidston 68 H11
Reikorangi 33 A4
Reischek Hut 50 F12 51 F3
Remarkables Skifield 65 H6
Remarkables, The 65 J5
Remuera 7 E5 90 C4
Renata Hut 33 B5
Renown 9 G4
Renwick 44 C9
Reotahi Bay 4 H13
Repia 5 B3
Reporoa 20 A8
Reporua 16 E12
Rere 21 C7
Rere Falls - Bay of Plenty 21 C7
Rerekapa Falls 17 G6 24 A11
Rerekapa Track 17 F5 24 A10
Rerewhakaaitu 13 J6
Reservoir, The 78 H10
Resolution Island 69 G3 75 A3
Retaruke 18 J9 24 C14
Retaruke Upper 18 J10
Rewa 26 J13 27 J1
Rewanui 45 E5
Rewarewa 11 H7
Rewiti 5 J7 7 C2
Riamaki (Upper Ruatiti) 18 J10 26 A10
Riccarton 53 H7 56 D9 120 D3
Riccarton Park 120 C3
Richard Pearse Airport - near Timaru 61 H4
Richardson Track 52 E13 53 E4 55 A6
Richmond (Christchurch) 120 F3
Richmond (Invercargill) 68 G12 127 A5 128 B3
Richmond (Tasman) 39 H3 43 A4 116 D3
Richmond Downs 12 C10
Richmond Heights 98 C5
Richmond Hill 120 H1
Richmond Hut 66 E12 67 E1
Right Branch Wairoa Hut 43 C3
Rigney 72 F14 73 F3
Rileys Lookout - Panau Island 48 E11
Rimariki Island 4 C13
Rimu (Southland) 77 E6
Rimu (Westland) 45 J2
Rimutaka Forest Park 33 E5 33 F3 35 A4
Ringway 76 F14 77 C2
Riordons Hut 37 G7
Ripiro Beach 3 H5
Riponui 4 E10
Ripponvale 66 H8
Rissington 28 D10
Riverdale 100 A2
Riverhead 6 J9 7 C3
Riverlands 35 J6 44 C11
Riverlea 23 F5
Riversdale (Blenheim) 117 A6
Riversdale (Central Otago) 72 J8
Riversdale Beach 34 D12
Riverside 84 B5
Riverside, SI 62 E9
Riverstone Terraces 111 A5
Riverton 76 H14 77 E2
Riwaka 38 G9 39 E1
Roa 45 D5
Roaring Lion Hut 37 H5 42 A10
Roaseneath 110 E2
Robinsons Bay 56 G12
Rock and Pillar 74 B9
Rockdale 128 A4
Rockford 52 F12 53 F3 55 B5
Rocks Ahead Hut 27 B7
Rocks Hut 39 H4 43 A5
Rocks, The 77 E2
Rockville 37 C6
Rocky Creek Hut 45 J5
Rodedale 128 B2
Rodgers Inlet Hut 70 J9 76 C9
Rogers Hut (Te Wairoa) 20 E11
Rokeby 55 G4 62 B10
Rokeby Hut 46 E14 47 E2
Rolleston 53 J6 56 E8
Rolling Junction Hut 42 C11
Romahapa 79 F3
Rona Bay 110 D3
Rona Island 70 E10

Rongahere 72 J14 73 J3 79 B1
Rongoiti Junction 26 F14 27 F2
Rongokokako 30 H8 31 H2
Rongomai 30 G9 31 G3
Rongotai 110 E2
Rongotea 29 D6
Rosebank Road 89 C3
Rosebery 68 G11
Roseneath (Dunedin) 74 G12 124 B2
Rosewill 61 H4
Roslyn (Dunedin) 124 E3
Roslyn (Palmerston North) 30 D8 31 D2 105 A4
Roslyn Bush 77 E6
Ross 50 B11 51 B2
Rosvalls Track 27 H5
Rotherham 47 H6
Rothesay Bay 88 F4
Rotoehu 13 F6
Rotoiti 13 F6
Rotokakahi 3 B2
Rotokare Walkway 24 F8 25 C3
Rotokauri 9 J5 11 C6 92 E1
Rotokautuku 16 E11
Rotokawa (Bay of Plenty) 13 G5 96 A6
Rotokawa (Waikato) 19 C7
Rotokino 49 E7
Rotokohu 41 J5
Rotomahana 13 J5
Rotomanu 45 H7
Rotongaro 9 G4
Rotongata (Bay of Plenty) 13 E4
Rotongata (Waikato) 12 G9
Rotoorangi 12 E8
Rotoroa 42 G11
Rotoroa Island 8 D8
Rotoroa Track 42 H12
Rotorua 13 G4
Rotorua Airport 13 G5 96 B6
Rotorua Central 95 D3
Rotorua Museum 13 G4 96 C3
Rototuna (Northland) 5 D4
Rototuna (Waikato) 9 J6 11 B7 92 C3
Rotowaro 9 H4
Round Hill (Clutha) 73 J6 79 C4
Round Hill (Southland) 76 H13
Round Hill Skifield 60 C11
Round the Island Track North West Circuit
77 J2 80 C4
Round the Mountain Track 26 A13 27 A1
Routeburn Falls 64 E10
Routeburn Flats Hut 64 E11
Routeburn Track - Great Walk 64 D11 65 D1
Rowan 23 E5
Roxburgh 72 D13 73 D2
Roxburgh East 72 D13 73 D2
Royal Oak 90 D4
Ruahine Corner Hut 27 E6
Ruahine Forest Park 27 F5 30 A11 31 A5
Ruahine Hut 27 E7
Ruahine, NI 27 H3
Ruahine, SI 76 H12
Ruakaka 4 J13
Ruakituri 21 E5
Ruakiwi 9 J2 11 B3
Ruakokoputuna 33 F7
Ruamahunga 8 F11 10 A8
Ruanui 26 E13 27 E1
Ruapani Track 21 E2
Ruapekapeka 4 D10
Ruapuke 11 D2
Ruapuke Island 77 J6
Ruapuna 61 C5
Ruarangi 4 J11
Ruaroa (Manawatu) 30 B11 31 B5
Ruaroa (Northland) 1 J7
Ruas Track 21 C3
Ruatahuna 20 C13 21 C1
Ruataniwha 28 J8
Ruataniwha Conservation Park 59 F6
Ruatapu 45 J1 50 A11 51 A2
Ruatiti 26 A9
Ruato 13 F6
Ruatoki North 14 G11
Ruatoria 16 E11
Ruawai 5 B4
Ruawaro 9 G4
Ruawhata 30 E10 31 E4
Rugged Islands 80 C2
Rukuhia 11 D7 92 J5
Rukuwai 4 G13
Runanga 45 E4
Runanga Lake 28 E10

Runaruna 3 B3
Runciman 7 G6 9 B3
Rurima Island 14 D10
Ruru 45 G6
Russell 4 B10 81 A3
Russell Forest 4 C11
Russells Flat 52 G11 53 G2 55 C4
Russley 120 C3
Rutherglen 45 F3
Ryal Bush 77 D4

S

Sabine Hut 42 H12
Sabine Track 42 J12
Saddle Hill 74 H10 124 H5
Saddle Hut 65 C6
Saddle Rocks 40 A10
Saies 2 H10
Sainsburys Hut 65 F4
Saint Albans 54 H8 56 D10 120 E4
Saint Andrews Hill 120 G2
Saint Arnaud 42 G13 43 F1
Saint Arnaud Track 42 G13 43 F1
Saint Bathans 66 F13 67 F2
Saint Clair 74 H11 124 E5
St Heliers 90 C5
St Jacob's Hut 46 G12
Saint James Walkway 46 D14 47 D2
St Johns 90 C5
Saint Johns Hill 26 H8 109 B3
St Johns Park 90 C5
Saint Kilda 74 H11 124 D5
St Leonards 103 C5 102 A1
Saint Leonards, SI 74 G12
St Lukes 89 C3
St Martins 120 F2
St Marys Bay 87 C1
Saint Patricks 71 H7
St Winifred Hut 50 G10
Salisbury 61 J4 68 A13
Saltwater Creek 54 E8 56 A10
Saltwater Lagoon 49 D7
Sandringham 89 C3
Sandspit 6 E10
Sandstone 71 H7
Sandy Bay Hut 21 E3
Sandy Knolls 52 J14 53 J5 55 E7
Sandymount 74 H12 124 A3
Sanson 29 C6
Santoft 29 B5
Sapphire Springs - Katikati 10 H11
12 A12 13 A1
Sawyers Bay 74 G12 124 B2
Saxon Hut 37 E4
Sayers Hut 33 B7
Scarborough (Christchurch) 120 J1
Scarborough (Timaru) 61 J5 68 A14
Scargill 54 B10
Scone Hut 50 G9
Scotsman Valley 12 C8
Scotts Gap 76 E13 77 B1
Scow Landing 4 F13
Scroggs Hill 74 H10 124 J5
Seacliff 74 E12
Seadown 61 H5
Seafield 55 J4 62 D10
Seaford 37 B7
Seaforth 61 H5
Seagrove 7 G4 9 B1
Seagull Lake 51 H5
Seal Island 45 A5
Seal Islands 69 H2 75 B2
Seal Rocks 77 J7
Seatoun 33 F2 35 B4
Seaview (Timaru) 121 C3
Seaview (Wellington) 110 D3
Seaward Downs 78 E8
Secretary Island 69 B5
Seddon 44 E11
Seddonville 41 D6
Sedgemere 55 H7 62 C13
Sefton 54 E8 56 A10
Sefton Bivvy 59 A6
Selwyn Heights 96 B2
Selwyn Huts 56 F8 62 A14
Selwyn, NI 5 D4
Selwyn, SI 52 J13 53 J4 55 F6 62 A12
Sentry Box Hut 27 F7
Sentry Hill 17 H1 23 B6

Sergeants Hill 41 G3
Serpentine Hut 50 C13 51 C4
Shaftesbury 10 H10 12 A11
Shag Lake 3 G5
Shag Point 74 C13
Shag Rock 48 J9 54 A13
Shallow Bay Hut 70 D10
Shamrock Hut 58 G14 59 G3
Shamrock Park 90 D6
Shannon, NI 29 F6
Shannon, SI 74 E8
Shantytown 45 F4
Sharks Tooth Hut 65 C5
Sheffield 52 G12 53 G3 55 C5
Shelly Beach 5 G7 7 A1
Shelly Park 90 D6
Shelter Islands 69 B5
Shelter Rock Hut 64 C13 65 C3
Shenandoah 42 H8
Sherenden 28 D9
Sherwood 55 G3 62 B9
Shiel Burn Hut 65 D5
Shiel Hill 124 D4
Shingle Creek 72 C12 73 C1
Shirley 54 H8 56 D10 120 F4
Shoe Island / Motuhoa 10 A11
Shorts Track 30 A11 31 A5
Shutes Hut 27 D7
Shy Lake 69 F5
Siberia Hut 58 H9
Silver Island 66 A9
Silver Peaks Route 74 F11
Silverdale 88 B2
Silverdale (Auckland) 6 H10 7 B4
Silverdale (Hamilton) 92 F5
Silverhope 26 J12
Silverstream 111 B5
Simmonds Islands 1 E5
Sir Robert Hut 50 C13 51 C4
Sisters, The 80 H1
Six Foot Track 21 B2
Six Mile 42 H9
Six Mile Walkway & Track 42 H9
Skippers 65 F4
Skippers Canyon 65 F4
Skyline Track 24 J14 26 F9
Slaty Creek 45 D6
Slipper Island 10 B12
Slyburn Hut 64 G11 65 G1
Smithfield 61 J5
Smiths Ponds 57 G5
Smiths Stream Hut 27 H6
Snells Beach 6 F10
Sockburn 53 H7 56 D9 120 C2
Somerfield 120 E2
Somerton 55 G4 62 B10
Somerville 90 D6
Somes Island / Matiu 33 E2 35 B3
South Bay 48 E12
South Beach 45 F4
South Dunedin 124 E4
South Head 5 F6
South Hill 122 D5
South Hillend 77 A4
South Malvern 52 H11 53 H2 55 D4
South Mavora Lake 71 B4
South New Brighton 120 H3
South Oamaru 122 D6
South Ohau Hut 29 H6
South Temple Hut 59 G4
Southbridge 55 G6 62 B12
Southbrook 53 F7 56 B9
Southburn 68 A12
Southdown 90 D5
Southern Alps / Ka Tiritiri o te Moana 58 J8
Southern Coastal Track 76 F9
Southshore 54 H8 56 D10 120 H2
Spar Bush 77 D4
Speargrass Hut 42 H12
Speargrass Track 42 G13
Spectacle Lake 6 C9
Spence Hut 70 G13 71 G2 76 A13
Spencerville 54 G8 56 C10 120 G6
Sphinx Lake 69 J7 75 C7
Sportswood 107 C2
Spotswood, NI 23 B4
Spotswood, SI 48 J9
Spreydon 53 J7 56 E9 120 D2
Spring Creek 35 J5 40 J10 44 B11
Spring Grove 39 H2 43 A3
Springbank 53 F6 56 B8
Springbrook 68 A13
Springburn 61 A6

Springdale 10 G8
Springfield (Rotorua) 96 D2
Springfield, NI 4 H12
Springfield, SI 52 F11 53 F2 55 B4
Springhill 27 H7
Springhills 77 C6
Springlands 35 K6 44 C10 117 B1
Springs Flat 4 F11
Springs Junction 46 D12
Springston 53 J6 56 F8 62 A14
Springston South 56 F8 62 A14
Springvale (Otago) 66 J10 72 A13 73 A2
Springvale (Wanganui) 108 A1 109 C3
Spye 54 B10
Square Top Island 36 G4
Stafford 45 H3
Stafford Hut 57 E5
Stag Flat Shelter 42 C9
Staglands Wildlife Park - Cloustonville 33 B4
Staircase 52 E11 53 E2 55 A4
Stanfield Hut 30 B11 31 B5
Stanley Bay 90 B4
Stanley Brook 42 B13 43 A1
Stanley Point 90 B4
Stanmore Bay 88 B3
Stanway 29 B7 31 B1
Station Hut 59 E5
Staveley 61 A6
Stephens Island / Takapourewa 40 A10
Stephenson Island 2 G11
Stevensons Island 66 C8
Stewart Island / Rakiura 77 J1 80 C3
Stewarts Gully 54 G8 56 C10
Steyning Hut 47 F3
Stillwater 88 C3
Stillwater, NI 6 H10 7 B4
Stillwater, SI 45 E5
Stirling 79 E4
Stirling Falls, The 64 D8
Stockton 41 E5
Stodys Hut 66 B10
Stoke 39 H3 43 A4
Stokes Valley 33 D3 111 C4
Stone Hut 42 C10
Stoneburn 74 C11
Stony Creek 79 D3
Stony River Walk 23 C3
Stony Stream Hut 46 J11
Strandon 107 B4
Stratford 23 E7 25 B2
Strathern 128 B4
Strathmore 24 D9 25 A4
Strathmore Park 110 E2
Streamlands 6 E9
Stronvar 34 C11
Stuarts 78 F13 79 H1
Studholme 68 D13
Studholme Saddle Hut 28 B8
Styx 120 D5
Subritsky Homestead 1 F5
Sudden Valley Bivvy 52 B9
Sugar Loaf Islands / Nga Motu 23 B5
Summer Hill 79 F4
Summerfield (Canterbury) 52 E14 53 E5 55 A7
Summerhill (Palmerston North) 105 D4
Summerlea 41 D6
Sumner 54 J9 56 E11 120 J1
Sundale 110 C2
Sunnybrook 96 C2
Sunnyhills 90 C5
Sunnynook 88 H4
Sunnyvale (Auckland) 89 C2
Sunnyvale (Dunedin) 124 G5
Sunrise Hut 27 G6
Supper Cove Hut 69 G5 75 A5
Surfdale 7 D7
Sutherland Falls 63 F7
Sutherlands 60 H14 61 H3
Sutton 74 D8
Swan Lagoon 59 H5
Swannanoa 53 G6 56 C8
Swanson 7 D3 89 C1
Sweetwater 1 H6
Sydenham 119 G6 120 D2
Sylvia Flat Hot Springs 46 F13 47 F1

T

Tablelands (Bay of Plenty) 14 F13 15 F2
Tablelands (Wellington) 34 E8
Tadmor 42 C12
Taemaro 2 G9

Tahaia 11 H6
Tahakopa 78 F13 79 H1
Taharoa 11 G2
Tahatika 78 E14 79 G2
Tahawai 10 G11
Taheke 3 D5
Tahekeroa 6 G9 7 A3
Tahere 4 F13
Tahora (Bay of Plenty) 14 J12
Tahora (Taranaki) 17 H6 24 B11
Tahoraiti 30 C12 31 C6
Tahorakuri 19 C7
Tahuna 10 G8
Tahunanui 38 J12 39 G4 43 A5 116 B4
Tahunga 21 D6
Tahuroa 10 J8 12 B9
Taieri Beach 79 C7
Taieri Island / Moturata 79 C7
Taieri Mouth 79 C7
Taihape 27 F2
Taiharuru 4 G14
Taihoa 12 C11
Taikirau 4 D9
Taiko 60 J14 61 J3
Taikorea 29 D6
Taingaehe 5 C4
Tainui 124 D5
Taipa 2 H8
Taipo Hut 42 C9
Taipoiti 46 B9
Taipuha 5 A6
Tairua 8 F14 10 A11
Taita 33 D3 35 A2 111 C4
Tai Tapu 56 F9
Taitville 110 E1
Taka Ra Haka Conservation Park 71 C5
Takahiwai 4 H12
Takahue 1 K7 3 A3
Takaka 38 E8
Takaka Hill 38 F8
Takamatua 56 G12
Takamore 16 E11
Takanini 7 F6 9 A3
Takapau (East Cape, NI) 16 F11
Takapau (Gisborne) 22 A12
Takapau (Manawatu) 30 A14 32 A8
Takapou 38 D9 39 B1
Takapu Rd 110 C2
Takapu Valley 110 B3
Takapuna 7 D5 90 A4
Takaputahi 15 G5
Takapuwahia 110 B2
Takaro 29 D7 31 D1 105 B3
Takarua Hut 20 B13 21 B1
Takatu 6 E10
Takou 24 F10 25 C5
Takou Bay 2 J12
Takutai 45 J2
Tamahere 11 C7 92 H6
Tamaki 7 E5 90 C5
Tamaki Maori Village - Rotorua 13 H4
Tamarau 100 D5
Tamaterau 4 G12
Tamihana 10 J10 12 B11
Tanatana 14 H11
Tane 30 G10 31 G4
Taneatua 14 F11
Tanehopuwai 11 J5 18 A9
Tanekaha 4 E11
Tangahoe 24 E12 25 B7
Tangarakau 17 G7 24 A12
Tangarakau Gorge 17 G6 24 A11
Tangihua 4 H10
Tangihua Forest 4 H10
Tangimoana 29 D5
Tangiteroria 4 H9
Tangitu 18 C10
Tangiwai 26 C13 27 C1
Tangoake 1 C3
Tangoio 28 B12
Tangowahine 4 H8
Taniwha 9 F6
Tanoa 5 C7
Tanupara 26 D10
Taonui 30 C8 31 C2
Taoroa Junction 27 F4
Taotaoroa 12 D10
Tapanui 72 J13 73 J2
Tapapa 12 E11
Tapawera 42 C13 43 B1
Tapora 5 E6
Tapu 8 F11 10 A8
Tapuhi 4 D11

Tapui 68 G9
Tapuiwahine 18 C10
Taputeranga Island 33 F1 35 C4
Tapuwae (Northland) 3 C4
Tapuwae (Waikato) 18 B11
Tara 6 B8
Tara Hills 74 G10 124 J1
Taradale 28 E12 103 C2
Tarakohe 38 D9
Taramakau 45 H4
Taramea Bay 76 H14 77 E2
Taramoa 77 E4
Taranga Island 6 A10
Taranui 68 J11
Tarara 78 F14 79 H2
Tararu 8 G11 10 B8
Tararua Forest Park 29 H7 29 J5 31 H1 33 A6
Tarata 17 J2 23 C7
Taraunui 4 G13
Tarawera 20 H9
Tarawera Hot Springs 20 H9
Tariki 23 D6 25 A1
Taringamotu 18 F10
Taringamotu Valley 18 E11
Tarn Hut (Canterbury) 52 C13 53 C4
Tarn Hut (Mt Richmond CP) 43 C4
Tarn Ridge Hut 29 J6
Taronui Bay 2 J13
Tarras 66 E10
Taruheru 100 A1
Tarukenga 12 F14 13 F3
Tarurutangi 23 B6
Tasman 38 H10 39 F2
Tasman Lake 59 B7
Tasman Saddle Hut 49 H7
Tata Islands 38 D9 39 B1
Tataiahapi Pa 14 H12
Tatapouri 22 D11
Tataraimaka 23 C3
Tataramoa 30 B12 31 B6
Tatarariki 5 A3
Tatare 49 G6
Tataweka Hut 21 B3
Tatu 17 F7 24 A12
Tatuanui 10 H8 12 A9
Tauanui Hut 33 G6
Tauhara 98 B5
Tauhei 9 H7 12 A8
Tauherenikau 33 D6
Tauhoa 6 E8
Taumaka Island 57 D7
Taumarere 4 C9
Taumaruiti 18 F10
Taumarunui 18 F10
Taumata 78 B13 79 D1
Taumatatahi 24 G11 25 D6
Taumatawhakatangihangakoauauotamatea-
pokaiwhenuakitanatahu - New Zealand's
longest place name 32 E10
Taumutu 55 H7 62 C13
Taungatara 23 F4
Taungatara Track 23 E4
Taunoka 24 G12 25 D7
Taupaki 7 D2
Taupiri 9 H5 11 A6
Taupo 19 D5 97 B3 98 B4
Taupo Airport 19 E5 98 D4
Taupo Bay 2 H10
Taupo Hot Springs 19 D5
Tauranga 10 J13 13 B3 94 B2
Tauranga Bay 2 H11
Tauranga Central 93 D5
Tauranga Mission House 13 C4
Tauranga Valley 2 H11
Tauranganui 7 J5 9 E2
Taurangaruru 7 J3 9 D1
Tauraroa (Northland) 4 H11
Tauraroa (Waikato) 12 H8
Taurawharana Hut 20 B14 21 B2
Taurewa 18 H13
Tauriko 10 J13 12 B14 13 B3 94 D1
Taurikura 4 H13
Tautoro 3 D7
Tautuku 78 G13 79 J1
Tauweru 34 B10
Tauwhare (Bay of Plenty) 14 J11
Tauwhare Pa 12 C8
Tauwharemanuka 21 A2
Tauwhareparae 16 J9
Tawa 33 D2 35 B2 110 B2
Tawa Hut 21 B4
Tawai 68 F12
Tawanui 78 E14 79 G2

Tawataia 30 G9 31 G3
Tawhana 21 B2
Tawharanui 6 E11
Tawharekiri Lakes 58 C9
Tawhata 18 H8 24 B13
Tawhero 108 C1
Tawhiti, NI 23 G7 25 D2
Tawhiti, SI 72 C12 73 C1
Tawhiwhi 24 H11 25 E6
Tawhiwhi Hut 20 B13 21 B1
Taylor Dam 35 K6 44 D10
Taylors Mistake 54 J9 56 E11 120 J1
Taylorville 45 E5
Te Ahuahu 3 B7
Te Akatea 9 H4 11 A5
Te Akau 9 J2 11 B3
Te Akau South 9 J2 11 B3
Te Anau 70 D11
Te Anau Downs 70 A12 71 A1
Te Anga 11 H3
Te Angiangi Marine Reserve 32 C12
Te Aputa 18 E14 19 E2
Te Arai 6 C9
Te Arai Point 6 C9
Te Arakura 29 C7 31 C1
Te Araroa 16 B12
Te Ariuru 16 H11
Te Aro 110 E2 112 E5
Te Aroha 10 G9
Te Aroha Aerodrome 10 F9
Te Aroha West 10 H10 12 A11
Te Atatu North 7 D3
Te Atatu Peninsula 89 B2
Te Atatu South 89 C2
Te Awa (Canterbury) 61 G5
Te Awa (Napier) 103 A2
Te Awaatu Channel Marine Reserve 69 C5
Te Awamutu 11 E7
Te Awanga 28 F13
Te Ekaou Hut 30 B10 31 B4
Te Hana 6 D8
Te Hapara 100 B2
Te Hapua 1 B3
Te Haroto 20 J10
Te Hauke 28 G10
Te Haumi 81 C2
Te Henga / Bethells Beach 7 E1
Te Henga Goldie Bush Walkway 7 D1
Te Henui 23 C5
Te Hihi 7 G5 9 B2
Te Hoe 9 G6
Te Horo 29 J3
Te Horo Beach 29 J3
Te Horoa 26 E13 27 E1
Te Houka 79 E3
Te Huahua 3 B4
Te Hue Track 20 C13 21 C1
Te Huia 2 J11
Te Hutewai 11 D3
Te Iringa 3 D7
Te Kaha 15 C6
Te Kahui Kaupeka Conservation Park 60 A11
Te Kainga 110 D2
Te Kakaho Island 40 C11
Te Kao 1 D3
Te Karae 3 B4
Te Karaka (Gisborne) 22 B9
Te Karaka (Northland) 3 C3
Te Karanga-a-Hape (Cornwallis) 7 F3 89 E2
Te Kauri 9 G4
Te Kauwhata 9 E5
Te Kawa 11 F7
Te Kawa West 11 F6
Te Kinga 45 G6
Te Kiri 23 F4
Te Kiteroa 72 J11
Te Kohanga 7 J5 9 D2
Te Kopua (Bay of Plenty) 15 C6
Te Kopua (Waikato) 11 F6
Te Kopuru 5 A3
Te Koraha 11 G3
Te Kouma 8 D11
Te Koura 18 E10
Te Kowhai (Northland) 5 B4
Te Kowhai (Waikato) 9 J5 11 B6
Te Kuha 41 G3
Te Kuiti 11 J5
Te Kumi 11 J5
Te Mahia 35 J3 40 G10
Te Mahoe 14 G9
Te Maika 11 F2
Te Maire 18 G9
Te Mapara 18 A9

Te Marua, NI 33 C4
Te Marua, SI 40 B10
Te Mata (Waikato - Coromandel) 8 F11 10 A8
Te Mata (Waikato) 11 D3
Te Mata Peak Walkway 28 F12
Te Matai 13 C5
Te Matawai Hut 29 J6
Te Maunga 13 B4
Te Mawhai 11 F7
Te Miko 45 A5
Te Miro 12 C9
Te Moana 61 E3
Te Moananui 10 F9
Te Moehau Junction 27 E3
Te Motu Island 11 F2
Te Mutu Kairangi / Miramar Peninsula 110 E2
Te Namu 41 B7
Te Ngae 13 F5
Te Ngaire 2 H11
Te Ngaru 74 G12
Te Ohaki Pa 12 C12
Te Oneone Rangatira Beach 5 G5
Te Opai Lagoon 33 F5
Te Ore Ore 34 B9
Te Pahu 11 D5
Te Paki 1 B2
Te Paki Recreation Reserve 1 B1
Te Panaa Hut 21 B2
Te Papa Museum - Wellington 33 F1 35 C4
Te Papanui Conservation Park 73 F5
Te Papapa 90 D4
Te Papatapu 11 D3
Te Peka 78 F9
Te Pirita 52 J11 53 J2 55 F4 62 A10
Te Pohue 28 A10
Te Poi 12 D12
Te Popo 23 D7 25 A2
Te Pourewa Hut 21 A2
Te Pouwhakatutu 19 C5
Te Pu 13 E4
Te Pua 5 H7 7 B1
Te Pua Hut 21 B3
Te Puhi 2 J8
Te Puia Hut 28 A8
Te Puia Lodge 20 J8 28 A8
Te Puia Springs 16 G11
Te Puia Springs - Kawhia 11 F2
Te Puia Springs Hot Pools - East Cape 16 G11
Te Puka 16 H11
Te Puke 13 C5
Te Puna 10 J13 12 B14 13 B3
Te Puninga 10 G8 12 A9
Te Puru 8 G11 10 B8
Te Rae 37 A7
Te Rahu 11 E7
Te Raina 18 E14 19 E2
Te Ranga (Bay of Plenty) 12 C14 13 D4
13 C3 94 D1
Te Rangiita 19 F4
Te Rapa 9 J5 11 B6 92 D2
Te Rauamoa 11 F5
Te Raumauku 11 G5
Te Raupo 1 E5
Te Reinga 21 F6
Te Rerenga 8 C12
Te Rerepahupahu Falls 17 F7
Te Rore (Northland) 2 K7 3 A3
Te Rore (Waikato) 11 D6
Te Roti 23 G6 25 D1
Te Rou 43 C6
Te Tahi 11 E5
Te Taho 50 E8
Te Teko 14 F9
Te Tii 2 J13
Te Tipua 78 C8
Te Toro 7 H3 9 C1
Te Totara Hut 20 E12
Te Tua 76 F11
Te Tuhi Junction 24 H12 25 E7
Te Tumu 13 C5
Te Uku 11 C4
Te Uku Landing 11 C4
Te Urewera National Park 14 H10 20 A13 21 A1
Te Uri 32 C8
Te Waewae 76 F11
Te Waiiti 20 D13 21 D1
Te Waikoropupu Springs / Pupu Springs 38 E8
Te Waimate Mission 4 B8
Te Waiotukapiti Hut 20 F12
Te Wairoa 13 H5
Te Waitere 11 G2
Te Waiti Hut 14 H14 15 H3
Te Wakatehaua Island 1 D3

Te Wera 24 D9 25 A4
Te Whaiti 20 C11
Te Whakarae 18 F10
Te Whanga 34 C9
Te Wharau (Northland) 4 J8
Te Wharau (Wellington) 34 E10
Te Whau 2 J12 4 A8
Teal Bay Hut 76 E8
Teardrop Lake 69 B7
Teddington 56 F10
Telford Hut 70 G12 71 G1 76 A12
Temple Basin Skifield 52 A8
Temple View 11 C6 92 G2
Templeton 53 J6 56 E8 120 A2
Temuka 61 G5
Tennyson Inlet 40 F8
Tentpoles Hut 48 D10
Tepene 2 H12
Terrace End 30 D8 31 D2 105 B4
Teschemakers 68 J11
Teviot 72 E13 73 E2
Thames 8 H11 10 C8
Thames North 8 H11 10 C8
The Brothers (Marlborough) 35 E2 40 F14
The Brothers (Stewart Island) 80 H3
The Hermitage 59 B6
Theta Tarn 57 H4
Third House Hut 39 H4 43 A5
Thomsons Crossing 77 C4
Thor Hut 42 B10
Thornbury 77 D3
Thorndon 110 D2 112 C5
Thornton 14 E10
Thornton Bay 8 G11 10 B8
Thorpe 38 J8 42 A13
Three Bridges 3 E6
Three Kings 90 C4
Three Mile Bush 85 B1
Three Mile Lagoon 49 F5
Three Mile Stream Hut 46 H12
Three Steeples 41 F2
Three Streams 11 C3
Thrillseekers Canyon 47 G5
Ti Point 5 D11
Ti Tree Point 32 F8
Tia Island 80 G6
Tiakitahuna 29 E7
Tihaka 16 H14 77 E2
Tihiroa 11 F6
Tihoi 18 C14 19 C2
Tikinui 5 B3
Tikipunga 4 F12
Tikitere 13 F5
Tikitiki 16 D12
Tikokino 28 H8
Tikorangi 17 G2 23 A7
Tikotiko 9 F3
Timaru 61 J5 121 B3
Timber Bay 30 C12 31 C6
Timberlea 111 A6
Timpanys 77 F6
Tindalls Beach 88 B4
Tiniroto 21 F6
Tinkertown 70 J14 71 J3 76 C14 77 A2
Tinopai 5 D6
Tinui 34 A12
Tinui Island 40 B10
Tinwald 55 J2 62 D8
Tipapakuku 30 C12 31 C6
Tipunga 85 A2
Tiratu 30 C13 31 C7
Tirau 12 E11
Tiraumea 30 H11 31 H5
Tiraumea Hut 42 J11
Tiraumea Track 42 H11
Tiriraukawa 26 G13 27 G1
Tiritiri Matangi Island 6 H11 7 B5
Tiroa 18 B12
Tirohanga (Bay of Plenty) 14 F14 15 F3
Tirohanga (Wellington) 110 C3
Tirohanga, SI 79 G4
Tirohia 10 F9
Tiroiti 74 A9
Tiromoana 45 A5
Tiroroa 41 H4
Tisbury 128 B5
Titahi Bay 32 D2 35 B2 110 A2
Titi Island 40 D11
Titirangi 7 E3 89 D2
Titirangi Beach 89 D2
Titirangi North 89 D2
Titirangi Park 100 C4
Titirangi South 89 D2

Titiroa 78 F8
Titoki 4 G9
Toa Bridge 11 H7
Toatoa (Bay of Plenty) 15 G4
Toatoa (Northland) 2 H8
Todds Valley 38 J12 39 G4
Toetoe 4 G11 85 D2
Tohunga Junction 26 B11
Toi Flat 30 D13 31 D7
Tokaanu 19 G2
Tokanui, NI 11 F7
Tokanui, SI 78 G9
Tokaora 23 G6 25 D1
Tokarahi 68 F9
Tokata 16 B12
Tokata Island 14 D10
Tokatoka 5 A3
Tokerau 13 E5
Tokerau Beach 1 F7
Tokirima 18 G8 24 A13
Toko 24 E8 25 B3
Toko Mouth 79 E6
Tokoiti 79 D5
Tokomaru 29 F7 31 F1
Tokomaru Bay 16 H11
Tokomaru Steam Engine Museum 29 F7 31 F1
Tokorangi 29 A7
Tokoroa 12 H12
Tolaga Bay 22 A13
Tomarata 6 C9
Tomarata Lake 6 C9
Tomoana 103 C5
Tonga Island 38 E10 39 C2
Tonga Island Marine Res 38 E10 39 C2
Tongaporutu 17 E4
Tongariro 18 H13 19 H1
Tongariro Crossing 18 H13 19 H1
Tongariro National Park 18 H13 19 H1
26 A13 27 A1
Tongariro Northern Circuit 18 J14 19 J2
26 A14 27 A2
Top Branch Hut 43 H3
Top Butler Hut 50 G8
Top Crawford Hut 51 B5
Top Dingle Burn Hut 58 H13 59 H2
Top Forks Hut 58 H8
Top Gorge Hut 27 J5
Top Hope Hut 46 G12
Top Hut 58 F14 59 F3
Top Kokatahi Hut 50 B14 51 B5
Top Maropea Hut 27 G6
Top Robinson Hut 46 F12
Top Timaru Ck Hut 66 A11
Top Toaroha Hut 50 C13 51 C4
Top Trent Hut / Lagoon Hut 46 H9
Top Tuke Hut 50 D11 51 D2
Top Wairoa Hut 43 D3
Top Waitaha Hut 50 D11 51 D2
Tophouse 42 G14 43 F2
Topuni 6 C8
Torbay 6 J10 7 C4 88 F4
Torehape 9 E7
Torere 15 E4
Torlesse Tussocklands Park 52 E10 52 F9
Totara Flat 45 D7
Totara Heights 90 E6
Totara North 2 H10
Totara Park 33 D4 111 A6
Totara Valley 60 G14 61 G3
Totara, NI 8 H11 10 C8
Totara, SI 68 H11
Totaranui 38 D10 39 B2
Towai 4 D10
Town Basin - Whangarei 4 G12
Townsend 117 C5
Townsend Hut 46 J9
Townsend Huts 52 B12 53 B3
Travers - Sabine Track 42 J13
Traverse Hut 30 B11 31 B5
Treaty House - Waitangi 4 B9
Treble Cone Skifield 65 C6
Trentham, NI 33 D4 111 B5
Trentham, SI 60 E13 61 E2
Trevor Carter Hut 42 C9
Triangle Hut 27 H5
Trilobite Hut 37 H6
Trinity Lakes 19 H1
Trio Islands / Kuru Pongi 40 B10
Triplex Hut 27 G6
Tripp Settlement 61 E4
Trotters Gorge 74 B13
Trust/Poulter Hut 52 A10 53 A1
Tryphena 36 E5

Tuai 21 F3
Tuakau 7 J6 9 D3
Tuamarina 35 J5 40 J10 44 B11
Tuapeka Flat 73 J4 79 B2
Tuapeka Mouth 73 J4 78 A14 79 C2
Tuapeka West 73 J4 79 B2
Tuatapere 76 F11
Tuatapere Hump Ridge Track 76 E9
Tuateawa 8 B12 36 J6
Tuatini 16 H11
Tuhara 21 H6
Tuhikaramea 11 D6
Tuhipa 4 C8
Tuhitarata 33 F6
Tuhua 18 E9
Tui 42 D12
Tui Brewery Tower - Pahiatua 30 E10 31 E4
Tui Glen 38 J12 39 G4
Tukaki Marae - Te Kaha 15 C6
Tukemokihi 21 G6
Tukino Skifield - Mt Ruapehu 26 B13 27 B1
Tumahu 23 D3
Tumai 74 D12
Tumunui 13 H5
Tuna 23 D7 25 A2
Tunakotekote 18 F10
Tunnel Creek Hut 58 C13 59 C2
Tuparehuia 4 C12
Tuparoa 16 E12
Turakina 29 A4
Turangaomoana 10 J10 12 C11
Turangarere 26 E14 27 E2
Turangi 19 G3
Turitea 30 E8 31 E2
Turiwhate 45 J5
Turiwiri 4 J8
Turoa Skifield - Mt Ruapehu 26 B12
Turua 8 J11 10 D8
Tussock Creek 77 D5
Tussock Hut 19 J6
Tutaematai 4 B11
Tutaenui 26 J11 29 A6
Tutaki 42 G10
Tutamoe 3 F6
Tutekehua 3 B4
Tutira 28 A12
Tutu Hut 47 F3
Tutukaka 4 E13
Tuturau 78 C9
Tuturumuri 34 G7
Tututawa 24 E9 25 B4
Tutuwai Hut 33 C6
Tuwhakairiora Marae - Hicks Bay 16 B11
Twelve Mile Delta 64 H13 65 H3
Twin Bridges 3 F7
Twizel 59 H6
Twyford 28 E11 103 D3

U

Ulva Island 80 E5
Umawera 3 B5
Umere 37 J3 42 A8
Umutaoroa 30 B12 31 B6
Umutoi 27 J4 30 A11 31 A5
Unahi 1 H6
Underwood 77 E4
Unwin Hut 59 B6
Upokongaro 26 H9
Upokorau 2 J11
Upper Atiamuri 12 J13 13 J2
Upper Atiamuri Hot Pools 12 J13 13 J2
Upper Charlton 78 B8
Upper Deception Hut 52 A8
Upper D'Urville Hut 47 B3
Upper Hutt 33 D4 111 B6
Upper Junction 74 G12 124 C2
Upper Kawhatau 27 G4
Upper Makaroro Hut 27 F6
Upper Mangatawhiri Reservoir 8 G8 9 B5
Upper Matakitaki 42 J9 46 A13 47 A1
Upper Matakuhia Hut 20 F10
Upper Moutere 38 J10 39 G2
Upper Princhester Hut 70 F13 71 F2
Upper Riccarton 120 D2
Upper South Branch Hut 46 J10
Upper Spey Hut 69 F7
Upper Takaka 38 G8
Upper Tama Lake 18 J13 19 J1 26 A13 27 A1
Upper Te Hoe Hut 20 F11
Upper Travers Hut 42 J12 47 A4
Upper Wairaki Hut 70 G13 71 G2 76 A13

Upper Waitati 74 F11
Upper Waitohi 61 G3
Upper Whirinaki Hut 20 F10
Upper Windley Hut 71 D4
Urenui 17 G3 24 A8
Uretane 68 D12
Uretara Island 14 F12
Urquharts Bay 4 H13
Urquhart's Hut 51 C6
Urrall 55 F2 62 A8
Urungaio 3 B4
Urupukapuka Island 4 A11
Uruti 17 G4 24 A9
Uruwhenua 38 F8
Utakura 3 C6
Utiku 27 G3
Utuhina 96 C2
Utuwai 30 A11 31 A5

V

Valetta 61 B6
Vauxhall (Auckland) 90 B4
Vauxhall (Dunedin) 123 J6 124 D4
Venison Tops Hut 27 A7
Venus Hut 42 B10
Victoria 100 C3
Victoria Conservation Park 46 A12
Victoria Valley 2 J7
Victory Island / Moutiti 40 A9
View Hill 52 F12 53 F3 55 B5
Vinegar Hill 26 J13 27 J1
Vinetown 84 C3
Virginia 52 A14 53 A5
Vogeltown (New Plymouth) 23 B5 107 C4
Vogeltown (Wellington) 110 E1

W

Waddington 52 G12 53 G3 55 C5
Wade Heads 88 C4
Wadestown 33 E1 35 C3 110 D2
Waenga 66 H9
Waerenga 9 E5
Waerengaahika 22 D9
Waerengaokuri 22 E8
Waewaetorea Island 4 A11
Waharoa 10 J10 12 C11
Wai O Taiki Bay 90 C5
Waiake 88 F3
Waianakarua 74 A13
Waianiwa 77 D4
Waiapi 61 G4
Waiare 2 J11
Waiareka Junction 68 H11
Waiaririkiki 78 D10
Waiaro 8 B10 36 J4
Waiaruhe 30 D11 31 D5
Waiatarua 7 E3 89 D1
Waiatoto 57 E7
Waiau Beach 7 H4 9 C1
Waiau Falls - Coromandel 8 D11
Waiau Pa 7 G4 9 B1
Waiau, NI 8 D11
Waiau, SI 47 H7
Waiaua 14 F14 15 F3
Waiaua Gorge Hut 23 E4
Waiawa Hut 20 C14 21 C2
Waihaha (Northland) 4 B11
Waihaha (Waikato) 19 D2
Waihaha Hut 18 D13 19 D1
Waihao Downs 68 E11
Waihao Forks 68 D11
Waihaorunga 68 D10
Waihapa 2 J10
Waiharakeke (Waikato - Coromandel) 8 J14 10 D11
Waiharakeke (Waikato) 11 G3
Waiharara 1 G5
Waiharuru Hut 20 E14
Waihau Bay 16 B8
Waiheke Island 8 D8 6 J13
Waihemo 74 B11
Waihi (Bay of Plenty) 10 F11
Waihi (Waikato) 19 G2
Waihi Beach 10 F12
Waihi Falls 30 E13 31 E7
Waihi Hot Springs 18 G14 19 G2
Waihirere 22 D10
Waihoaka 76 G12
Waihohonu Hut 18 J14 19 J2 26 A14 27 A2
Waihohonu Track 18 J13 27 A1 26 A13 27 A1

Waihoki 30 G13 31 G7
Waihoki Valley 30 H12 31 H6
Waihola 74 J8 79 B6
Waihopai 128 B2
Waihopo 1 E4
Waihou 10 H9 12 A10
Waihou Valley 3 B6
Waihua 21 J4
Waihua Hut 14 J10
Waihuahua Swamp 1 F6
Waihue 3 H7
Waihuka 2 J11
Waiinu Beach 25 H5
Wai-iti 39 J1 43 B2
Waikaia 72 G9
Waikaka 72 J11
Waikaka Valley 78 A10
Waikakahi 68 E12
Waikakaho - Cullen Creek Track 40 H9 44 A10
Waikamaka Hut 27 G5
Waikana 78 C9
Waikanae 33 A4
Waikanae Beach 33 A4
Waikaraka 4 G12 85 D3
Waikare 4 B11
Waikare Junction Hut 20 A13 21 A1
Waikaremoana 21 E3
Waikaretu 9 G2
Waikari (Canterbury) 54 B8
Waikari (Dunedin) 124 E3
Waikato 37 B7
Waikaura 68 E9
Waikawa (Marlborough) 35 J3 40 G10
Waikawa (Southland) 78 G11
Waikawa Beach 29 H4
Waikawa Museum 78 G11
Waikawa Valley 78 F11
Waikawau (Waikato - Coromandel Coast) 8 E11 10 A8
Waikawau (Waikato - Coromandel) 8 B11 36 J5
Waikawau (Waikato) 17 A5
Waikeria 11 G7
Waikiekie 4 J11
Waikino 10 F10
Waikirikiri 14 H11
Waikite Valley 13 J4
Waikite Valley Hot Pools & Thermal Area 13 J4
Waikiwi 77 E5 128 C1
Waikoau 28 A11
Waikoikoi 72 J12 78 A11
Waikokopu 22 J8 22 AA1
Waikokowai 9 G4 11 A5
Waikorea 9 G2
Waikouaiti 74 E12
Waikoukou Valley 6 J8 7 C2
Waikouro 76 E14 77 B2
Waikowhai 89 D3
Waikuku 54 F8 56 B10
Waikuku Beach 54 F8 56 B10
Waikune 18 J11 26 A11
Waima 89 D2
Waima (East Cape, NI) 16 G11
Waima (Northland) 3 D5
Waima Forest 3 D4
Waima Main Range Track 3 E5
Waima Valley 3 D5
Waimahaka 78 F8
Waimahana 19 B7
Waimahora 11 H7
Waimairi Beach 54 H8 56 D10
Waimakariri Falls Hut 51 B7
Waimamaku 3 E4
Waimana 14 G11
Waimangaroa 41 F4
Waimangu 13 J5
Waimangu Volcanic Valley 13 J5
Waimanoni 1 H6
Waimanu Bay 89 B2
Waimapu 10 J13 94 D1 13 C3
Waimarama 28 H13
Waimari Beach 120 H4
Waimarie 41 D6
Waimata (Bay of Plenty) 10 F11
Waimata (Gisborne) 22 C11
Waimate 68 D12
Waimate Aerodrome 68 D12
Waimate Historical Museum 68 D12
Waimate Island 8 C10
Waimate North 4 B8
Waimate Walkway 68 D12
Waimatenui 3 E6
Waimatua 77 F6
Waimatuku 77 D3

Waimauku 6 J8 7 C2
Waimaunga 46 C8
Waimea 72 H8
Waimiha 18 C11
Waimimihia 19 E7
Waimiro 30 F13 31 F7
Waimotu 68 J10
Waimumu 78 B8
Waingake 22 F8
Waingarara 14 F11
Waingaro 9 J3 11 B4
Waingaro Forks Hut 37 G7
Waingaro Hot Springs 9 J3 11 B4
Waingaro Track 37 F7
Waingawa 34 B8
Wainihinihi 45 J5
Wainoni (Auckland) 88 H2
Wainoni (Christchurch) 120 G3
Wainono Lagoon 68 C13
Wainui Falls - Abel Tasman National Park 38 E9 39 C1
Wainui Hut 38 E9 39 C1
Wainui Junction (Manawatu) 27 E3
Wainui Junction (Northland) 1 J5 3 A1
Wainui Track 38 E9
Wainui, NI (Bay of Plenty) 14 F11
Wainui, NI (Gisborne) 22 E11 100 D6
Wainui, NI (Northland - Far North) 2 H11
Wainui, NI (Northland) 6 H9 7 B3
Wainui, SI 56 G12
Wainuiomata 33 E3 35 A3 111 D4
Wainuioru (Wellington) 34 C10 34 E9
Waioeka Gorge Scenic Reserve 14 H13 15 H2
Waioeka Pa 14 G13 15 G2
Waiohau 14 H9
Waiohiki 28 E11 103 C3
Waiomatatini 16 D12
Waiomio 4 C9
Waiomu 8 F11 10 A8
Waione 30 F13 31 F7
Waioneke 5 G6
Waiopaoa Hut 20 F13 21 F1
Waiopehu Hut 29 H5
Waiopehu Track 29 H5
Waiorongomai 10 G10 12 A11
Waiorore 15 C6
Waiotahi 14 F12 15 F1
Waiotahi Beach 14 F13 15 F2
Waiotahi Marae 14 F12 15 F1
Waiotahi Valley 14 G12 15 G1
Waiotama 4 H9
Waiotapu 13 J5
Wai-o-tapu Thermal Area 13 J5 20 A8
Waiotauru Hut 33 B5
Waiotehue 3 A2
Waiotemarama 3 E4
Waiotira 4 J10
Waiotu 4 E11
Waiouru 26 D14 27 D2
Waipa Valley 18 A11
Waipa Village 13 G4
Waipahi 3 B11
Waipahihi 19 D5 98 C4
Waipaipai 4 E13
Waipakihi Hut 19 J4
Waipango 76 G14 77 D2
Waipaoa 22 C9
Waipapa (Northland) 2 K12 4 A8
Waipapa (Waikato) 12 J10
Waipapakauri 1 H6
Waipapakauri Beach 1 H5
Waipara 54 C9
Waiparera 3 D3 4 G13
Waiparu 72 G9
Waipatiki 30 E13 31 E7
Waipatiki Beach 28 B13
Waipatu 103 B5
Waipawa 28 J9
Waipiata 67 J5
Waipipi 7 H3 9 C1
Waipiro Bay 16 G11
Waipopo 61 H5
Waipori Falls 73 H7 79 A5
Waipoua Forest 3 F5
Waipoua Forest (locality) 3 F5
Waipoua Settlement 3 F4
Waipounamu 72 H9
Waipu 4 J13 6 A8
Waipu Caves 4 J12
Waipu Cove 6 A8
Waipuku 23 D6 25 A1
Waipukurau 28 J9 32 A10
Waipuna, NI 26 D9

Waipuna, SI 46 D8
Waipunga Falls 20 G9
Waipuru 26 H14 27 H2
Wairakau 10 H10 12 A11
Wairakei 19 C5
Wairakei Village 19 C6
Wairamarama 9 F2
Wairapukao 20 B10
Wairata 14 J14 15 J3
Wairau Bar 35 J6 44 C11
Wairau Pa 35 J5 40 J10 44 B11
Wairau Park 88 H3
Wairau Valley 43 C7
Wairaurahiri Hut 76 G8
Waireia 3 C3
Waireka 12 H14 13 H3
Wairere (Northland - Far North) 3 C5
Wairere (Northland) 5 B6
Wairere Boulders Nature Park 3 C5
Wairere Waterfall - Whakatane 14 E11
Wairio 76 D14 77 A2
Wairoa (Bay of Plenty) 10 J13 12 B14 13 B3
Wairoa (Dunedin) 124 G2
Wairoa (Gisborne) 16 D12
Wairoa (Hawke's Bay) 21 H5
Wairoa Pa 10 J13 12 B14 13 B3 94 C1
Wairoa Reservoir 7 G7 9 B4
Wairua Falls - Whangarei 4 G9
Wairuna 78 B12
Wairunga 74 D13
Waitaanga 17 E6
Waitaha 50 C10 51 C1
Waitahanui 19 E5
Waitahora 30 D13 31 D7
Waitahu 46 A9
Waitahuna 73 J5 79 B3
Waitahuna Gully 73 J6 79 B4
Waitahuna West 73 J4 79 B2
Waitakaruru 8 J10 9 D7
Waitakere 7 D2 89 B1
Waitakere Regional Park 7 E2
Waitakere Reservoir 7 E2
Waitaki Bridge 68 F12
Waitane 78 C8
Waitangi 4 B9 81 A2
Waitangirua 110 B3
Waitanguru 11 J3 17 A7
Waitao 13 B4 94 D3
Waitapu, NI 3 D3
Waitapu, SI 38 D8
Waitara 17 G1 23 A6
Waitarere 29 F4
Waitaria Bay 35 J2 40 F10
Waitaruke 2 H10
Waitati 74 F12
Waitawa 61 H4
Waitawheta 10 F10
Waiteitei 6 D9
Waitekauri 10 E10
Waitepeka 79 E3
Waiterimu 9 F6
Waiteti (Bay of Plenty) 13 F4
Waiteti (Waikato) 11 J6 18 A10
Waitetoki 2 G8
Waitetoko 19 F4
Waitetuna 11 C4
Waitewaewae Hut 29 J5 33 A6
Waiti 10 G7
Waitiki Landing 1 B2
Waitoa 10 H9 12 A10
Waitohi, NI 29 C6
Waitohi, SI 61 G4
Waitoki 6 H8 7 B2
Waitomo Caves (locality) 11 H5
Waitotara 25 G5
Waituhi 22 D9
Waituna (Invercargill) 77 E7
Waituna (Waimate) 68 D12
Waituna Lagoon 77 G7
Waituna West 30 A8 31 A2
Waitutu Hut 75 G7
Waitutu Track 75 G7
Waiuku 7 J4 9 D1
Waiuna Lagoon 57 J2
Waiuta 46 D9
Waiuta - Big River Track 46 C9
Waiwaka 30 H8 31 H2
Waiwera (Auckland) 6 G10 7 A4
Waiwera (Manawatu) 30 G8 31 G2
Waiwera Hot Springs 6 G10 7 A4
Waiwera South 78 C13 79 E1
Waiwhetu 111 C4
Waiwhiu 6 E9

Wakamarina - Onamalutu Track 39 J7 44 B8
Wakanui 55 J3 62 D9
Wakapatu 76 H13
Wakapuaka 38 H13 39 F5
Wakarara 27 G6
Wakari 74 G11
Wakatipu Heights 125 B5 126 B3
Wakatu 116 B4
Wakefield 39 J2 43 B3
Wakelings Hut 27 G5
Waldronville 74 H10 124 G6
Walker Island 1 G6
Wall Island 41 G2
Wallacetown 77 D4
Wallaceville 111 B5
Wallingford 32 C10
Waltham 120 F2
Walton 10 J9 12 B10
Wanaka 66 D8
Wangaloa 79 E5
Wanganui 26 J8 108 B4
Wanganui East 26 H8 109 B5
Wangapeka Track 42 C9
Wanstead 32 B10
Waoku Coach Road Walk 3 E5
Waotu 12 G10
Warawara Forest 3 C3
Ward 44 F12
Ward / Makaro Island 110 D3
Wardville 10 J10 12 B11
Warea 23 D3
Warepa 79 E2
Warkworth 6 E9
Warkworth District Museum 6 E10
Waro 4 E11
Warren, The 52 F13 53 F4 55 B6
Warrington 74 F12
Warwick Junction 46 B12
Washdyke 61 J5
Washdyke Lagoon 61 J5
Washington Valley 115 B1
Watchdog Hut 50 G11 51 G2
Waterfall Hut (Mackenzie Region) 59 C5
Waterfall Hut (Mt Cook) 50 J9 60 A10
Waterfall Hut (Ruahine FP) 27 H5
Waterloo 34 E3 35 A3 111 C4
Waterton 62 E8
Waterview 89 C3
Watlington 61 J4
Wattle Bay 7 F3
Wattle Downs 7 F5 9 A2
Waverley, NI 24 J9 25 G4
Waverley, SI (Dunedin) 74 H11 124 D4
Waverley, SI (Invercargill) 128 B2
Wawa 12 J12 13 J1
Wayby 6 D8
Wayby Valley 6 D9
Waynes 74 B12
Weavers Crossing 9 G4
Weber 30 E14 32 E8
Wedderburn 67 G4
Weedons 53 J6 56 E8
Weka Pass 54 C8
Wekaweka 3 E4
Welbourn 106 D6 107 C4
Welcome Bay 10 J13 13 B4 94 D2
Welcome Flat Hot Pools 59 A5
Welcome Flat Hut 59 A5
Wellington 33 F1 35 C4 110 D2 112 D5
Wellington Zoo 33 F1 35 C4
Wellsford 6 D8
Wendon 72 H9
Wendon Valley 72 H10
Wendonside 72 G8
Wentworth Falls - Whangamata 8 J13 10 D10
Weraroa 29 G5
Wesley 89 C3
West End 104 D1 105 C3
West Eweburn Dam 67 G4
West Eyreton 53 F5 55 B7
West Harbour 89 B2
West Harper Hut 52 D8
West Melton 53 H5 55 D7
West Plains 77 E4 128 D1
West Sabine Hut 42 J12 47 A4
Westerfield 55 H1 61 C7
Western Heights (Auckland) 89 C2
Western Heights (Rotorua) 96 B2
Western Springs 89 C3
Westfield 90 D5
Westhaven (Christchurch) 120 F4
Westhaven (Te Tai Tapu) Marine Reserve 37 B5

Westhaven (Wellington) 110 B2
Westlake (Auckland) 88 H4
Westlake (Christchurch) 120 C1
Westland Tai Poutini National Park 49 F6
Westmere (Auckland) 89 C3
Westmere (Waikato) 9 G4 11 A5
Westmere (Wanganui) 26 H8 109 A2
Westmere (Wellington) 34 C10
Westmorland 120 D1
Weston 68 H11
Westown 23 B5 107 C3
Westport 41 G3
Westshore 28 D12 103 B1
Westwood 74 H10 124 H6
Wetheral 53 G7 56 C9
Wetherstons 73 H5 79 A3
Weymouth 7 F5 9 A2
Whakaari/White Island 14 A13
Whakahoro 18 H8 24 B13
Whakahoro Hut 18 H8 24 B13
Whakaki 21 H6
Whakaki Lagoon 21 J6
Whakamara 24 H8 25 E3
Whakamarama 10 J12 12 B13 13 B2
Whakamaru 19 A3
Whakanui Track 33 F3
Whakapapa Skifield - Mt Ruapehu 26 A13
Whakapapa Village 18 J12 26 A12
Whakapapaiti Hut 26 A12
Whakapapaiti Hut Track 18 J12 26 A12
Whakapara 4 E11
Whakapirau 5 C6
Whakapourangi 16 E11
Whakarae 14 J11
Whakarewarewa 13 G4 96 D3
Whakarewarewa Thermal Valley - Rotorua 13 G4 96 D3
Whakarongo 30 D8 31 D2
Whakataka Hut 20 D13 21 D1
Whakataki 34 A13
Whakatane 14 E11
Whakaterepapanui Island 40 B10
Whakatete Bay 8 G11 10 B8
Whakatina 24 E13 26 B8
Whakatiwai 8 G9 9 B6
Whakatu 28 E12 103 B4
Whakawhitira 16 D11
Whale Stream Hut 59 D6
Whananaki 4 D13
Whananaki South 4 D13
Whanarua Bay 15 B7
Whangaahei 8 B11 36 J5
Whangae 4 B9
Whangaehu Hut 26 A13
Whangaehu (Wanganui) 26 J9 29 A4
Whangaehu (Wellington) 34 B10
Whangaimoana 33 G5
Whangamarino (Bay of Plenty) 13 F5
Whangamarino (Waikato) 9 E4
Whangamata 8 J14 10 D11
Whangamomona 17 J6 24 C11
Whanganui 18 E14 19 E2
Whanganui Hut 20 E14 21 E2
Whanganui Island 8 D10
Whanganui National Park 18 J8 24 D12 25 A7
Whangaparaoa (Auckland) 6 H10 7 B4
Whangaparaoa (East Cape, NI) 16 A9
Whangaparapara 36 E4
Whangape 3 B2
Whangapoua 8 C12
Whangara 22 D12
Whangara Island (Auckland) 36 E4
Whangara Island (Gisborne) 22 D12
Whangarata 7 J6 9 D3
Whangarei 4 G11 84 B4
Whangarei Airport 4 G12
Whangarei Falls 4 F12
Whangarei Heads 4 H13
Whangaripo 6 D9
Whangaroa 2 H10
Whangaruru 4 C12
Whangaruru South 4 C12
Whangateau 6 D10
Wharanui 44 H12
Whare Creek Hut 70 F12 71 F1
Whare Flat 74 G11 124 F1
Whareama 34 B12
Wharehine 5 D7
Wharehuanui 65 G5
Wharehuia 23 D7 25 A2
Wharekahika Hut 14 H11
Wharekaho Beach / Simpsons Beach 8 D13
Wharekaka 22 A13

Wharekakahu Island 74 H13
Wharekauhau 33 G4
Wharekawa (Auckland) 8 G9 9 B6
Wharekawa (Waikato) 8 H14 10 C11
Wharekohe 4 G10
Wharekopae 21 C6
Wharepaina 20 A8
Wharepapa 5 J7 7 C1
Wharepapa South 12 G9
Wharepoa 8 J12 10 D9
Whareponga 16 F12
Wharepuhunga 12 H8
Whareroa 23 H7 25 E2
Wharetoa 78 A13 79 C1
Wharewaka 19 D5 98 D4
Wharfedale Hut 52 E12 53 E3 55 A5
Wharfedale Track 52 E12 53 E3 55 A5
Whariwharangi Hut 38 D9 39 B1
Whataroa 49 F7
Whatatutu 22 A9
Whataupoko 100 B4
Whatawhata 11 C5
Whatipu 7 F2
Whatipu Caves 7 F2
Whatitiri 4 G10
Whatoro 3 G6
Whatuwhiwhi 2 F7
Whau Valley 85 B1
Whawharua 11 H6
Wheatstone 62 E9
Wheki Valley 4 H10
Whenuahou 30 A14 32 A8
Whenuakite 8 E13
Whenuakura 24 J9 25 F4
Whenuanui 5 B4
Whenuapai 6 J9 7 C3 89 A2
Whenuapai Airforce Base 6 J9 7 D3
Whetukura 30 B14 32 B8
Whirinaki (Hawke's Bay) 28 C12
Whirinaki (Northland) 3 D4
Whirinaki Forest Park 20 D10
Whiritoa 8 J14 10 D11
Whiriwhiri 7 J4 9 D1
Whitby 110 A3
White Hut 50 B14 51 B5
White Island 14 A13
White Pine Bush 14 F10
White Rock 80 G5
White Rocks 35 F1 40 E13
Whitecliffs 52 H11 53 H2 55 D4
Whitecliffs Walkway 17 F4
Whitecraig 68 H11
Whitemans Valley 33 D4
Whiterigg 78 A9
Whiterock 53 D6
Whitford 7 E6 9 A3
Whitiaga Airfield 8 D12
Whitianga (Bay of Plenty) 15 D5
Whitianga (Waikato) 8 D13
Whitikahu 9 H6 11 A7
Whitikau 15 H4
Whitiroa 91 C3 92 E3
Whitstone 68 H11
Whymper Hut 49 H7
Wigram Aerodrome - Christchurch 53 J7 56 E9 120 C2
Wigram Park 120 V2
Wilden 72 G13 73 G2
Wilder Settlement 32 D9
Wilkinson Hut 50 D12 51 D3
Willowbank 78 A10
Willowbridge 68 D13
Willowby 55 J2 62 D8
Willowford 28 C8
Willows Hut 48 C9
Wills Hut 58 F12 59 F1
Wilsons Crossing 77 D5
Wilsons Siding 53 G7 56 C9
Wilsonville 4 E11
Wilton 110 D1
Wiltsdown 12 G11
Wimbledon 32 F9
Winchester 61 G5
Winchmore 55 H2 62 C8
Windermere 55 J1 61 D7
Windsor (Invercargill) 68 G10 127 A5 128 B2
Windsor Park 68 G11
Windwhistle 52 H9 55 D2
Windy Hill 4 J8
Windy Ridge 88 J3
Wingate 33 E3 35 A3 111 C4
Wingatui 74 H10 124 G4

Winiata 27 F3
Winscombe 60 F12 61 F1
Winslow 55 J2 62 D8
Winton 77 B4
Wiri 7 F5 9 A2 90 E5
Wither Hills Walkway 35 K6 44 C10
Woburn 110 C3
Womens Island 80 D6
Wood Bay 89 D2
Wood, The 115 B5
Woodaugh 123 A4 124 D3
Woodbourne 44 C10
Woodbury 61 E4
Woodcocks 6 F9
Woodend (Invercargill) 77 F5
Woodend (Waimakariri) 54 F8 56 B10
Woodend Beach 54 F8 56 B10
Woodhill 5 J7 7 C1 84 C2
Woodlands Park 89 D2
Woodlands, NI (Bay of Plenty) 10 G11 14 F13 15 F2
Woodlands, SI 77 E6
Woodlaw 76 D14 77 A2
Woodleigh 9 G2
Woodridge 110 C2
Woodside, NI 33 C7
Woodside, SI 74 H9 79 A7
Woodstock (Tasman) 38 J8 42 A13
Woodstock (Westland) 45 J2
Woodville 30 D10 31 D4
Woolleys Bay 4 E13
Woolston 54 J8 56 E10 120 F2
Woolwich 103 D4
Worsley Bivvy 52 A10
Wreys Bush 77 A3
Wrights Bush 77 D4
Wyllies Crossing 74 H10 124 J3
Wyndham 78 D9

Y

Yaldhurst 53 H7 56 D9 120 A3
Yaldhurst Museum of Transport & Science - Christchurch 53 H7 56 D9
Yankee River Hut 77 J1 80 C3
Yeates Track 29 H6
Yeats Ridge Hut 50 B13 51 B4
Yellow Hut 74 F11
Yeoman Track 27 G6
York Track 23 D5
Young Hut 58 G9
Youngman Stream Hut 52 C13 53 C4
Yourk Bay 110 D3